# Youth in Education

*Youth in Education* explores the multiple, interrelated social contexts that young people inhabit and navigate, and how educational institutions cope with increasing ethnic, cultural and ideological diversity. Schools, families and communities represent important settings in which young people must make successful transitions to adulthood, and the classroom often becomes a battleground in which these contexts and values interact.

With contributions from the UK, Belgium, Germany and Canada, the chapters in this book explore rich examples from Europe and North America to suggest strategies that can help to counter negative perceptions, processes of stigmatization and disengagement, instead prioritising peer support and cooperative learning to give pupils a renewed sense of worth.

This book takes the growing ethnocultural diversity in education systems to heart and studies the various related educational processes from a multidisciplinary and multi-method approach. It aims to offer more insight into underlying mechanisms that are often implicit, but can be important factors that positively or negatively influence educational trajectories and outcomes. It is essential reading for researchers, academics and postgraduate students in the fields of education, sociology, higher education, policy and politics, and social and cultural geography.

**Christiane Timmerman** is Research Professor and Director of the Interdisciplinary Research Centre on Migration and Intercultural Studies, University of Antwerp, Belgium.

**Noel Clycq** is Professor in a chair on European Values and a CeMIS Postdoctoral Researcher and Academic Coordinator within the EU-FP7-project 'Reducing Early School Leaving in Europe', University of Antwerp, Belgium.

**Marie Mc Andrew** is Professor in the Department of Educational Administration and Foundations and Director of the Research Group on Immigration, Equity and Schooling (GRIES) at the University of Montreal, Canada.

**Alhassane Balde** is Lecturer in the Department of Education and Specialized Training, University of Quebec in Montreal, Canada.

**Luc Braeckmans** is Professor in the Department of Philosophy at the University of Antwerp, and Director of Academic Affairs of the University Centre Saint Ignatius Antwerp, Belgium.

**Sara Mels** is Project Co-ordinator at the University Centre Saint Ignatius Antwerp, Belgium.

# Routledge Research in Educational Equality and Diversity

Books in the series include:

### Youth in Education
The necessity of valuing ethnocultural diversity
*Edited by Christiane Timmerman, Noel Clycq, Marie Mc Andrew, Alhassane Balde, Luc Braeckmans and Sara Mels*

### Identity, Neoliberalism and Aspiration
Educating white working-class boys
*Garth Stahl*

### Faces of Discrimination in Higher Education in India
Quota policy, social justice and the Dalits
*Samson K. Ovichegan*

### Inequality, Power and School Success
Case Studies on Racial Disparity and Opportunity in Education
*Edited by Gilberto Q. Conchas and Michael A. Gottfried with Briana M. Hinga*

### Youth and Inequality in Education
Global Actions in Youth Work
*Edited by Michael Heathfield and Dana Fusco*

### Social Justice and Transformative Learning
Culture and Identity in the United States and South Africa
*Edited by Saundra M. Tomlinson-Clarke and Darren L. Clarke*

# Youth in Education
The necessity of valuing
ethnocultural diversity

Edited by
Christiane Timmerman, Noel Clycq,
Marie Mc Andrew, Alhassane Balde,
Luc Braeckmans and Sara Mels

LONDON AND NEW YORK

First published 2016
by Routledge
2 Park Square, Milton Park, Abingdon, Oxon OX14 4RN

and by Routledge
711 Third Avenue, New York, NY 10017

*Routledge is an imprint of the Taylor & Francis Group, an informa business*

© 2016 selection and editorial matter, Christiane Timmerman, Noel Clycq, Marie Mc Andrew, Alhassane Balde, Luc Braeckmans and Sara Mels; individual chapters, the contributors.

The right of Christiane Timmerman, Noel Clycq, Marie Mc Andrew, Alhassane Balde, Luc Braeckmans and Sara Mels to be identified as the authors of the editorial material, and of the authors for their individual chapters, has been asserted in accordance with sections 77 and 78 of the Copyright, Designs and Patents Act 1988.

All rights reserved. No part of this book may be reprinted or reproduced or utilised in any form or by any electronic, mechanical, or other means, now known or hereafter invented, including photocopying and recording, or in any information storage or retrieval system, without permission in writing from the publishers.

*Trademark notice*: Product or corporate names may be trademarks or registered trademarks, and are used only for identification and explanation without intent to infringe.

*British Library Cataloguing in Publication Data*
A catalogue record for this book is available from the British Library

*Library of Congress Cataloging in Publication Data*
Names: Timmerman, Christiane, editor.
Title: Youth in education : the necessity of valuing ethnocultural diversity / edited by Christiane Timmerman, Noel Clycq, Marie McAndrew, Alhassane Balde, Luc Braekmans, and Sara Mels.
Description: London ; New York : Routledge is an imprint of the Taylor & Francis Group, an Informa Business, [2016] | Series: Routledge research in educational equality and diversity | Includes bibliographical references and index.
Identifiers: LCCN 2015030674| ISBN 9781138999602 (hardback) | ISBN 9781315658148 (e-book)
Subjects: LCSH: Educational sociology. | Multicultural education. | Community and school. | Home and school.
Classification: LCC LC191 .Y68 2016 | DDC 370.117--dc23LC record available at http://lccn.loc.gov/2015030674

ISBN: 978-1-138-99960-2 (hbk)
ISBN: 978-1-315-65814-8 (ebk)

Typeset in Bembo
by Florence Production Ltd, Stoodleigh, Devon, UK

# Contents

| | |
|---|---|
| *List of figures* | vii |
| *List of tables* | viii |
| *List of contributors* | ix |
| *Preface* | xv |

Introduction    1
NOEL CLYCQ AND CHRISTIANE TIMMERMAN

## PART 1
## Values, relationships and institutions in a context of diversity    9

1 The influence of socioeconomic change and culture on intergenerational relations    11
GISELA TROMMSDORFF

2 Horizontal transmission of value orientations in adolescence    27
KLAUS BOEHNKE AND DAVID SCHIEFER

3 Educational structures and the curriculum: reproducing or transforming ethnic boundaries?    45
MARIE MC ANDREW

## PART 2
## Educational pathways    65

4 Does congruence between the school and the home/community environment make a difference?    67
CHRISTIANE TIMMERMAN, NOEL CLYCQ,
KENNETH HEMMERECHTS AND JOHAN WETS

5  The Quebec youth of immigrant origin in secondary education: educational pathways and the factors influencing graduation  89
   JACQUES LEDENT AND MARIE MC ANDREW

6  Culture, narratives and upward educational mobility  111
   NICOLAS LEGEWIE

## PART 3
## Peers, family and community  137

7  Parents, schools and diversity: challenges and opportunities for parental involvement in a changing global context  139
   GILL CROZIER

8  Aspirations disclosed: the case of Turkish-Belgian parents in Brussels  153
   FATMA ZEHRA ÇOLAK

9  The Polish community school in Flanders: bridging the gap between school and home environment  171
   EDITH PIQUERAY, NOEL CLYCQ AND CHRISTIANE TIMMERMAN

## PART 4
## Social, systemic and school dynamics  193

10  Aspirations and stigmatization as factors of school success  195
    NOEL CLYCQ, WARD NOUWEN AND MARJOLEIN BRASPENNINGX

11  Partnership between schools and immigrant families and communities  215
    GENEVIÈVE AUDET, MARIE MC ANDREW AND MICHÈLE VATZ LAAROUSSI

12  Rethinking values and schooling in white working-class neighbourhoods  233
    RUTH LUPTON

Conclusion: major contributions of the book and the complementarity of its chapters: a critical reflection  249
ALHASSANE BALDE AND MARIE MC ANDREW

Index  255

# Figures

| | | |
|---|---|---|
| 1.1 | Parent–child relations in three generations (the VOC-IR Study) | 18 |
| 2.1 | Schwartz value circumplex (10 value types) | 30 |
| 2.2 | Correlations of Schwartz values and differences between individual preferences and school class means | 38 |
| 2.3 | Schematic design for nested ANOVAs | 39 |
| 5.1 | Percentage distribution by region of origin: first- and second-generation students | 94 |
| 5.2 | Graduation two years after expected, first and second generations by regional origin vs. third generation and more, with and without control for student characteristics | 99 |
| 6.1 | Concept structure of the promotive narratives | 119 |
| 10.1 | Correspondence analysis representing the association of specific student characteristics in our sample | 203 |

# Tables

| | | |
|---|---|---|
| 2.1 | Portrait Value Questionnaire (25-item version) | 32 |
| 2.2 | Results table for hierarchic ANOVA | 39 |
| 2.3 | Results table for hierarchic ANOVA | 40 |
| 4.1 | Descriptive statistics of the sample (n = 7940) | 77 |
| 4.2 | Multilevel binary logistic regression of grade retention (odds ratios) | 80 |
| 4.3 | Multilevel binary logistic regression of grade retention and networks of students: native and immigrant students | 81 |
| 5.1 | Immigrant background characteristics: first- and second-generation students by region of origin | 94 |
| 5.2 | Indicators of educational pathways: first- and second-generation students by region of origin | 97 |
| 5.3 | Factors influencing graduation two years after expected: first and second generations versus third generation and more | 102 |
| 6.1 | Co-occurrence of promotive narratives and the outcome | 112 |
| 6.2 | Case selection scheme | 116 |
| 6.3 | Illustrative quotes for the promotive narratives | 120 |
| 6.4 | Distribution of narrative types over parents' origin | 123 |
| 9.1 | Research population and methodology | 178 |
| 9.2 | The percentage of ethnic minorities within different educational tracks | 180 |
| 10.1 | Standardized regression parameter estimates for a two-step regression analyses on relation between GPA and academic self-concept ($\star$ = $p<.05$) | 208 |

# Contributors

**Geneviève Audet** is an Associate Professor in the Department of Educational Administration and Foundations at the University of Montreal. She also coordinates the Research Group on Immigration, Equity and Schooling. She holds a Ph.D. in psycho-pedagogy at the Université Laval and Université Paris 8. After her postdoctoral research at the Canada Research Chair on Education and Ethnic Relations, she became the coordinator of the first research centre within a school setting, the Centre for Pedagogical Intervention in a Diversity Context at the Commission Scolaire Marguerite-Bourgeoys.

**Alhassane Balde** is Lecturer in the Department of Education and Specialized Training at the Université du Québec à Montréal (UQAM). He holds a Ph.D. in Demography and Social Sciences from Université Paris Descartes. He works on the academic success of immigrant students in Quebec high schools and on the social demand of education in Sub-Saharan Africa (education policy, local knowledge, strategies of education). His current research focuses on the relationship between immigration, equity and schooling. He most recently co-published a book by the P.U.M, *La réussite éducative des élèves issus de l'immigration: Dix ans de recherche et d'intervention au Québec* (2015).

**Klaus Boehnke** studied English (major), Russian (minor) and psychology (double major) for MA-equivalent degrees. In 1985 he earned his Ph.D. in psychology at Berlin University of Technology; in 1992 he was awarded the habilitation degree at the Free University of Berlin, traditionally necessary in Germany to become a tenured full professor. From 1993 to 2002 he was Professor of Socialization Research and Empirical Social Research at t-he Department of Sociology of Chemnitz University of Technology. Since 2002 he holds the Chair of Social Science Methodology at Jacobs University Bremen. Since 2007 he is Vice Dean of the Bremen International Graduate School of Social Sciences (BIGSSS), an interuniversity institution of doctoral education (with Universität Bremen) funded in the German Excellence Initiative. In very general terms, his research deals with political socialization processes.

**Luc Braeckmans** (Ph.D. in Philosophy) is Director of Academic Affairs at the University Centre Saint Ignatius Antwerp (UCSIA). He is Professor at the Department of Philosophy at the University of Antwerp, where he is also Chair of the Centre for Andragogy. The focus of his research is in the field of the philosophy of religion, the philosophy of education and metaphysics.

**Marjolein Braspenningx** obtained a Master's degree in Sociology (University of Antwerp, 2012) and has written her Master's thesis about social inequality in Flemish higher education. After obtaining her teacher's degree, she started working as a teacher in human sciences in secondary education in 2013. Since then, she has become a researcher and Ph.D. candidate for the Centre for Migration and Intercultural Studies (CeMIS) in the Resl.eu research project on early school leaving.

**Noel Clycq** is Professor in a chair on European Values and a CeMIS Postdoctoral Researcher and Academic Coordinator within the EU-FP7-project 'Reducing Early School Leaving in Europe', University of Antwerp, Belgium. His Ph.D. (2007) project studied the identification and socialization processes in majority and minority families in Flanders. He coordinated the four-year, interuniversity project 'Bet You! Boosting the Educational Trajectories of YOUth in Flanders' (2009–2012). Currently, he is a co-teacher of the bachelor courses 'Introduction to Anthropology' and 'Interdisciplinary Perspectives on Migration and Integration' and has published on diverse topics in books and journals, such as *Current Sociology*, *Ethnography* and *British Educational Research Journal*.

**Fatma Zehra Çolak** is a Ph.D. candidate in the Faculty of Psychology and Educational Sciences in KU Leuven. She received her M.Sc. degree in the Social and Cultural Anthropology Department at the same university. Her Master's thesis looked into the aspirations, experiences and choices of Turkish-Belgian parents in Brussels regarding their children's education. Her primary research interests are in the area of migration, interethnic contact, identity and acculturation. Currently, she has been investigating the dynamics of contact between Flemish students and Turkish-Belgian students from a qualitative perspective while analysing the parameters of acculturation in the lives of migrant-origin young adults.

**Gill Crozier** is Professor of Education, former Director of the Centre for Educational Research in Equalities, Policy and Pedagogy (2012–2015), School of Education, University of Roehampton, London, and a Fellow of the Royal Society of Arts. As a sociologist of education, she has researched and written extensively about parents/families and school relationships, young people, access to and participation in higher education and the sociocultural influences upon identity formation and learner experiences. Her work is underpinned by a deep concern for social justice and is informed by the analysis of race, class and gender and the ways these social locations and identities intersect and impact on life chances. Her books include: *Parents and Schools: Partners or Protagonists?* (2000); *Activating Participation: Parents and teachers working towards partnership* (2005) co-edited with Diane Reay; *White Middle Class Identities and Urban Schooling* (2011 and 2013, second revised edition), co-authored with Diane Reay and David James.

**Kenneth Hemmerechts** is a Doctoral Researcher at the Free University of Brussels in Etterbeek (VUB) where he is currently working in the field of the sociology of education. Previously, he has worked at different universities in Belgium on a variety of topics, including migration; criminal recidivism; fraud; police capacity; employment and trade unionism; genocide; and social theory.

**Jacques Ledent**, recipient of a Ph.D. in urban planning from Northwestern University in Evanston, Illinois, is Research Professor at the Centre Urbanisation-Culture-Société of the Institut de la recherche scientifique (INRS), in Montreal, Quebec. Primarily interested in population problems and issues at the urban and regional levels, he specializes in a resolutely quantitative analysis of human migration. After focusing for some years on the patterns and characteristics of interregional migration in Canada, his research now revolves around international migration and, more specifically, the integration of the immigrant-origin population in Quebec society. His most recent writings deal with (1) the overqualification of workers who are immigrants or belong to the visible minorities and (2) the academic success of first- and second-generation students in secondary school.

**Nicolas Legewie** is a Research Associate at the German Institute for Economic Research (DIW Berlin). He earned his doctorate from Humboldt University of Berlin, where he focused on combinations of personal network factors as explanations of upward educational mobility. Currently, he is involved in research projects on the life courses of second-generation Germans and on the effects of the minimum wage in Germany. His research interests include social inequality and mobility, immigration and integration, education, research methodology, as well as Qualitative Comparative Analysis (QCA).

**Ruth Lupton** is a Professor of Education at the University of Manchester. She researches and writes on poverty and inequality in the UK, with a particular focus on education and on low-income neighbourhoods. Much of her work has examined the effects of local socioeconomic contexts on the organization and processes of schools. Relevant publications include *Poverty Street: The Dynamics of Neighbourhood Decline and Renewal* (Policy Press 2003), and *The Importance of Teaching: Pedagogical Constraints and Possibilities in Working Class Schools* (with Amelia Hempel-Jorgensen in the *Journal of Education Policy* 27(5), 2012).

**Marie Mc Andrew** is Professor in the Faculty of Education at the Université of Montréal and Director of the Research Group on Immigration, Equity and Schooling. She has published numerous books and articles which have received recognition and awards: *Immigration et diversité à l'école: le cas québécois dans une perspective comparative* (Immigration and diversity in school: Quebec case in a comparative perspective) which received the Donner Prize in 2001 attributed to the best book on Canadian public policy, and *Les majorités fragiles et l'éducation: Belgique, Catalogne, Irlande du Nord, Québec* (Fragile Majorities and Education: Belgium, Catalonia, Northern Ireland, Quebec) nominated for the Governor Generals' Award in 2010 in the category for Essays and Studies.

**Sara Mels** holds a Master's degree in Modern History and in International Relations and Conflict Resolution from the KU Leuven. Since 2004 she is Project Coordinator at the University Centre Saint-Ignatius Antwerp (UCSIA) where she develops academic programmes on various topics of contemporary relevance to society.

**Ward Nouwen** attained a Master's degree in Sociology (University of Leuven, 2008) and since 2013 has worked as Ph.D. Researcher for the Centre for Migration and Intercultural Studies (University of Antwerp) in the Resl.eu research project on Reducing Early School Leaving in Europe. Ward Nouwen previously worked in research on segregation in Flemish primary education (SinBa, FWO) and school careers of pupils with and without an immigrant background in Flemish secondary education (Oprit14, IWT).

**Edith Piqueray**, with a Master's in Social and Cultural Anthropology (KUL), has been a research staff member at CeMIS since March 2008. She was involved in an action research on the needs for creating a training in Islamic studies in Flanders. From 2009 to 2012 she worked on BET YOU!, a research project on the school careers of youngsters with and without a migration background in Flanders. She was subsequently involved in an action research on improving the trajectories of newcomers in education and on the Belgian labour market, and in a study about the school careers of immigrant students at the University of Antwerp. She is currently writing a Ph.D. about the role of the Polish community school in the school careers of Polish youngsters in Flanders.

**David Schiefer** worked as a Research Associate at the School of Humanities and Social Sciences at Jacobs University Bremen following his studies in psychology at the University of Potsdam. He earned his Ph.D. in 2012. He was a Postdoctoral Fellow at the Bremen International Graduate School of Social Sciences from 2013 to 2014. Since 2015 he is a Researcher at the Research Unit of the Expert Council of German Foundations on Integration and Migration (Berlin). David Schiefer's research expertise spans the fields of individual and cultural values, acculturation, bicultural identities, intergroup relations and refugee research.

**Christiane Timmerman** holds a Master's in Psychology, an Advanced Master's in Social and Cultural Anthropology and a Ph.D. in Social and Cultural Anthropology for which she conducted extended field research in Turkey. She is a Research Professor (ZAPBOF) at the University of Antwerp and Director of the internationally recognized Centre of Migration and Intercultural Studies (CeMIS), which focuses on multidisciplinary research on migration, integration and ethnic minorities. As Director, she has built extensive experience coordinating large-scale research projects on international migration and integration: EU FP7 project RESL.eu 'Reducing Early School Leaving in Europe' (2013–2018), EU FP7 project EUMAGINE 'Imagining Europe from the outside' (2009–2013), Policy Centre on Civic Integration (2012–2015). She is also supervisor of numerous (accomplished) Ph.D. projects in the field of international migration and integration. She is a member of the Board of Directors of the European Research Network on Migration, IMISCOE.

**Gisela Trommsdorff** received her doctoral degree and venia legendi from the University of Mannheim. She was Professor at the Technical University of Aachen from 1977 to 1987. She then served as Chair for Developmental and Cross-Cultural Psychology at the University of Konstanz before her 2007 appointment as Research Professor at the German Institute for Economic Studies, Berlin. Gisela Trommsdorff's research interests are focused on intergenerational relations over the lifespan, transmission of values, and children's socioemotional and prosocial development, including adaptation to sociocultural change, with a primary focus on cultural contexts. Over the past twenty years, she has established an international and interdisciplinary collaborative research team involving Japan, Korea, China, Indonesia, India, the United States and several Eastern and Western European countries. She has co-edited more than twenty books, authored numerous book chapters and articles and served on the boards of international journals and scientific institutions. Dr Trommsdorff is a member of the Academy of Sciences in Erfurt and a recipient of the German Federal Cross of Merit, 1st Class.

**Michèle Vatz Laaroussi** holds a Ph.D. in intercultural psychology and is a Professor at the School of Social Work at the University of Sherbrooke. Her research explores immigration and social action with immigrants. She is interested both in family patterns related to immigration and in local dynamics that occur when populations are faced with cultural diversity outside of large urban centres. She co-directs the research field 'Welcoming Organizations' of the Quebec Metropolis Centre – Immigration and Metropolis. Her recent studies have considered the geographical and social mobility of immigrant and/or refugee families in Quebec and in Canada, and the transnational networks of these families.

**Johan Wets** (Ph.D.) is Migration Expert and Research Manager Migration at the Research Institute for Labour and Society (HIVA), an interdisciplinary research institute from the University of Leuven, Belgium (KU Leuven). His fields of research are international migration and related issues: migration and the labour market, irregular migration, migrant integration, migration and integration policy, migration and development (brain drain, remittances), and the attitude towards (new) migrants. The research conducted is policy-oriented research as well as fundamental research. Johan Wets is also Visiting Professor at the Université Saint Louis, Brussels, where he teaches political sociology.

# Preface

As an international and interdisciplinary platform for scholarly debate on issues related to religion and worldview as well as justice and value change in society, the University Centre Saint Ignatius Antwerp (UCSIA) develops on average 15 projects each year (a yearly summer school, international workshops, seminars, congresses, lectures, etc.).

In November 2013, UCSIA organized an international multidisciplinary academic workshop on the topic of youth, education and value change. The centre convened a select group of researchers to investigate how ethnocultural diversity is valued today, as well as how different values and behavioural patterns of young people influence their educational achievement.

There is a growing consensus among sociologists that a more complete understanding of how youth achieve social competency requires taking into account the multiple and interrelated social contexts that young people inhabit. Families, schools, peer groups and neighbourhoods each represent important contextual settings where youth must master the tasks necessary to make a successful transition to adulthood. UCSIA is particularly interested in understanding how different spheres of influence can encompass either a congruent or a contrasting set of values. Whereas a youngster with an immigrant background, a weak socioeconomic status etc. may consider school as just one sphere of influence in competition with other spheres, it may not appear to be such a dramatic clash of contexts to a middle-class autochthonous/native youngster, as their cultural capital is mostly validated at schools. Furthermore, the aspirations and schooling values of youngsters and families with an immigrant and/or weak socioeconomic background may threaten their school success and jeopardize their future chances in society.

Now, two years later, and thanks to the academic commitment of Christiane Timmerman, Noel Clycq, Marie Mc Andrew and Alhassane Balde, we are proud to present the collection *Youth in Education: The necessity of valuing ethnocultural diversity*. We wish to thank all the authors who contributed. Without their dedication and expertise, this volume would not exist.

Luc Braeckmans
Sara Mels

# Introduction

*Noel Clycq and Christiane Timmerman*

Today, young people encounter both the opportunities and the challenges of an increasingly globalizing world. This is particularly true for metropolitan areas around the world that are changing into majority–minority cities characterized by a majority group composed of various ethnic minority groups. Continuing immigration and emigration flows are fundamentally changing the demographic and ethnocultural outlook of cities and this will have a major impact on all involved, especially on society's crucial social institutions such as the labour market and the educational system. In particular the latter is – and will increasingly be – confronted with these changing social patterns. All in all, this is a rather confusing phenomenon. In general, people experience strong centripetal tendencies towards global cultural homogenization, intense economic integration, and a globalization of consumption and media, but they also face centrifugal tendencies and the development of new forms of 'closed' communitarism – often framed within 'nationalistic', 'ethnic', 'cultural – religious' or ideological idioms – which cultivate the difference from 'the other'.

Especially young people have to find their way in this world of growing and ever more diversifying spaces. One of the main responsibilities societies have towards young people is to prepare them to become 'efficient' citizens, well equipped to meet the challenges of the contemporary world. To a large extent, societies entrust schools with this major task. Here, centrally established educational systems complement the socialization processes at work in families. They rely upon the educational system to raise and educate their children and vice versa, at least when one implicitly assumes that both social institutions to a large extent share common goals, values and strategies. Therefore, the questions as to how these educational institutions cope with growing diversity and how these efforts reach out, especially to those who are difficult to reach, become highly relevant. Educational systems are often perceived as social institutions that constitute the foundation of societies, institutions that build up and reproduce social cohesion in a society over time.

Social cohesion might be endangered, however, if large disparities and inequalities between specific categories of pupils in these systems should emerge. This is indeed what research shows. In most Western societies, the 'democratization' process of the educational system has only partially succeeded. During the last decades, the participation rate strongly increased and ever more students enrol in higher education (Eurostat, 2014; Finnie *et al.*, 2010). However, this tendency has not been able to remove inequalities. Socially vulnerable children, mainly those with a lower socioeconomic and/or belonging to certain ethnic minorities – although we must never forget the diversity within these categories – often experience troubled school careers and do not easily find their way to higher education, or do not even obtain an upper secondary education qualification. Such inequalities are found at different levels or moments in the course of life: the age at which children start attending nursery school, the quality and outcomes of their school career, the extent to which they participate and succeed in higher education, etc. (Eurostat, 2014; Rumberger & Ah Lim, 2008). The social cost of these inequalities is high: besides widening significant knowledge gaps between vulnerable and privileged groups in society, these inequalities also impact labour and housing opportunities, well-being and health (NESSE, 2010).

There is a growing consensus among social scientists that for a better understanding of how youth achieves competencies, it is necessary to take into account the multiple and interrelated social contexts that young people inhabit and navigate. Schools, families, peer groups and neighbourhoods represent important contextual settings where youth must learn to master the tasks necessary to make a successful transition to adulthood (Bronfenbrenner, 1989; Feinstein *et al.*, 2004). These different spheres of influence can encompass either a congruent or a contrasting set of values. So, the classroom may become a contested space in which these different contexts and value patterns interact. Whereas a youngster with a vulnerable socioeconomic status or belonging to a marginalized ethnic minority may consider the school as just one sphere of influence in competition with other spheres, a middle-class youngster from the majority group or from an immigrant family whose educational and/or cultural capital is rather similar to that valued in schools may not experience it as so much of a 'clash' of contexts and battle of values (Bourdieu & Passeron, 1977; Roosens, 1995). Such struggles and contrasts may jeopardize the school success of specific categories of youngsters, as they 'do not fit' in educational systems where recognition and appreciation of different forms of capital or resources may be low or absent (Yosso, 2005).

Indeed, several studies have shown that there is a strong tendency in educational systems to aim to let immigrant children and youngsters participate by way of subtractive acculturation or subtractive schooling processes, although this trend may be more pronounced in Europe than in North America where ideologies and practices promoting pluralism are more widespread, albeit not dominant (Alba & Holdaway, 2013; Antrop-Gonzalez, 2006; Clycq *et al.*, 2013; Mc Andrew, 2013; Valenzuela, 1999). These processes approach youngsters with an immigrant background mainly from a deficit perspective and focus on having them learn the language and culture of the region of immigration as soon as possible. The underlying assumption is that these youngsters' social and cultural capital is inadequate to allow them to be successful in the educational system and that they should therefore become more like their autochthonous counterparts (Gibson, 1988; Roosens, 1995). This vision is sometimes advocated based on earlier theories on the integration of immigrants, theories that assumed that immigrants who are determined to settle permanently in their new country – and who wish to benefit from the opportunities provided by the new society (i.e. the labour market and education) in order to build a better future for themselves and their children – should and will ultimately assimilate completely into the dominant society. This idea is the core of classical assimilation theory as formulated by Gordon (1964). Segmented assimilation models, however, reject the idea of a single straight-line assimilation path, which eventually leads to equal outcomes for all groups (Portes & Zhou, 1993; Rumbaut, 1997). They do show that if this strategy tends to work for some immigrant groups, it is often detrimental to others. In the same context, many studies have highlighted the importance of 'cultural markers' in immigrants' ability to establish a niche within the host country – references to the language, history and religion of the culture of origin, with the caveat that one should not fall into essentialized visions in this regard (Clycq, 2012, 2014; Portes & Fernandez-Kelly, 2006; Roosens, 1998; Timmerman, 2000). Research points out that minority groups whose language and culture receive sufficient recognition feel more appreciated as participants in society and will consequently develop stronger ties with the society in which they are living. Social psychologists have already shown that accommodation of diversity in the 'new' country can have a positive effect on adaptation because it reduces 'acculturative stress' (Berry, 2001). In the same vein, political philosophers argue that accommodation of diversity can stimulate participation in the institutions of the host society and create a sense of belonging (e.g. Kymlicka, 1995; Modood, 2007; Parekh, 2000). Many of these arguments lie at the foundation of the Multiculturalism Policy in Canada, the oldest official policy in this regard in the Western world, which stresses that the whole society is enriched by the preservation of some elements of immigrant culture and the thriving of a pluralist common heritage (Juteau et al., 1998).

In line with this, some scholars argue that, contrary to subtractive schooling, additive schooling approaches could have a positive influence on the school performances of minority groups, especially when they belong to marginalized communities whose history and contribution has been undervalued, both at the international and national levels (Gibson et al., 2013). As Portes and Fernandez-Kelly (2006) claim:

> unlike the full assimilation approach emphasized by public school personnel, [. . .] it is not necessary to reject one's own culture and history to do well in school. On the contrary, such roots can provide the necessary point of reference to strengthen the children's self-esteem and aspirations for the future.
> (p. 19)

Although many immigrant children and youngsters navigate smoothly between competing worlds, especially when their families exhibit positive characteristics supporting school success (such as a higher valorization of education, literacy and discipline than in the average native family) researchers have found that in some groups, underachievement is higher when students feel that their culture is not fully accepted in the school. This refers, for example, to the acceptance and status of their native language, teacher attitudes, the feeling of being welcomed at school or the legitimization of the students' own background within the classroom and the school (Gibson, 1988; Mc Andrew et al., 2015; Yosso, 2005). Research also suggests that some straightforward strategies can help counter negative perceptions, processes of stigmatization and disengagement (Benard, 1991; Inzlicht et al., 2011). Peer helping and cooperative learning give pupils a renewed sense of worth by developing the sense that their input and resources are valuable and can make a difference.

The findings discussed above provided the point of departure for UCSIA to organize an international academic workshop on 'Youth, Education & Value Change', which took place on 20–22 November 2013 at the University of Antwerp (Belgium). Based upon the various, interesting presentations, we selected those chapters that allow us to discuss the idea of valuing ethnocultural diversity in educational settings from a variety of perspectives while bringing them together in one, coherent framework. Therefore, in this book we mainly apply the aforementioned broad cultural-ecological approach to education and from a multilevel perspective we study the educational trajectories of youngsters and the transmission of different forms of capital, values and attitudes within educational and home/community environments.

The book is divided into four parts. The first part focuses on 'Values, relationships and institutions in a context of diversity' and discusses the vertical transmission of values over generations (Chapter 1) or the horizontal transmission of values between peers (Chapter 2). While the contribution of Gisela Trommsdorff's 'The influence of socioeconomic change and culture on intergenerational relations' deals with the question of whether early parent–child relations can predict the quality of intergenerational relations over the lifespan in the family, Klaus Boehnke and David Schiefer's chapter 'Horizontal transmission of value orientations in adolescence', presents an innovative method of operationalizing horizontal value transmission. Their research also disentangles the impact that different 'layers' of environments have on adolescents' values, examining how these 'layers' interact. Both studies apply a mainly quantitative approach to study these transmission processes while offering new insights into the similarities and differences between horizontal versus vertical value transmission. Marie Mc Andew's chapter 'Educational structures and the curriculum: reproducting or transforming ethnic boundaries?' looks at the impact of educational structures themselves on the reproduction or transformation of ethnic boundaries in the school. In modern, pluralistic societies, formal schooling plays a major role in the production and redefinition of identities and values through two of its main functions: the transmission of knowledge, and the formal and informal socialization of students. Marie McAndrew emphasizes the nature of school as a contested site, while stressing some differences between North America and Europe in this respect.

The second part of the book focuses more concretely on the 'Educational pathways' of immigrant youngsters. Chapter 4, 'Does congruence between the school and the home/community environment make a difference?' by Christiane Timmerman, Noel Clycq, Kenneth Hemmerechts and Johan Wets, builds on research conducted in Flanders/Belgium. This study also affirms the significance of socioeconomic and immigrant background in predicting school success. More interestingly, it was also found that elements indicating congruence between school, home and peer's contexts are related to having experienced uninterrupted, and thus more successful school careers. Chapter 5, 'The Quebec youth of immigrant origin in secondary education: educational pathways and the factors influencing graduation', by Jacques Ledent and Marie Mc Andrew presents a broad overview of the results stemming from a large, comprehensive study of the pathways and performance of immigrant-origin students in Quebec. Among other things, it shows that although the selective nature of the Canadian/Québecois immigration policies clearly has an impact on the overall positive school careers of minority youth, differences between ethnic groups are still important, especially for the second generation. Chapter 6, 'Culture, narratives and upward educational mobility' by Nicolas Legewie adds an interesting perspective to this idea of educational success, and uses German data to grasp individuals' narratives on educational success and upward social mobility. He demonstrates how narratives of upward mobility work as mechanisms for upward mobility in two ways: pushing an internalization of norms, and managing social relations and social distance.

The third part of the book redirects its attention towards the meso-level factors and contexts of 'Peers, family and community' that influence educational trajectories. Chapter 7, 'Parents, schools and diversity: challenges and opportunities for parental involvement in a changing global context' by Gill Crozier, focuses on the relations between minority parents and school personnel in a British context. For understanding the role of parents/families (and primary carers/guardians) in relation to schools, particularly with respect to diversity, she locates her analysis in the context of globalization and neoliberal education policies. Chapter 8, 'Aspirations disclosed: the case of Turkish-Belgian parents in Brussels' by Fatma Zehra Çolak also delves into the relations between minority parents and school. Çolak uses the concept of 'aspirations', as both a framework and useful tool in conceptualizing and analysing the future dreams and experiences of these parents regarding the educational career of their children. Chapter 9, 'The Polish community school in Flanders: bridging the gap between school and home environment' by Edith Piqueray, Noel Clycq and Christiane Timmerman highlights the case of a Polish community school and its relation with mainstream schools in Flanders. With their study, the authors demonstrate the relevance of community schools in enhancing the social, cultural and linguistic capital of Polish youngsters in Flanders.

The fourth and final part of the book discusses the 'Social, systemic and school dynamics' and zooms in on several specific processes emerging in and across the different contexts discussed above. Chapter 10, 'Aspirations and stigmatization as factors of school success' by Noel Clycq, Ward Nouwen and Marjolein Braspenningx, studies the influence of teacher respect and/or stigmatization on pupils' aspirations. Data from a survey and ethnographic research demonstrates that the interactions between teachers and pupils can have significant effects on pupils' identification with school. Chapter 11, 'Partnership between schools and immigrant families and communities' by Geneviève Audet, Marie Mc Andrew and Michèle Vatz Laaroussi, turns the focus to one of the most important levers of schools in fostering equal opportunity and school success for minority youth: their relationship with parents and the wider milieu. The chapter studies this question in the context of Quebec's, and especially Montreal's, highly diversified schools and proposes innovative avenues in this regard to transform challenges into assets. Chapter 12, 'Rethinking values and schooling in white working-class neighbourhoods' by Ruth Lupton, focuses on the experiences and trajectories of white working-class pupils and families in education. Organized around the case of a deindustrialized neighbourhood in Northern England, Lupton argues that 'neighbourhood effects' need to be rethought as 'spatial injustices' and that 'justice as recognition' needs to take its place with 'justice as distribution' in the way teachers and school leaders think about their roles in these neighbourhoods.

In the conclusion, Alhassane and Mc Andrew offer a critical reflection on the main theoretical and practical contributions of this book with a special emphasis on the complementary nature of the various chapters. They highlight primarily the four assets of the collective endeavour offered in this book: the variety of disciplines and methodological approaches, the complementarity of various levels of analysis, the diversity of political and social contexts, as well as the identification of 'promising practices' on the issues at hand.

This book takes the growing ethnocultural diversity in education systems to heart and tries to study the various related educational processes from a multi-disciplinary and multimethod approach. It aims to offer more insight into underlying mechanisms that are often implicit but can be important factors that positively or negatively influence educational trajectories and outcomes.

## References

Alba, R. & Holdaway, J. (2013). *The Children of Immigrants at School: A Comparative Look at Integration in the United States and Western Europe*. New York: New York University Press.

Antrop-González, R. (2006). Toward the school as sanctuary concept in multicultural small school urban education: Implications for small high school reform. *Curriculum Inquiry*, 36(3), 273–301.

Benard, B. (1991). *Fostering resiliency in kids: Protective factors in the family, school, and community*. Opinion papers. Retrieved from: http://eric.ed.gov/?id=ED335781.

Berry, J. (2001). A psychology of immigration. *Journal of Social Issue*, 57(3), 615–31.

Bourdieu, P. & Passeron, J.-C. (1977). *Reproduction in Education, Society and Culture*. London: Sage Publications.

Bronfenbrenner, U. (1989). Ecological systems theory. *Annals of Child Development*, 6, 187–249.

Clycq, N. (2012). 'My daughter is a free woman, so she can't marry a Muslim': The gendering of ethno-religious boundaries. *European Journal of Women's Studies*, 19(2), 157–71.

Clycq, N. (2014). 'You can't escape from it. It's in your blood': Naturalizing ethnicity and strategies to ensure family and in-group cohesion. *Ethnography*. (Published online 3 October 2014) DOI: 10.1177/1466138114552948.

Clycq, N., Nouwen, W. & Vandenbroucke, A. (2013). Meritocracy, deficit thinking and the invisibility of the system: Discourses on educational success and failure. *British Educational Research Journal*, 40(5), 796–819.

EUROSTAT. (2014). School enrolment and early leavers from education and training. Retrieved from: http://ec.europa.eu/eurostat/statistics-explained/index.php/School_enrolment_and_early_leavers_from_education_and_training.

Feinstein, L., Duckworth, K. & Sabates, R. (2004). *A model of inter-generational transmission of educational success*. London: Centre for Research on the Wider Benefits of Learning.

Finnie, R., Frenette, M., Mueller, R. E. & Sweetman, A. (2010). *Pursuing Higher Education in Canada: Economic, Social and Policy Dimensions*. Montréal/Kingston: McGill's-Queens University Press.

Gibson, M. (1988). *Accommodation Without Assimilation: Sikh Immigrants in an American High School*. New York: Cornell University Press.

Gibson, M., Carrasco, S., Pàmies, J., Ponferrada, M. & Ríos-Rojas, A. (2013). Different systems, similar results: Youth of immigrant origin at school in California and Catalonia. In R. Alba & J. Holdaway (eds), *The Children of Immigrants at School: A Comparative Look at Integration in the United States and Western Europe* (pp. 84–119). New York: New York University Press.

Gordon, M. M. (1964). *Assimilation in American life: The Role of Race, Religion, and National Origins*. New York: Oxford University Press.

Inzlicht, M., Tullett, A. M., Legault, L. & Kang, S. K. (2011). Lingering effects: Stereotype threat hurts more than you think. *Social Issues and Policy Review*, 5(1), 227–56.

Juteau, D., Mc Andrew, M. & Pietrantonio, L. (1998). Multiculturalism 'à la Canadian' and intégration 'à la québécoise': Transcending their limits. In R. Baubœck & J. Rundell (eds), *Blurred Boundaries* (pp. 95–110). Avebury: The European Centre.

Kymlicka, W. (1995). *Multicultural Citizenship: A Liberal Theory of Minority Rights*. Oxford: Oxford University Press.

Mc Andrew, M. (2013). *Fragile Majorities and Education: Belgium, Catalonia, Northern Ireland, and Quebec*. Montréal: McGill-Queen's University Press.

Mc Andrew, M., Balde, A., Bakhshaei, M., Tardif-Grenier, K., Audet, G., Armand, F., Guyon, S., Ledent, J., Lemieux, G., Potvin, M., Rahm, J., Vatz, L., Michelle, C. A. & Rousseau, C. (2015). *La réussite éducative des élèves issus de l'immigration: Dix ans de recherche et d'intervention au Québec*. Montréal: Presses de l'Université de Montréal.

Modood, T. (2007). *Multiculturalism: A Civic Idea*. Cambridge: Polity Press.

NESSE. (2010). Early school leaving, lessons from research for policy makers: An independent expert report submitted to the European Commission. Luxembourg: Publications Office of the European Union.

Parekh, B. (2000). *Rethinking Multiculturalism: Cultural Diversity and Political Theory*. Basingstoke: Macmillan.

Portes, A. & Fernandez-Kelly, P. (2006). *No margin for error: Educational and occupational achievement among disadvantaged children of immigrants*. CMD-Working Paper. Princeton, NJ: Princeton University.

Portes, A. & Zhou, M. (1993). The new second generation: Segmented assimilation and its variants. *Annals of the American Academy of Political and Social Science*, 530, 74–96.

Roosens, E. (1995). *Rethinking Culture, 'Multicultural Society' and the School*. Oxford: Pergamon.

Roosens, E. (1998). *Eigen grond eerst? Primordiale autochtonie: Dilemma van de multiculturele samenleving*. Leuven: Acco.

Rumbaut, R. G. (1997). Assimilation and its discontents: Between rhetoric and reality. *International Migration Review*, 31(4), 923–60.

Rumberger, R. & Ah Lim, S. (2008). Why students drop out of school: A review of 25 years of research. Santa Barbara, CA: University of California Santa Barbara.

Timmerman, C. (2000). Secular and religious nationalism among young Turkish women in Belgium: Education may make the difference. *Anthropology and Education Quarterly*, 31(3), 333–54.

Valenzuela, A. (1999). *Subtractive Schooling: U.S. Mexican Youth and the Politics of Caring*. Albany, NY: State University of New York Press.

Yosso, T. J. (2005). Whose culture has capital? A critical race theory discussion of community cultural wealth. *Race Ethnicity and Education*, 8(1), 69–91.

# Part 1
# Values, relationships and institutions in a context of diversity

# 1 The influence of socioeconomic change and culture on intergenerational relations[1]

*Gisela Trommsdorff*

## Introduction

Why is a culture-contextual lens important for the study of intergenerational relations? Intergenerational relations can be viewed from a structural perspective focusing on the relationships among different cohorts who share the same historical and sociocultural background in their socialization experiences (Mannheim, 1929/1964). Different from this approach is the psychological perspective on biologically and psychologically related individuals from different generations within a family. Intergenerational relations influence one's individual development by transmitting cognitive, motivational, social and emotional resources. Furthermore, intergenerational relations may also influence the sociocultural and economic context, e.g. economic exchange among generations, stability of families, changes of cultural values. At the same time, taking an ecocultural perspective, intergenerational relations are influenced by the sociocultural and economic context. Accordingly, intergenerational relations are related to cultural values in several ways. They function to transmit certain values from one generation to the next, and they are shaped by the respective value orientation in a culture.

Adolescents play a major role in this process since they are developing value preferences as part of their identity development, which in turn is influenced partly by the quality of the parent–child relationship. The parent–child relationship influences the child's social, cognitive, and emotional development, which in turn is relevant in the development of intergenerational relations throughout the lifespan (Albert & Trommsdorff, 2014; Trommsdorff, 2006). For example, attachment relationships in early childhood are the basis of further developmental outcomes, including the later relationship with one's ageing parents.

Additionally, parents and their children generally share the same cultural context and related developmental conditions that influence parenting, the parent–child relationship, and the relationships with family members from different generations. Thus, we conceive of parent–child relationships as a specific element within a network of extended intergenerational relationships that is in turn embedded in a particular cultural context and its value system. This view is informed by Bronfenbrenner's (1979) ecocultural model of development.

In line with Schwartz (1992, 2007, 2012), we understand value orientations as motivating and guiding individual behaviour (Trommsdorff, 2012b). Schwartz claims universality of ten basic human values with distinct goals. The relative importance of these values may change over time, especially in times of socioeconomic and cultural changes. Here, the question arises about what kind of value changes adolescents are experiencing, and how these changes are affecting adolescent development and also intergenerational relations in a society. Part of such value changes are preconditions for and consequences of intergenerational relations, particularly with respect to the current widespread globalization. All over the world, ongoing fundamental demographic changes – increasing life expectancy and decreasing birth rate – are interrelated with major economic and social changes, and respective changes in value orientations and intergenerational relations in the family.

Until after the Second World War, a typical traditional family consisted of three generations – grandparents, parents and children – with all three generations usually living together in one household. However, during the last decades ongoing socioeconomic, demographic and cultural changes have affected this family structure significantly (Bertram & Ehlert, 2012). Changing economic and social resources, and related value orientations of the older and younger generation have also affected changes in intergenerational relations.

For example, the increasing life expectancy implies a potentially longer life span shared among generational cohorts differing in age. However, decreasing birth rates as part of the demographic change are giving rise to sociopolitical concerns, e.g. regarding justice in the distribution of resources among the generations. It is discussed whether conflicts between the generations may arise due to the economic strain of young cohorts who are supposed to carry the burden of supporting the elderly.

Sociocultural changes imply questions about how parent–child relationships will change, and how and on which basis family members, especially children and ageing parents, can expect to receive and provide care and support. Ongoing sociocultural changes may cause more individualization related to a dissolution of family bonds, or it may activate a revival of fruitful and mutually supportive intergenerational relations. Here, psychological and sociological approaches are needed to clarify the complexity of the ongoing changes, the conditions for and the consequences of changes in intergenerational relations, and the role of adolescents and their value orientations in this process.

Here, I conceptualize intergenerational relations as relationships between individual, biologically connected members of a family who belong to different generations. Accordingly, my interest is in children's relations to their parents and grandparents, and parents' relations to their own parents (children's grandparents). These relations are asymmetrical and bidirectional, and they imply a long-term commitment usually based on trust and reciprocity.

Bengtson (2000) and Bengtson and Roberts (1991) have suggested a model of family solidarity to characterize intergenerational relations in the family. However, social change in families due to individualization, geographic mobility, separation, step-parenting and changes during the individual life course may undermine lifelong solidarity relations among family members and thereby affect children's sense of responsibility with respect to supporting their ageing parents (Silverstein & Conroy, 2009). The question remains: what effect does the dissolution of both sociocultural norms as well as biological and economic bonds have on the parent–child relationship? Is its socioemotional quality perhaps thereby affected?

Moreover, since parent–child relations do not remain the same over time, studies of intergenerational relations need a lifespan approach that takes various age groups into account: beyond extending the notion of parent–child relations to more than only two generations (including grandparents, parents, and children), I argue that the developmental age and the developmental process in parent–child relations should be considered (Trommsdorff, 2006).

This perspective borrows from psychological research that shows how closely individual development is related to the family and the cultural context. The quality of the early parent–child relationship sets the tone for further developmental outcomes of the child, including internalization of values, social and emotional competence, resilience to risks, coping with challenges, and prosocial motivation for supporting ageing parents. Therefore, early parent–child relations (based on attachment, see Bowlby, 1969, 1988) can partly predict the quality of intergenerational relations in the family through the generations. Furthermore, the quality of relations among generations is assumed to be an important factor in the structure of societies, and the socialization function of the family, affecting the continuity of cultural values.

Most research on intergenerational relations have studied Western, European-American samples, largely ignoring the diversity of cultures and the impact of the cultural context on societal and interpersonal phenomena (named 'WEIRD: Western, Educated, Industrialized, Rich, and Democratic' by Henrich et al., 2010). This is especially problematic given the ongoing trends in demographic changes, migration and urbanization, and continuous political and socioeconomic changes in most parts of the world. In order to avoid an ethnocentric bias, more cross-cultural studies that focus specifically on culture are needed (Trommsdorff & Nauck, 2005, 2006, 2010). These could test the universality and culture-specificity of intergenerational relations and their socioeconomic and culture-psychological correlates. Cultures are not homogeneous entities; they are continuously changing in various aspects and directions, which makes it difficult to form a culture-informed theory on intergenerational relations. However, one may start from some general psychological assumptions and their empirical validation and focus on to what extent psychological implications of the context influence the theoretically interesting relations among the variables under study. Using this framework, the present study deals with intergenerational relations in diverse cultural contexts, partly based on theoretical perspectives and results from the international Value-of-Children and Intergenerational Relations Study (VOC-IR) (Trommsdorff & Nauck, 2010).

My focus is first and foremost on demographic and value change in diverse cultures. Second, I discuss issues of intergenerational transmission of values. Third, I deal with questions of support in the family between the generations.

## Demographic change and changing values of the family

Globalization and demographic shifts are affecting societies and families all over the world, especially in terms of value changes (Bertram & Ehlert, 2012). Life expectancy in most industrialized countries is continuously rising, while fertility rates are continuously declining. This ongoing pattern implies an increase in the relative number of old people and a relative decrease of the younger generation. Additionally, the divorce rate and different patterns of family structure (e.g. living apart together) have been increasing (Nave-Herz, 2012). As a consequence, people are facing the prospect of living in their old age without close family ties. In all European countries, persons above age 80 are reported to be living alone (Börsch-Supan et al., 2005). Whether this implies loneliness and dependency on professional care is an empirical question. Recent studies show considerable differences in loneliness between South-European and North-European countries (Börsch-Supan et al., 2005).

Regarding non-European countries, significant changes also abound. Japan has undergone enormous transformations in a short time, from being an agrarian to an industrial and a post-industrial society. At present, it is experiencing a shrinking population due to low birthrate, and at the same time the highest percentage of elderly in the world. These changes have significant effects on the family and on intergenerational relations, partly also since traditional values of 'filial piety' are declining (Linhart, 2012).

Fertility rates in less economically developed countries such as those in Sub-Saharan Africa remain rather high, while the life expectancy of the population increases due to improved medical care. An increasing number of young people who are facing unemployment and poverty choose to migrate, leaving their ageing parents. Thus, socioeconomic and demographic change affect family as well as care of the older generation (e.g. Ntozi, 2012).

Socioeconomic changes are related to demographic changes, especially insofar as both imply value changes. Values have been conceived of as motivating individuals to achieve certain goals. Values may differ between individual societies, and also depend on the cultural context and related cultural values (e.g. rather individualistic goals of independence, autonomy, and self-reliance are in contrast to rather collectivistic goals of interdependence and relatedness). On the cultural level, values function as a basis for social rules and legitimation of institutions integrating individuals into the society (see Trommsdorff, 2012a) and characterizing culture-specific general tendencies. Considerable value change from materialistic (e.g. security) to post-materialistic values (e.g. self-fulfilment) has been observed in European industrialized societies (Inglehart, 1997). This change has been accompanied by changes in family values (e. g. decreasing preference of extended to increasing preference of nuclear families and single households), and changes in the value of children in society (Kagitcibasi, 2007; Trommsdorff, 2012b; Trommsdorff & Nauck, 2005).

Trommsdorff and Nauck (2005, 2006) relate demographic changes to changes in parent–child relationships and in the value of children in different cultural contexts. In traditional societies with less economic development, children are valued in terms of how much social status and old-age security they provide. Here, one can say that the economic and social value of children is higher than in more industrialized societies, where children are primarily valued for how much emotional reward they provide the parents. This may explain the decreasing fertility rate in industrialized countries, since more than one or two children would not necessarily provide a higher degree of emotional satisfaction (Mayer et al., 2005). In contrast, in less industrialized countries, each child is potentially contributing to the parents' old age security, thereby reinforcing the economic or material value of children (Kim & Park, 2005; Mishra et al., 2005; Trommsdorff & Mayer, 2012). In his cross-cultural study on adolescents' family models, Mayer (2009, 2013) has shown how the interdependent family model is related to the material value of children, while the independent family model is related to the emotional value of children (Mayer & Trommsdorff, 2010, 2012). Furthermore, in a cross-cultural and multi-level study we have shown how adolescents' value of children is related to the intention to have children in the future. Most adolescents from diverse cultures wish to have children and are motivated by expecting close and satisfying emotional relationships with their offspring – thus clearly giving priority to an emotional (in contrast to an economic or social) value of children (Mayer & Trommsdorff, 2010).

## Transmission of values

Intergenerational relations in the family are an important basis of socialization processes. Here, the transmission of values and behavioural preferences between the generations are grounded. Values can be transmitted from the older to the younger generation and vice versa, thereby influencing the direction of value change or cultural continuity (Trommsdorff, 2009a). The transmission of values follows both vertical (e.g. parent–child relations) and horizontal (e.g. peer relations; dyadic partnership; 'Zeitgeist') directions. Transmission is based on interaction processes among components of the microsystem – that is, in the family, school, peers and neighbourhood. According to Bronfenbrenner's (1979) ecosystem approach, the microsystem is embedded in and interacting with the meso- and exosystem (mass media, friends of family, legal and social welfare services), while these are interacting with the macrosystem (cultural values, religion, ideologies). An ecosystem approach assumes bidirectionality in the transmission of values.

Under which conditions are values transmitted within the family, between parents and grandparents, and children (grandchildren)? According to culture-informed studies on the transmission of values, the quality of intergenerational relations is a relevant predictor for successful internalization of the respective parental values (Albert & Trommsdorff, 2014; Trommsdorff, 2009a). Parenting and parent–child relations are the transmission belt for the culture-specific transmission of parental values. However, parenting alone cannot explain whether the intended transmission of values is successful or not. In order to understand the transmission process and successful internalization of the parents' values, it is necessary to study the features of parental disciplinary behaviour, whether the parents' intentions are accurately perceived by the child, and also whether the child accepts the parents' message (Grusec & Goodnow, 1994). The child's acceptance of parents' goals and values in turn depends on the parent–child relationship, especially the quality of attachment (Trommsdorff, 2009a). This model for the process of internalization is useful to describe the successful transmission of values from the parents to their children.

In empirical studies, several difficulties have to be solved. Whether the child accurately perceives parental values, and whether the child accepts the parental message, probably depends on the quality of the parent–child relationship and the cultural context. For example, in our studies on adolescents' perception of parental control, German adolescents overall felt rejected with respect to their parents' control and monitoring, while Japanese adolescents felt accepted and satisfied (Trommsdorff, 1985, 2015).

Furthermore, the empirical assessment of parenting is difficult due to its complex multifaceted characteristics of e.g. warmth and control or acceptance and rejection (Maccoby, 2000; Rohner & Cournover, 1994; Rohner & Pettengill, 1985). Baumrind's (1968) distinction among authoritarian, authoritative and permissive parenting has been the dominant approach of studies based on Western samples. However, cross-cultural and culture-informed studies have shown that authoritarian parenting has a very different meaning in Asian cultures (Chao & Tseng, 2002). Moreover, recent research underlines that global measures of parenting neglecting the situational context are insufficient. Therefore, Grusec and Davidov (2010) have suggested a domain-specific approach to parenting.

Of special importance for further development is the early mother–child relationship; this can evoke secure or insecure attachment, the basis for an internal working model of the self and the world (Bowlby, 1969, 1988). Attachment research has shown that sensitive mothers can build an attachment relationship with their child which fosters a secure working model (Grossmann & Grossmann, 1990). However, again, sensitivity with respect to mothering takes on different meanings in different geographical contexts due to situational and cultural differences (Rothbaum et al., 2006; Trommsdorff & Friedlmeier, 2010; Ziehm et al., 2013).

Therefore, cross-cultural and domain-specific approaches should be combined for a better understanding of parenting as a transmission belt for values, and the quality of parent–child relations should be specified to predict the transmission and the internalization of values (Albert et al., 2011; Trommsdorff, 2009b). Furthermore, due to the effects of cultural norms and developmental changes, it is not easy to empirically assess whether value transmission was successful or not. For example, correlations between verbal measures of parents' and their children's values should be related to behavioural measures and perceived cultural norms.

Finally, bidirectional influences should be taken into account: children come of age in a particular peer group and adopt values that in turn organize their individual and social development, including their interaction with their parents – thereby influencing their parents' value orientations and resulting intergenerational relations. Bidirectional influences can differ among different cultures (Trommsdorff & Kornadt, 2003).

## Intergenerational relations

Intergenerational relations differ among individuals and also among cultures. Rothbaum et al. (2000) have discussed the cultural differences in intergenerational relations over the lifespan, distinguishing the path of generative tension and the related lens of individuation, and the path of symbiotic harmony with preference for the lens of accommodation. For example, in cultures where individualism and independence is highly valued, the parent–child relationship develops from separation and reunion experiences with the caregiver in early childhood. In childhood, personal preferences are built up; in adolescence and adulthood, negotiations serve as the basis of trust in the relationship. In contrast, in cultures where interdependence and relatedness are highly valued, infancy is characterized by union (mother–child 'oneness'). In childhood, the development of intergenerational relations is based upon understanding and accepting the expectations of others, which in turn furthers the processes of internalization. In adolescence, when stability of the intergenerational relationships is achieved, the assurance of secure relatedness in adulthood is promoted (Rothbaum et al., 2000). The culture-informed perspective thus allows the analysis of intergenerational relationships over the lifespan by taking cultural values and their transmission in the socialization process into account.

Since intergenerational relations in the family have only rarely been studied cross-culturally, we have started the 'Value of Children and Intergenerational Relations' Study (VOC-IR) (Trommsdorff & Nauck, 2005, 2006, 2010) including three-generation samples from 20 countries (in each country about 1,000 adolescents, 1,000 mothers and 100 grandparents) (in some countries intracultural comparisons of urban and rural samples were carried out). This project has been designed to study the quality of intergenerational relations in the cultural context for predicting value transmission and support for ageing parents (Schwarz & Trommsdorff, 2005a). We started from a lifespan perspective in order to be able to study later stages in the parent–child relation as well as relations between non-adjacent generations, such as grandchildren and grandparents. Therefore, our theoretical framework is based on an ecocultural and developmental approach. Our culture-informed model of intergenerational relationships across the lifespan considers parent–child relationships as embedded in the socioeconomic and cultural context (Trommsdorff, 2006).

The model to be tested includes (1) *contextual factors*, e.g. cultural values and socioeconomic factors, (2) *person variables* such as attachment and individual value orientations, (3) *relationship variables* regarding the child (e.g. preferred child-rearing practices and investments in the child) and regarding the parents as well (e.g. given support to pursue these goals) (Trommsdorff, 2001; Albert & Trommsdorff, 2014)

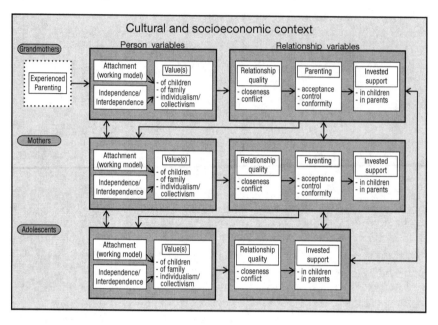

*Figure 1.1* Parent–child relations in three generations (the VOC-IR Study)

(see Figure 1.1). The relationships among these three aspects (context, person, parent–child relationship) were studied for three (biologically related) generations: adolescents, mothers, and grandmothers. Originally, six cultures were included in the study (Germany, Israel, Turkey, Republic of Korea, China and Indonesia). In the meantime, researchers from different parts of the world have joined the project, and currently, a large dataset ($N = 16.461$ participants) is available from nineteen different countries on four continents (Trommsdorff & Nauck, 2005, 2006, 2010). Multilevel analyses take context, person and relationships into account (e.g. Mayer & Trommsdorff, 2010).

The main question was whether socioeconomic changes affect value change (individualism/collectivism; family values; the value of children) and the quality of intergenerational relations. The basic hypothesis is as follows: there is mutual interaction between parents' and their children's values in all three generations, and that interaction is in turn influenced by the extent to which it is embedded in its sociocultural context. Accordingly, the analyses focused on person variables and relationship variables and their respective interrelations (see Figure 1.1). Some selected results from the VOC-IR Study are summarized in the following.

### Value of children and the family

The emotional value of children was high in all countries, however, significant differences occurred with respect to the utilitarian (socioeconomic) value of children: the more economically developed countries (e.g. Germany, France) are less in favour of utilitarian values of children as compared to less economically developed countries (e.g. China, India, Russia). Furthermore, in all countries, the older generation (grandparents) favour utilitarian values of children more than their adult daughters do (Trommsdorff & Mayer, 2012). Whether this difference in values depends on a value change or on the developmental age remains an open question.

Value orientations (measured on the individual level) are related to certain macro-level factors (measured on the cultural level). The Human Development Index (HDI) is positively associated with the emotional value of children and negatively associated with family values for both grandmothers and adult daughters. Additionally, individualism (measured as cultural dimension according to Hofstede, 1980) is negatively related to collectivism and family values, again, for both generations (Trommsdorff & Mayer, 2012).

Post-materialistic values (measured according to the World Value Survey 1990–1992) correlate negatively with the socioeconomic (utalitarian) value of children in Germany and France and positively in South Africa and India, while Japan, Korea and China are about in-between these two groups (cluster analyses) (Trommsdorff, 2006).

### *Giving and receiving support between the generations*

According to Bengtson (2000), solidarity should characterize the families even in times of individualization. However, the question is whether respective positive results for European-American families also hold for other countries (Bengtson *et al.*, 2000). The VOC-IR study allows the comparison of mean values of giving and receiving support across diverse cultures. The results show that in East Asian and Western countries, support given to the elderly mother (grandmother) by her adult daughter is lower than the support given by the grandmother to the adult daughter. However, in Germany, the given and received support is much lower than in China and Indonesia, while Korea is situated in the middle (Schwarz & Trommsdorff, 2005b). A closer look at the kind of support given by the adult daughters to their elderly mothers (grandmothers) shows that German adult daughters give less emotional, even less instrumental, and much less financial support as compared to Chinese and Korean adult daughters. German adult daughters distinguish clearly among the different kinds of support. When they do provide support, they prefer to give emotional support.

Adolescents in traditional, collectivistic cultures (Indonesia, India, Turkey, South Africa) who experience a conflict between helping their parents or meeting friends tend to prefer to help their parents. However, in individualistic cultures, adolescents facing the same/similar conflict prefer to meet up with their friends (Mayer & Trommsdorff, 2012; Schwarz *et al.*, 2012).

It is known from studies in lifespan intergenerational relations in Western countries that the anticipation of giving support to one's elderly parents can be a burden for children, adolescents and adults. In Asian cultures, children are normatively expected to support their elderly parents. Based on the Confucian tradition of filial piety, this filial duty is strongly established. However, in Western countries, the intention to support one's elderly parents is based on the individual decision and related prosocial motivation. Research in prosocial motivation has shown that a positive relationship with the person in need facilitates the motivation to help and give support (e.g. Eisenberg *et al.*, 2006; Staub, 1980). Therefore, more individual differences in support should be expected in those countries where values of individualism are high as compared to more traditional and collectivistic countries. More psychological conflict should also be expected in individualistic cultures since support is based on individual decision-making and related prosocial motivation. Empirical results from the VOC-IR study clearly show significant differences in the correlation between individualism (Hofstede's cultural dimension) and filial anxiety among the diverse countries with low individualism associated with low filial anxiety. This is the case for China, Turkey and India, while in Germany and France individualism is higher and at the same time filial anxiety is more pronounced.

Do these results indicate less intraindividual and intergenerational conflicts in traditional compared to more modern societies? Here, cultural differences in the conditions and functions of emotions (such as anxiety) have to be taken into account as part of culture-specific effects of socioemotional development (Trommsdorff & Cole, 2011). Therefore, it should be noted that our results show more filial anxiety when intergenerational relations are based on personal decisions, as is the case in individualistic cultures. In contrast, in traditional and collective cultures where cultural values of filial piety prevail, the normative expectation to support one's elderly parents is very strong; moreover, the general value to stabilize harmony in one's in-group and the emotional bond that underlies that value contribute to the very low probability of intra-individual conflicts. Our data clearly demonstrate that intergenerational conflicts are less pronounced in traditional, norm-oriented societies such as India, in contrast to Germany and France (Trommsdorff & Mayer, 2012).

## Summary and outlook

### Summary

So far, the empirical studies across different cultures have shown that intergenerational relations in the family as well as cultural values are important in the individual's development over his/her lifespan. They serve as a transmission belt for the transmission and internalization of values, but also serve the function of giving and receiving support between the generations. Our results have also shown that the quality of the relationship is important for both the transmission of values, and for the mutual support between the generations.

The results from our VOC-IR study are clearly in line with the assumptions based on the model of pathways for intergenerational relations over the lifespan by Rothbaum *et al.* (2000). The intergenerational relationship in individualistic cultures is more characterized by generative tension, while in collectivistic and interdependent cultures, it is more characterized by symbiotic harmony. The results from our VOC-IR study are only partly in line with the assumptions by Kagitcibasi (2007), since we could not observe the predicted direct change of cultures (high in independence and of cultures high in interdependence) towards a symbiosis of emotional interdependence. Our results are based on multilevel analyses involving very different cultures. However, in future research, the processes and effects of ongoing multi-facet cultural changes should be assessed.

The results of our studies do in general fit to Bengtson and Roberts's (1991) model of intergenerational solidarity, which had not previously been tested in large-scale cross-cultural comparisons. This underlines the assumption that socioeconomic changes do not disrupt family solidarity and mutual support among the generations in the family.

*Outlook*

In the present chapter, I could not report about gender effects in intergenerational relations. However, this is a very interesting issue, deserving more attention in culture-informed studies. Much of ongoing gender-related value change and change in intergenerational relations can be directly linked to cultural values. For example, in many traditional societies (e.g. in East and South East Asia), the eldest son is obliged to be in charge of honouring the ancestors, thus contributing to the continuity of the family. Or in India, the daughter has to leave her family of origin after marriage and live in her husband's household, fulfilling duties of a daughter to the mother-in-law. Cultural change of the patriarchal family system in Japan has resulted in substantial change with respect to the value of children and the value of family, including the role of men and women: three-generation households are decreasing, an increasing number of men and women do not marry (or get divorced at a later age), while the value of having a daughter instead of having a son (who has to fulfil duties in the service of the family and the ancestors) has been increasing (e.g. Linhart, 2012).

The transmission of values depends among other variables on the 'Zeitgeist' and the homogeneity of the context. Hence, the intergenerational relations in migrant families is an important area for future research, especially regarding questions of support and transmission of values (see Albert & Trommsdorff, 2014; Barni et al., 2012). For example, studies on migrants and non-migrants in Germany, in the Netherlands (Phalet & Schönpflug, 2001; Schönpflug, 2001), and in Israel (Knafo et al., 2009) found more similarities than differences between cultural groups. These studies clarified the importance of the culture-specific meaning of parenting variables for value transmission.

Since the transmission of values has implications for intergenerational relations and well-being, culture-informed studies on migrant families are of special importance. Hadjar et al. (2012) who have compared adolescents from migrant and minority families to majority families in Germany and Israel were able to show that value similarity between adolescents and their parents might promote well-being in families from the majority culture. Adolescents' well-being from migrant (or minority) families depends on the similarity of their families' values with the general cultural value orientation ('goodness-of-fit'). A related question has been asked by Albert, Ferring and Michels (2013) in their study on the function of intergenerational value similarity for intergenerational solidarity in migrant and non-migrant families in Luxembourg. Their results show that shared values within the family promote supportive intergenerational relations. However, sharing values does not mean 'absolute' value similarity (independent of situations), which is less preferable for intergenerational solidarity, while 'relative' value similarity (taking into account given circumstances) allows for flexibility between generations.

These studies aim to contribute to a better understanding of universal and culture-specific processes of development over the lifespan, the transmission of values over several generations in the family and the basis of support between the generations. The conditions and consequences of intergenerational relations and sociocultural change may thereby be clarified.

## Note

1   This chapter is based on the international 'Value of Children and Intergenerational Relations Study (VOC-IR)', PI: Gisela Trommsdorff and Bernhard Nauck, supported by the German Research Council (Tr 169/1–4).

## References

Albert, I. & Trommsdorff, G. (2014). The role of culture in development over the life span: An interpersonal relations approach. *Online Readings in Psychology and Culture*, 6. doi: http://dx.doi.org/10.9707/2307-0919.1057.

Albert, I., Ferring, D. & Michels, T. (2013). Intergenerational family relations in Luxembourg: Family values and intergenerational solidarity in Portuguese immigrant and Luxembourgish families. *European Psychologist*, *18*(1), 59–69. doi: 10.1027/1016-9040/a000125.

Albert, I., Trommsdorff, G. & Sabatier, C. (2011). Patterns of relationship regulation: German and French adolescents' perceptions with regard to their mothers. *Family Science*, 2, 58–67.

Barni, D., Knafo, A., Ben-Arieh, A. & Haj-Yahia, M. M. (2012, March). Parent–child value similarity within and across cultures. In W. Friedlmeier (Chair), Intergenerational Relations and Transmission of Values in Cross-cultural Comparison. Symposium conducted at the Value of Children and Intergenerational Relations Workshop, University of Konstanz, Germany.

Baumrind, D. (1968). Authoritarian vs. authoritative parental control. *Adolescence*, 3, 255–72.

Bengtson, V. L. (2000). Beyond the nuclear family: The increasing importance of multi-generational bonds (The Burgess Award Lecture). *Journal of Marriage & the Family*, 63, 1–16.

Bengtson, V. L. & Roberts, R. E. L. (1991). Intergenerational solidarity in aging families: An example of formal theory construction. *Journal of Marriage and the Family*, 53, 856–70.

Bengtson, V. L., Kyong-Dong, K., Myers, G. C. & Eun, K.-S. (eds). (2000). *Aging in East and West: Families, States, and Elderly*. New York: Springer Publishing Company.

Bertram, H. & Ehlert, N. (eds). (2012). *Family, Ties and Care: Family Transformation in a Plural Modernity*. Opladen, Germany; Barbara Budrich.

Börsch-Supan, A., Brugiavini, A., Jürges, H., Mackenbach, J., Siegrist, J. & Weber, G. (2005). *Health, Aging and Retirement in Europe: First Results from the Survey of Health, Aging and Retirement in Europe*. Mannheim: Mannheim Research Institute for the Economics of Aging (MEA).

Bowlby, J. (1969). *Attachment and Loss: Vol. 1. Attachment*. London: Hogarth Press.

Bowlby, J. (1988). *A Secure Base: Parent–Child Attachment and Healthy Human Development*. New York: Basic Books.

Bronfenbrenner, U. (1979). *The Ecology of Human Development: Experiments by Nature and Design*. Cambridge, MA: Harvard University Press.

Chao, R. & Tseng, V. (2002). Parenting of Asians. In M. H. Bornstein (ed.), *Handbook of Parenting: Vol. 4. Social Conditions and Applied Parenting* (2nd edn, pp. 59–93). Mahwah, NJ: Lawrence Erlbaum Association.

Eisenberg, N., Fabes, R. A. & Spinrad, T. L. (2006). Prosocial development. In W. Damon, R. M. Lerner & N. Eisenberg (eds), *Handbook of Child Psychology: Social, Emotional, and Personality Development* (pp. 646–718). New York: Wiley.

Grossmann, K. E. & Grossmann, K. (1990). The wider concept of attachment in cross-cultural research. *Human Development*, *33*, 31–47.

Grusec, J. E. & Davidov, M. (2010). Integrating different perspectives on socialization theory and research: A domain-specific approach. *Child Development*, *81*, 687–709.

Grusec, J. E. & Goodnow, J. J. (1994). Impact of parental discipline methods on the child's internalization of values: A reconceptualization of current points of view. *Developmental Psychology*, *30*, 4–19.

Hadjar, A., Boehnke, K., Knafo, A., Daniel, E., Musiol, A.-L., Schiefer, D. & Möllering, A. (2012). Parent–child value similarity and subjective well-being in the context of migration: An exploration. *Family Science*, *3*, 55–63.

Henrich, J., Heine, S. J. & Norenzayan, A. (2010). The weirdest people in the world? *Behavioral and Brain Science*, *33*, 61–83.

Hofstede, G. H. (1980). *Culture's Consequences: International Differences in Work-related Values*. Los Angeles, CA: Sage Publications.

Inglehart, R. (1997). *Modernization and Postmodernization: Cultural, Economic, and Political Change in 43 Societies*. Princeton, NJ: Princeton University Press.

Kagitcibasi, C. (2007). *Family, Self, and Human Development Across Cultures: Theory and Application* (2nd edn). Mahwah, NJ: Erlbaum.

Kim, U. & Park, Y.-S. (2005). Family, parent–child relationships, fertility rates, and values of children in Korea: Indigenous, psychological, and cultural analysis. In G. Trommsdorff & B. Nauck (eds), *The Value of Children in Cross-cultural Perspective: Case Studies from Eight Societies*. Lengerich, Germany: Pabst Science.

Knafo, A., Assor, A., Schwartz, S. H. & David, L. (2009). Culture, migration, and family value socialization: A theoretical model and empirical investigation with Russian-speaking youth in Israel. In U. Schönpflug (ed.), *Cultural Transmission: Developmental, Psychological, Social, and Methodological Perspectives* (pp. 269–96). New York: Cambridge University Press.

Linhart, S. (2012). Intergenerational relations in Japan's aged society. In H. Bertram & N. Ehlert (eds), *Family, Ties and Care: Family Transformation in a Plural Modernity* (pp. 379–92). Opladen, Germany: Barbara Budrich.

Maccoby, E. E. (2000). Parenting and its effects on children: On reading and misreading behavior genetics. *Annual Review of Psychology*, *51*(1), 1–27. doi: doi:10.1146/annurev.psych.51.1.1.

Mannheim, K. (1929/1964). *Das Problem der Generationen* (*The Problem of Generations*). Köln, Germany: Westdeutscher Verlag.

Mayer, B. (2009). Adolescents' family models: A cross-cultural study (doctoral dissertation, University of Konstanz). Konstanz, Germany: Universitätsbibliothek, KOPS.

Mayer, B. (2013). Family change theory: A preliminary evaluation on the basis of recent cross-cultural studies. In I. Albert & D. Ferring (eds), *Intergenerational Relations: European Perspectives on Family and Society* (pp. 167–87). Cambridge: Policy Press.

Mayer, B. & Trommsdorff, G. (2010). Adolescents' value of children and their intentions to have children: A cross-cultural and multilevel analysis. *Journal of Cross-Cultural Psychology*, 41, 671–89. doi: 10.1177/0022022110372195.

Mayer, B. & Trommsdorff, G. (2012). Cross-cultural perspectives on adolescents' religiosity and family orientation. In G. Trommsdorff & X. Chen (eds), *Values, Religion, and Culture in Adolescent Development* (pp. 341–69). New York: Cambridge University Press.

Mayer, B., Albert, I., Trommsdorff, G. & Schwarz, B. (2005). Value of children in Germany: Dimensions, comparison of generations, and relevance for parenting. In G. Trommsdorff & B. Nauck (eds), *The Value of Children in Cross-cultural Perspective: Case Studies from Eight Societies* (pp. 43–65). Lengerich, Germany: Pabst Science.

Mishra, R. C., Mayer, B., Trommsdorff, G., Albert, I. & Schwarz, B. (2005). The value of children in urban and rural India: Cultural background and empirical results. In G. Trommsdorff & B. Nauck (eds), *The Value of Children in Cross-cultural Perspective: Case Studies from Eight Societies* (pp. 143–70). Lengerich, Germany: Pabst Science.

Nave-Herz, R. (2012). *Familie heute: Wandel der Familienstrukturen und Folgen für die Erziehung* (Family today: Change of family structure and consequences for parenting) (Vol. 5). Darmstadt, Germany: WBG.

Ntozi, J. (2012). The demographic situation of Sub-Saharan Africa. In H. Bertram & N. Ehlert (eds), *Family, Ties and Care: Family Transformation in a Plural Modernity* (pp. 465–80). Opladen, Berlin: Barbara Budrich Publ.

Phalet, K. & Schönpflug, U. (2001). Intergenerational transmission of collectivism and achievement values in two acculturation contexts: The case of Turkish families in Germany and Turkish and Moroccan families in the Netherlands. *Journal of Cross-Cultural Psychology*, 32, 186–201.

Rohner, R. P. & Cournoyer, D. E. (1994). Universals in youths' perceptions of parental acceptance and rejection: Evidence from factor analyses within eight sociocultural groups worldwide. *Cross-Cultural Research*, 28, 371–83.

Rohner, R. P. & Pettengill, S. M. (1985). Perceived parental acceptance-rejection and parental control among Korean adolescents. *Child Development*, 56, 524–8.

Rothbaum, F., Nagaoka, R. & Ponte, I. C. (2006). Caregiver sensitivity in cultural context: Japanese and U. S. teachers' beliefs about anticipating and responding to children's needs. *Journal of Research in Childhood Education*, 21, 23–39.

Rothbaum, F., Pott, M., Azuma, H., Miyake, K. & Weisz, J. (2000). The development of close relationships in Japan and the United States: Paths of symbiotic harmony and generative tension. *Child Development*, 71, 1121–42. doi: 10.1111/1467-8624.00214.

Schönpflug, U. (2001). Intergenerational transmission of values: The role of transmission belts. *Journal of Cross-Cultural Psychology*, 32(2), 174–85. doi: 10.1177/0022022101032 002005.

Schwartz, S. H. (1992). Universals in the content and structure of values: Theoretical advances and empirical tests in 20 countries. In M. P. Zanna (ed.), *Advances in Experimental Social Psychology*, Vol. 25 (pp. 1–65). San Diego, CA: Academic Press. doi:10.1016/S0065-2601(08)60281-6

Schwartz, S. H. (2007). Value orientations: Measurement, antecedents and consequences across nations. In R. Jowell, C. Roberts, R. Fitzgerald & G. Eva (eds), *Measuring Attitudes*

Cross-nationally: Lessons from the European Social Survey (pp. 169–203). London: Sage. doi: 10.4135/9781849209458.n9.
Schwartz, S. H. (2012). Values and religion in adolescent development: Cross-national and comparative evidence. In G. Trommsdorff & X. Chen (eds), *Values, Religion, and Culture in Adolescent Development* (pp. 97–122). New York: Cambridge University Press.
Schwarz, B., Mayer, B., Trommsdorff, G., Ben-Arieh, A., Friedlmeier, M., Lubiewska, K., Mishra, R. C. & Peltzer, K. (2012). Does the importance of parent and peer relationships for adolescents' life satisfaction vary across cultures? *Journal of Early Adolescence*, 32, 55–80.
Schwarz, B. & Trommsdorff, G. (2005a). The relation between attachment and intergenerational support. *European Journal of Ageing*, 2, 192–9.
Schwarz, B. & Trommsdorff, G. (2005b). Intergenerationaler Austausch von Unterstützung und Reziprozität im Kulturvergleich. In A. Steinbach (ed.), *Generatives Verhalten und Generationenbeziehungen* (pp. 199–212). Wiesbaden: VS Verlag für Sozialwissenschaften.
Silverstein, M. & Conroy, S. J. (2009). Intergenerational transmission of moral capital across the family life course. In U. Schönpflug (ed.), *Cultural Transmission: Psychological, Developmental, Social, Methodological Aspects* (pp. 317–37). New York: Cambridge University Press.
Staub, E. (1980). Social and prosocial behavior: Personal and situational influences and their interactions. In E. Staub (ed.), *Personality: Basic Aspects and Current Research* (pp. 237–94). Englewood Cliffs, NJ: Prentice-Hall.
Trommsdorff, G. (1985). Some comparative aspects of socialization in Japan and Germany. In I. Reyes Lagunes & Y. H. Poortinga (eds), *From a Different Perspective: Studies of Behavior Across Cultures* (pp. 231–40). Amsterdam: Swets & Zeitlinger.
Trommsdorff, G. (2001). *Value of Children and Intergenerational Relations: A Cross-Cultural Psychological Study*. University of Konstanz, Department of Psychology, Developmental and Cross-Cultural Psychology.
Trommsdorff, G. (2006). Parent–child relations over the life-span: A cross-cultural perspective. In K. H. Rubin & O. B. Chung (eds), *Parenting Beliefs, Behaviors, and Parent–Child relations: A Cross-Cultural Perspective* (pp. 143–83). New York: Psychology Press.
Trommsdorff, G. (2009a). Intergenerational relations and cultural transmission. In U. Schönpflug (ed.), *Cultural Transmission: Psychological, Developmental, Social, and Methodological Aspects* (pp. 126–60). New York: Cambridge University Press.
Trommsdorff, G. (2009b). A social change and a human development perspective on the value of children. In S. Bekman & A. Aksu-Koc (eds), *Perspectives on Human Development, Family and Culture: Essays in Honor of Cigdem Kagitcibasi* (pp. 86–107). Cambridge: Cambridge University Press.
Trommsdorff, G. (2012a). Development of "agentic" regulation in cultural context: The role of self and world views. *Child Development Perspectives*, 6(1), 19–26. doi:10.1111/j.1750-8606.2011.00224.x.
Trommsdorff, G. (2012b). Cultural perspectives on values and religion in adolescent development: A conceptual overview and synthesis. In G. Trommsdorff & X. Chen (eds), *Values, Religion, and Culture in Adolescent Development* (pp. 3–45). New York: Cambridge University Press.
Trommsdorff, G. (2015). Cultural roots of values, and moral and religious purposes in adolescent development. In L. A. Jensen (ed.), *The Oxford Handbook of Human Culture and Development*. New York: Cambridge University Press.
Trommsdorff, G. & Cole, P. M. (2011). Emotion, self-regulation, and social behavior in cultural contexts. In X. Chen & K. H. Rubin (eds), *Socioemotional Development in Cultural Context* (pp. 131–63). New York: The Guilford Press.

Trommsdorff, G. & Friedlmeier, W. (2010). Preschool girls' distress and mothers' sensitivity in Japan and Germany. *European Journal of Developmental Psychology*, 7, 350–70. doi: 10.1080/17405620802252742.

Trommsdorff, G. & Kornadt, H.-J. (2003). Parent–child relations in cross-cultural perspective. In L. Kuczynski (ed.), *Handbook of Dynamics in Parent–child Relations* (pp. 271–306). London: Sage.

Trommsdorff, G. & Mayer, B. (2012). A cross-cultural study of intergenerational relations: The role of socioeconomic factors, values, and relationship quality in intergenerational support. In H. Bertram & N. Ehlert (eds), *Family, Ties, and Care: Family Transformation in a Plural Modernity* (pp. 315–42). Berlin, Germany: Barbara Budrich Publishers.

Trommsdorff, G. & Nauck, B. (eds) (2005). *The Value of Children in Cross-Cultural Perspective: Case Studies from Eight Societies*. Lengerich, Germany: Pabst Science.

Trommsdorff, G. & Nauck, B. (2006). Demographic changes and parent–child relationships. *Parenting: Science and Practice*, 6, 343–60.

Trommsdorff, G. & Nauck, B. (2010). Introduction to special section for Journal of CrossCultural Psychology: Value of children: A concept for the better understanding of cross-cultural variations of fertility behavior and intergenerational relationships. *Journal of Cross-Cultural Psychology*, 41, 637–51.

Ziehm, J., Trommsdorff, G., Heikamp, T. & Park, S. Y. (2013). German and Korean mothers' sensitivity and related parenting beliefs. *Frontiers in Psychology*, 4, 561. doi: 10.3389/fpsyg.2013.00561.

# 2 Horizontal transmission of value orientations in adolescence

*Klaus Boehnke and David Schiefer*

## Introduction

One of the core topics of the social sciences is the question how social entities secure their continuity. A crucial feature of an intact social entity is that its members share certain values. Values are frequently seen as defining the fundamental nature of a given culture at a given time (Hitlin & Piliavin, 2004). There also appears to be sufficient consensus that across history, equilibrium between value continuity and value change seems to be the best guarantor of the continued existence of social entities. The family is often perceived as one of the breeding places of the balance of continuity and change in value preferences. A number of studies on the intergenerational transmission of values within the family have been published in recent years (e.g. Boehnke *et al.*, 2007; Hitlin, 2006; Schönpflug, 2009). However, values are not only transmitted intergenerationally and not only in families, but also institutionally (e.g. in schools), via various types of media, in neighbourhoods and other living contexts, and, last but not least, from peer to peer.

## Three types of transmission

The transmission literature (Boyd & Richerson, 1985; Cavalli-Sforza & Feldman, 1981) sees three distinguishable types of transmission – namely, vertical transmission, horizontal transmission and oblique transmission. Vertical transmission refers to an intergenerational process: How (and to what extent) does it happen that parents and offspring have similar (or, for that matter, dissimilar) value orientations? Horizontal transmission refers to a peer-to-peer process: How (and to what extent) does it happen that members of the same generation have similar (or dissimilar) value orientations? Within the realm of horizontal transmission, similarity between related peers (siblings) and unrelated peers (e.g. class mates, neighbours, etc.) should be distinguished. Oblique transmission refers to an intergenerational process between unrelated individuals (e.g. teachers and students).

From a research design perspective, studies on all three types of transmission need at least two measurement points (repeated measurement) in order to assess the transmission *process* and thereby answer the question *how* two (or more) bearers of certain value orientations impact each other. Such studies, however, are very rare in the transmission literature (cf. Kohn et al., 1997). Typically, studies on value transmission take the degree of similarity of value orientations between two bearers of certain value preferences as evidence of transmission. However, when similarity is taken as a proxy for transmission, it remains unclear what different reasons/sources account for such a possible covariation in value orientations. These sources differ for the three types of transmission. The main difference lies in the genetic relatedness of the bearers of value orientations. In families there are typically four sources of similarity. First, values may be similar because parents have influenced children. Second, they may also be similar because children have influenced their parents. Third, they may be similar because both parents and offspring are exposed to a given value-related life context (value transmission studies often call this the *Zeitgeist* (Vedder et al., 2009)). But fourth, there also is the common genetic make-up of parents and offspring that can be a source of value similarity. In studies of horizontal transmission, this source of covariation only exists for transmission among siblings but not in studies of horizontal transmission among unrelated peers. In studies of oblique transmission, a common genetic make-up of the different bearers of value orientations does not play a role as a source of covariation.

The question arises, then, how it might be possible to disentangle the three sources[1] of similarity between different bearers of value orientations in studies that have no process element in their design. As mentioned, a process element in the design of a transmission study could be a repeated measurement that allows cross-lagged analyses.[2] Or it could be the availability of sociometric network data, where study participants are not only asked to indicate their value orientations, but are also asked about their relationships to others and the perceived impact of those others' value orientations on own value orientations. This can provide insights into whether social closeness is indeed related to higher value similarity. An experimental element in the design of a study could also be a way to disentangle the different sources of similarity in value orientations. In such an experimental setting, participants are randomly assigned to groups which then receive material (e.g. texts) that makes a particular value content more salient and emotionally important (so-called priming methods). Most of the time, transmission studies do not have these elements. They are simple one-shot studies that have surveyed a sample of parents and offspring (vertical transmission), of teachers and students (oblique transmission), or simply a sample of peers interacting in a certain context, e.g. a school class (horizontal transmission).

For the case of such one-shot studies, several suggestions have been made regarding how to disentangle the different sources of transmission. These suggestions, however, involve only studies of vertical and oblique transmission. An attempt to estimate the size of the impact of the common context on intergenerational value similarity (i.e. vertical transmission) has been made by Boehnke, Ittel and Baier (2002). In their research they correlated values of parents and their offspring and then used the value preferences of a randomly selected third participant (e.g. the data entry that is next to a particular person's entry in a randomly ordered data file) as a proxy variable for assessing the impact of the common context of a family (the Zeitgeist). The assumption behind this approach is that correlations between a person and an unrelated, randomly chosen person in a data file cannot originate from intrafamilial transmission but only from the fact that both persons live in the same general context.

A way to disentangle the direction of vertical transmission (parent-on-offspring vs. offspring-on-parent influence) is path modelling with mediating variables. In such models, the impact of a variable x on a variable y (here: values of parents and their offspring) is transmitted through a third variable (the mediator): the link between variables x and y results from the fact that x is related to a mediator, which in turn is related to y. In the case of intra-familial value transmission, additional family variables (e.g. parenting style) can be included as mediators. Different models can be compared that either test the effect of parents' values on their offspring's values or the opposite direction. The direction of the impact can be evaluated using the strength of the relationships. For example, certain additional variables can mediate the impact of x on y, but not (or oppositely so) the impact of y on x. This strategy has successfully been utilized by the first author to offer clues in one-shot studies as to whether high self-esteem leads to improved academic performance or whether a good academic performance leads to increased self-esteem (Boehnke, 1996): the parenting style of caring lenience buffered the detrimental effect of low academic performance on self-esteem, while it enhanced the positive impact of self-esteem on academic performance. Thus, when taking parental style into account in analyses predicting academic performance on the grounds of self-esteem and vice versa, the strength of the impact of self-esteem on to academic performance differed from the impact of academic performance on to self-esteem. Such strategies have, however, rarely been applied in value transmission studies (cf. Schönpflug & Silbereisen, 1992).

For research on oblique transmission, multilevel modelling can be utilized if only one-shot data are available. This approach has become a powerful tool to disentangle the three sources of value similarity between, for example, teachers and their students. Teacher values can in such analyses be used as group-level predictors of individual student values and vice versa. Analyses also allow for additional (predictor) variables on either the group or the individual level.

With regard to horizontal transmission, however, it has rarely if ever been discussed how it might be possible to corroborate peer-to-peer value transmission in one-shot studies in the absence of any additional data on the transmission process. The central question is how one can show that inter-student value similarity can be taken as indication for peer-to-peer value transmission if no overt information is available on mutual influence among peers.

## Value orientations as a social science concept

The remainder of the chapter will address this question by suggesting a method for finding an answer and by offering empirical material from a study conducted by the authors to illustrate the suggested approach. Before we turn to our methodological chain of arguments, it must be clarified, however, what we mean by 'value orientations'. Although this is not the place to extensively review the development of empirical value research in the social sciences, a brief account is offered. It seems fair to say that four approaches dominate contemporary value research. One comes from political science and is primarily associated with the work of Ronald Inglehart (Inglehart, 1997; Inglehart & Welzel, 2005). Inglehart's concept can be traced back to one of the godfathers of humanistic psychology, Abraham Maslow (1954). Inglehart distinguishes two orthogonal dimensions on which value orientations can vary – namely, self-expression as opposed to survival values and secular-rational as opposed to traditional values. The central body of empirical data available for these values is the World Values Survey.[3] A second highly influential approach to assessing individual value orientations is the one by social psychologist Shalom Schwartz (1992). Schwartz builds upon work by anthropologist Clyde Kluckhohn (1951) and psychologist Milton Rokeach (1968, 1973). His conceptual approach is that of a value circumplex that originally distinguished 10 value types (Schwartz, 1992), and has recently been refined to now distinguish 19 different types of values (Schwartz et al., 2012) collapsible into the original 10, which themselves can be grouped into four higher-order value orientations. The circumplex of the ten original value types distinguished by Schwartz is documented in Figure 2.1.

The most easily accessible body of data on Schwartz value orientations originates from the European Social Survey (ESS)[4]. Two further approaches to

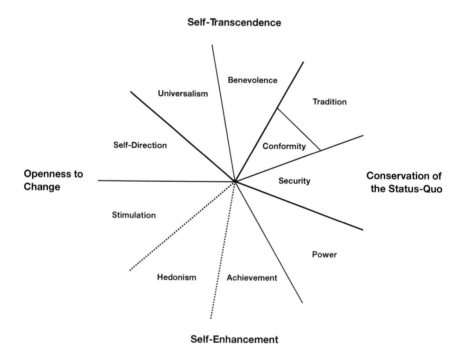

*Figure 2.1* Schwartz value circumplex (10 value types)

assessing value orientations across cultures make the distinction between collectivist and individualist values their point of departure. The first approach is that of Geert Hofstede (2001), who is predominantly concerned with distinguishing cultures, institutions and organizations (not individuals) on five to six dimensions. Hofstede made parts of his data accessible to the public as well.[5] The second highly influential author in the field of individualism/collectivism is Harry C. Triandis (1995). However, an easily accessible archive of his data does not exist.

The present chapter relies on data obtained with a 25-item version of the Portrait Value Questionnaire (PVQ; Schwartz *et al.*, 2001) that assesses individuals' preferences for each of the 10 value types suggested by Schwartz. Table 2.1 documents the instrument.

## How to assess horizontal transmission in simple survey studies

We now return to the topic of horizontal transmission of value orientations with a particular focus on adolescents. Three quasi-axiomatic assumptions govern our further elaborations: (1) Peer-to-peer transmission among adolescents needs a common space of personal interaction. (2) Horizontal transmission effects manifest themselves in the level of similarity of value preferences among members of this common interaction space. (3) The extent of horizontal transmission effects is influenced not only by the immediate members of the common interaction space, but also by the general context in which the interaction space is situated (i.e., culture, institution/organization). In principle, horizontal transmission can take place without direct interaction among peers – for example, in social media or via the classical media. In order to be able to interpret similarity data in one-shot studies as evidence for transmission – lacking any further information from participants than that on their value preferences – one does, however, need structural evidence that peers have interacted and thus had a chance to impact each other's values. This reasoning is the basis of the first assumption stated above. The second assumption suggests that one can interpret homogeneity of value preferences among peers interacting in a common interaction space as evidence for transmission. The third assumption refers us back to sources of similarity that have been addressed before, in particular the Zeitgeist as a source of similarity. It reminds us that inter-peer value similarity can not only originate from processes of influencing each other in the common interaction space, but also from the fact that that interaction space is part of a larger – cultural – context.

Based on the first two assumptions, one can go on and operationalize inter-peer value similarity, our proxy for horizontal value transmission, as being determined by the degree of value homogeneity/heterogeneity in a given interaction space of adolescents. We focus here on the school class as the classic adolescent interaction space. For single individuals, susceptibility to peer-to-peer influence on value orientations is conceptualized as the absolute difference of a given member of a given school class from the mean of that school class. The closer the value preferences of an individual adolescent are to the average of his or her classmates,

Table 2.1 Portrait Value Questionnaire (25-item version)[a]

*Intro*

**Person Profiles**
Here we briefly describe some people. Please read each description and think about how much each person is or is not like you. Tick the box to the right that shows how much the person in the description is like you.

| Item[b] | Value type |
|---|---|
| Thinking up new ideas and being creative is important to her. She likes to do things in her own original way. | Self-direction |
| It is important to her to be rich. She wants to have a lot of money and expensive things. | Power |
| She thinks it is important that every person in the world should be treated equally. She believes everyone should have equal opportunities in life. | Universalism |
| It is important to her to show his abilities. She wants people to admire what she does. | Achievement |
| It is important to her to live in secure surroundings. She avoids anything that might endanger her safety. | Security |
| She likes surprises and is always looking for new things to do. She thinks it is important to do lots of different things in life. | Stimulation |
| She believes that people should do what they are told. She thinks people should follow rules at all times, even when no-one is watching. | Conformity |
| It is important to her to listen to people who are different from her. Even when she disagrees with them, she still wants to understand them. | Universalism |
| It is important to her to be humble and modest. She tries not to draw attention to herself. | Tradition |
| Having a good time is important to her. She likes to 'spoil' herself. | Hedonism |
| It is important to her to make her own decisions about what she does. She likes to be free and not depend on others. | Self-direction |
| It is very important to her to help the people around her. She wants to care for their well-being. | Benevolence |
| Being very successful is important to her. She hopes people will recognize her achievements. | Achievement |
| It is important to her that the government ensures her safety against all threats. She wants the state to be strong so it can defend its citizens. | Security |
| She looks for adventures and likes to take risks. She wants to have an exciting life. | Stimulation |
| It is important to her always to behave properly. She wants to avoid doing anything people would say is wrong. | Conformity |
| It is important to her to get respect from others. She wants people to do what she says. | Power |

*continued . . .*

*Table 2.1* Continued

| Item[b] | Value type |
|---|---|
| It is important to her to be loyal to her friends. She wants to devote herself to people close to her. | Benevolence |
| She strongly believes that people should care for nature. Looking after the environment is important to her. | Universalism |
| Tradition is important to her. She tries to follow the customs handed down by her religion or her family. | Tradition |
| She seeks every chance she can to have fun. It is important to her to do things that give her pleasure. | Hedonism |
| She thinks it is important to be interested in things. She likes to be curious and to try to understand all sorts of things. | Self-direction |
| Forgiving people who have hurt her is important to her. She tries to see what is good in them and not to hold a grudge. | Benevolence |
| Getting ahead in life is important to her. She strives to do better than others. | Achievement |
| She believes she should always show respect to her parents and to older people. It is important to her to be obedient. | Conformity |

a Respondents were requested to respond to the question 'How much like you is this person' on a response scale ranging from 'very much like me' (6) to 'not like me at all' (1).
b Items are taken from the questionnaire version for girls; there obviously also is a version for boys.

the more – we assume – he or she has been influenced by the value orientations of fellow students. Note that this assumption is also quasi-axiomatic, because from one-shot questionnaire studies we have no information as to whether an influence process has really taken place. In a certain way, we do process tracing here: from the fact that a student has value preferences very similar to the preferences of the average of his/her classmates, we infer that a transmission process is likely to have taken place. We cannot prove this, but as the following sections document, we will set out to make the legitimacy of such an inference plausible.

How do we assess homogeneity/heterogeneity? These are our calculation rules: in Step 1, we calculate subscale mean scores for the 10 value types by averaging the raw scores across all items that belong to one particular value type (see Table 2.1). Before doing so, however, the item scores needed to be corrected for scale use, as suggested by Schwartz.[6] In Step 2, we calculate means of the school classes for the ten value types by averaging the scale scores across all members of a particular school class. In Step 3, we determine the absolute difference between individual scale scores for the 10 value types and the respective class mean within each school class. Importantly, one has to calculate the *absolute* difference between individual scores and the class mean, because only the amount of deviation signals high or low similarity, not its direction/sign (higher or lower scores compared to the average class score). Finally, in Step 4, we average the 10 absolute difference scores across all 10 values in order to determine an overall measure of within-school-class value similarity.

Our calculation rules imply that we eventually determine only one score that we see as assessing the individual adolescent's inclination to join the average value climate in his or her school class. The lower this score (low difference from class mean) is, the more the value preferences of the individual resemble the average of his or her school class. The higher the score is (higher difference from mean), the more the individual adolescent is an outsider in his or her class with regard to value orientations. We could have worked with absolute discrepancy scores for the ten different value orientations as well, but we refrain from doing so for the sake of parsimony: we seek to present evidence that a low discrepancy between the values of an individual and the average values held in his or her school class can be seen as a proximal measurement of the size of horizontal value transmission that has taken place in that school class. Should we succeed in finding empirical evidence for the plausibility of our argumentation, the strength of our argument is obviously enhanced by the fact that we speak of all possible values together and do not have to qualify our findings as being valid only for this or the other particular value.

## Hypotheses

In order to support our assertion that high homogeneity of values in a school class is a sign for high degrees of horizontal value transmission, we test three hypotheses. First, we assume that the susceptibility of an individual to be influenced by the average value climate of his or her school class depends itself on the kind of values this individual prefers. We hypothesize that large differences should be related to openness values (self-direction, stimulation and, to a lesser degree, hedonism), whereas small differences should be positively related to conservation values (tradition, conformity, security). Whereas individuals oriented towards openness tend to emphasize individual choice and independent thought, those oriented towards conservation values have a higher tendency to follow the norms and behavioural codes they are exposed to in their group. A correlation between individuals' value preferences with their distance from the class average, in turn, can be seen, in our view, as an indicator that the latter is indeed an indicator of value transmission. It would indicate that value orientations are indeed the substantive basis of the difference measure.

Second, if school classes are interaction spaces for horizontal transmission, homogeneity of value preferences should be more sizable in school classes than in schools, or in school types. In line with Bronfenbrenner's (1986) ecological socialization theory, school classes are microsystems, where members interact with each other continuously. Schools are so-called mesosystems, where members are able to personally interact with each other but do not do so on a regular or frequent basis. School types are exosystems in Bronfenbrenner's terms, where members are subject to comparable ecological conditions but do not personally interact with each other. If school classes are indeed interaction spaces for horizontal transmission, belonging to a particular school class should explain more variance in individual-group similarity scores than being the student of a particular school or attending a particular type of school.

Third, if differences of individuals from the mean of their school class are measures of horizontal transmission, they should be related linearly to the average values prevalent in the cultural environment (i.e. the country). In other words, whether or not values of students within a class are similar depends on how similar this class is to the value climate of the larger cultural environment. We expect school classes that exhibit more similarity with the average values of the culture to show a higher level of within-class value homogeneity. In more technical terms, the lower the discrepancy score of a school class' values is compared to the average value preferences of the surrounding culture (in the present case: Germany), the lower the difference scores of the class' students' values are compared to the class average. The theoretical argument behind this assumption could be that in classes that more strongly resemble the cultural value climate (in other words, in classes that more strongly match general cultural expectations), there is less need for within-group disagreements and negotiations. Conversely, individuals that are far away from the cultural group's average values might be more inclined to justify and defend their value preferences on an everyday basis, which leads to more disagreement in classes farther away from the mean of the superordinate cultural group. How do we operationalize this: for each of the ten value types, we first determine the absolute difference of the average scores of a school class from those of the general German population. The latter we derive from a representative country sample from the European Social Survey (ESS). Then we average these ten difference scores across the ten values in order to obtain one score that measures the degree to which a given school class differs from the German average value preferences. Our hypothesis is that the mean discrepancy between individual value preferences and the mean score of their school class (within-class homogeneity) and the discrepancy between class means and the culture mean should be linearly related: the lower the within-school-class discrepancy, the lower the difference between the class average and the country average should be. We see a confirmation of this hypothesis as another piece of evidence that what we measure with the individual's absolute difference to the average value preferences in his or her school class is indeed a proximal measurement of the degree of horizontal value transmission that has taken place in a given class.

Lastly, a final plausibility check is offered: in school classes with higher percentages of students with a migration background, value homogeneity should be smaller than in school classes consisting mostly of non-immigrant German adolescents. From the literature on the values of migrant adolescents (e.g. Daniel et al., 2012; Daniel et al., 2014), we know that modal values of migrants differ from those of the autochthonous population. Homogeneity should thus be higher in diverse school classes than in largely autochthonous classes.

To sum up, we suggest that within-school-class value homogeneity is a proximal measure of horizontal value transmission; and we attempt to make this plausible by showing that discrepancies between an individual's value preferences and the average preferences of a school class are correlated with the type of values the individual adheres to. Second, we suggest that discrepancy scores are impacted more by belonging to a particular school class than to a particular school or school type.

Third, we assume that within-class value homogeneity is linearly related to the difference between this class' mean values and the German average: the closer a school class' mean value preferences are to the average German value preferences, the higher homogeneity is expected to be. Fourth, heterogeneity of values should be higher in classes with larger percentages of immigrant youth, but the previously sketched systematic relationships should persist even when one partials for this effect.

## The current study

The data we present here stem from a German-Israeli study 'Identity development and value transmission among veteran and migrant adolescents and their families in Germany and Israel: Life transitions and context', funded by the German Ministry of Education and Science. We will only be reporting data from Germany in this chapter. Data collection for the German leg of the study took place in Bremen, Germany, and nearby areas in the surrounding state of Lower Saxony. As the study focused on migrants, students with a migration background were oversampled by targeting schools with a high percentage of migrants. As migrants are typically economically underprivileged in comparison to non-immigrant Germans, the oversampling of migrants resulted in a sample that is likely to have a below-average SES. Altogether, data from 1,596 students were included in the present analysis; there were more participants but we included only those who came from school classes where at least 10 students participated in the study. Students came from 97 school classes, nested in 19 schools, nested in 3 school types.

School types were *not* defined along the lines of pedagogical tracking systems, but were classified according to their socio-organizational set-up. In our sample there are schools where students can *only* obtain the typical university-bound German school-leaving certificate (the *Abitur*). These schools are the classical German *Gymnasium* schools. Then there are schools where students can *only* obtain lower level degrees (these schools have different names; what unites them is the fact that you cannot obtain an *Abitur* in such a school). And then there are schools where you can obtain all levels of school leaving certificates (these schools also have different names). In a way, the differentiation can be seen as a separation by social class.

Students from Grades 5, 6 and 10 were sampled. The overall age mean of the sample was 12.3, with a range from 9 to 18 years of age (age 9: 0.2%; 10: 16.8%; 11: 34.7%; 12: 20.0; 13: 3.7%; 14: 0.4%; 15: 6.3%; 16: 13.9%; 17: 3.6%; 18: 0.3%). Of all participants, 48.9% were boys, 51.1% were girls. Altogether, 39.3% of the sampled students had a migration background,[7] while 50.8% were non-immigrant Germans; for the remaining students, their migration status could not clearly be determined due to missing information.

The current chapter only reports information obtained with a 25-item PVQ version of the Schwartz value survey (Table 2.1). As mentioned, to prepare the data for our analyses, we first performed a mathematical correction for scale use (see Note 6). Scores for the 10 Schwartz (1992) values were then calculated in accordance with the assignment rules of the author (see also Table 2.1). Subsequently, two difference scores were calculated. The first one assesses the absolute difference of an individual's value preferences from the value mean of his or her school class averaged across all 10 values. We see the resulting score as a measure of value homogeneity in a school class and want to show that low difference scores in a school class can be seen as a proxy for horizontal value transmission having taken place in that school class. To ease comprehension, we label this difference score *distance to class*.

The second difference score calculates the absolute difference between the mean value ratings of a school class and the value preference score obtained for a particular value for Germany in the European Social Survey (ESS). The absolute differences were once again averaged across all 10 values. This measure is assumed to assess the cultural prototypicality of a specific school class in terms of values. One could also rephrase this as suggesting that the measure assesses the degree to which value preferences in a given school class are compatible with the current German Zeitgeist. It should be noted that for this variable only 97 different scores exist (= 97 studied school classes). Each student of a particular class receives the same score – the difference score of the class to the German average. Again, to ease readability, we label this with the term *distance to culture*.

## Analytic approach and results

In Step 1 of our analyses, we correlated the value preferences of study participants with their distance to class. As stated earlier, if difference scores measure value-related aspects of within-class processes, there should be a correlation of value preferences and difference scores that follows the predicted pattern: negative correlations should be found with conformity and other conservation values, positive correlations with self-determination and other openness values, correlations with self-transcendence and self-enhancement values in between and close to 0. Figure 2.2 documents results; for the four higher-order value orientations, multiple correlations are documented.

The correlation pattern suggests that distance to class is indeed a reflection of individual value preferences. Students with larger distances prefer openness values (hedonism: $r = 0.9$, $p \leq 0.01$; stimulation: $r = .07$, $p \leq 0.05$; self-direction: $r = 0.11$, $p \leq 0.01$), whereas students with smaller distances exhibit conservation values (security: $r = -0.09$, $p \leq 0.01$; conformity: $r = -0.10$, $p \leq 0.01$; tradition: $r = -0.13$, $p \leq 0.01$). The correlations certainly are not very sizeable, but the pattern of correlations perfectly matches expectations, so that the results clearly support the proposition that individuals' distance to class reflects personal values.

In Step 2 of our analyses, we checked whether individuals' distance to class varied across school types, schools, and school classes. In order to interpret homogeneity scores as indeed an indicator of horizontal transmission processes, homogeneity scores should differ between school classes more so than between schools or even school types, because it is primarily the – in Bronfenbrennerian terminology – microsystem 'school class' that resembles a permanent interaction space of students, relevant for horizontal value transmission. For the mesosystem 'school' and the exosystem 'school type' this is much less or even not at all the case.

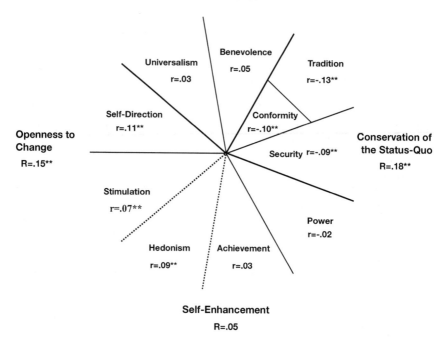

*Figure 2.2* Correlations of Schwarz values and differences between individual preferences and school class means

In order to comprehensively test this assumption, we conducted nested analyses of variance, in which 'school class' is nested within 'school', which itself is nested within 'school type'.

Schematically, such an ANOVA design has the characteristic portrayed in Figure 2.3. Readers should note that the number of lower level units need not be the same under each higher level unit (in other words, the data can include e.g. three classes from school A and five classes from school B). A hierarchic ANOVA separately calculates the amount of variance in the dependent variable (here, individuals' value distance to the class average) that is due to membership in the categories at different levels (here, membership in a particular class, school, and school type).

Hierarchic ANOVAs fully confirm our hypotheses that distance to class scores should differ significantly between school classes, should differ less pronouncedly between schools, and should not differ significantly between school types. This again supports the proposition that distance to class is a proxy measure of horizontal transmission. It furthermore supports the assumption that the school class is an interaction space for horizontal transmission, whereas the school is only so to a much lesser degree, and the exosystem school type is not such an interaction space. ANOVA details are documented in Table 2.2.

| Exosystem (here 'School Type') | A | | | | | | B | | | | | | C | | | | | |
|---|---|---|---|---|---|---|---|---|---|---|---|---|---|---|---|---|---|---|
| Mesosystem (here 'School') | A | | B | | C | | D | | E | | F | | G | | H | | I | |
| Microsystem (here 'School Class') | 1 | 2 | 3 | 4 | 5 | 6 | 7 | 8 | 9 | 10 | 11 | 12 | 13 | 14 | 15 | 16 | 17 | 18 |
| Individual (here 'Student') | $n_{11}$ to $n_{1n}$ | $n_{21}$ to $n_{2n}$ | $n_{31}$ to $n_{3n}$ | $n_{41}$ to $n_{4n}$ | $n_{51}$ to $n_{5n}$ | $n_{61}$ to $n_{6n}$ | $n_{71}$ to $n_{7n}$ | $n_{81}$ to $n_{8n}$ | $n_{91}$ to $n_{9n}$ | $n_{101}$ to $n_{10n}$ | $n_{111}$ to $n_{11n}$ | $n_{121}$ to $n_{12n}$ | $n_{131}$ to $n_{13n}$ | $n_{141}$ to $n_{14n}$ | $n_{151}$ to $n_{15n}$ | $n_{161}$ to $n_{16n}$ | $n_{171}$ to $n_{17n}$ | $n_{181}$ to $n_{18n}$ |

*Figure 2.3* Schematic design for nested ANOVAs

*Table 2.2* Results table for hierarchic ANOVA

| Source[a] | | F | df | p |
|---|---|---|---|---|
| School type | Hypothesis | .180 | 2 | .839 |
| | Error | | 8.113 | |
| School (school type) | Hypothesis | 1.702 | 16 | .061 |
| | Error | | 87.311 | |
| School class (school (school type)) | Hypothesis | 1.358 | 78 | .023 |
| | Error | | 1.484 | |

a Dependent variable: distance to class

The table shows that there are no significant differences in average value homogeneity between school types (p = 0.839). Between schools, differences in value homogeneity are marginally significant (p = 0.061). Between school classes, however, homogeneity differs on the 5% significance level (p = 0.023).

Step 3 of our analyses was to include three covariates: age, gender and migration background. For the variable migration background there were numerous data missing, cases where we were unable to obtain information from respondents. In principle, the variable is dichotomous (0 = 'autochthonous', 1 = 'with a migration background'). Respondents for whom the information was missing were assigned a 0.5 score. Results of the pertinent hierarchic ANOVA are documented in Table 2.3.

Table 2.3 Results table for hierarchic ANOVA

| Source[a] | | F | df | p |
|---|---|---|---|---|
| Age | Hypothesis | .961 | 1 | .331 |
| | Error | | 52.233 | |
| Gender | Hypothesis | .032 | 1 | .859 |
| | Error | | 1442.243 | |
| Migration status | Hypothesis | 6.875 | 1 | .010 |
| | Error | | 144.712 | |
| School type | Hypothesis | .034 | 2 | .966 |
| | Error | | 8.354 | |
| School (school type) | Hypothesis | 1.690 | 16 | .065 |
| | Error | | 83.456 | |
| School class (school (school type)) | Hypothesis | 1.325 | 78 | .033 |
| | Error | | 1422 | |

a Dependent variable: distance to class

The table shows that – as can be expected – migration status does have a significant impact on the within-class value homogeneity (p = 0.010); migrants, on average, differ more from the school class mean than do non-immigrant Germans. Gender and age, however, are not significantly related to individuals' distance to class (p = 0.859/p = 0.331). The main effect findings at the same time remain essentially unchanged (school type: p = 0.966; school: p = 0.065; school class: p = 0.033).

In Step 4 of our analyses, we take one further step to support our interpretation that what we measure by assessing the degree of within-class value homogeneity is indeed horizontal value transmission (or, in simpler words, students influencing each other). We investigate whether within-class value homogeneity varies as a function of the class' distance to culture (the mean value score of the German population). For this analytic step we had to first organize the data in a way that allows us to test the hypothesis: all 97 school classes were put in an order according to their distance to the average value preference evident in the German population (taken from the representative German sample of the ESS). The class with the smallest distance to the German value mean (averaged across all 10 values) received the Number 1, the one with the largest distance, the Number 97. We assume that value homogeneity should be higher in classes closer to the average German values. For this analysis we conducted a one-way ANOVA and consulted so-called polynomial trend coefficients. The latter indicate the significance of a trend towards more within-class value homogeneity, the closer a class is to the German average. The ANOVA was conducted with school class as the only independent variable; this is necessary, because polynomial trend tests cannot be conducted for nested factors (classes nested within schools, which are nested within school types).[8] A significant contrast estimate of 0.222 (p = 0.001) suggested that there is indeed a linear relationship between a class' distance to culture and its within-class value homogeneity. Students from classes that are less prototypical for German value preferences exhibit less value homogeneity. We take this finding as another indication that value homogeneity in a class can be interpreted as an indication for horizontal value transmission, since – as our assumption described above – students in classes that differ more from the German average need to negotiate, justify, and defend their values more strongly, leading to more disagreement within those classes.

## Concluding discussion

This chapter set out to describe a way to assess the horizontal transmission of value preferences among adolescents. We suggested that under certain conditions the absolute difference score between the value preferences of an individual adolescent and the average value preferences of his/her classmates can be used as a proxy variable assessing the degree to which the adolescent has been influenced by classmates in his or her value preferences. Our line of argumentation commenced with the proviso that research on the *process* of horizontal transmission is impossible without *process data* (in the form of repeated-measures data, sociometric data or experimental data). In the absence of such data, interindividual similarity data can – as per our assertion – be used as a proxy for assessing the degree of horizontal value transmission among adolescents. The assertion has to be qualified, however: in simple survey studies, the utilization of interindividual similarity data as a proxy for horizontal transmission only makes sense when the sampling strategy of a study was that of cluster sampling. Only when it can be ascertained that groups of participants of a study had a common interaction space, does it make sense to interpret interindividual similarity scores as evidence for horizontal transmission. A common microsystem allowing peer-to-peer interaction is necessary in order to trace similarity among individuals back to a transmission process that has likely taken place. In the present study, the school class set the frame for peer-to-peer transmission. Of course, school classes are not the only microsystems that constitute an interaction space for horizontal transmission. Neighbourhoods, friendship circles in social media, sports clubs and the like can also constitute such a space.

Sharing an interaction space is a necessary but in actuality not a sufficient precondition for interpreting interindividual similarity as evidence for horizontal value transmission. Only if it can additionally be shown that sizes of interindividual similarities of value preferences in a common interaction space (like a school class) are themselves related to (a) individual value preferences and (b) to the value climate in the larger cultural context, should researchers really take (small vs. large) differences between individual values and mean values of a school class as evidence for a small vs. large amount of horizontal value transmission. In the study reported here, measures of absolute differences between individual value preferences and mean value preferences of a school class can – according to our argument – indeed be interpreted as standing for horizontal transmission of values among adolescents. Peers seemingly impact each other's values in the school class, the core context of their everyday life outside the family. Our empirical evidence supports this conclusion, because (a) individual difference scores were correlated with individual value preferences (openness to change vs. conservation of the status quo), (b) homogeneity scores varied by school class (a real interaction space of students), much less so by school, and not at all by school type, (c) differences between school classes did not vanish when important controls were included (gender, age, migration status), and, most importantly, (d) value homogeneity in a school class covaried linearly with the size of discrepancy between a class' mean value preferences and those representative for Germany.

In conclusion, readers should be reminded of the fact that this chapter sees itself as an account of a methodological inquiry, and thus, a contribution to an ongoing discussion. Further research is obviously needed concerning substantive questions of horizontal transmission research: which properties of school classes increase transmission and which properties reduce it? Can the overall finding that there is evidence for within-school-class horizontal value transmission among adolescents be generalized to all value types equally? Does horizontal value transmission also take place in other adolescent interaction spaces, and if yes, are transmission effects smaller, similar, or larger in other interaction spaces? Are there contextual variables and/or interindividual difference variables that enhance or impede horizontal value transmission in adolescence? These are just a few research questions that remain open after this introductory methodological contribution.

## Notes

1 Including the possible impact of (1) Bearer A on Bearer B, (2) Bearer B on Bearer A, and (3), the impact of the common context on both A and B, where A can be a parent and B an offspring, A a teacher, B a student, or both A and B same-generation peers.
2 This method incorporates both the assumed predictor(s) and the assumed outcome variable(s) at both measurement points in the analyses and tests which direction of the relationship is statistically stronger.
3 Available at: www.worldvaluessurvey.org/wvs.jsp.
4 Available at: www.europeansocialsurvey.org.
5 Available at: http://geert-hofstede.com/dimensions.html.
6 This correction is suggested by Shalom Schwartz to account for idiosyncratic effects of scale use by individual study participants (see Schwartz, 2009). According to him, people may be prone to mark all values relatively high or all values relatively low due to reasons other than their value preferences. This is likely to distort correlations between items, which should be avoided. Schwartz suggests a procedure to correct for these individual response habits: a participant's average score across all 25 value items (i.e. his or her general tendency to agree or disagree with the items) is subtracted from the score of each individual item, and the resulting difference scores are used for the subsequent analyses.
7 Having a migration background was defined with reference to the German Bureau of Statistics as someone who either him/herself or one of his/her parents was born in a country other than Germany.
8 With this kind of ordering of the classes, the statistical programme recognizes the differences between two pairs of classes (e.g. between Class 1 and 2 and between Class 90 and 91) to be equal (a difference of one in each case). This obviously does not resemble reality, since the difference between Class 1 and 2 in terms of their similarity to the German average is unlikely to be identical to the difference between, e.g. Class 90 and 91. Our analyses take these unequal differences between classes into account by applying weighting procedures based on exact similarity scores of the classes.

# References

Boehnke, K. (1996). *Is intelligence negligible? The relationship of family climate and school behavior in a cross-cultural perspective*. Münster: Waxmann.

Boehnke, K., Hadjar, A. & Baier, D. (2007). Parent–child value similarity: The role of Zeitgeist. *Journal of Marriage and Family*, 69, 778–92.

Boehnke, K., Ittel, A. & Baier, D. (2002). Value transmission and Zeitgeist: An underresearched relationship. *Sociale Wetenschappen*, 45, 28–43.

Boyd, R. & Richerson, P. J. (1985). *Culture and the Evolutionary Process*. Chicago: University of Chicago Press.

Bronfenbrenner, U. (1986). Recent advances in research on the ecology of human development. In R. K. Silbereisen, K. Eyferth, & G. Rudinger (eds), *Development as Action in Context* (pp. 287–309). Heidelberg: Springer.

Cavalli-Sforza, L. L. & Feldman, M. W. (1981). *Cultural Transmission and Evolution: A Quantitative Approach*. Princeton, NJ: Princeton University Press.

Daniel, E., Benish-Weisman, M., Boehnke, K. & Knafo, A. (2014). Personal and culture-dependent values as part of minority adolescent identity. In R. K. Silbereisen, P. F. Titzmann & Y. Shavit (eds), *The Challenges of Diaspora Migration: Interdisciplinary Perspectives on Israel and Germany* (pp. 103–26). Farnham: Ashgate.

Daniel, E., Schiefer, D., Möllering, A., Benish-Weisman, M., Boehnke, K. & Knafo, A. (2012). Value differentiation in adolescence: The role of age and cultural complexity. *Child Development*, 83(1), 322–36.

Hitlin, S. (2006). Parental influences on children's values and aspirations: Bridging theories of social class and socialization. *Sociological Perspectives*, 49(1), 25–46.

Hitlin, S. & Piliavin, J. A. (2004). Values: Reviving a dormant concept. *Annual Review of Sociology*, 30, 359–93.

Hofstede, G. (2001). *Culture's Consequences: Comparing Values, Behaviors, Institutions and Organizations Across Nations*. 2nd edn. Thousand Oaks, CA: Sage.

Inglehart, R. (1997). *Modernization and Postmodernization*. Princeton, NJ: Princeton University Press.

Inglehart, R. & Welzel, C. (2005). *Modernization, Cultural Change and Democracy: The Human Development Space*. Cambridge, MA: Cambridge University Press.

Kluckhohn, C. (1951). Values and value-orientations in the theory of action: An exploration in definition and classification. In T. Parsons & E. Shils (eds), *Toward a General Theory of Action*. Cambridge, MA: Harvard University Press.

Kohn, M. L., Slomczynski, K. M., Janicka, K., Khmelko, V., Mach, B. W., Paniotto, V., Zaborowski, W., Gutierrez, R. & Heyman, C. (1997). Social structure and personality under conditions of radical social change: A comparative analysis of Poland and Ukraine. *American Sociological Review*, 62, 614–38.

Maslow, A. H. (1954). *Motivation and Personality*. New York: Harper.

Rokeach, M. (1968). *Beliefs, Attitudes, and Values: A Theory of Organization and Change*. San Francisco, CA: Jossey-Bass.

Rokeach, M. (1973). *The Nature of Human Values*. New York: The Free Press.

Schönpflug, U. (ed.) (2009). *Cultural Transmission: Psychological, Developmental, Social, and Methodological Aspects*. New York: Cambridge University Press.

Schönpflug, U. & Silbereisen, R. K. (1992). Transmission of values between generations in the family regarding societal keynote issues: A cross-cultural longitudinal study on Polish and German families. In S. Iwawaki, Y. Kashima & K. Leung (eds), *Innovations in Cross-cultural Psychology* (pp. 269–78). Lisse, Netherlands: Swets & Zeitlinger.

Schwartz, S. H. (1992). Universals in the content and structure of values: Theoretical advances and empirical tests in 20 countries. *Advances in Experimental Social Psychology*, 25, 1–65.

Schwartz, S. H. (2009). Instructions for computing scores for the 10 human values and using them in analyses. Retrieved from: www.europeansocialsurvey.org/docs/methodology/ESS1_human_values_scale.pdf.

Schwartz, S. H., Cieciuch, J., Vecchione, M., Davidov, E., Fischer, R., Beierlein, C., Ramos, A., Verkasalo, M., Lönnqvist, J.-E., Demirutku, K., Dirilen-Gumus, O. & Konty, M. (2012). Refining the theory of basic individual values. *Journal of Personality and Social Psychology*, 103, 663–88.

Schwartz, S. H., Melech, G., Lehmann, A., Burgess, S., Harris, M. & Owens, V. (2001). Extending the cross-cultural validity of the theory of basic human values with a different method of measurement. *Journal of Cross-Cultural Psychology*, 32, 519–42.

Triandis, H. C. (1995). *Individualism & Collectivism: New Directions in Social Psychology*. Boulder, CO: Westview Press.

Vedder, P. H., Berry, J. W., Sabatier, C. & Sam, D. (2009). The intergenerational transmission of values in national and immigrant families: The role of Zeitgeist. *Journal of Youth and Adolescence*, 38, 642–53.

# 3 Educational structures and the curriculum

Reproducing or transforming ethnic boundaries?

*Marie Mc Andrew*

## Introduction

In modern, pluralistic societies, formal schooling plays a major role in the production and redefinition of identities and values through two of its main functions: the transmission of knowledge, and the formal and informal socialization of students. In the first instance, one often witnesses a competition between majority and minority groups, in order to maximize the benefits of schooling for the preservation of their defining markers. This is exemplified by the numerous controversies in diverse contexts regarding the legitimacy of various languages, cultures and religions in the curriculum. In the second instance, schools significantly contribute to the formation of identities and attitudes towards diversity among youth, as well as promote the sharing of common, yet pluralistic values at the national level and within minority groups. In this regard, divergent conceptions of citizenship lead to divergent views about the respective relevance of attending common schools or institutions controlled by specific ethnic minorities.

In this chapter, I review some of these controversies in the North American and European contexts, as well as the results of several empirical studies that contribute to a better understanding of the dynamics at stake. Given the central role played by contextual differences in comparing debates and practices, I will first give an overview of the distinct origins of ethnocultural diversity within Western school systems, as well as of the educational consequences of various markers defining specific groups. The importance of common institutions, the role of immigrant languages in the curriculum, as well as the legitimacy of cultural and religious diversity in school programmes and practices will then be addressed. Finally, in my conclusion, I will reflect on the rather bold question raised in the title of this chapter, emphasizing the nature of school as a contested site, while stressing some differences between North America and Europe in this respect.

## The origin and markers of diversity: consequences for education

At least three distinct historical roots are at the origin of ethnocultural diversity in Western school systems (Gibson & Ogbu, 1991; Juteau, 2000a; Rex, 2006; Schermerhorn, 1970). First, one can identify the presence, prior to the emergence of a political community, of national groups that would eventually come together, through a more or less democratic process, to form new states. The Walloons and Flemings in Belgium, and French and English Canadians are examples of this. Other groups became minorities against their will, through conquest or forced displacement. This is the case, for example, with Aboriginal communities in many societies, as well as with populations of African origin in North and South Americas. These are often considered involuntary minorities. The third root is linked to the more or less recent migration of individuals seeking, among other reasons, to improve their economic situation or fleeing from political persecution. Such individuals joined a pre-existing political community and, for that reason, are often considered voluntary minorities, although this label varies in the nuances of its definition depending on the extent of post-colonial relationships between immigrant-sending and immigrant-receiving countries. National minorities (or national communities where two or more groups have the same demographic weight) often enjoy constitutional rights or international protection to control educational choices offered, although the extent to which this is implemented at the ground level often raises tension and mobilization. This is also often the case for Aboriginal populations, but rarely for groups resulting from involuntary displacement or individual migration.

By the same token, national or involuntary minorities often enjoy greater political power and legitimacy with regard to education. From an ethical standpoint, the fact that indigenous peoples or groups who are the product of slavery were violently incorporated into the host society, gives them some moral grounds to claim community control of education as does the fact that their cultural contribution to world heritage is often unique (OSCE, 1999). This is especially the case for Aboriginal peoples whose languages and cultures are threatened or limited to a specific territory, a situation very different from that of immigrants. In the case of national minorities, the legitimacy of their claims is linked to respect for the original contract that a majority group made with them. Meanwhile, when it comes to immigrant-origin groups, the right to have one's language and culture reflected in schools is justified from an individual rights perspective, and not that of collective rights. Host societies do not have a formal obligation to ensure the long-term survival of immigrant communities, even if the maintenance of culture and language is often supported, either for historical reasons of for the sake of national interest, such as economic competitiveness (Kymlicka, 1995; Mc Andrew, 1999).

However, a group's socioeconomic status and its demographic importance are often more reliable predictors of the ability to influence decision-makers than is constitutional status. As widely documented in the broader society as well as within immigrant communities (Apple, 2013; Bourdieu & Passeron, 1990; Putnam, 2000), some groups are able to achieve more status, power and influence in the educational field due to their higher social and cultural capital. Moreover, in the case of immigrants, the legitimacy of their presence as perceived by members of host populations is strongly influenced by the existence or absence of proactive immigrant recruiting policies (Bloemraad, 2006; Inglis, 2008). In this matter, a distinction emerges between on the one hand, Canada, the United States, Australia, and New Zealand, and on the other, Western Europe. In this latter case, the fact of belonging to a supra national entity also has a significant impact on the one hand, on the depolarization of national groups who were once in competition, and on the other hand, on the increased status gap between immigrant communities belonging or not to the European Union (Khader *et al.*, 2006; Zapata, *et al.* 2005).

The predictive value of the nature of historical contact that led to the genesis of a given group, to determine its socioeconomic status, may appear more unequivocal. Indeed, in Western countries, the same hierarchy generally prevails. National minorities or communities have a better status, followed more or less closely (depending on the selective nature of immigration policy) by minorities of immigrant origin, while involuntary minorities such as aboriginal groups and others subjected to forced displacement are at the bottom. Nevertheless, variations exist in the relative socioeconomic and educational status of national minorities when compared to immigrant-origin minorities. For example, in Canada, French-speaking minorities (e.g. outside Quebec), some of whom have very old roots in Western Canada, are on average less privileged than are the Western and Eastern European communities who migrated in the latter part of the 19th and early 20th Centuries (Juteau, 2000b). In the same vein, although they are usually at the bottom of a hierarchy, involuntary minorities are often characterized by an internal polarization, especially when some have benefited from special economic or educational supports, such as equity programmes or quotas. This is the case, for example, with the 'Black *bourgeoisie*' in the United States, whose emergence in the last fifty years has not fundamentally questioned the difficult socioeconomic situation lived by a majority of the Black population (Lacy, 2007).

Understanding the challenges undermining adaptation to diversity in schools also requires addressing the variety of markers that groups use to assert their specificity, as well as markers that serve as a basis for their 'Othering' by majority groups. These include religion, language, culture, 'race' and specific historical trajectories, with these often but not necessarily experienced in a compounded manner. At one end of the spectrum, Aboriginal groups often differ from the majority in all of these respects, and at the other end, some groups are almost indistinguishable, except for one or two dimensions, for example with the travellers' community in Ireland.

From a theoretical point of view, in the constructivist perspective that currently dominates the sociology of ethnic relations (Barth, 1969; Jenkins, 2008) the nature of these markers should not matter greatly. This perspective insists that boundaries between groups, and not specific differences, create and maintain ethnicity, which is a dynamic phenomenon. Rejecting essentialism, which postulates that difference exists in and of itself, constructivists focus essentially on various factors explaining why these tend to generally be resilient to change, considering that boundaries between groups are sometimes redefined. The role of schooling in the preservation or the fluctuation of distinct identities is of special interest here, whether one focuses on the function of cultural reproduction (preservation or disappearance of minority cultures, languages, religions), of socialization (promotion of a common sense of belonging and identity), or of selection (maintenance, increase or reduction of educational and subsequently socioeconomic inequalities).

However, in education, differences in the nature of various markers of diversity lead to differences in the way public policy issues are addressed (Glenn & De Jong, 2011; Inglis, 2008). For instance, compared to other markers, language represents a more absolute impediment to communication. The accommodation of linguistic differences is also more complex. Indeed, the concepts of interracial or interfaith education have no equivalent in the area of language, where the aim is to strike a balance between multilinguicism and the common language, rather than to produce an interlingua.

Some markers, such as religion, are intricately related to freedom of conscience. These are protected by major international conventions and national constitutions. Moreover, historically, the separation between the state (and therefore schools) and one or several predominant religions has had much greater legitimacy, at least in certain countries, than the utopia of a linguistically or culturally neutral state (or school). Debates over the place of religion in educational institutions are therefore generally more complex and often more acrimonious, especially in the current international context, where Islam has clearly emerged as the 'significant other' in the so-called 'clash of civilization' (Gottschalk & Greenberg, 2008; Milot, 2010; Milot & Koussens, 2009).

Although all markers can be essentialized, as is currently the case with Islam in many countries, 'race' holds a special status, as it is clearly, more than any other, the product of stigmatization, and not of specific beliefs or practices to which given groups can identify (Dei, 1996; Van den Berghe, 1967). Thus, one could assume that instead of active inclusion through curriculum change, such differences require combative action on the part of educational decision-makers and practitioners. Yet, in the last fifty years, paradoxical valorization strategies have grown in this area, such as the 'Black is Beautiful' movement in the United States. These strategies have relied more on an imagined cultural identity, such as a return to an African origin, than on the current cultural specificities of the group, but have nevertheless become the focus of an important mobilization for recognition in schools.

## Policy debates in a comparative perspective

### The importance of sharing common educational institutions

In the West, over the past thirty years, this broad issue has been addressed in the context of two distinct debates (Mc Andrew, 2001, 2013). The first relates to the right for various minorities to control specific educational institutions. The second debate focuses on undesired school segregation; since most *de jure* segregation has been abolished over the last fifty years in Western countries, this essentially refers to a de facto segregation largely influenced by socioeconomic status but also by immigrant, ethnic and racial affinities.

*Community control over education*

With respect to the first debate, three factors influence the political response among both minority and majority groups to claims for and the popularity of educational services controlled by specific communities. The first factor relates to the nature of the minority and the markers by which the group is defined. Whether by virtue of constitutional, national or international protections, or as a result of a stronger tendency to be territorialized, it is generally national or Aboriginal minorities, rather than immigrant groups or minorities resulting from involuntary displacements, who enjoy the right to specific institutions (Ballantine, 2009; Inglis, 2008; Lê Than Khoi, 1981). Nevertheless, the degree of such control varies considerably. At one end of the spectrum, we observe entirely separate systems, from the Department of Education to intermediary structures, all the way down to schools. At the other end, a mere de facto control over specific schools occurs. In the case of minorities of immigrant origin, the specific markers that define them play an important role in their educational autonomy. When compared to minorities defined only through linguistic or cultural criteria, religious minorities are more likely to control their own institutions (whether publicly funded or not). In addition to the higher legal and constitutional legitimacy and protection granted to religious diversity referred to in the first section, this trend can paradoxically be linked to the secular nature of many school systems, which is considered by some parents to be incompatible with the requirements of their denominational commitments. Historically, this has favoured longer-standing religions, creating a space for more recent religious groups to claim similar status (Allouche-Benayoun, 2009; Thiessen, 2001).

The second factor is the divergent conceptions of integration and of the nature of pluralism that should be recognized in any given society. In this regard, the supporters of *pluralistic integration* (Carens, 1995; Kymlicka, 1995), which promotes an intercultural blue-print through the sharing of common educational and social spaces, are seen to oppose supporters of *radical pluralism* (Gagnon-Tessier, 2011; Taylor, 1992). The latter contend that a viable form of citizenship can be built on the aggregation of distinct groups, provided that a minimal legal and constitutional framework is guaranteed. Although these two conceptions are in opposition, they are considered compatible in many societies, where the first is applied to relations between the majority and minorities of immigrant origin, and the second serves as a framework for the historical modus vivendi to which the majority is bound towards national or Aboriginal minorities. However, generally speaking, partisans of pluralistic integration take a dim view on the medium-term effects of radical pluralism, perceived to be a threat to social cohesion. In contrast, those who favour radical pluralism claim that pluralistic integration is, at best, a soft assimilation strategy of minority groups to the values and cultural characteristics of the majority.

In societies having experienced violent conflicts, such as in Northern Ireland during the Troubles or in the former Yugoslavia, citizens are more likely to take a critical stance on the role of separate schooling than when the control of specific educational institutions by distinct groups has allowed for a relatively stable, if not enthusiastic, co-existence such as in Canada, and to a large extent in Belgium (Mc Andrew, 2013).

The third factor is the relative weight placed on the various mandates of schooling. In most Western countries, the issue has rarely been discussed around the equalization of opportunities role of education, but has been heavily focused on striking the balance between the functions of cultural reproduction and common socialization. There are some exceptions here, especially among disadvantaged and disenfranchised minorities, who often seek control over their own institutions to promote educational mobility of their youth, even if they may use, to various extents, the rhetoric of cultural distinctiveness to justify their causes. This has been the case, for example, with African Americans who have consistently wavered for the last fifty years between the fight for school integration and a struggle to return to community-control based in an ideology of Afro-centrist schools (Banks, 2010).

Nevertheless, the general trend (Gallagher, 2004; Mc Andrew, 2013) is that citizens and groups who think that education should contribute more to the preservation and dynamism of minority cultures are more inclined to view separate institutions positively, while those who insist on the importance of co-existence between youth of all origins, at ages where values, attitudes and behaviours are shaped, tend to value common institutions. These choices are also influenced by the assessment one makes, on the one hand, of the potential of a segregated educational service to promote harmonious intercultural relations, and on the other hand, of the potential of an integrated school to preserve cultural and linguistic diversity.

*De facto segregation*

Regarding the impact of de facto segregation (e.g. which is not desired by the groups themselves), we tread on somewhat less normative ground (Mahieu, 1999; Orfield & Eaton, 1996; Payet, 1999). First, we know that the degree to which certain minorities are over-represented in certain schools is not solely the product of socioecological factors, such as the concentration of immigrants in big cities and in some neighbourhoods, nor of their socioeconomically lower status. Indeed, the school system also contributes to segregation through both explicit and implicit policies, such as the clustering of immigrant services into specific institutions or the definition of school recruitment areas in the first case, and a de facto specialization of educational institutions attracting different school populations in the second. In countries and regions with the freedom to choose educational institution, parental school choices can also contribute to segregation.

There is also a strong consensus among scholars around the fact that the educational consequences of de facto segregation are, first and foremost, influenced by the socioeconomic characteristics of the populations concerned. This explains why European research and discourse are far more alarmist than Canadian or

American counterparts regarding the negative impact of the phenomenon, at least with respect to immigrant origin populations (Christensen, 2004; Christensen & Segeritz, 2008). In both instances, though, one should keep in mind that it is not the current socioeconomic status of immigrants that predicts their schooling success, but rather the family's cultural capital linked to its situation in the country of origin (Mc Andrew et al., 2008; Suárez-Orozco, 2011). This explains the paradoxical, but widely supported finding, that underprivileged schools with high ethnic density often perform better than do schools where students come from native-born families that have shared a culture of poverty across generations. Nevertheless, there are other contributing factors, such as the strong valorization of education among many immigrant families.

However, what is less clear is the extent to which there is an added value for students of immigrant origin to attend schools with a high concentration of immigrants, once we control for their socioeconomic background. Research (De Rycke & Swyngedouw, 1999; Mc Andrew et al., 2015; Suárez-Orozco et al., 2008) is inconclusive, because results are likely to be linked to the cultural characteristics of distinct groups. High-density schools can therefore be either positive or negative for some immigrant students, but most of the time that factor is much less significant than social class. Moreover, level of concentration also plays a certain role. A significant but not dominant presence of immigrant students may help raise the issue of their school integration as an institutional priority, thus ensuring the availability of necessary resources. On the contrary, the presence of too few, or too many students of diverse immigrant origin, can potentially have a negative impact on their school integration (Inglis, 2008; Leman, 1997).

Finally, even in settings where de facto segregation does not seem to have a negative impact on school success, concerns arise nonetheless over the more long-term effect of a lack of social networks within the host society (Driessen & Bezemer, 1999; Mc Andrew et al., 1999) with respect to social integration and the production of a common identity, which then raises questions largely similar to those discussed around community control over education.

## *The place of immigrant languages in the curriculum*

Most Western countries have one, two or even three 'official' languages – that is, languages that have a privileged status within public institutions and in the interactions between the State and citizens. There is a broad consensus, among both minorities and majorities, that school systems need to promote the learning of these languages, regardless of the preferred schooling model, for the dual purpose of equalizing opportunities and promoting intergroup exchanges (Eurydice, 2005; Grin & Vaillancourt, 1999).

Therefore, the debate over the place of minority languages relates to more specific issues (Mc Andrew, 2009, 2013). First, when there is more than one official language, is it legitimate for some regions of the country to give special weight to one language over the other, as is the case in Quebec within Canada and in Catalonia within Spain? In such cases, what rights should be granted to local minorities who belong to the national majority? Similarly, what rights should be accorded to immigrant groups regarding the choice of language of instruction?

The second issue is the pedagogical status of the common language(s) to be taught to linguistic minorities: should these be considered second language(s) or schooling language(s)? Generally, since national or aboriginal minorities often control their own institutions, these are more likely to adopt the first model, while the second is most often imposed on minorities of immigrant origin.

When this is the case, a third important question emerges with regard to the extent to which mastering the common language at the level of a schooling language requires the loss of one's mother tongue, or whether to the contrary, skills in each language are interrelated. On this point, the debate among specialists is nearly closed. The need to promote a balanced additive bilingualism – that is, as much as possible a comparable mastery of both languages, so as to promote the transfer of metalinguistic and metacognitive skills from the first language to the second – is today largely corroborated by fundamental and applied research (Armand et al., 2011; Cummins, 2000). Consequently, one must also reject subtractive bilingualism, where the learning of one language occurs at the expense of the others. Yet, even among decision-makers who claim to be convinced of these realities, the logical choices are not always made. For example, responding positively to parents' requests, some authorities may develop programmes for the teaching of the mother tongue of immigrant or minority groups that would not otherwise have a place in the school curriculum, but then limit the services to the transmission of oral skills, responding to teacher concerns about the potential 'mixing-up' of languages by students. Moreover, research on the attitudes of school professionals, as well as content analysis of media debates and of public opinion, show that the view that a dichotomous opposition exists between first and second languages still has many supporters.

Moreover, experiencing immigrant or minority languages as a threat to the national language is far from limited to societies where that language has experienced, or is still experiencing, challenges to this status, such as Quebec, Catalonia or Flanders (Mc Andrew, 2013). Indeed, resistance to the recognition of multilingualism is also high in societies whose common language is dominant, such as in the United States and France. This seems to point to the fact that the issue here has more to do with power and control, than merely with identity concerns. Nevertheless, today, immigrant or minority languages play some role in most Western school systems, whether it be treated as a schooling language (on its own or together with another language), as a taught subject matter or as a mere afterschool activity. In the second case, a wide variety of objectives are accorded to this teaching, which, in part, determine the preferred model (Bale, 2010; Kibbee, 2012; Mc Andrew, 2009).

A first objective is to favour the return to the parents' country of origin. It is around this objective, especially in Europe, that the first official support for the teaching of heritage languages emerged at the end of the 1970s. It has been increasingly questioned following the growing acknowledgement of the permanent settlement of migratory waves who were expected to be temporary. Thus, the recognition of immigrant languages in the school system is increasingly advocated as a support for the learning of the host language and for the development of a harmonious identity among youth. Such an aim usually induces the temporary teaching in/or of the immigrant language, such as the American bilingual education programmes, where the second language is taught only when students have mastered English language skills. In some instances, though, European and North American authorities also put forward multilingual programmes for the sake of preserving minority communities and cultures, considered to be assets for the host country. In such cases, programmes are funded by national or local authorities, not by the country of origin, and are often reserved for speakers of the target language. This objective often appeals not only to newcomers, who are generally more concerned with mastering the host language, but also to long-standing communities who for political or religious reasons may wish to preserve their heritage languages. But several programmes aimed first and foremost at supporting the learning of majority language(s) can also contribute to the maintenance of minority languages and cultures, often under pressure from the minority groups themselves, who may resist the transitory character of certain bilingual programmes, for example in the United States.

While the three objectives above are essentially concerned with minority students, a growing awareness of the potential enrichment of all students through the presence of a multiethnic student body, as well as some criticisms directed towards the segregating nature of some programmes, have given momentum to a fourth aim: the promotion of multilingualism and of intercultural education within the entire school population. In some instances, such as the Heritage Language Programme in the Canadian province of Ontario, educational institutions have evolved towards instructional programmes open to non-native speakers, coupled with the recognition of third languages for certification purposes. In other instances, especially when too many languages are spoken in a given classroom, this objective can be pursued through diverse multilingual activities offered to all students within the same classroom, often inspired by the Language Awareness Movement (Armand & Maraillet, 2013; Candelier, 2003).

In many instances, the same model can serve complementary purposes. This is the case for bilingual programmes, as mentioned above, which, depending on their transitory or permanent nature, may aim for mastery of the host language or play a wider role in the maintenance of a community's language and culture. But, except for a few languages with important international status, such programmes have limited impact on the promotion of multilingualism among the full student body, as it is usually difficult to convince majority parents to involve their children. The teaching of heritage languages offered by communities usually fosters the maintenance of languages and cultures, sometimes in an outdated form that corresponds neither to the values of the second generation youth, nor to the actual characteristics of teaching in the country of origin. Programmes within public schools differ in status, depending on whether they are offered within regular school hours or outside. However, these usually put more stress on mastering the host language, often by ensuring the harmonization between pedagogical approaches and content to the mainstream and the heritage languages. Also, majority parents are more likely to enrol their children in such programmes, as the commitment is less intense than for bilingual education programmes, which turn them into good vehicles for the promotion of multilingualism and intercultural rapprochement in schools. However, one encounters major differences in the popularity of dominant and less powerful languages in this regard.

Debates and tensions over the choice of models and/or the prioritization of objectives are influenced by local power relationships (e.g. the weight and status of various immigrant groups within the collectivity), national priorities and issues (e.g. the need to counteract declining economic competitiveness or to fight high school drop-out), and, as already mentioned, the international status of various languages.

Thus, the American debate (Bale, 2010; Crawford, 1999) is focused on contrasting evidence showing that bilingual education (especially English/Spanish) yields better results than English immersion with respect to the learning of that language. This clearly shows the social priority that the integration of the Spanish minority enjoys in America, given its demographic significance, as well as the resistance of some segments of that population to linguistic assimilation. Fundamental research lends credit to the proponents of bilingual education as the more efficient tool for mastering English. Nevertheless, American bilingual programmes are fragmented and diversified, and meta-analytical research is limited in many ways, undermining the comparability of measures. Thus, it is often the second camp that wins out in the court of public opinion, including among Spanish-speaking parents themselves. In fact, when Resolution 227 outlawed bilingual programmes in California in 1993, it was supported by more than 70% of the electorate, indicating a minority support for such a position.

In other contexts, such as Canada and Australia (Inglis, 2008; Mc Andrew, 2009), where the host society supports the maintenance of heritage languages and cultures for their own sake, even if they may also seek beneficial impacts on the mastery of host languages, the debate has focused on the legitimacy of various organizing powers. While one could assume that heritage language teaching integrated into public schools may be more favourably viewed by immigrant groups, some communities prefer to retain control over such programmes, even when faced with inadequate funding, fewer resources and less universal access. Such is the case in particular for religious minorities, who are then able to supplement language instruction with a promotion of faith or of traditional values. Immigrant communities may also consider programmes aimed at the promotion of multilingualism in the full student population as a threat to the quality of heritage language teaching, either because the presence of non-speakers in structured programmes is likely to lower the level of instruction, or because language awareness activities may not be fully conducive to mastering a given language.

On the other end of the spectrum, the weak status of immigrant origin populations, combined with a higher need for multilingual skills among all students, has led most European countries, when they moved away from a model of heritage language teaching geared towards the return to the country of origin, to prefer inclusive multilingual approaches. Indeed, the negative consequences of full bilingual programmes or even structured heritage language programmes are often feared with regard to segregation, but also to school performance, in a context where the social capital of minority languages is not fully recognized (Office for Standards in Education, 1999; Roosens, 2007).

## *The legitimacy of cultural and religious diversity in school programmes and practices*

Of all the debates considered in this chapter, this has been the most controversial during the last ten years in the West, especially regarding accommodation for religious diversity (Baubérot, 2007; Eid *et al.*, 2009; Mc Andrew, 2011, 2013). In a post-9/11 context, where both religious fundamentalism and Islamophobia are on the rise, this complexity can be linked, as mentioned above, to some specific characteristics of the relationship between public institutions and religious markers (Boyd, 2007; Bramadat & Seljak, 2009). First, the requirement of State neutrality when it comes to religion is, with a few historical exceptions, much more absolute than in matters of language or culture. Compared to mere cultural traditions, the absolutism of religious beliefs is also far less amenable to the critical review of facts needed for the acquisition of knowledge. However, international conventions and several national constitutions and charters of rights often attribute more weight to religious freedom than to the mere right to further one's cultural life. This often leads to deeper conflicts over legitimacy between an educational institution attempting to generate common practices and identities, and parents or students who emphasize their right to develop their faith.

The place of cultural and religious diversity in school programmes and practices is also the issue where educational response is broadest, whether such responses are initiated by the State, the institutions or school actors themselves, and coherence often lacks in this respect. The intensive nature of compulsory schooling, which spans for some 25 hours per week during approximately twelve years, also often prevents the consistency of institutional responses (Mc Andrew, 2010). Thus, for better or worse, practices in the field often appear more multiform and more supportive of a merger approach than the political and programmatic discourse that purports to guide them. For the sake of clarity, these can be divided into five major groups of practices, according to their prevalence and the consensus they generate (Banks, 2010; Gillborn, 1995; Glenn & De Jong, 2011; Mc Andrew *et al.*, 1997; Pagé, 1993).

### *A continuum of practices*

The first group is the *selective integration of elements pertaining to minority cultures and religions for an integrative purpose*, which refers to practices such as the inclusion of student characters of all origins or various cultural elements in the learning materials or in school decorations, the presence of teaching staff of various origins, as well as the celebration of various cultural or religious events and holidays. These measures are widely found in most immigrant-receiving countries, giving little rise to debate. However, while potentially having an impact on the sense of belonging among immigrant students who are not especially marginalized, such as those from educated families with a good socioeconomic status, these measures are often criticized as being merely tokenistic by minority groups who are more heavily disenfranchised from society and school.

A step forward in a stronger recognition of cultural and religious diversity is thus exemplified by *the implementation of activities specially tailored to the needs and characteristics of religious and cultural minorities, with the aim of fighting inequalities*. Under this approach, authorities may develop multilingual and/or culturally adapted informational documents about the school system, implement special school outreach activities directed toward the community, or organize the intercultural training of teachers to help them better understand immigrant students' characteristics, in turn enabling instructors to vary their teaching strategies. These practices are also relatively widespread, but in many European countries, they are implemented based on a rationale of socioeconomic disadvantage (e.g. Priority Education Zones in France and French-speaking Belgium), rather than justified explicitly by the presence of religious and cultural minorities. When and if these measures succeed in bridging the gap between low-achieving minorities and the majority, they can contribute in the long run to the development of more inclusive identities and societies. Nevertheless, many analysts argue that compensatory approaches are insufficient when groups are particularly alienated from the school curriculum, be it for their position in the world order or their current situation in a given country.

*The integration of specific minority content or perspectives in the regular school curriculum, where radical differences are acknowledged* is thus sometimes implemented, although at this tipping point between the promotion of common values and the taking into account of diversity, one already finds more resistance and less consensus. Responses vary depending on the nature of the groups at stake. For example, for aboriginal minorities in many countries, an adaptation to their culture and worldview is found almost across all disciplines, including Mathematics and Sciences. However, in the case of national and immigrant minorities, adaptation is usually limited to Social Sciences, such as History and Geography, where the contribution and interpretation of various groups are emphasized and, to a lesser extent, where conflicts over values may occur, such as in the realm of moral or sexual education. These practices are more common in contexts of long-standing division, where the dimensions of dissent within the political community cannot be ignored, such as the interpretation of various historical facts by Blacks and Whites in the United States, or Catholics and Protestants in Northern Ireland.

The last two sets of practices are concerned more with the informal and hidden curriculum. *The adaptation of standard norms and regulations governing school life in response to individual religious or culture-based claims* is more frequent than the high-profile controversies they give rise to would have us believe, especially with regard to Islam. In societies that recognize the legitimacy of diversity in public spaces, practices such as adapting school cafeteria menus to religious requirements, allowing for the absence of minority students during major religious holidays, and making school uniforms acceptable to a variety of cultural and religious perspectives are regularly found. Such an approach is usually governed by an individual rights and not a group rights perspective. However, such demands are met with greater resistance when they appear to encroach on the mandates that lie at the very heart of educational activity, such as the critical transmission of knowledge, the promotion of fundamental democratic values (including gender equality), and the preservation of a public space where common identity outweighs differences. There is also usually a much higher support for *additive pluralism*, which allows all students to be exposed to more diversity, than for *subtractive pluralism*, which allows for censorship and limited exposure of some contents, values and materials to minority students.

Finally, in some instances, such as during the peak years of anti-racist education in Great Britain and in English Canada, one could encounter – and still can, in some local settings – *the tailoring and transformation of various elements of the curriculum in response to the claims of the 'organized' community*. Such practices include exempting minority students from elements deemed offensive in sexual education, setting up segregated male/female classes for physical education or for the teaching of all subject matters, and warning teachers about any value judgements on elements that could be deemed racist or sexist within minority cultures or works of art (though teachers are often asked to be critical when dealing with similar elements within majority culture or works of art). Although triggering some resistance, these questionable practices are often justified by the competition between the public sector and ethno-religious schools, especially when they are partly funded by the State. Proponents of such a radical adaptation argue that it ensures that minority students stay in common schools. The level of interethnic contact it preserves is considered preferable to isolation, even if not all students are exposed to exactly the same teaching or bound by the same regulations.

*Some influencing factors*

The position that educational specialists, decision-makers and staff, as well as parents and concerned citizens, take on this continuum regarding cultural and religious adaptation is influenced by many dynamics.

One of these influences is the preferred citizenship model, relating to the State's role in the promotion of a conception of 'the common good' and expressions of diversity in the public space (Kymlicka, 2000; Miller & Walzer, 1995; Taylor, 1992; Touraine, 1994). Two of these models, the republican and the liberal, relegate diversity to the private sphere, promoting instead the neutrality of schools. However, they differ on the extent to which they put forward substantive or procedural values, or, to use here Kymlicka's classical opposition, a 'thick' or a 'thin' culture. The republican model considers that schools must promote values of involvement, solidarity, and a sense of national belonging, as these are necessary for living together in a common society. Proponents of such an approach will usually limit themselves to the selective integration of elements pertaining to minority culture and religion for an integrative purpose, although they may also implement activities specially tailored to the needs and characteristics of a religious and cultural minority, but only with the aim of fighting inequalities. Meanwhile, the liberal model views the State, and therefore the school, as an arbitrator between various conceptions of the 'good'. This distinction provokes differences in the response to claims for cultural or religious accommodation from minority students and parents, as well as in curriculum content, especially with regard to civic, moral and value-based education. Proponents of the classical liberal models tend not to favour the use of education by the State to transform ethnic relations, as they are in principle less interventionist. At the other end of the spectrum, two other models, the communitarian and the renewed liberal, both recognize the legitimacy of a representation of diversity in public spaces, including in schools, but advocate it from a rather different perspective. Communitarians, who question the mere existence of a neutral State, see diversity as a collective right of any group to influence the nature of public services and especially the content of schooling, while renewed liberals support it as a requirement for realizing the equitable treatment of all individuals, especially those belonging to marginalized groups. Here again, this difference of perspective has evident consequences for educational programmes and practices. In the first instance, adaptation to diversity in schools is paramount, and the legitimacy that services be structured according to the language, culture and values of various subgroups is promoted. In the second instance, the limits of adaptation are much more clearly fixed within the framework of civic values, such as the expectation that any adaptation stems from individual will and not community pressure, and that it is compatible with other rights and freedoms, as well as with the major mandates of schooling.

The second factor influencing the extent to which cultural and religious adaptation is promoted lies in ethical positions taken on conflicts of values, which often oppose minority students, their families and school staff. These are influenced by the citizenship models described above, but there is no absolute congruence in this regard. For example, *cultural relativists* are usually proponents of the communitarian model, advocating respect for those elements perceived by immigrant minorities as requirements of their culture and their religion, even if some of these would seem to contradict major social goals. *Minimalist democrats* tend to support the liberal and renewed liberal models, stressing the importance of democratic values and of the actual state of the law (even if it is likely to be modified over time) as limits to school accommodation to diversity. *Substantive democrats* are often proponents of the republican model, emphasizing that adapting to diversity should also be weighed through more substantive values, even if these are not embraced by all subgroups of society, but are deemed necessary to promoting important social objectives. Such values would include broad social solidarity, an involvement in institutions and networks outside one's own group, and identity moderation (e.g. accepting some limits on the expression of religious or political beliefs) for the sake of preserving neutrality and harmony. A fourth ethical position that cannot be linked to a democratic legitimate model of citizenship is also encountered, and often dominant in everyday positioning. *Majority supremacists* consider that the definition of schools, programmes, norms and practices must reflect the central role that the historically dominant group has played in the building of a national identity. These advocate that in response to the growing diversity of a society, schools play a conservative role – e.g. protecting some values and cultural characteristics that members of the majority wish to remain unchanged, even if this implies to a certain extent unequal treatment for newly established groups.

The third and last influencing factor we wish to point out here is the conception of knowledge itself, which has a significant impact on positions adopted regarding curriculum content (Apple, 1979; Dei, 1996; Grinter, 1992). At one end of the spectrum, *epistemological realists* believe that knowledge can be neutral and universal, and thus also believe in the possibility to define a school curriculum based on a consensus between all social groups. At the other end of the spectrum, *antiracist constructivists* consider that knowledge is socially constructed, and that given the current and past world orders, 'mainstream' school knowledge is strongly marked by Western ethnocentrism. Several positions in-between exist in this respect, and are influenced, among other things, by the discipline at stake. For example, while Mathematics and Science are today considered cultural constructs, their universality is much less questioned than knowledge in the Social Sciences, especially in History teaching, where many studies have shown that a selective narrative reproduction of dominant or specific group perspectives prevails. Moreover, both camps adopt sharply contrasting views regarding the relation between the nature of school knowledge and the prevalence of school failure among some groups. Epistemological realists see school failure as stemming mainly from family or student deficits, and advocate for compensatory measures and programmes to support access to 'knowledge' by such students. Anti-racist constructivists argue, on the contrary, that the gap between school and family regarding what constitutes relevant knowledge is at the core of the disengagement and disenfranchisement of minority students.

## Conclusion

Through this review of issues and policy surrounding education and ethnic relations, we hope to have illustrated the extent to which education is a battleground, on one hand between majority and minority groups, and on the other hand between proponents of various perspectives for reshaping ethnic relations. Whether one considers the necessity of sharing common institutions, the role of immigrant languages in the curriculum or the legitimacy of cultural and religious diversity in school programmes and practices, it appears that a pessimistic and deterministic perspective, such as that of reproduction, does not render justice to the central role of conflicts in education in the redefinition of ethnic boundaries. Nevertheless, our analysis also shows that an overly optimistic vision of schools as agents of social and ethnic transformation is not realistic, either. *Schools as contested sites* is clearly the concept that best describes the current situation of educational institutions questioned by the diversification of their student body and by the debates on the 'common good' to be transmitted. The languages, cultures, identities and values that will thrive tomorrow are being negotiated today through a relationship reflecting but also contributing, to a certain extent, to the modification of current inequalities.

I also hope to have demonstrated that there is no simple solution in what is often framed as the pluralistic dilemma, this being the balance to be found between the recognition of pluralism and the promotion of common values that renders its expression possible. Indeed, any policy response that moves decision-makers and practitioners a little too much towards either side of the continuum between unity and diversity is likely to provoke perverse effects. We have seen this with regard to the control of specific institutions by minorities, a solution that one should not disallow in a context where segregation and inequality prevail within public schools, but which needs to be set within a clear framework in order to avoid the reproduction of essentialized and fixed identities through segregation. By the same token, while multilingualism and the maintenance of immigrant languages are important social objectives, some programmes that support such aims can reinforce the boundaries between 'Us' and the 'Other', fashioning perpetual foreigners. The pluralism dilemma is also important with regard to the place of cultural and religious diversity in schools. Indeed, one slips quite quickly from folklore and tokenism into an essentialization of culture and a legitimation of anti-democratic practices. Thus, the suitable balance always needs to be redefined.

In this chapter, I have looked at a variety of experiences reflecting both North American and European contexts. While the aim was not a systematic comparison, some questions warrant further investigation. The first is whether the classical distinction between New World countries, where immigration and pluralism are integral parts of the process of nation-building, and the countries of Old Europe, where history has created more traditional and cohesive identities, is still relevant. Some trends identified in the chapter would seem to show that indeed it is, such as the slightly more problematic relationship one finds in Europe with ethnic concentration, multilingualism, and the recognition of cultural and religious diversity in education. Nevertheless, commonalities appear more significant. In both contexts, there is a growing polarization between advocates of social cohesion based on linguistic, cultural, and religious homogeneity, and proponents of a pluralist and multilingual redefinition of civic and school spaces. Another question that is especially interesting for a North American observer, is the role that the European construction plays in the openness or resistance to the taking into account of diversity. In some instances, such as the place of immigrant languages, it could be seen as an agent of legitimation of diversity within the school space. In others, especially with regard to religious diversity, it appears more as a complicating factor that feeds defensive reactions.

As a concluding remark, one can wonder why in so many contexts, debates regarding the socialization function of schools seem to generate greater academic, public and media interest than those focusing on the socioeconomic improvement of immigrant students. Most of the time the majority group controls the agenda, even if in countries where access to citizenship is quicker, minorities enjoy more political power. Nevertheless, in both instances, if one wishes to reinforce the role of schools as a central agent in the transformation of ethnic boundaries, it is essential that the concerns of marginalized groups be more recognized.

## References

Allouche-Benayoun, J. (2009). *L'enseignement privé juif*. In C. Béraud & J.-P. Willaime (eds), *Les jeunes, l'école et la religion* (pp. 219–50). Paris: Bayard.

Apple, M. W. (1979). *Ideology and Curriculum*. London: Routledge & Kegan Paul.

Apple, M. W. (2013). *Can Education Change Society?* New York: Routledge.

Armand, F. & Maraillet, É. (2013). *Éducation interculturelle et diversité linguistique*. Retrieved from: www.elodil.umontreal.ca.

Armand, F., Thi Hoa, L., Combes, É., Sabounjian, R. & Thamin, N. (2011). *L'enseignement de l'écriture en langue seconde: Synthèse des connaissances*. Report submitted to the Ministère de l'Éducation, du Loisir et du Sport. Québec.

Bale, J. (2010). International comparative perspective on Heritage Language Education Policy Research. *Annual Review of Applied Linguistic*, 30, 42–65.

Ballantine, J. H. (2009). *The Sociology of Education: A Systematic Analysis* (6th edn). Upper Saddle River, NJ: Prentice Hall.

Banks, J. A. (2010). *Multicultural Education: Issues and Perspectives* (7th edn) (with C. A. McGee-Banks). New York: John Wiley & Sons.

Barth, F. (ed.). (1969). *Ethnic Groups and Boundaries*. Boston, MA: Little, Brown & Co.

Baubérot, J. (2007). *Les laïcités dans le monde*. Paris: PUF.

Bloemraad, I. (2006). *Becoming a Citizen: Incorporating Immigrants and Refugees in the United States and Canada*. Oakland, CA: University of California Press.

Bourdieu, P. & Passeron, J. P. (1990). *Reproduction in Education: Society and Culture*. New York: Sage Publications.

Boyd, M. (2007). Religion-based alternative diffuse resolution: A challenge to multiculturalism. In K. Banting, T. Courchesne & S. L. Seidle (eds), *Belonging? Diversity, Recognition and Shared Citizenship in Canada*. Montréal: The Art of the State/IRPP.

Bramadat, P. & Seljak, O. (2009). *Religion and Ethnicity in Canada*. Toronto: Toronto University Press.

Candelier, M. (2003). *L'éveil aux langues à l'école primaire. Evlang: Bilan d'une innovation européenne*. Bruxelles: De Boeck, Pratiques pédagogiques.

Carens, J. H. (1995). Complex justice, cultural difference, and political community. In D. Miller & M. Walzer (eds), *Pluralism, Justice and Equality*. Oxford: Oxford University Press.

Christensen, G. (2004). What matters for immigrant achievement cross-nationally? A comparative approach examining immigrant and non-immigrant student's achievement. Unpublished dissertation. Stanford, CA: Stanford University.

Christensen, G. & Segeritz, M. (2008). An international perspective on student's achievement. In Bertelsmann Stiftung (ed.), *Immigrant Students Can Succeed: Lessons from Around the Globe* (pp. 11–33). Gütersloh, Germany: Verlag Bertelsmann Stiftung.

Crawford, J. (1999). *Bilingual Education: History, Politics, Theory and Practice*. Los Angeles, CA: Bilingual Education Services.

Cummins, J. (2000). *Language, Power and Pedagogy: Bilingual Children in the Crossfire*. Clevedon: Multilingual Matters.

Dei, G. J. (1996). *Anti-racist Education: Theory and Practice*. Halifax: Fernwood Publishing.

De Rycke, L. & Swyngedouw, M. (1999). The value of concentration schools as appreciated by Morrocans, Turks, and unskilled Belgians in Brussels. *International Journal of Education Research*, 31(4), 267–81.

Driessen, G. W. J. M. & Bezemer, J. J. (1999). Background and achievement levels of Islamic schools in the Netherlands: Are the reservations justified? *Race, Ethnicity and Education*, 2(2).

Eid, P., Bosset, P., Milot, M. & Lebel-Grenier, S. (2009). *Appartenance religieuse, appartenance citoyenne: Un équilibre en tension*. Québec: Presses de l'Université Laval.

Eurydice. (2005). *Key Data on Teaching Languages at School in Europe*. Brussels: Eurydice.

Gagnon-Tessier, L. C. (2011). *La philosophie du pluralisme radical chez Chantal Mouffe: Théorie, critique et enjeux*. Sarrebruck: Éditions universitaires européennes.

Gallagher, T. (2004). *Education in Divided Societies*. Basingstoke: Palgrave Macmillan.

Gibson, M. A. & Ogbu, J. U. (eds). (1991). *Minority Status and Schooling: A Comparative Study of Immigrant an Involuntary Minorities*. New York: Garland.

Gillborn, D. (1995). *Racism and Anti-racism in Real School: Theory, Policy, Practice*. Buckingham: Open University Press.

Glenn, J. U. & De Jong, E. (2011). *Educating Immigrant Children: Schools and Language Minorities in Twelve Nations*. New York: Garland.

Gottschalk, P. & Greenberg, G. (2008). *Islamophobia: Making Muslims the Enemy*. Lanham, MD: Rowman & Littlefield.

Grin, F. & Vaillancourt, F. (1999). *The Cost-effective Evaluation of Minority Language Policies: Case Studies on Wales, Ireland and the Basque Country*. Flensburg, Germany: European Centre for Minority Issues.

Grinter, R. (1992). Multicultural or antiracist education? The need to choose. In J. Lynch, C. Modgill & S. Modgil (eds), *Cultural Diversity and the Schools*, vol. 1, *Education for Cultural Diversity: Convergence and Divergence* (pp. 95–111). London/Washington, DC: The Falmer Press.

Inglis, C. (2008). *Planning for Cultural Diversity*. Paris: UNESCO, International Institute for Educational Planning.

Jenkins, R. (2008). *Rethinking Ethnicity: Arguments and Exploration* (2nd edn). Thousand Oaks, CA: Sage Publications.

Juteau, D. (2000a). *L'ethnicité et ses frontières*. Montréal: PUM, Collection Trajectoires sociales.

Juteau, D. (2000b). Du dualisme canadien au pluralisme québécois. In M. Mc Andrew & F. Gagnon (eds), *Relations ethniques et éducation dans les sociétés divisées: Québec, Irlande du Nord, Catalogne et Belgique* (pp. 17–38). Montréal: L'Harmattan.

Khader, B., Martiniello, M., Rea, A. & Timmerman, C. (2006). *Penser l'immigration et l'intégration autrement*. Belgique: Bruylant.

Kibbee, D. A. (2012). International perspective on bilingual education: Policy, practice and controversy. *The Modern Language Journal*, 96(3), 471–2.

Kymlicka, W. (1995). *Multicultural Citizenship*. Oxford: Clarendon Press.

Kymlicka, W. (2000). Les droits des minorités et le multiculturalisme: L'évolution du débat anglo-américain. *Comprendre*, 1, 141–71.

Lacy, K. (2007). *Blue-chip Black: Race, Class, and Status in the New Black Middle Class*. Berkeley, CA: University of California Press.

Lê Than Khoi. (1981). *L'éducation comparée*. Paris: Armand Colin.

Leman, J. (1997). School as socializing and corrective force in inter-ethnic European relations. *Journal of Multilingual Development*, 18(2), 125–35.

Mc Andrew, M. (1999). Sens et limite du principe de non-discrimination en matière éducative: Une réflexion critique. *Revue québécoise de droit international*, 12(1), 225–40.

Mc Andrew, M. (2001). *Immigration et diversité à l'école: Le débat québécois dans une perspective comparative*. Montréal: Presses de l'Université de Montréal.

Mc Andrew, M. (2009). Ensuring proper competency in the host language: Contrasting formula and the place of Heritage Languages. *Teacher College Review*, Teacher College, Columbia University, 111(6), 1528–54.

Mc Andrew, M. (2010). *Diversité, éducation au Québec et au Canada: Un ou plusieurs modèles?* In M. Mc Andrew, M. Milot & A. Triki-Yamani (eds), *L'école et la diversité: Perspectives comparées* (pp. 7–20). Québec: Presses de l'Université Laval.

Mc Andrew, M. (2011). Le débat sur le voile à l'école à la lumière des diverses conceptions de l'ethnicité et des rapports ethniques. *Alterstice*, 1(1), 19–34.

Mc Andrew, M. (2013). *Fragile Majorities and Education: Belgium, Catalonia, Northern Ireland, and Quebec*. Montréal: McGill Queen's Press.

Mc Andrew, M., Balde, A., Bakhshaei, M., Tardif-Grenier, K., Audet, G., Armand, F., Guyon, S., Ledent, J., Lemieux, G., Potvin, M., Rahm, J., Vatz Laaroussi, M., Carpentier, A. & Rousseau, C. (2015). *La réussite éducative des élèves issus de l'immigration: Dix ans de recherche et d'intervention au Québec*. Montréal: Presses de l'Université de Montréal.

Mc Andrew, M., Cicéri, C. & Jacquet, M. (1997). La prise en compte de la diversité culturelle et religieuse dans les normes et pratiques de gestion des établissements scolaires: Une étude exploratoire dans cinq provinces canadiennes. *Revue des sciences de l'éducation*, 23(1), 209–32.

Mc Andrew, M., Garnett, B., Ledent, J., Ungerleider, C., Adumati-Trache, M. & Aït-Saïd, R. (2008). La réussite scolaire des élèves issus de l'immigration: Une question de classe sociale, de langue ou de culture? *Éducation et francophonie*, 36(1), 177–96.

Mc Andrew, M., Pagé, M., Jodoin, M. & Lemire, F. (1999). Densité ethnique de l'école et intégration des sociale des élèves néo-québécois. *Canadian Ethnic Studies*, 31(1), 5–25.

Mahieu, P. (1999). Minorities, policies and strategies in Europe: A Belgian (Flemish) view. In D. Turton & J. Gonzalez (eds), *Cultural Identities and Ethnic Minorities in Europe* (pp. 35–45). Bilbao: University of Deusto.

Miller, D. & Walzer, M. (1995). *Pluralism, Justice and Equality*. Oxford: Oxford University Press.

Milot, M. (2010). Conception of the good: Challenging promises of deliberative democracy. In D. Kahane, D. Weinstock, D. Leydet & M. William (eds), *Deliberative Democracy in Practice* (pp. 21–34). Vancouver/Toronto: UBC Press.

Office for Standards in Education. (1999). *Raising the attainment of minority ethnic pupils, schools and LEA responses*. London: OFSTED.

Orfield, G., Eaton, S. E. & The Harvard Project on School Desegregation. (1996). *Dismantling Desegregation: The Quiet Reversal of Brown v. Board of Education*. New York: The New Press.

Organization for Security and Cooperation in Europe (OSCE). (1999). *Report on the linguistic rights of persons belonging to national minorities in the OSCE area*. OSCE: High Commissioner on National Minorities.

Pagé, M. (1993). *Courants d'idées actuels en éducation des clientèles scolaires multiethnique*. Québec: Conseil supérieur de l'éducation.

Payet, J. P. (1999). L'école et la question de l'immigration en France: Une mise à l'épreuve. In M. Mc Andrew, A. C. Découfflé & C. Cicéri (eds), *Les politiques d'immigration et d'intégration au Canada et en France: Analyses comparées et perspectives de recherche* (pp. 353–69). Paris/Ottawa: Ministère de l'Emploi et de la Solidarité sociale, CRSH.

Putnam, R. (2000). *Bowling Alone, the Collapse and Revival of American Community*. New York: Simon & Schuster.

Rex, J. (2006). *Les fondamentaux d'une théorie de l'ethnicité: Ethnicité et citoyenneté, la sociologie des sociétés multiculturelles*. Paris: L'Harmattan.

Roosens, E. (2007). First-language and -culture learning in light of globalization: The case of Muslims in Flanders and in the Brussels area, Belgium. In M. Suárez-Orozco (ed.), *Global Understandings: Learning and Education in Troubled Times* (pp. 256–71). Berkeley, CA/London/New York: University of California Press/Ross Institute.

Schermerhorn, R. A. (1970). *Comparative Ethnic Relations: A Framework for Theory and Research*. New York: Random House.

Suárez-Orozco, C. (2011). Understanding diversity student's trajectories in American schools. In M. Mc Andrew, M. Potvin & A. Triki-Yamani (eds), *The Academic Achievement of Immigrant Origin Students. Canadian Issues*, 77–84.

Suárez-Orozco, C., Suárez-Orozco, M. & Todorova, T. (2008). *Learning a New Land: Immigrant Children in American Society*. Cambridge, MA: Harvard University Press.

Taylor, C. (1992). *Multiculturalism and the Politics of Recognition: An Essay*. Princeton, NJ: Princeton University Press.

Thiessen, E. (2001). *In Defence of Religious Schools and Colleges*. Montréal: McGill-Queen's University Press.

Touraine, A. (1994). *Qu'est-ce que la démocratie?* Paris: Fayard.

Van den Berghe, P. L. (1967). *Race and Racism: A Comparative Study*. New York: Wiley & Sons.

Zapata, R., Requijo, R. & Giménez, A. (2005). *La immigració en estats plurinacionals: El cas de Catalunya en perspectiva*, Rapport de recherche, Barcelona, Universitat Pompeu Fabra, Fundació Trias Fargas.

# Part 2
# Educational pathways

# 4 Does congruence between the school and the home/community environment make a difference?

*Christiane Timmerman, Noel Clycq, Kenneth Hemmerechts and Johan Wets*

## Introduction

The 'democratization' process of the educational system in Flanders[1] has only partially succeeded. The participation rate strongly increased during the last decades, with more students enrolling in higher education and Flemish pupils scoring very highly in international comparative school performance research.

Yet this tendency has not been able to remove inequalities. Many children with an immigrant background and/or lower socioeconomic status – though we must never forget the diversity among ethnic minorities – have a troubled school career and often do not find their way to higher education or do not even obtain an ISCED level 3 qualification (Van Landeghem *et al.*, 2013). This concerns inequalities at different levels: the age at which children start attending nursery school, the quality and outcomes of the school career, the extent to which they participate and succeed in higher education, etc. (Hirtt, 2006; Mahieu, 2002).

A consequence of these inequalities is the development of a knowledge gap between youth with an immigrant background and/or a lower socioeconomic status and those without. This socioethnic stratification also hampers success on the labour market and their chances in life in general. In Belgium, there is a huge overlap between migration background and socioeconomic status. The disadvantage of non-EU migrants in Belgium tends to be large in absolute and in relative terms. The risk of poverty they face is more than three times the risk of the local population. In absolute terms, only Finland presents worse figures than Belgium (Lelkes & Zolyomi, 2010, p. 12). The proportion of persons (18 years and older) born outside the EU27 with a household income below the national poverty line, is 37 per cent in Flanders, compared to 8 per cent for the local population. From the EU15 countries only Wallonia (the southern part of Belgium) and Greece score worse. If the nationality is taken into account instead of the place of birth, 48 per cent of the non-EU citizens in Belgium are living with a household income below the national poverty line (Vanduynslager *et al.*, 2013, p. 153). The two largest groups of non-EU citizens in Belgium are Moroccans and Turks. A large share of pupils with a non-EU migration background are thus situated within the lower socioeconomic strata of society.

Although the Flemish educational system is rated one of the best in the world (de Boyser, 2003) and the participation rate is high, the gap between the results of the best performing and the worst performing students is much higher than in our neighbouring countries, even controlled for socioeconomic status[2] (see also De Meyer & Warlop, 2010; Jacobs et al., 2009). A large majority of the worst performing students are youngsters with an immigrant background (Duquet et al., 2006). Already in the first year of secondary education, for instance, students with an immigrant background are over-represented in technical and vocational education. The study of Duquet et al. (2006) shows that almost 50 per cent of the Turkish and North African girls start secondary education in the vocational track. On average, 15 per cent of all students leave secondary education without any qualification, but this increases to 50 per cent when considering only the Turkish and North African students. In this respect, more in-depth knowledge of the educational status and the school career of youngsters with an immigrant background is needed. Yet a focus solely on the pupil is insufficient. Major socializing institutions such as the school, family, peer group and neighbourhood play crucial roles in these processes. The insights presented in this chapter have been obtained from a large, interuniversity, mixed-method research project on the educational trajectories of pupils (approximately 14–15 years old) with and without an immigration background in secondary education in three major cities in Flanders (Antwerp, Ghent, Genk).[3] For this chapter, we have focused on the concrete educational careers of youngsters in secondary education. We will demonstrate that besides the already well-documented evidence of the influences of gender, socioeconomic status and immigration history, elements that relate to the school and home environment and peer groups are also significantly related to doing well at school.

However, how to define educational success? The educational system has its own definitions of success (getting good points, being able to pass, being in a 'good track'). The students and their significant others (parents, family, peers, community) also have their own definitions of educational success. Data generated within the context of this study revealed that teachers, but also parents and students, share more or less the same ideas about what constitutes a successful student (Clycq et al., 2014). In this chapter we start from the assumption that an uninterrupted school career – i.e. without experiencing grade retention[4] – is generally preferred by pupils, their families, the school and society, rather than an 'interrupted' school career, i.e. experiencing grade retention.

## The embedded context approach: when the school environment meets the home/community environment

Educational systems – as centrally organized social institutions – have long been seen as important means of social continuity and social reproduction (Bourdieu & Passeron, 1977; Hannerz, 1992). Research shows that also in Flanders, social stratification processes and differences between groups with a different socioeconomic status and/or ethnic minority groups tend to endure over decades (De Meyer & Warlop, 2010; Jacobs *et al.*, 2009). To understand these persisting social patterns, scholars have focused on the surrounding contexts of individuals (such as the cultural ecological model of Ogbu & Simons, 1998), the cultural resources and social networks of individuals and groups (such as the cultural repertoire theory of Lamont, 1992), or the power relations between majority and minority groups (such as the subtractive acculturation/schooling theory of Roosens, 1998 or Valenzuela, 1999). These theories and approaches can be seen as being part of the research traditions elaborated on by scholars such as Epstein (1987), Bronfenbrenner (1989) and Portes and Rumbaut (2001). They are all devoted to explaining educational trajectories by studying different actors in different contexts and social networks, and as such counter the idea that the individual pupil is solely responsible for his school career. This multicontext approach, which has its origins in developmental psychology (Bronfenbrenner, 1979), distinguishes different (f)actors, groups and institutions influencing the school career of (immigrant) youngsters and is as such a social network approach. In highlighting the importance of particular institutional characteristics that are situated on different levels of analysis, the literature reveals the usefulness of employing an 'embedded context' (McLaughlin & Talbert, 2001) or 'ecological' approach (Feinstein *et al.*, 2004: Stevens, 2007). Individuals grow up and live in multiple contexts including family, peer groups, school and neighbourhood, as well as the broader political/legal and socioeconomic context. To fully understand the (un)successful school careers of students, we need to examine the influence of these multiple contexts. We also need to examine how the specific characteristics of these contexts interact and influence students and how students in turn shape the multiple contexts in which they live.

One of the most important background variables influencing educational outcomes is the socioeconomic status of the individual, which is often based upon the educational and labour market background of the parents (Duquet *et al.*, 2006; Glick & Hohmann-Marriott, 2007; Kao & Thompson, 2003). Several scholars (Bourdieu & Passeron, 1977; Giroux, 1980; Reay, 1998) have stated that especially middle-class parents possess the financial, social and cultural resources – or have access to them through their social networks – that allow them to be more assertive and influential in relationships with schools. Their middle-class habitus corresponds most with the habitus often found in the educational system, which is manifested in its curriculum, its personnel and its policy (Bourdieu, 1990). As mentioned above, people with a Moroccan or Turkish migration background are often found in the lower socioeconomic stratus in Belgium. This brings us to a second important difference often found in educational studies: performance differences between the majority group and specific ethnic minorities also tend to endure over decades (De Meyer & Warlop, 2010). Even when controlling for socioeconomic status, strong differences remain between ethnic groups (Driessen, 2001). However, while there is often a focus on the underperformance of pupils with an immigration background in Flanders, there are also indications in international literature that 'specific' minority and/or immigrant groups tend to overperform when compared to the ethnic majority group. Based upon their (assumed) overperformance, new critical theories such as the 'model minority' theory are developed to engage with these findings (Song & Wang, 2003).

Thus, children from different social as well as ethnic backgrounds arrive at school with a different habitus from that exemplified by the school itself. The degree to which the youngster's family habitus is congruent with the school habitus will have an impact on the educational achievement barriers experienced by the youngster. Because the school habitus reflects the habitus of the dominant class, it is easier for a child from this class to acquire the values, dispositions and cultural capital that characterize the school and promote school success (Webb et al., 2002). An interesting elaboration on Bourdieu's capital theory is the notion of cultural repertoire, as mentioned earlier, which lays out broader sets of frames of reference and cultural resources, and which emphasizes processes of cultural and social exclusion.[5]

As a consequence, the interplay of different social dimensions is important to consider; in the context of educational studies the intersection of socioeconomic status and ethnicity is one of the most important social axes (Yuval-Davis, 2010). In Belgium as well as in many other European countries, compared with the dominant group, families with an immigrant background often combine both a lower socioeconomic status and a different ethnocultural background (Latuheru & Hessels, 1996; Roossens, 1998). Research makes clear that there is very little to no difference between the school careers of youngsters of immigrant versus Belgian origin within the same socioeconomic context (Hustinx & Meijnen, 2001; van der Veen, 2001). They achieve the same results and are found in the same educational tracks. Yet, the influence of the socioeconomic status on the school career of immigrants is more limiting than on the school career of youngsters of Belgian origin with a similar profile (Duquet et al., 2006). The relation between their educational achievement and the socioeconomic status of their parents is less pronounced than for youngsters with a Belgian origin. This implies that next to the socioeconomic background, other factors intervene in influencing the school results of students with a migration background. Another finding in the literature is that in general, girls do better in school than boys. Gender marks a major social division in society, also in education. Also from a gender perspective it is crucial to take into account the interplay of different social dimensions in the educational context. Several studies focused on the intersection between gender and ethnicity (Archer et al., 2005; Dillabough, 2003). In a study on the Turkish immigrant communities in Belgium, for example, it was found that young girls saw a successful educational career as the most important and feasible instrument for emancipating themselves from patriarchal dominance (Timmerman, 1999).

## Hypotheses

We discern several structural factors in the literature that confront every student, factors that he or she can do little to change, namely socioeconomic and immigration background, and gender. Based on the literature discussed above, we formulate the following hypotheses in a specific order. We start with a discussion and study of some of the more structural elements found in educational studies and in our research sample: educational differences related to SES, immigration background and gender. This analysis reveals whether our research sample is representative with respect to the findings of studies mentioned above. In a second stage, we broaden our perspective and argue that an embedded approach enables us to link some of the most important contexts such as the family, the peer group and the school to the educational trajectories of students. This gives us more ideas about how to influence educational trajectories.

> H1: Students with a lower socioeconomic background are more likely to experience an interrupted school career than pupils from a higher SES background.
> H2: Students with an immigration background are more likely to experience an interrupted school career than students without an immigration background.
> H3: Boys are more likely to experience an interrupted school career than girls.

So far, the main structural constraints have already been extensively proven to be of great relevance in explaining educational achievements. As important as they might be, they are all elements that are quite fixed and stable. Therefore, let us look at factors that might be easier to work with from a policy perspective.

Several studies found that the effects of socioeconomic status on social outcomes and school success are partially mediated by a series of variables that refer to the educational situation at home (Harnish et al., 1995; Opdenakker & Hermans, 2006). A relevant insight that gains importance is that 'culture' is known in its practice; applied to the educational context it means that it is important to study the concrete practices in learning environments, as e.g. classrooms or home settings (Gutiérrez, 2002; Mehan, 1992). Parental involvement in the school career is considered to have a positive impact on children's school experiences (Coleman, 1988). Children seem to benefit from their parents showing interest in what is going on at school and supervising or helping them with their homework. At the very least it demonstrates that both worlds – the one of the school and the one at home – share several school-related ambitions (Clycq et al., 2014). It might also be the case that grade retention results in lower parental involvement; that parents become less inclined to follow up on their children as a result of previous failure or lack of resources or skills on behalf of the parent(s) or student. Notwithstanding the several possible scenarios, we assume a positive relation between parental involvement and school performance of the child because of the shared perspective between school and home that this implies. Therefore, we postulate the following:

> H4: Students who have experienced an interrupted school career are less likely to experience parental involvement than students who have not experienced an interrupted school career.

Another important school characteristic is the school atmosphere or the school ethos, meaning the messages transferred to the students, the academic expectations held by the teachers, and the attitudes of the teachers towards the students. An important element is the attitude of the school (teachers, staff members) towards the culture and language of origin of the students (Driessen, 2002; Opdenakker & Hermans, 2006; Rhamie, 2007; Van Houtte, 2002). Pupils who experience that their background, identity, the world they belong to, is appreciated by the school personnel, feel themselves more 'at home' and accepted within the school context. This kind of respectful attitude from the school staff towards students means that there is a common ground between school and home/community. As mentioned earlier, we believe that a shared perspective between school and home environment translates in a better performance of the students. Therefore, we assume that a positive relation exists between feeling respected by the school and doing well at school. However, an important expectation from the school is that students make sufficient progress. Students who do not perform as well as others academically might feel devalued or experience a lowering of their self-esteem. We assume this may also mean they may feel less respected by the school. This assumption does not exclude that any disrespectful attitudes from the school staff towards the student can precede and exacerbate his poor performance. Therefore, we formulate the following hypothesis:

> H5: Students who have experienced an interrupted school career are less likely to feel themselves respected by the school than students who have not experienced an interrupted school career.

Theories of Bourdieu, Portes and others demonstrated extensively the importance of social networks for explaining educational success. Peers play a crucial role in the social networks of students. It is known that social networks can be significant at an emotional, instrumental, or informative level (Berg & Piner, 1990; Thoits, 1995). They can function as protective environments in more hostile or unknown settings. Being friends with students who are doing well at school can be beneficial from several perspectives. Aligning oneself with students who are well regarded at school – because of their positive achievements – gives one the opportunity of sharing in this positive evaluation. Besides this emotional benefit, having successful friends might also be instrumental in enhancing one's esteem within the school context. Successful friends might also be informative because they have relatively good insight into what is offered in the school curriculum (Derks *et al.*, 2007; Ward *et al.*, 2001). Having experienced grade retention might also result in moving to schools or tracks where other unsuccessful students tend to gather (for example a technical track). Therefore we put forward the following hypothesis.

> H6: Students who have experienced an interrupted school career are less likely to have friends who are doing well at school than students who have not experienced an interrupted school career.

Several studies demonstrated already that peer groups matter when understanding school achievements (Sussman et al., 2007). A recent study conducted in the Belgian school context came to the remarkable finding that children with an immigrant background who have at least one friend with no migration background have 50 per cent more chance to enrol in higher education than those who have no such friends. This finding is controlled for family SES, study advice received and experience of grade retention (in primary and secondary education) (Baysu et al., 2009; for similar findings, see Shook & Fazio, 2008). Having friends who are successful at school and having friends at school with no immigrant background seem to be important variables. Students without grade retention, in other words, more successful students and students without an immigrant background, probably have easier access to the dominant culture – including the dominant school culture – than students with an immigrant background and/or unsuccessful students. Students who can align themselves with the 'dominant school culture' have the opportunity of sharing in the more positive appraisal from the school staff in particular, compared to students who are more aligned with 'unsuccessful school cultures' and/or 'immigrant school cultures' within the school context (Roosens, 1998). Besides this emotional gain, being friends with students who belong to the 'dominant school culture' is also instrumental and informative for gaining information about and access to several domains that are easier to access by members belonging to the 'dominant school culture'. We also know that experiencing grade retention can result in moving to, for example, a technical track and that in these type of tracks there are more students with immigrant backgrounds. The benefits of the networks that we just discussed might be missing for these students because of grade retention. Therefore we postulate the following:

> H7: Students who have experienced an interrupted school career are less likely to have friends who have no immigration background.

To sum up, we start from the assumption that socioeconomic status, gender and immigration background matter. We also hypothesize that – after controlling for these variables – elements related to the family environment (in this case parental involvement), peer group (number of friends who are successful at school and/or number of friends without an immigrant background), and school (perception of negative attitude of schoolteachers), are relevant for researching (the effects of) uninterrupted school careers – i.e. without experiencing grade retention – of students enrolled in secondary education in Flanders (Antwerp, Ghent and Genk).

## Methodology

The research project on which this chapter is based reports on the school careers of students with and without an immigrant background in Flemish secondary education. To gain sufficient descriptive and in-depth data on these school careers, different methodologies were applied. One of the methodologies used was a survey, aiming at questioning the entire student population of the so-called 'second grade'[6] of secondary education in the three aforementioned cities (Antwerp, Ghent and Genk).

All secondary schools in the three selected cities were asked to collaborate (136 schools). Two out of three of the schools responded positively (90 schools: 52 in Antwerp, 26 in Ghent and 10 in Genk). The exact response rate among schools was 66.2 per cent. The majority of the responding schools (76 schools) offer normal, full-time education, whereas 6 are part-time vocational schools and 8 offer special (needs) education (BuSO). The questionnaires were distributed in the 930 classes over the 90 collaborating schools. Over 11,000 pupils filled out the questionnaire (11,070), which resulted in 11,015 usable documents.

The students were given a written questionnaire in Dutch during school hours, asking about a broad set of background variables, their school career, ambitions and other characteristics. They were distributed in the classes in the presence of a member of the educational staff and a member of the research team. In some cases the classes were grouped. The questionnaire was conceived in a way that the pupils could fill it out in one teaching hour. To avoid answering many questions in the brief hour we had for the survey, we adapted the design of the questionnaire to the different schools. Thus, there are three types of questionnaires. The first type is a limited questionnaire aiming at the part-time vocational schools and 'special (needs) education'. The other two types contained the core questions of the limited questionnaire as well as some supplementary questions. This results in a database containing questions answered by all pupils, questions answered by half of the pupils and questions answered by the other half of the pupils. The final database is composed of 11,015 unique, non-blank records, representing just about 50 per cent of the potential population.

The Flemish full-time secondary education consists of three consecutive stages of two years each. After the second year (in the first stage) students have to choose between four different types of specialization: general, technical, artistic or vocational education. The current study focuses on the second stage or 'second grade'. The survey only collected data on students who are in the second grade of secondary school. The resulting total number of respondents is 11,015 (approximately 44 per cent boys and 55 per cent girls), around 14 and 15 years old if they do not have experienced grade retention. Around half of the students were third-year students (first year of the second grade) and approximately 47 per cent of the students in the survey were fourth-year students (second year of the second grade). The remaining 2 per cent were students in a system of part-time vocational education. They were excluded from further analysis.

In this chapter, we focus specifically on students who are in the general (approximately 42 per cent of the dataset), technical (approximately 25 per cent) and artistic tracks (approximately 5 per cent). The students in the vocational track have a rather different profile from the students in the other tracks and were therefore excluded. The final number of respondents is therefore 7,949 (around 51 per cent of the students are in the first year of second grade and around 49 per cent of the students are in the second year of second grade). A further description of the dataset can be found in the next section.

The data were analysed with the statistical software R, Mplus, SAS and SPSS. We use multilevel model specifications to account for variation of grade retention of students in second grade within and between schools.

## Variables

The dependent variable used in this chapter is 'uninterrupted school career'. This means a school career without grade retention. A student has an interrupted school career when he or she experienced grade retention. Students indicated in which year and grade they experienced grade retention (in the first, second and/or third year of kindergarten, the first, second, third, fourth, fifth and/or sixth year of primary school, the first, second, third and/or fourth year of secondary school). The dependent variable is dichotomous. It has a zero value when a student experienced no grade retention and value one when they experienced grade retention in kindergarten/primary school and/or secondary school.[7] Of 7,940 students, around 71.1 per cent or 5,647 students experienced no grade retention. Around 28.9 per cent, or 2,293 students, experienced grade retention. The rest were marked as missing.

The following independent variables are used on the student level (the first level of analysis): socioeconomic status, immigration background, gender, track, year of the second grade, city of the school, parental involvement, number of friends with an immigrant background at school, number of friends who are successful at school, the perception of being respected by teachers. On the level of the second grade of each school (first and second year of the second grade in each school), we calculated the composition of students with an immigration background and the socioeconomic composition of students (see also Table 4.1).

*Immigration background*: The survey included questions on the country of birth of the students' two grandmothers. They could choose between 13 different possible answers (Belgium, Poland, other Eastern European country, other non-Eastern European country, Turkey, other country in the Middle East, Morocco, other Maghreb country, China, other Asiatic country, Congo, Rwanda, other country). On the basis of these questions, we calculated the number of students with an immigrant background. The data consists of approximately 62 per cent 'Belgian' students (both grandmothers born in Belgium: 4,918 students) and 38 per cent 'non-Belgian' students when both grandmothers were born in Morocco, Turkey, Europe (not Belgium or an Eastern European country), Eastern Europe, Asia or another country. Students have a mixed background when grandmothers have different origins. According to this coding, we have 5.5 per cent Moroccan, 4.9 per cent Turkish, 3.3 per cent EU, 2.8 per cent Eastern European, 2 per cent Asian and 19.3 per cent other or mixed background students in our data. We coded the variable into four dummy variables: Belgian students, Moroccan and Turkish students, and students with a different background (EU, Eastern-European, other country and Asian) and students with a mixed background (at least one grandmother with a non-Belgian origin).

*Gender*: This variable is dichotomous. Male students are coded as 1 (approximately 44 per cent, or 3,503 students) and female students (around 56 per cent, or 4,416 students) are coded as 0.

*Socioeconomic status*: we used Mplus software to perform factor analyses and estimate factor scores for items referring to the socioeconomic status of the student. The factor scores reflect the labour market situation of the parents, their educational attainment, the availability of a quiet room at home, as well as the availability of a computer and Internet at home. The variable was then rescaled. It has continuous values between 0 (high socioeconomic status) and 1 (low socioeconomic status).

*Track*: We distinguish three groups: the general, technical and artistic track. The largest group of students, at 59 per cent, can be found in the general track, 34 per cent in the technical track and 7 per cent in the artistic track.

*Year of the second grade:* Students can be in the first year (0) or second year of second grade (1): 51 per cent, or 4,055 of the students, are in year one of the second grade; 49 per cent, or 3,894 of the students, are in year two of the second grade.

*City of the school:* this variable shows the city where the students receive their schooling (Ghent: around 33 per cent, or 2,657 students; Genk: around 17 per cent, or 1,331 students; Antwerp: 50 per cent, or 3,952 students).

*Parental involvement*: this variable is based on a set of 7 questions asking to what degree parents are committed to school-related activities, are informed about achievements, and are interested in the content of the courses.[8] The items were summed and the missing values were mean imputed. When there were a maximum 3 out of 7 items missing, we used the mean of the other items to impute. The resulting scale is internally consistent (cronbach alpha is 0.79). The continuous variable is coded from 0 (frequent parental involvement) to 1 (no parental involvement).

*Feeling of being respected by teachers:* one question in our survey measured the perceived respect by teachers.[9] This variable was rescaled and is continuous between 0 (respect from the teacher) and 1 (no respect from the teacher).

*Peers*: students were asked to report on the proportion of friends at school with an immigrant background.[10] Students also had to indicate the proportion of friends who are successful at school.[11] Both variables were rescaled to a scale between 0 (almost all) native friends or friends who are successful at school) and 1 (almost no native friends or friends who are successful at school). The variable is continuous.

*Socioeconomic composition of students in second grade:* the variable indicating socioeconomic status of students was binned in four equal parts (25 per cent each). The part indicating the students with the lowest socioeconomic status was then used to calculate percentages. These percentages were calculated for each second grade of the schools. The variable was then rescaled. It has continuous values between 0 (no students with the lowest socioeconomic background) and 1 (all students have the lowest socioeconomic status).

The percentage of missing values of the variables indicating socioeconomic status, proportion of friends with immigrant background, immigration background and proportion of friends who are successful at school is not higher than 3 per cent.[12] Except for the variable that measures parental involvement, 5.49 per cent values were missing. We decided to mean impute this scale. When there were maximum 3 out of 7 items missing, we used the mean of the other items of the same scale to impute the missing values.

Table 4.1 Descriptive statistics of the sample (n = 7940)[1]

| Student level variables | Mean/ proportions | Standard deviation |
|---|---|---|
| Ethnic background | | |
|   Belgian | 0.62 | / |
|   Moroccan or Turkish | 0.10 | / |
|   Other (EU, Eastern Europe, Asia, other) | 0.08 | / |
|   Mixed | 0.19 | / |
| Socioeconomic status | 0.30 | 0.18 |
| Male | 0.44 | / |
| Track | | |
|   Artistic | 0.07 | / |
|   Technical | 0,34 | / |
|   General | 0.59 | / |
| Presence in the second year of second grade | 0.49 | / |
| Parental involvement | 0.46 | 0.20 |
|   (from frequent to none) | | |
| Perception of respect from teachers | 0.30 | 0.24 |
|   (from respect to no respect) | | |
| Proportion of friends with immigrant background | 0.30 | 0.31 |
|   (from all to no native friends) | | |
| Proportion of friends who are successful at school | 0.32 | 0.23 |
|   (from all to no successful friends) | | |
| School level variables | | |
| City of the school | | |
|   Antwerp | 0.50 | / |
|   Genk | 0.17 | / |
|   Ghent | 0.33 | / |
| Percentage of students with low socioeconomic status in second grade | 0.34 | 0.23 |
| Percentage of students with an immigrant background in second grade | 0.47 | 0.29 |

1 Note: in some instances, n is lower due to missing values.

## Results

We analysed the data with multilevel binary logistic regression. More specifically, we constructed two varying intercept models. In a baseline model, we included 7,940 individuals on the student level. On the second level (the second grade level), we have 74 observations.

The residual variance on the second grade level in an empty model (without independent variables) is 0.95. The intraclass correlation is therefore 0.22 (see also Hox, 2010, p. 128; Ruiter & Van Tubergen, 2009, p. 878).[13] We conclude that in a randomly drawn second grade in our sample, the correlation in grade retention between two randomly chosen individuals is 0.22.

We constructed three models. The first model includes only immigrant background, track, year of second grade, location of the school, percentage of students with low socioeconomic status in second grade and percentage of students with an immigrant background in second grade. The second model includes gender, socioeconomic status and immigration background, track, year of second grade, location of the school, percentage of students with low socioeconomic status in second grade and percentage of students with an immigrant background in second grade. Variables referring to peers, parents and teachers were added in a third model. The results of both models are listed in Table 4.2.

Model one was included to check whether the negative effect of immigrant background changes with the inclusion of gender and socioeconomic status in model 2 and 3. This was the case: immigrant background has a separate and independent effect on grade retention, even after controlling for gender and socioeconomic status.

We find that students from a lower socioeconomic background more often experience an interrupted school career than students from a higher socioeconomic background (see model 2 and 3). The results of the multilevel models indicate that the likelihood to have a school career without grade retention decreases significantly with increasing scores on the measure of socioeconomic backwardness. The higher the educational qualifications of parents, the better jobs they have, the more likely that children experience a school career without grade retention. This finding confirms our first hypothesis. This finding is in line with the study of Agirdag *et al.* that demonstrated that children's socioeconomic status is a rather good predictor of an uninterrupted school career (Agirdag *et al.*, 2012).

The likelihood of experiencing a school career without grade retention as a student in the second grade is also significantly related to immigrant background (hypothesis two). The likelihood of having an uninterrupted school career is much higher for the Belgian students than for students with an immigrant background. This is true when we compare the Belgian students with the students from a Moroccan or Turkish background, students with a European, Asian or East European background, and students with a mixed background (at least one grandparent with an immigrant background). This finding is in line with earlier research conducted in Flanders, which demonstrated that especially children from Moroccan and Turkish descent were doing relatively poorly in the Flemish educational system (Duquet et al., 2006). In addition to socioeconomic and immigrant background, we also confirm that male students will more often experience grade retention than female students (hypothesis three). Our analyses demonstrated that less parental involvement is significantly and positively related with having experienced grade retention in the past. This confirms hypothesis four: students who have experienced an interrupted school career are less likely to experience parental involvement than students who have not experienced an interrupted school career. These findings are consistent with Reynolds (1992), Suárez-Orozco and Suárez-Orozco (2001) and Thoits (1995). In the analysis of the current chapter, parents who are reported to be involved – in one way or another – in the school career of the student probably share several educational ambitions with the school. The relevance of congruence of shared values was emphasized in the analyses of Clycq, Nouwen and Vandenbroucke (2014) in the same research project.

We also found statistical evidence that students who have experienced an interrupted school career are less likely to feel themselves respected by schoolteachers than students who have not experienced an interrupted school career (hypothesis five). The connection between having experienced grade retention and feeling respected by schoolteachers suggests the importance of sharing the same perspectives, appreciations, which might translate into mutual respect – in this case between the student and the school. We note the importance of the school respecting the student's sociocultural environment (Driessen, 2002; Opdenakker & Hermans, 2006; Rhamie, 2007; Van Houtte, 2002).

Being friends with students who are successful at school relates to a lower likelihood of having experienced grade retention in the past. The same applies to being friends with students at school without an immigration background (hypothesis six and seven). These two relations exist after controlling for the socioeconomic and immigrant composition of the second grade of school (Baysu & Phalet, 2012).

We also included 'track', as a control variable. It is more likely to find students with an interrupted school career in the technical and artistic track compared to the general track, considering how the Flemish educational system functions.

In separate analyses for native and immigrant students and their reported structure of networks (see Table 4.3), we found that the proportion of friends with an immigrant background at school has a positive relation with the previous occurrence of grade retention. This is so for the native and non-native students analysed separately (under control of different background variables).

One important difference between native and non-native students exists with regards to the proportion of friends who are successful at school. The variable that measures an increasing proportion of no friends who are successful at school has only a significant relation with the previous occurrence of grade retention in the subsample of students with an immigrant background.

Table 4.2 Multilevel binary logistic regression of grade retention (odds ratios)

| | Model 1 Odds ratio (S.E.) | Model 2 Odds ratio (S.E.) | Model 3 Odds ratio (S.E.) |
|---|---|---|---|
| Intercept | 0.1 (0.17)*** | 0.07 (0.18)*** | 0.05 (0.18)*** |
| Ethnic background | | | |
| Moroccan or Turkish background | 2.51 (0.1)*** | 2.1 (0.1)*** | 1.98 (0.11)*** |
| Other background | 1.84 (0.1)*** | 1.71 (0.1)*** | 1.58 (0.11)*** |
| Mixed background | 1.88 (0.07)*** | 1.79 (0.07)*** | 1.71 (0.08)*** |
| Male | | 1.34 (0.06)*** | 1.32 (0.06)*** |
| Socioeconomic status | | 3.08 (0.18)*** | 2.73 (0.19)*** |
| Track | | | |
| Artistic track | 3.03 (0.22)*** | 3.08 (0.23)*** | 3.01 (0.22)*** |
| Technical track | 3.1 (0.09)*** | 2.98 (0.09)*** | 2.99 (0.09)*** |
| Presence in the second year of second grade | 1.14 (0.06)* | 1.15 (0.06)** | 1.13 (0.06)** |
| City of the school | | | |
| Attending a school in Genk | 0.86 (0.18) | 0.85 (0.19) | 0.87 (0.17) |
| Attending a school in Ghent | 1.31 (0.27)+ | 1.31 (0.16)* | 1.31 (0.15)* |
| % students of low socio-economic status in second grade | 8.76 (0.61)*** | 6.62 (0.62)*** | 5.09 (0.59)*** |
| % students of non-Belgian background in second grade | 0.72 (0.45) | 0.68 (0.45) | 0.63 (0.43) |
| Parental involvement (from frequent to none) | | | 1.76 (0.15)*** |
| Perception of respect from teachers (from respect to no respect) | | | 1.6 (0.12)*** |
| Proportion of friends with an immigrant background at school (from all to no native friends) | | | 1.43 (0.12)*** |
| Proportion of friends who are successful at school (from all to no successful friends) | | | 1.23 (0.13)* |
| Variance (second grade level) | 0.19 | 0.2 | 0.16 |
| N | 7702 | 7671 | 7446 |
| J | 74 | 74 | 74 |

Significance: ***: $p < 0.001$. **: $p < 0.01$. *: $p < 0.05$. +: $p < 0.10$

Table 4.3 Multilevel binary logistic regression of grade retention and networks of students: native and immigrant students

|  | Model 1 (only native students) Odds ratio (S.E.) | Model 2 (only non-native students) Odds ratio (S.E.) |
|---|---|---|
| Intercept | 0.04 (0.22)★★★ | 0.17 (0.23)★★★ |
| Ethnic background |  |  |
| Other background |  | 0.76 (0.12)★ |
| *(Ref. Cat.: Moroccan or Turkish background)* |  |  |
| Mixed background |  | 0.83 (0.11)+ |
| *(Ref. Cat.: Moroccan or Turkish background)* |  |  |
| Male | 1.48 (0.09)★★★ | 1.17 (0.09)+ |
| Socioeconomic status | 3.67 (0.26)★★★ | 2.27 (0.26)★★ |
| Track |  |  |
| Artistic track | 4.31 (0.24)★★★ | 2.44 (0.26)★★★ |
| Technical track | 4.18 (0.13)★★★ | 2.36 (0.11)★★★ |
| Presence in the second year of second grade | 1.26 (0.08)★★ | 1.07 (0.08) |
| City of the school |  |  |
| Attending a school in Genk | 0.7 (0.23) | 0.84 (0.17) |
| Attending a school in Ghent | 1.34 (0.17)+ | 1.4 (0.16)★ |
| % students of low socioeconomic status in second grade | 2.46 (0.81) | 7.17 (0.68)★★ |
| % students of non-Belgian background in second grade | 1.63 (0.63) | 0.46 (0.48) |
| Proportion of friends with an immigrant background at school *(from all to no native friends)* | 1.48 (0.19)★ | 1.58 (0.15)★★ |
| Proportion of friends who are successful at school *(from all to no successful friends)* | 1.21 (0.18) | 1.63 (0.17)★★ |
| Variance (second grade level) | 0.19 | 0.12 |
| N | 4700 | 2813 |
| J | 70 | 72 |

Significance: ★★★: $p < 0.001$. ★★: $p < 0.01$. ★: $p < 0.05$. +: $p < 0.10$.

## Conclusion

In this chapter, we started from the general assumption that educational achievements of students are influenced by an interplay of elements situated at different levels: macro-level elements such as institutions and policies, meso-level elements like social networks such as the family, the school, the community and the peer groups (and in particular by processes occurring in these networks), and individual elements like capabilities and attitudes.

More specifically, the evidence that there is a high level of inequality in the Flemish educational system triggered this chapter. A lot of research already demonstrated the relevance of structural constraints in explaining unequal educational outcomes. It is known, for example, that the socioeconomic background of students has an important impact on school achievements. Moreover, their specific immigration background also proved to be an additional element in explaining inequalities in school results. And, lastly, girls, compared to boys, are also known for better performance in secondary schools in the Flemish part of Belgium.

Our analyses confirmed the relevance of these structural constraints and the relevance of studying the resources present in pupils' and parents' networks. The influence of students' socioeconomic background and immigrant background (both based upon the situation and background of the parents and family as a social network) on school career proved to be highly significant, in that students from a lower socioeconomic background experienced an interrupted school career more often than those from a higher socioeconomic background. A similar high influence was confirmed for specific immigration backgrounds compared to students without an immigration background. Students from Moroccan and Turkish descent experienced more often an interrupted school career than students without an immigration background; the same applied to students from other immigration backgrounds, but to a lesser extent. It is relevant to emphasize these structural constraints. This clarifies that Flemish native and middle-class pupils experience the least problems in education, and their counterparts – lower class Moroccan and Turkish pupils – experience the most problems. However, it is also important – at least from a policy perspective – to identify other elements that are more susceptible to change and might therefore be starting points to alter the educational achievements of these low-performing groups.

We notice that elements indicating congruence or no congruence between school, home and peer's contexts are related to having experienced uninterrupted school careers. For example, we see that students who indicate that their parents show an interest and/or involvement in their school experiences have performed better at school in the past. The same applies to being friends with students without an immigration background and who are successful at school. In both cases, the student aligns with someone who is familiar with and even well regarded within the 'dominant school culture'– namely, the 'successful student' and the 'student without an immigration background'. These social networks (in casu peer groups) are definitely helpful from an emotional, instrumental and informative perspective. These findings suggest the relevance of the congruence between these different environments (school, home, peers). Feelings of being respected and receiving fair chances within the educational context also prove to relate significantly with having experienced a smooth school career. However, we might assume that the relevance of feeling being treated correctly and fair for understanding educational achievements is not limited to the individual student. Parents who feel respected by the school in their role of parenting might also be more eager to align with the school in their mutual ambition to attain the best educational context for their children. On a final note, our research stresses the importance of incorporating different macro-, meso- and micro-level factors in the analysis in order to sufficiently grasp the influence of processes intersecting these various levels. Only a holistic approach can offer the necessary broad and in-depth insights to tackle socioeconomic and ethnocultural differences in the educational system and wider society.

## Notes

1. In this research project, we focus on the Belgian region of Flanders. The Brussels-Capital Region and Walloon Region are not included in our project.
2. In 2012, immigrant students in Belgium performed 52 score points below that of non-immigrant students, after taking into account the socioeconomic background of students. This difference is significantly higher than the OECD average but has significantly improved since 2003, when it was 67 score points (results from PISA 2012; country note Belgium).
3. In this four-year research project (2009–2012) four research groups from three Flemish universities applied a mixed method approach to survey around 11,000 pupils and interview, observe and follow-up on 110 pupils and (as much as possible) their parents, peers, principals and teachers during a two-year ethnographic fieldwork period.
4. Some pupils are advised or sometimes obliged to repeat an educational year when the school decides that they have not sufficiently mastered what is required to pass on to a next level.
5. Lamont and Lareau proposed to define cultural capital as 'widely shared, high status cultural signals (attitudes, preferences, formal knowledge, behaviors, goods and credentials) used for social and cultural exclusion' (Lamont & Lareau, 1988, p. 156).
6. In Flanders, the second grade of secondary education comprises the 3rd and 4th year of secondary education. Unless held back a year, these pupils are around 14 and 15 years old.
7. We calculated four mutually exclusive categories: no grade retention (0), only in kindergarten/in primary school and not in secondary school (1), only in secondary school and not in kindergarten/primary school (2) and the fourth category indicating grade retention in kindergarten/primary school as well as in secondary school (3).
8. The questions are 'how often do your parents participate in school activities (for example, school parties, open house days, . . .)?', 'how often do your parents go to a parents evening?', 'how often do your parents pay attention whether you do your homework or not?', 'how often do your parents pay attention whether you study or not?', 'how often do your parents know which points you have on assignments, tests and exams?', 'how often are your parents interested in what happens at school?', 'how often are your parents interested in what you learn at school?' The answer categories were on a Likert scale (never, sometimes, often, most of the time, always).
9. 'Teachers respect me.' The answer categories are 'totally not applicable, rather not applicable, neutral, rather applicable, totally applicable'.

10 The question is 'how many of your friends at school have a non-Belgian background (parents or grandparents are, for example, born in Turkey, Morocco, Poland, ...?'). Possible answers are '(almost) none', 'less than half', '(close to) half', 'more than half', '(almost) all'.
11 The question is 'how many of your friends at school have the same ethnic (cultural) background as you?' Possible answers are '(almost) none', 'less than half', '(close to) half', 'more than half', '(almost) all'.
12 More specifically, 0.09 per cent of the values of the socioeconomic status variable were missing. Around 0.83 per cent of the values of the variable measuring the perception of respect from teachers were missing. Concerning the variable measuring the proportion of friends with immigrant background: 1.61 per cent was lacking/missing, and 3 per cent of the values of the variable that measures immigrant background were also missing. Finally, 1.28 per cent of the values of the variable measuring the proportion of friends who are successful at school were also missing.
13 The level 1 variance term is constrained to 3.29 ($\pi 2/3$). We calculate the intraclass correlation as follows: (0.95578/(0.95578 + 3.29)): 0.2251129.

## References

Agirdag, O., Van Houtte, M. & Van Avermaet, P. (2012). Why does the ethnic and socioeconomic composition of schools influence math achievement? The role of sense of futility and futility culture. *European Sociological Review, 28*(3), 366–78.

Archer, L., Halsall, A., Hollingworth, S. & Mendick, H. (2005). Dropping out and drifting away: An investigation of factors affecting inner-city pupils' identities, aspirations and post-16 routes. London: IPSE.

Baysu, G. & Phalet, K. (2012). Staying on or dropping out: The role of the school environment in minority and non-minority school careers. *Teachers College Record, 114*(5), 1–25.

Baysu, G., Phalet, K. & Swyngedouw, M. (2009). *Segregatie in het onderwijs: Schoolloopbanen van Turkse en Marokkaanse Belgen.* Retrieved from http://soc.kuleuven.be/web/files/6/34/EtnischestratificatieonderwijsZegeneratieAntwerpenBrussel.pdf.

Berg, J. H. & Piner, K. E. (1990). Social relationships and the lack of social relationships. In S. Duck (ed.), *Personal Relationships and Social Support* (pp. 140–58). London: Sage.

Bourdieu, P. (1990). *The Logic of Practice.* Cambridge: Polity Press.

Bourdieu, P. & Passeron, J.-C. (1977). *Reproduction in Education, Society and Culture.* London: Sage Publications.

Bronfenbrenner, U. (1979). *The Ecology of Human Development: Experiments by Nature and Design.* Cambridge, MA: Harvard University Press.

Bronfenbrenner, U. (1989). Ecological systems theory. *Annals of Child Development, 6,* 187–249.

Clycq, N., Nouwen, W. & Vandenbroucke, A. (2014). Meritocracy, deficit thinking and the invisibility of the system: Discourses on educational success and failure. *British Educational Research Journal, 40*(5), 796–819.

Coleman, J. (1988). Social capital in the creation of human capital. *American Journal of Sociology, 94,* 95–120.

de Boyser, K. (2003). *De blik op uitsluiting op diverse domeinen van het maatschappelijk leven.* In J. Vranken (ed.), *Armoede en sociale uitsluiting: Jaarboek 2003.* Leuven: Acco.

De Meyer, I. & Warlop, N. (2010). *PISA: Leesvaardigheid van 15-jarigen in Vlaanderen: De eerste resultaten van PISA 2009.* Ghent: Universiteit Gent, Vakgroep Onderwijskunde/Brussel: Departement Onderwijs en Vorming, Afdeling Strategische Beleidsondersteuning.

Derks, B., van Laar, C. & Ellemers, N. (2007). The beneficial effects of social identity protection on the performance motivation of members devalued groups. *Social Issues and Policy Review*, 1(1), 217–56.

Dillabough, J. (2003). Gender, education, and society: The limits and possibilities of feminist reproduction theory. *Sociology of Education*, 76, 376–9.

Driessen, G. (2001). Ethnicity, forms of capital, and educational achievement. *International Review of Education*, 47, 513–37.

Driessen, G. (2002). *Sociaal-etnische schoolcompositie en onderwijsresultaten: Sociaal-economische en etnisch-culturele factoren, met speciale aandacht voor het Onderwijs. Eigen Taal en Cultuur*, Nijmegen: ITS.

Duquet, N., Glorieux, I., Laurijssen, I. & Van Dorsselaer, Y. (2006). *Wit krijt schrijft beter: Schoolloopbanen van allochtone jongeren in beeld*. Antwerp, Apeldoorn: Garant.

Epstein, J. L. (1987). Toward a theory of family-school connections: Teacher practices and parent involvement. In K. Hurrelmann, F. Kayfnabb & F. Losel (eds), *Social Interventions: Potential and Constraints*. New York: De Gruyter.

Feinstein, L., Duckworth, K. & Sabates, R. (2004). *A model of inter-generational transmission of educational success*. London: Centre for Research on the Wider Benefits of Learning.

Giroux, H. A. (1980). Beyond the correspondence theory: Notes on the dynamics of educational reproduction and transformation. *Curriculum Inquiry*, 10(3), 225–47.

Glick, J. E. & Hohmann-Marriott, B. (2007). Academic performance of young children in immigrant families: The significance of race, ethnicity, and national origins. *International Migration Review*, 41(2), 371–402.

Gutiérrez, K. D. (2002). Studying cultural practices in urban learning communities. *Human Development*, 45, 312–21.

Hannerz, U. (1992). *Cultural Complexity: Studies in the Social Organization of Meaning*. New York: Columbia University Press.

Harnish, J. D., Dodge, K. A. & Valente, E. (1995). Mother–child interaction quality as a partial mediator of the roles of maternal depressive symptomatology and socioeconomic status in the development of child behavior problems. *Child Development*, 66(3), 739–53.

Hirtt, N. (2006). *Culturele handicap, slechte integratie of sociale segregatie*. Brussels: OVDS.

Hox, J. (2010). *Multilevel Analysis: Techniques and Applications*. New York: Routledge.

Hustinx, P. & Meijnen, W. (2001). Allochtone leerlingen in het voortgezet onderwijs: De rol van enkele gezinsfactoren nader geanalyseerd. In W. Meijnen, J. Rupp & T. Veld (eds), *Succesvolle allochtone leerlingen* (pp. 47–72). Leuven/Apeldoorn: Garant.

Jacobs, D., Rea, A., Teney, C., Callier, L. & Lothaire, S. (2009). *De sociale lift blijft steken: De prestaties van allochtone leerlingen in de Vlaamse Gemeenschap en de Franse Gemeenschap*. Brussels: Koning Boudewijnstichting.

Kao, G. & Thompson, S. (2003). Racial and ethnic stratification in educational achievement and attainment. *Annual Review of Sociology*, 29, 417–42.

Lamont, M. (1992). *Money, Morals and Manners: The Culture of the French and the American Upper Middle Class*. Chicago/London: University of Chicago Press.

Lamont, M. & Lareau, A. (1988). Cultural capital: Allusions, gaps and glissandos in recent theoritical developments. *Sociological Theory*, 6(2).

Latuheru, E. J. & Hessels, M. G. P. (1996). *Schoolprestaties en de invloed van etnische en sociaal-economische herkomst*. *Sociologische Gids*, 2, 100–13.

Lelkes, O. & Zolyomi, E. (2010, November). Detailed analysis of the relative position of migrants. Research Note 1/2010. European Centre for Social Welfare Policy and Research.

McLaughlin, M. W. & Talbert, J. E. (2001). *Professional Communities and the work of High School Teachers.* Chicago: University of Chicago Press.

Mahieu, P. (2002). Desegregatie in functie van integratie. In C. Timmerman, P. Hermans, & J. Hoornaert (eds), *Allochtone jongeren in het onderwijs: Een multidisciplinair perspectief* (pp. 205–32). Leuven, Apeldoorn: Garant.

Mehan, H. (1992). Understanding inequality in schools: The contribution of interpretive studies. *Sociology of Education, 65*(1), 1–20.

Ogbu, J. U. & Simons, H. (1998). Voluntary and involuntary minorities: A cultural-ecological theory of school performance with some implications for education. *Anthropology & Educational Quarterly, 29,* 155–88.

Opdenakker, M. & Hermans, D. (2006). Allochtonen in en doorheen het onderwijs: Cijfers, oorzaken en verklaringen. In S. Sierens et al. (eds), *Onderwijs onderweg in de immigratiesamenleving* (pp. 33–66). Ghent: Academia Press.

Portes, A. & Rumbaut, R. G. (2001). *Legacies: The Story of the Second Generation.* Berkeley, CA: University of California Press.

Reay, D. (1998). *Class Work.* London: University College Press.

Reynolds, A. J. (1992). Grade retention and school adjustment: An explanatory analysis. *Educational Evaluation and Policy Analysis, 14*(2), 101–21.

Rhamie, J. (2007). *Eagles Who Soar: How Black Learners Find Paths to Success.* Stoke on Trent: Trentham.

Roosens, E. (1998). *Eigen grond eerst? Primordiale autochtonie: Dilemma van de multiculturele samenleving.* Leuven: Acco.

Ruiter, S. & Van Tubergen, F. (2009). Religious attendance in cross-national perspective: A multilevel analysis of 60 countries. *American Journal of Sociology, 115*(3).

Shook, N. J. & Fazio, R. H. (2008). Roommate relationships: A comparison of interracial and same-race living situations. *Group Processes and Intergroup Relations, 11,* 425–37.

Song, D. W. & Wang, J. T. (2003). *Modelling the Model Minority: Educational Investment and Returns for Asian Americans.* Durham, NC: Duke University.

Stevens, P. (2007). Exploring the importance of teachers' institutional structure on the development of teachers' standards of assessment in Belgium. *Sociology of Education, 80,* 314–29.

Suárez-Orozco, C. & Suárez-Orozco, M. (2001). *Children of Immigration.* Cambridge, MA: Harvard University Press.

Sussman, S., Pokhrel, P., Ashmore, R. & Brown, B. B. (2007). Adolescent peer group identification and characteristics: A review of the literature. *Addictive Behaviors, 32*(8), 1602–27.

Thoits, P. A. (1995). Stress, coping, and social support processes: 'Where are we? What next?'. *Journal of Health and Social Behavior,* extra issue, 53–79.

Timmerman, C. (1999). *Onderwijs maakt het verschil: Socio-culturele praxis en etniciteitsbeleving bij Turkse jonge vrouwen.* Leuven/Amersfoort: Acco.

Valenzuela, A. (1999). *Subtractive schooling: U.S. Mexican youth and the politics of caring.* Albany, NY: State University of New York Press.

van der Veen, L. (2001). Succesvolle Turkse, Marokkaanse en autochtone leerlingen in het voortgezet onderwijs. In W. Meijnen, J. Rupp & T. Veld (eds), *Succesvolle allochtone leerlingen* (pp. 13–30). Leuven/Apeldoorn: Garant.

Van Houtte, M. (2002). *Zo de school, zo de slaagkansen? Academische cultuur als verklaring voor schoolverschillen in falen van leerlingen in het secundair onderwijs.* Ghent: Ghent University.

Van Landeghem, G., De Fraine, B., Gielen, S. & Van Damme, J. (2013). *Vroege schoolverlaters in Vlaanderen in 2010: Indeling volgens locatie, opleidingsniveau van de moeder en moedertaal rapport nr. SSL/2013.05/1.2.0.* Leuven: Steunpunt Studie-en Schoolloopbanen (SSL).

Vanduynslager, L., Wets, J., Noppe, J. & Doyen, G. (2013). *Vlaamse migratieën integratiemonitor 2013*. Antwerpen: Steunpunt Inburgering en Integratie.

Ward, C., Bochner, S. & Furnham, A. (2001). *The Psychology of Culture Shock*. London: Routledge.

Webb, J., Schirato, T. & Danaher, G. (2002). *Understanding Bourdieu*. Sydney: Allen & Unwin.

Yuval-Davis, N. (2010). Theorizing identity: Beyond the 'us' and 'them' dichotomy'. *Patterns of Prejudice, 44*(3), 261–80.

# 5 The Quebec youth of immigrant origin in secondary education

Educational pathways and the factors influencing graduation

*Jacques Ledent and Marie Mc Andrew*

## Introduction

Quebec, like the rest of Canada, has always been an immigration society, but in the last 40 years, two major changes have occurred. First, immigrants to Quebec used to come essentially from Europe, but now they are highly diversified, originating mostly from non-Western societies (MIDI, 2014). Second, whereas in the past immigrants integrated mostly into the anglophone community and its institutions, since the adoption of the Charter of the French Language in 1977, immigrant youth are required to attend French-language schools. As a result, these schools have become multicultural settings which provide equal benefits to all segments of their clientele, a rather daunting challenge in view of their traditionally homogeneous character (Mc Andrew, 2012).

The educational experience of the youth of immigrant origin is thus a central indicator of the extent to which the incorporation of immigrants into a pluralistic and yet francophone Quebec is deemed successful. Over the years, this question has been the topic of many qualitative studies (Icart, 2010; Kanouté & Lafortune, 2011; Kanouté et. al. 2008; Livingstone et al., 2010). Several quantitative studies based on alternative definitions of immigrant origin students have been carried out as well. Among such studies, early ones carried out within Quebec's Ministry of Education and elsewhere – see, for example, Moisset et al. (1995) – focused on graduation rates in secondary schools by linguistic group (Chamberland & Mc Andrew, 2011). But using mother tongue or home language (French, English and other) as a marker of immigrant originhas its limits, and thus when they faced the task of examining the secondary school educational experience of the students from Black communities, the authors of this chapter had to look for a different marker in order to describe such students (Mc Andrew & Ledent, 2009). Using the databanks maintained by Quebec's Ministry of Education, those students were identified as the ones who them-selves were born or had at least one parent born in the Caribbean or Sub-Saharan Africa, whereas immigrant-origin students as a whole were defined as all students born outside Canada (first generation) or born in Canada with at least one parent born abroad (second generation). Although some recent studies still used mother tongue/home language as the marker of ethnic origin (Ledent et al., 2013; Mc Andrew et al., 2009; Provencher, 2008), this definition of immigrant-origin students is now dominant in immigration research in Quebec and is therefore used in the comprehensive study of the school success of immigrant-origin students (Mc Andrew et al., 2012) on which this chapter is based.

This chapter pursues a threefold objective:

1.  Characterize the educational pathways of first- and second-generation students with an emphasis on the differences observed 1) with regard to students of the third generation and more – that is, students who were born in Canada and whose parents were also both born in Canada – and 2) among subgroups by region of origin.
2.  Evaluate the influence of student characteristics on the graduation of first and second generations and compare that with the corresponding influence on the graduation of the third generation and more.
3.  Contrast the results obtained in the course of pursuing these two objectives with theoretical considerations and empirical evidence available in the existing literature.

## Literature review

Unlike other social categories such as gender or social class, ethnicity – whether measured using immigrant status, national origin, language, 'race' or religion (Juteau, 1999) – does not hold an easy-to-predict unidirectional relationship with educational achievement (Rumbaut, 2005). Canadian and international literature clearly illustrates the wide variety of educational profiles and experiences that can be associated with various subgroups defined by either of these markers. In societies in which immigration and poverty are closely linked, this complex reality is sometimes masked by the overlapping of these two phenomena, but in contexts in which immigration is more class-balanced, such as in Canada and the United States, variability is the norm (OCDE, 2006; Suárez-Orozco & Carhill, 2008).

In this regard, there are several systems of explanation sometimes considered to be antithetic but which in our opinion complement each other. Socioeconomic theories stress the close relationship between socioeconomic status (SES) and school results, both among all students (Bourdieu, 1970; Bradley & Corwin, 2002; Charlot, 2005) and among immigrant students (Portes, 1994; Rumbaut, 2005; Zady & Portes, 2001). This school of thought identifies poverty as the main explanatory factor of school failure, because it is generally associated with a deficit of cultural capital among families, as well as with a lack of active involvement in the educational promotion of their children. It also shows the contribution of schooling to the segmented assimilation of different groups of immigrants. Such a school of thought also pays significant attention to the segregation of students in specific schools, although the negative impact of attending a school in an underprivileged milieu is much more established than that of mere ethnic concentration (Christensen & Segeritz, 2008; Inglis, 2008; Mc Andrew, 2001).

Nevertheless, many datasets lead one to conclude that among immigrant students, SES does not have the overwhelming impact it has among all students. On one hand, even among immigrants with a higher socioeconomic status, mastery of the language of schooling is a rather long process. Thus, many factors linked to the specific educational experiences of immigrant students in their country of origin or during the migration process must also be considered, such as (1) prior exposure to the host language and literacy in the mother tongue (Armand et al., 2011; Cummins, 2000); (2) age at arrival and level of entry within the host school system (Gibson et al., 2004; Stiefel et al., 2010) – which gives a clear advantage to students who were born in the host country or who entered the primary level; and (3) educational delay when entering the host school system, whether it is linked to actual under-schooling or to limits in the evaluation process (Alspaugh, 1998; Lucas, 2001).

On the other hand, many Canadian and European studies show that under-privileged immigrant or second-generation students tend to over-perform when compared with native peers with the same socioeconomic background (Bouteyre, 2004; Kamanzi et al., 2007; Mc Andrew et al., 2009; Zhou & Kim, 2007). Some of these studies use the fact that migrants represent a subsample of particularly motivated individuals to explain this phenomenon, while others insist that it has to do with (1) the role that schooling opportunities for children play in the family decision to migrate, and (2) the high educational expectations that immigrant parents usually hold for their children and the consequent pressure exerted upon these children to succeed. This over-performance is especially pronounced among immigrant girls who overall enjoy the same advantages as their longer established peers (OCDE, 2003; Qin, 2006; Suárez-Orozco et al., 2008). By contrast, immigrant or visible minority boys seem to face more obstacles, either linked to factors and dynamics common to all boys in Western school systems or specific to their situation in the host country.

Nevertheless, this migratory effect is inconsistent and a variety of sociocultural explanations have been put forward for the inconsistency. Ogbu (1992) links it to the existence of either a conflictual or a positive relationship with the host society and the integration model it proposes (Ogbu & Simmons, 1998). Immigrants who belong to voluntary minorities – that is, groups whose settlement in a new country is primarily for socioeconomic reasons – would strongly adhere to an ideology of social mobility through schooling and would consider the obstacles they encounter as temporary. By contrast, immigrants who could be categorized as 'involuntary' minorities – that is, groups whose presence in the host country is the result of conquest, colonialism (or neocolonialism) or slavery – would distrust majority institutions and the dominant culture, not believing that schooling could actually be a way out for their children. But other researchers focus on the characteristics of the home country culture, especially the values that are closely linked to school success, even in our modern school system: conformism, respect for authority, hard work as well as the valorization of the written word (Samuel et al., 2001; Chow,

2004; Costigan et al., 2010). In some communities, therefore, ethnicity constitutes a strong cultural capital that generates many practices that lead to school success, both in the family and within the community.

Finally, the importance of systemic factors, either common to all students or specific to immigrant youth, cannot be overlooked. Those common to all students include the extent to which the school system is one that is genuinely shared – for example, the importance of the private versus the public sectors and the occurrence of early versus late selection in specific streams (Crul et al., 2012; Hume, 2009) – as well as a variety of pedagogical characteristics supporting resilience among at-risk groups (Archambault et al., 2009; Johnson & Acera, 1999; UNESCO, 2009). As for the factors specific to immigrant youth, they focus on the reaction of the school system and of specific schools to immigrants in general and to various subgroups (Dei, 1996; Gillborn & Gipps, 1996; Sharkey & Layzer, 2000). This school of thought is especially interested in the impact of the attitudes and expectations of teachers on the success of various students who are largely influenced by an unstated pecking order reflecting national and international dynamics. It also carefully examines various indicators of institutional discrimination, such as the variance between schools with similar characteristics as well as early streaming of immigrant students into less prestigious courses.

## Data considerations

The study reported in this chapter not only adopts the ethnic marker defined in Mc Andrew & Ledent (2009), it also utilizes another feature set forth in the same paper – namely, the use of longitudinal rather than cross-section data, which enables one to follow the students entering secondary school over the years. The said research was carried out with the help of a database which includes all the students who began their secondary schooling in a French-language school at the secondary 1 level in either 1998 or 1999, as well as those who entered a higher grade later on, generally considered to belong to the same cohort.[1] For each student in the database, the information obtained comprises various variables representative of his/her characteristics as well several indicators representative of his/her educational pathways.

Student characteristics are divided into four categories: (1) immigrant background characteristics, (2) socio-demographic characteristics, (3) schooling process characteristics and (4) school characteristics.

*Immigrant background characteristics* consist of birthplace within or outside Canada as well as mother tongue and home language, which together enable one to break down first- and second-generation students into three separate linguistic subgroups: (1) students whose mother tongue is French, (2) students whose mother tongue is not French, but who speak it at home, and finally (3) students whose mother tongue and home language are not French. *Socio-demographic characteristics* reflect gender, location of the school attended as well as family socioeconomic status (hereafter referred to as family SES). The latter variable, it should be noted, is not observed but is instead proxied by a socioeconomic index specific to the small territorial unit in which the student's family resides.[2]

*Schooling process characteristics* include the level of entry into the Quebec system of education (primary or secondary), the grade of arrival in secondary school and the student's age upon such an arrival, thereby allowing one to estimate the possible delay with regard to the normal age of entry (12 years in secondary 1). In addition, they contain other characteristics pertaining to educational experience within secondary school, such as receiving *soutien linguistique* – that is, French language services – or being identified as having learning disabilities. Finally, the *characteristics of the school* in which each student is enrolled include the concentration of immigrant-origin students, the school's public or private character and, in the case of a public school, the degree of the socioeconomic challenge it faces, as evaluated on the basis of a socioeconomic index consisting of the average value of the students' family SES. A public school is deemed socioeconomically challenged if it falls within the deciles 8–10 representative of low family SES. Location on the island of Montreal rather than in the rest of Quebec is also accounted for,[3] as well as the school board – one of three – for those attending a public school in Montreal.

Educational pathways are accounted for by several variables which, for reasons explained later on, concern only those students who entered secondary 1. Basically, these variables enabled one to estimate the proportion of students who did not reach secondary 3 in time – that is, within two years – and the proportion of those who graduated on time (within five years in the Quebec context) as well as no later than two years after the normal time (within seven years). They were also used to estimate two drop-out rates relating to a nine-year horizon: a gross rate which is the complement to 100 of the cumulated graduation rate and a net rate derived from the gross one by subtracting the proportion of students who had no chances of graduating, either because they left Quebec prematurely or because they were still seeking to complete their secondary schooling in adult education.

## The target group and its regional subgroups

Out of the 158,460 students included in the cohort under study, 24,099 (15.1 per cent) belong to the first and second generations. They constitute the target group, whereas the remaining students, those of the third generation and more, constitute the comparison group.

As shown in Figure 5.1, close to half the students in the target group have their origin in three of the seven regions corresponding to the main source regions of recent immigration to Quebec: the Caribbean and Sub-Saharan Africa (4,847 or 20.1 per cent), North Africa and the Middle East (3,715 or 15.4 per cent), and Central and South America (2,792 or 11.6 per cent). Furthermore, one in six has his/her origin in one of the other four regions, leaving about one in three with an origin in the rest of the world, which largely consists of Europe (minus Eastern Europe) and the United States.

Whereas by definition none of the students in the comparison group was born abroad, three in five (58.6 per cent) of those in the target group were born abroad. This proportion is, however, an average that conceals wide variations among the various regional subgroups (see Table 5.1). The differences observed between the

94  J. Ledent and M. Mc Andrew

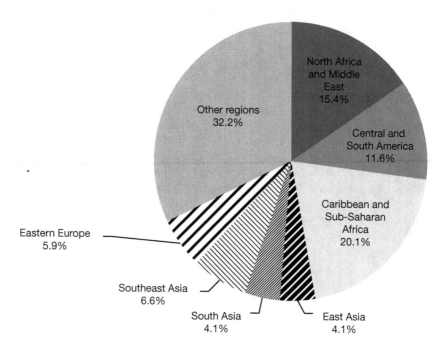

*Figure 5.1* Percentage distribution by region of origin: first- and second-generation students

*Table 5.1* Immigrant background characteristics: first- and second-generation students by region of origin

| Region of origin | Born outside Canada (%) | Per cent distribution by linguistic group | | |
|---|---|---|---|---|
| | | MT = French | MT ≠ French, HL = French | MT and HL ≠ French |
| Third generation and more | 0 | 97.8 | 0.4 | 1.8 |
| First and second generations | 58.6 | 35.4 | 12.3 | 52.3 |
| North Africa and Middle East | 62.1 | 29.0 | 16.0 | 54.9 |
| Central and South America | 68.2 | 18.6 | 15.5 | 65.9 |
| Caribbean and Sub-Saharan Africa | 53.1 | 45.9 | 18.2 | 35.9 |
| East Asia | 75.8 | 20.6 | 7.4 | 72.0 |
| South Asia | 88.2 | 4.2 | 2.2 | 93.6 |
| Southeast Asia | 41.9 | 13.0 | 13.0 | 74.1 |
| Eastern Europe | 84.8 | 10.5 | 11.5 | 78.1 |

Notes: MT = mother tongue; HL = home language.

seven subgroups are largely influenced by the timing of their respective establishment. Specifically, such a proportion ranges from lows of 41.9 per cent for Southeast Asia and 53.1 per cent for the Caribbean and Sub-Saharan Africa, two regions from which immigrants have come in large numbers since the early seventies, to highs of 84.8 per cent for Eastern Europe and 88.2 per cent for South Asia, two regions which have become prominent sources of immigrants to Quebec only in the recent past.

As one might expect, the quasi-totality of the students in the comparison group have French as a mother tongue or speak French at home. By contrast, that is true of just under half of the students in the target group (47.3 per cent), but again the figure pertaining to each regional subgroup may diverge somewhat from this average figure. Most likely, this figure depends on the subgroup's closeness to the French culture/language but also its timing of establishment. Thus the proportion of first- and second- generation students using French (because it is their mother tongue or because their family has adopted it as the home language) ranges from a low of 6.4 per cent for South Asia to a high of 64.1 per cent for the Caribbean and Sub-Saharan Africa.

The target group can be examined further with the help of a description of its other characteristics (socio-demographic, linked to the schooling process and school variables). Although such a description is worthwhile in its own right (see Mc Andrew et al., 2012), it is omitted here. Instead, we focus on the differences in such characteristics observed between the target and comparison groups as well as among the regional subgroups of the target group, because these differences have the potential of enlightening the graduation differences observed between the various (sub)groups.

First, contrasting the other characteristics of the target and comparison groups reveals that, for all of the relevant characteristics but one, the former group includes a higher proportion than the latter of individuals with an attribute which, according to Canadian and international literature, is conducive to lower graduation.[4] In comparison to students of the third generation and more, first- and second-generation students are more likely to belong to a family with a low SES, are more often late upon arrival in secondary school, are more likely to attend a public school that is socioeconomically challenged and more often attend schools with a high concentration of target group students. Moreover, when one considers the immigrant background characteristics specific to the target group which are likely to affect graduation in a negative way, it appears that the target group has a profile that is less favourable than that of the comparison group vis-à-vis graduation.

Second, the target group is far from being homogeneous, its regional subgroups exhibiting a wide diversity of profiles. A careful comparison of the profiles pertaining to the various regional subgroups with the one pertaining to the whole the group indicates that these subgroups possess characteristics which are not consistently less or more positive than those of the whole group. Indeed, the number of more positive characteristics varies widely from one group to another and leads to a very eloquent ranking of the regional subgroups (Mc Andrew et al., 2015, p. 50), thereby enabling one to divide the regional subgroups into two distinct sets:

1 a first set consisting of three subgroups (the Caribbean and Sub-Saharan Africa, Central and South America and especially South Asia), in which the student characteristics are more often less positive than those in the whole group;
2 a second set comprising the other four subgroups (Southeast Asia, Eastern Europe, East Asia and North Africa and the Middle East), in which the reverse is observed.

## Educational pathways

Because the students in the comparison group began their secondary schooling at the secondary 1 level (except for a few students having just transferred from the rest of Canada who began at a higher level), the focus here is on only those students who began at the secondary 1 level so as to make the contrast between the target and comparison groups more meaningful. Moreover, because the last year of observation was 2007, thus ruling out the possibility of estimating nine-year drop-out rates for those entering secondary 1 in 1999, only those students entering secondary 1 in 1998 are considered here. As can be seen from the left-hand side of Table 5.2, close to one in five among those students did not reach secondary 3 within two years, as would normally be the case; the actual proportion observed was slightly higher for the target group (20.3 per cent) than for the comparison group (18.8 per cent).

Moreover, within the target group, the frequency of being delayed in the first two years after entering secondary 1 varies somewhat among the regional subgroups. Observing the variations exhibited by such frequency leads us to gather the various subgroups in two sets which coincide with the two sets previously distinguished on the basis of the student characteristics. For the subgroups in the first set, the proportion of students additionally delayed within the first two years is largely above average, reaching 23.4 per cent for Central and South America and around 30 per cent for the Caribbean and Sub-Saharan Africa (29.7 per cent) and South Asia (30.6 per cent). On the contrary, it is below average in the other set of subgroups (Eastern Europe, East Asia, Southeast Asia, and North Africa and the Middle East), where it takes on values in the 12–16 per cent range.

Regarding graduation, it is striking that less than one half (48.9 per cent) of first- and second-generation students graduate on time – that is, within five years of entering secondary 1. Low graduation is not specific to the target group, but is also a feature of the comparison group, although to a lesser degree (55.9 per cent). In other words, the target group lags 7 percentage points behind the comparison group in terms of graduating on time. Naturally, some of the students who do not graduate on time are able to do so in the following years; thus, if one adds two more years to the five-year horizon, the graduation rates previously cited become substantially higher and differences between (sub)groups are reduced. In the target group, the graduation rate gains close to 15 percentage points, thereby reaching almost 64 per cent, whereas in the comparison group, it slightly surpasses 69 per cent, with a gain of 13 percentage points.

Table 5.2 Indicators of educational pathways: first- and second-generation students[a] by region of origin

| Region of origin | Additional delay after 2 years (%) | Graduation rate (%) | | Drop-out rate (%) | |
|---|---|---|---|---|---|
| | | On time | 2 years after expected | Gross[b] | Net[c] |
| Third generation and more | 18.8 | 55.9 | 69.1 | 26.4 | 20.8 |
| First and second generations | 20.3 | 48.9 | 63.7 | 32.9 | 21.7 |
| North Africa and Middle East | 15.8 | 58.6 | 72.3 | 25.1 | 17.9 |
| Central and South America | 23.4 | 38.7 | 55.5 | 40.7 | 27.7 |
| Caribbean and Sub-Saharan Africa | 29.7 | 36.1 | 55.2 | 40.1 | 25.5 |
| East Asia | 13.2 | 66.0 | 77.8 | 20.3 | 11.4 |
| South Asia | 30.6 | 28.7 | 46.1 | 50.3 | 28.7 |
| Southeast Asia | 15.0 | 56.5 | 69.6 | 28.3 | 19.2 |
| Eastern Europe | 12.4 | 60.3 | 71.3 | 26.3 | 17.4 |

Notes:
a Only for students who enrolled for the first time in secondary 1 in 1998–1999.
b Gross drop-out rate: 100 minus graduation rate four years after expected.
c Net drop-out rate: gross drop-out rate minus proportion of those who moved out of Quebec before reaching age 15 minus proportion of those attending adult education in fifth year after expected graduation.

Here again, the target group is not homogeneous and the differences observed according to the region of origin lead one to distinguish the same two sets of regional subgroups as before. On one hand, the regional subgroups in the first set have seven-year graduation rates, which are about 15 percentage points below that of the comparison group in two cases – the Caribbean and Sub-Saharan Africa (55.2 per cent) and Central and South America (55.5 per cent) – and close to 25 points below in the third case: South Asia (46.1 per cent). On the other hand, the regional subgroups in the second set present a seven-year graduation rate, which surpasses that of the comparison group, somewhat marginally (by up to 2 percentage points) in three cases (Eastern Europe, Southeast Asia and North Africa and the Middle East), but more substantially (by close to 9 percentage points) in the fourth case, East Asia, where it amounts to 77.8 per cent.[5]

Rather than look at graduating, we could instead look at dropping out; in this regard, it would seem that the complement to 100 of the graduation rate within seven years is not a true indicator of the propensity of dropping out. Indeed, after seven years, some students remain in the system, particularly in adult education, and may eventually graduate. Consequently, the time horizon for graduation is pushed forward another two years (the maximum made possible by the data available to us), which enables for the estimation of a graduation rate within nine years whose complement to 100 is labelled as the *gross drop-out rate*. But even after nine years, some students remain enrolled in adult education and thus should not be included in the estimation. Those students are thus subtracted from all those not graduating after nine years as are those students who had no chance of graduating at all because they left Quebec prematurely (before reaching 15 years of age), thereby leading to a more meaningful indicator labeled as the *net drop-out rate*.

The values of the gross and net drop-out rates estimated for all the (sub)groups are shown in Table 5.2. Because the proportion of students who were subtracted is understandably higher in the target group than in the comparison group, the net drop-out rate is only one percentage point higher for the former than for the latter (21.7 per cent vs. 20.8 per cent) – that is, a much smaller difference than the six to seven percentage point difference between the corresponding gross drop-out rates. Nevertheless, as the numerical importance of the two groups of students which were subtracted in the estimation of the net drop-out rates is relatively similar in all regional subgroups, the differences previously observed among regional subgroups on the basis of the gross drop-out rates remain largely in place, with one exception for South Asia.

In the latter regional subgroup, the proportion of students found to continue in adult education is much higher than in the other subgroups, to the point that, while its gross drop-out rate was 10 points higher than that of the two other subgroups included in the first set of regional subgroups distinguished earlier, its net drop-out rate is very similar. In this regard, supplementary analysis shows that students with an origin in South Asia who have graduated within the seven-year horizon have done so in adult education, at a rate which is approached by none of the other regional subgroups. Moving, as soon as they turn 16 years old, to adult education where the schooling requirement of the linguistic legislation does not apply could be, for the children of this community historically close to the British world, a strategy aimed at pursuing higher education in English.

## Graduation: target versus comparison groups

Given the earlier examination of the characteristics displayed by the students in the various (sub)groups, we could not help but think that 1) the graduation deficit exhibited by some (sub)groups is a consequence of their less positive characteristics and 2) this deficit might disappear once we control for the differences in the profile (composition according to the various student characteristics) of the various (sub)groups. To see whether this was the case, we ran a multivariate regression analysis using a logistic model in which the dependent variable is the dichotomous variable accounting for graduation or not within seven years of arrival in secondary 1.[6] As for the independent variables, they consist of a polytomous variable representative of the various regions of origin, as well as several variables representative of the student characteristics,[7] used as control variables, which were included out of necessity rather than by choice. Indeed, the immigrant background and socio-demographic characteristics available in the database stem from the (limited) information provided by students at the time of their initial enrolment in secondary education[8] and thus include only a small subset of the many variables mentioned in the literature review that are known to influence school success.

The results of this analysis are shown in Figure 5.2, in which the light grey bars depict the odds ratios of graduating for the target group and its various regional subgroups vis-à-vis the comparison group before adding the control variables; the dark grey bars represent the same odds ratios after inclusion of the control variables.

In sum, the information conveyed by the light grey bars (without inclusion of the control variables) is a reminder of the one suggested by our earlier observation of the graduation rates. In comparison to the students of the third generation and more, first- and second-generation students are less likely to graduate, in particular those belonging to three of the seven regional subgroups, whereas those belonging to the other four regional subgroups have a higher rate of graduation, especially those with an East Asian origin.

With inclusion of the control variables, the dark grey bars go higher than the corresponding light grey bars[9] in the case not only of the target group, but also of the three regional subgroups of the less achieving set, reaching a value of 1 or higher; meaning that after control for differences in other student characteristics, these (sub)groups show an equal if not higher propensity to graduate than those in the comparison group. The odds ratios associated with the target group reaches 1.14, whereas those associated with the less achieving regional subgroups reach 0.99 for

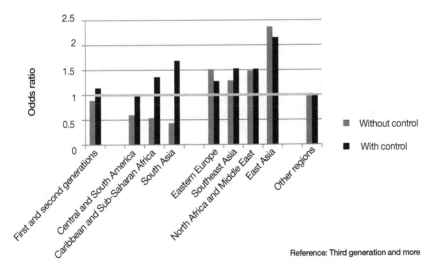

*Figure 5.2* Graduation two years after expected, first and second generations by regional origin vs. third generation and more, with and without control for student characteristics

Note: All odds ratios are significant at < 0.001 (< 0.05 for Eastern Europe w. control) except those for Other regions w/o and w. control and Central and South America w. control for which they are not significant at < 0.1

Central and South America, 1.36 for the Caribbean and Sub-Saharan Africa, and 1.69 for South Asia. If the students in the target group and in particular in the first set of regional subgroups have a lower graduation rate than their peers in the comparison group, this is only because they have a much less positive profile. Once their less positive characteristics are controlled for, they appear to be as likely to graduate (Central and South America) or even more likely to graduate (the Caribbean and Sub-Saharan Africa and especially South Asia). Student resilience appears to be strong in all three regional subgroups, in particular in the case of South Asia.

By contrast, in the case of the second 'more achieving' set, the dark grey bars are more or less similar in height to the corresponding light grey bars, meaning that controlling for the other student characteristics affects the associated odds ratios only slightly. Whereas it brings about a slight decrease in the odds ratio for East Asia and Eastern Europe, it leads to a marginal increase for North Africa and the Middle East and a more substantial increase for Southeast Asia. Such a result is in line with the earlier observation that the four regional subgroups concerned present a more positive profile than the whole target group.

## The factors influencing graduation

Following the above analysis of how regional origin influences graduation among first- and second-generation students, this section examines the influence of the other student characteristics, including a comparison with the corresponding influence among the students of the third generation and more. The best way to carry out such an examination is to begin with the comparison group and then to go on with the target group.

Basically, as suggested by the odds ratios (OR) in column (1) in Table 5.3, the impact of most characteristics on graduation in the comparison group is congruent with the results of national and international research. Indeed in this group, whereas more girls than boys tend to graduate (OR = 2.01), family SES influences graduation in a positive manner. Compared with students having a medium family SES, the students with a low family SES tend to have a lower graduation rate (OR = 0.76) while, on the contrary, those with a high family SES have a higher graduation rate (OR = 1.38). With regard to the schooling process characteristics, entering late by one year or more in secondary 1 results in a sharp reduction in graduation chances (OR = 0.12) and to a greater extent so does incurring some delay in the two years following arrival in secondary 1 (OR = 0.08). Moreover, changing school also has a negative impact on graduation, although to a much lesser extent (OR = 0.54). Finally, attending a private school rather than a public one is conducive to much higher chances of graduating (OR = 2.01). All of these influences, it should be noted, are not only substantial but also highly significant from a statistical viewpoint (at 0.001 or better). By contrast, the remaining characteristics included among the control variables do not appear to have an influence. Having attended a primary school in Quebec prior to enrolling in secondary 1 has no impact, nor does attending a public school that is socio-economically challenged.[10]

Interestingly, the various characteristics examined thus far operate in a similar fashion in the target group (see column (2) of Table 5.3). But, comparison with the odds ratios in column (1) readily suggests that the influence of socio-demographic characteristics has a lesser magnitude in the target group, as exemplified by the odds ratios of girls with respect to boys (1.76 instead vs. 2.01), and those of having a low family SES and symmetrically a high family SES rather than a medium family SES (respectively, 0.89 vs. 0.76 and 1.15 vs. 1.38). In addition, the influence of socio-demographic variables is statistically less significant in the target group, especially in the case of family SES, as is generally the case elsewhere (see studies mentioned above). This observation also applies to three of the schooling process characteristics (age upon arrival in secondary 1, additional delay incurred within the first two years in secondary school and changing schools) as well as to one school characteristic (enrolment in a private school). As for the remaining variables, entry level (whether the students attended primary school in Quebec beforehand) still has no impact on graduation, whereas being enrolled in a socioeconomically challenged school reduces the chances of graduating, despite it showing no influence in the comparison group.

Immigrant background characteristics are relevant only in the case of the target group. Their influence on graduation rates is as follows:

1  The first generation is not distinguishable from the second generation, as suggested by the absence of an impact for the birthplace variable.
2  When they are compared to the students who have French as a mother tongue, those who do not, in particular those who do not speak French at home, have a higher propensity to graduate. This result, perhaps surprising at first, may not be so at a second glance, given the fact that the reference category is the group of first- and second-generation students, and not the group of students of the third generation and more who have French as a mother tongue. It thus would appear that, among first- and second-generation students, having French as a mother tongue does not have a positive impact on graduation rates after controlling for the other characteristics.
3  Being identified during secondary schooling as needing *soutien linguistique* in French does not appear to have a significant impact on graduation. Such a result could be linked to the weakness of this indicator (one does not know if and how much support these students received) as well as its polysemic meaning (it is at the same time an indicator of how vulnerable students are).

Finally, a few words about the difference that schools make in the graduation of the two main groups. Since the regression analysis reported above was carried out in a multilevel setting, we were able to determine that the differences existing between schools with respect to the composition of the student body – according to the various characteristics entered in the model – explain about two-thirds (64.8 per cent) of the school variance in the case of the comparison group, but only about half (50.8 per cent) in the case of the target group (see last three lines in Table 5.3).

Table 5.3 Factors influencing graduation two years after expected: first and second generations versus third generation and more[a]

| Variables (reference value)[b] | (1) 3rd generation and more (N = 131,308) | | (2) 1st and 2nd generations (N = 19,157) | |
|---|---|---|---|---|
| | Odds ratio | Sig.[c] | Odds ratio | Sig.[c] |
| *Immigrant background characteristics* | | | | |
| Linguistic group[d] (MT = French) | | | | |
|   MT ≠ French and HL = French | — | — | 1.15 | * |
|   MT and HL ≠ French | — | — | 1.34 | *** |
| Birthplace (Canada) | | | | |
|   Outside Canada | — | — | 1.06 | |
| *Socio-demographic characteristics* | | | | |
| Gender (male) | | | | |
|   Female | 2.01 | *** | 1.76 | *** |
| Family SES (average) | | | | |
|   High | 1.38 | *** | 1.15 | ** |
|   Low | 0.76 | *** | 0.89 | ** |
| *Schooling process characteristics* | | | | |
| Entry level (primary) | | | | |
|   Secondary 1 | 0.83 | | 1.04 | |
| Late arrival (no) | | | | |
|   Yes | 0.12 | *** | 0.25 | *** |

| | | | | |
|---|---|---|---|---|
| *Soutien linguistique* in secondary school (no) | | | | |
| Yes | — | — | 0.86 | |
| Changed school (no) | | | | |
| Yes | 0.54 | *** | 0.71 | *** |
| Additional delay after two years (no) | | | | |
| Yes | 0.08 | *** | 0.09 | *** |
| *School characteristics* | | | | |
| Enrolled in a private school (no) | | | | |
| Yes | 2.10 | *** | 1.50 | *** |
| Enrolled in a socioeconomically challenged school (no) | | | | |
| Yes | 1.03 | | 0.85 | ** |
| School board (outside island of Montreal) | | | | |
| CSDM | 0.54 | *** | 1.17 | * |
| CSMB | 0.76 | *** | 1.47 | *** |
| CSPI | 0.69 | *** | 1.14 | |
| Intraclass correlation/empty model (%) | 22.3 | *** | 35.7 | *** |
| Intraclass correlation/full model (%) | 7.9 | *** | 17.6 | *** |
| % of school level variance explained by independent variables | 64.6 | | 50.8 | |

Notes:
a Includes only students who enrolled in secondary 1 and did not move out of Quebec before reaching age 15.
b Also includes regional origin and target group concentration in school, for which the results are not shown here.
c ***: significant at < 0.001; **: significant at < 0.05; *: significant at < 0.10.
d MT = mother tongue; HL = home language.

In other words, other student characteristics that are not amenable to quantitative analysis have an important influence on graduation rates, especially for immigrant-origin students.

## Conclusion

Although the administrative nature of the database used prevented it from examining all of its strands, the study of educational pathways among the Quebec youth with an immigrant origin reported in this chapter has nevertheless touched upon, to various degrees, the main explications of this phenomenon available in the literature. Its strength lies in its consideration of immigrant-origin factors, schooling process variables as well as characteristics of the school attended. In particular, with regard to the latter variables, we have examined the influence of a rather extensive set of indicators at a macro- or meso-level, such as the fact that schools belong to the private or public sector, the degree of educational challenge they face, or the concentration of the target group they experience. But neither could we identify which practices or attitudes explain the differences of results encountered between them, nor examine the many systemic and family dynamics considered in the literature. Moreover, our SES indicator, which was measured by means of a proxy representative of the socioeconomic status of the area of residence, is not very sensitive to immigrant realities, which limited our capacity to grasp fully the influence of this factor, especially with regard to the cultural capital of families.

Nevertheless, the breadth of this endeavour certainly sheds a rather encompassing light on the educational pathways of students with an immigrant background, as well as many of the factors that influence their graduation patterns:

1   Globally, first- and second-generation students have a lower graduation rate than the students of the third generation and more, mostly because their characteristics are comparatively less favourable, but also in part because, as shown by net drop-out rates, they may leave Quebec soon after entering secondary school or continue their schooling in adult education way into their early twenties. In particular, owing to circumstances linked to the immigration of their parents to Quebec, they tend to enter secondary school at a later age and also to experience additional delay in secondary school more frequently. But once their less positive characteristics are controlled for, they appear to have an even higher propensity to graduate. In other words, first- and second-generation students exhibit a stronger resilience than their peers of the third generation and more, which is clearly in line with the 'migratory' or voluntary migrants' bonus identified in the literature.
2   The graduation of first- and second-generation students is far from being uniform across the seven regional subgroups corresponding to the main source regions of recent immigration to Quebec. Globally, four of them, led by East Asia, have a higher graduation rate than the third generation and

more. However, since the students in these subgroups are endowed with characteristics which are globally positive, their propensity to graduate does not really go beyond what is suggested by their graduation rate. By contrast, the other three subgroups (Central and South America, the Caribbean and Sub-Saharan Africa, and South Asia) have a lower comparative graduation rate. But, after controlling for their less positive characteristics, such as a lower family SES and less frequent use of the French language, these subgroups have a propensity to graduate that is similar or even slightly higher than that of the third generation and more, which points toward a strong resilience, especially in the case of South Asia. In this regard, the fact that the pecking order of the various regional subgroups persists after controlling for differences in the student characteristics gives weight to the view, presented in the literature review, that historical, social and systemic factors may be at stake here, the reasons behind which remain unknown.

The first finding is rather positive. Since the social capital of families is one of the main predictors of school success, regardless of immigrant background, it is likely that this finding is linked to the selective nature of Quebec and Canadian immigration policies, insofar as they generate an immigration flow which is more socioeconomically and educationally diverse than in European countries. It also shows that the educational programmes and policies of the early 2000s, meant to integrate immigrants and foster intercultural education (MEQ, 1998), had the effect they were meant to have.

As suggested by the second finding, however, these programmes and policies may have not been equally effective for all communities. It could be that they did not adequately take into account the additional disadvantage in some communities of belonging to a low family SES, having a mother tongue other than French or being from a racialized minority group. They may also not have paid enough attention to the educational values and strategies of families, nor to the expectations and practices of teachers, which, in both cases, differ from one community to another.

We conclude that policy and programmes which work well for immigrant-origin students on the whole should be refined so as to benefit all subgroups in a similar fashion. To this aim, it is imperative to better understand the role of the parents, communities and schools in the educational performance of students from various origins, which calls for more qualitative studies, such as those already documenting the educational experiences of students with an origin in the Caribbean (Lafortune, 2012; Mc Andrew et al. , 2004), South Asia (Bakhshaei, 2013), and East Asia (Sun, 2014). Such qualitative studies have the potential of leading to useful findings, which could be translated into practical ways of helping (1) families faced with a particularly difficult context to develop proven and innovative strategies for ensuring the school success of their children; and (2) school decision-makers and teachers to combat the various obstacles to graduation, particularly those being generated by the educational system.

## Notes

1 Specifically, these additional students are those who began secondary 2 one year later (in 1999 or 2000), secondary 3 two years later, secondary 4 three years later and secondary 5 four years later (since secondary education in Quebec consists of five grades to be covered in as many years).
2 For each small territorial unit distinguished on Quebec territory, this socioeconomic index is evaluated on the basis of a formula which takes into account, for two-thirds, the proportion of mothers in two-spouse families with 9 years or less of education and, for one third, the proportion of such families in which neither parent works full-time. It is generally perceived as being not very well adapted to immigrant families (see, for example, Archambault et al., 2015).
3 Historically, immigrants to Quebec have settled in large numbers in the Montreal region, especially on the Island of Montreal where are located the central city and its nearest suburbs. Thus, the students in the target group attend by and large a school located on the Island of Montreal (65.2 per cent) contrary to those in the comparison group (10.5 per cent).
4 The exception alluded to here concerns attendance at a private school, known to have a positive influence on graduation. First- and second-generation students are more likely to be attending a private school than students of the third generation and more, but it should be noted that they are predominantly located in the Montreal area in which the majority of the private schools are to be found.
5 The graduation differences observed between the regional subgroups conform more or less to those substantiated outside Quebec. If the higher achievement of students from East Asia has been equally observed in the rest of Canada (Mc Andrew et al., 2009) and elsewhere, the lower achievement of students of South Asia does not agree with their high achievement in other Canadian provinces (Mc Andrew et al., 2009) for the very reasons mentioned earlier.
6 Note that this regression analysis was carried out for all students who entered secondary 1 not only in 1998 (as was the case in the above estimation of the gross and net drop-out rates) but also in 1999 and who moreover were still enrolled two years after arrival in view of including among the independent variables a variable reflecting possibility of an additional delay within the two years after arrival in secondary 1.
7 All of the characteristics introduced earlier in this chapter were used as explanatory variables with the exception of being identified as having learning disabilities, because this characteristic is highly correlated with graduation ($r = -0.84$) as well as the residential variable which did not appear to have an influence in preliminary testing.
8 This statement also applies to the school variables which are averages of some of the immigrant background and socio-demographic characteristics over the whole body of students in the school attended.
9 The sole exception concerns the residual regional subgroup for which the two bars have a similar height of about 1, meaning that graduation in this group is similar to that of the comparison group, whether or not the control variables are included or not in the regression model.
10 This is also the case of the concentration of the target group in the school attended which fails to display consistent results, for the target group as well as the comparison group, and thus the odds ratios concerning this characteristic are neither reported in Table 5.3, nor commented upon.

## References

Alspaugh, J. W. (1998). Achievement lost associated with the transition to middle-school and high school. *Journal of Education*, 92(1), 20–5.

Archambault, I., Janosz, M., Fallu, J.-S. & Pagani, L. S. (2009). Student engagement and its relationship with early high school dropout. *Journal of Adolescence*, *32*(3), 651–70.
Armand, F., Le Thi, H., Saboundjian, S. & Thamin, N. (2011). *L'enseignement de l'écriture en langue seconde: Synthèse des connaissances*. Rapport soumis au MELS, Montréal.
Bakhshaei, M. (2013). *L'expérience socio-scolaire d'élèves montréalais originaires de l'Asie du Sud: Dynamiques familiales, communautaires et systémiques*. Ph.D. thesis, Faculté des sciences de l'éducation, Université de Montréal, Montréal, Québec.
Bourdieu, P. (1970). *La reproduction*. Paris: Minuit.
Bouteyre, E. (2004). *Réussite et résilience scolaires chez l'enfant de migrants*. Paris: Dunod.
Bradley, R. H. & Corwin, R. F. (2002). Socio-economic status and child development. *Annual Review of Psychology*, *53*, 371–99.
Chamberland, C. & Mc Andrew, M. (2011). *La réussite scolaire des élèves issus de l'immigration au Québec: Engagement ministériel et résultats de recherches récentes*. Canadian Issues/Thèmes canadiens, Winter edition, 9–14.
Charlot, B. (2005). *Le rapport au savoir n'est pas une réponse, c'est une façon de poser le problem: Entretien*. Vie pédagogique, *135*, 11–15.
Chow, H. (2004). The effects of ethnic capital and family background on school performance: A case study of Chinese-Canadian adolescents in Calgary. *Alberta Journal of Educational Research*, *50*(3) (electronic version).
Christensen, G. & Segeritz, M. (2008). An international perspective on student achievement. In Bertelsmann Stiftung (ed.), *Immigrant Students Can Succeed: Lessons from Around the Globe* (pp. 11–33). Gütersloh, Germany: Verlag Bertelsmann Stiftung.
Costigan, C. L., Hua, J. M. & Su, T. F. (2010). Living up to expectations: The strengths and challenges experienced by Chinese Canadian students. *Canadian Journal of School Psychology*, *25*, 223–45.
Crul, M., Schneider, J. & Lelie, F. (eds). (2012). *The European Second Generation Compared: Does the Integration Context Matter?* IMISCOE Research Series. Amsterdam, Netherlands: Amsterdam University Press.
Cummins, J. (2000). *Language, Power and Pedagogy: Bilingual Children Caught in the Crossfire*. Toronto: Multilingual Matters.
Dei, G. (1996). *Antiracist Education: Theory and Practice*. Halifax: Fernwood Publishing.
Gibson, M. A., Gandára, P. & Peterson-Koyama, J. (2004). *School Connections: US Mexican Youth, Peers, and School Achievement*. New York: Teacher College Press.
Gillborn, D. & Gipps, C. (1996). *Recent Research on the Achievements of Ethnic Minority Pupils*. London: Office for Standards in Education.
Hume, K. (2009). *Pour une pédagogie différenciée au secondaire: La réussite scolaire pour tous*. Renouveau pédagogique, Québec.
Icart, J.-C. (2010). *Participation parentale et réussite scolaire – Les parents des communautés noires dans les écoles secondaires publiques francophones de Montréal*. Vivre Ensemble, *7*(59), 12–17.
Inglis, C. (2008). *Planning for cultural diversity*. International Institute for Educational Planning, UNESCO, Paris.
Johnson, J. & Acera, R. (1999). Hope for urban education: A study of nine high performing, high poverty urban elementary schools. Report of method to the US Department of Education, Planning and Evaluation Services, The Charles A. Dana Center, The University of Texas at Austin.
Juteau, D. (1999). *L'ethnicité et ses frontières*. Montreal: Presses de l'Université de Montréal.
Kamanzi, C., Ying Zhang, X., Deblois, L. & Deniger, M.-A. (2007). *L'influence du capital social sur la formation du capital humain chez les élèves résilients de milieux socioéconomiques défavorisés*. Revue des sciences de l'éducation, *33*(1), 127–45.

Kanoute, F. & Lafortune, G. (2011). *La réussite scolaire des élèves d'origine immigrée: Réflexions sur quelques enjeux à Montréal*. Éducation et francophonie, *39*(1), 80–92.

Kanoute, F., Vatz Laaroussi, M., Rachédi, L. & Tchimou Doffouchi, M. (2008). *Familles et réussite scolaire d'élèves immigrants du secondaire*. Revue des sciences de l'éducation, *34*(2), 265–89.

Lafortune, G. (2012). *Rapport à l'école et aux savoirs scolaires de jeunes d'origine haïtienne en contexte scolaire défavorisé à Montréal*. Ph.D. thesis, Faculté des sciences de l'éducation, Université de Montréal, Montréal, Québec.

Ledent, J., Aman, C., Garnett, B., Murdoch, J., Walters, D. & Mc Andrew, M. (2013). Academic performance and educational pathways of young allophones: A comparative multivariate analysis of Montreal, Toronto, and Vancouver. *Canadian Studies in Population*, *40*(2), 35–56.

Livingstone, A.-M., Celemencki, J., Calixte, M., Kofi-Duah, G., Julmeus-Leger, J., Thompson, T. & Dolphy, T. (2010). *Black Youths' Perspectives on Education Challenges and Policy*. Consortium for Ethnicity and Strategic Social Planning, McGill University. Montreal, Quebec.

Lucas, S. R. (2001). Effectively maintained inequality: Education transitions, track mobility and social background effects. *American Journal of Sociology*, *106*(6), 1642–90.

Mc Andrew, M. (2001). *Immigration et diversité à l'école: Le débat québécois dans une perspective comparative*. Montreal: Presses de l'Université de Montréal.

Mc Andrew, M. (2012). *Fragile Majorities and Education: Belgium, Catalonia, Northern Ireland, and Quebec*. Montreal: McGill-Queen's University Press.

Mc Andrew, M., Ait-Said, R., Ledent, J., Murdoch, J., Anisef, P., Brown, R., Sweet, R., Walters, D., Aman, C. & Garnett, B. (2009). Educational pathways and academic performance of youth of immigrant origin: Comparing Montreal, Toronto and Vancouver. Research Report to the Canadian Council on Learning.

Mc Andrew, M., Éphraïm, S., Lemire, F. & Swift, M. (2004). *La réussite scolaire des jeunes noirs anglophones dans les écoles de langue française à Montréal: Un bilan*. Rapport de recherche soumis au Ministère du Patrimoine canadien, Secteur Langues officielles et multiculturalisme, Montréal.

Mc Andrew, M. & Ledent, J. (2009). *La réussite scolaire des jeunes des communautés noires au secondaire*. WP No. 39, Centre Métropolis du Québec Immigration et métropoles, Montréal, Québec.

Mc Andrew, M., Ledent, J. & Murdoch, J., with collaboration of Ait-Said, R. (2012). *La réussite scolaire des jeunes Québécois issus de l'immigration*. Rapport soumis à la Direction des communautés culturelles du Ministère de l'éducation, du loisir et du sport. WP no. 47, Centre Métropolis du Québec Immigration et métropoles, Montréal, Québec.

Mc Andrew, M., Balde, A., Bakhshaei, M., Tardif-Grenier, K., Audet, G., Armand, F., Guyon, S., Ledent, J., Lemieux, G., Potvin, M., Rahm, J., Vatz, L., Michelle, C., A. & Rousseau, C. (2015). La réussite éducative des élèves issus de l'immigration: Dix ans de recherche et d'intervention au Québec. Montréal: Presses de l'Université de Montréal.

MEQ (Ministère de l'Éducation du Québec). (1998). *Une école d'avenir: La politique d'intégration scolaire et d'éducation interculturelle*. Gouvernement du Québec.

MIDI (Ministère de l'Immigration, de la Diversité et de l'Intégration). (2014). *L'immigration permanente du Québec selon les catégories d'immigration et quelques composantes, 2009–2013*. Gouvernement du Québec.

Moisset, J., Mellouki, M., Ouellet, R. & Diambomba, M. (1995). *Les jeunes des communautés culturelles du Québec et leur rendement scolaire*. Études et recherches, vol. 2, no. 4. Centre de recherche et d'intervention sur la réussite scolaire, Faculté des sciences de l'éducation, Université Laval, Québec.

OCDE (Organisation de coopération et de développement économiques). (2003). *Regards sur l'éducation: Les indicateurs de l'OCDE 2003.* Paris: OCDE.

OCDE (Organisation de coopération et de développement économiques). (2006). Where immigrant students succeed – A comparative review of performance and engagement in PISA 2003. *Intercultural Education, 17*(5), 507–16.

Ogbu, J. U. (1992). Adaptation to minority status and impact on school success. *Theory into Practice, 31*(4), 287–95.

Ogbu, J. U. & Simmons, H. (1998).Voluntary and involuntary minorities: A cultural-ecological theory of school performance with some implications for education. *Anthropology and Educational Quarterly, 29,* 155–88.

Portes, A. (1994). Immigration and its aftermath. *International Migration Review, 28*(4), 632–9.

Provencher, C., with collaboration of Deschênes, N. (2008). *Étude exploratoire du cheminement scolaire des élèves issus de l'immigration: Cohorte de 1994–1995 des élèves du secondaire.* Bulletin statistique de l'éducation, no. 34, Ministère de l'éducation, du loisir et du sport, Gouvernement du Québec.

Qin, D. B. (2006). The role of gender in immigrant children's educational adaptation. *Current Issues in Comparative Education, 9*(1), 8–19.

Rumbaut, R. G. (2005). Children of immigrants and their achievement: The roles of family, acculturation, social class, gender, ethnicity, and school context. In D. R. Taylor (ed.), *Addressing the Achievement Gap: Theory Informing Practice* (pp. 23–59). Series on Research in Educational Productivity, Information Age. San Diego, CA: Greenwich Publishing.

Samuel, E., Krugly-Smolska, E. & Warren, W. (2001). Academic achievement of adolescents from selected ethnocultural groups in Canada. *McGill Journal of Education, 36*(1), 61–73.

Sharkey, J. & Layzer, C. (2000). Whose definition of success: Identifying factors that affect English language learners access to academic success and resources. *TESOL Quarterly, 34*(2), 252–368.

Stiefel, L., Schwartz, A. E. & Conger, D. (2010). Age of entry and the high school performance of immigrant youth. *Journal of Urban Economics, 67*(3), 303–14.

Suárez-Orozco, C. & Carhill, A. (2008). Afterword: New directions in research with immigrant families and their children. *New Direction in Child and Adolescent Development, 121,* 87–104.

Suárez-Orozco, C., Suárez-Orozco, M. & Todorova, I. (2008). *Learning a New Land: Immigrant Students in American Society.* Cambridge, MA: Belknap Press of Harvard University Press.

Sun, M. (2014). The educational success of Chinese origin students in a French-speaking context: The role of school, family, and community. Ph.D. thesis, Faculté des sciences de l'éducation, Université de Montréal, Montréal, Québec.

UNESCO. (2009). *Principes directeurs pour l'inclusion dans l'éducation,* Paris: UNESCO.

Zady, M. & Portes, P. (2001). When low SES parents cannot assist their children in solving science problems. *Journal of Education for Students Placed at Risk, 6*(3), 215–29.

Zhou, M. & Kim, S. (2007). After-school institutions in Chinese and Korean immigrant communities: A model for Others? *Migration Information Source.* Retrieved from: www.migrationpolicy.org, Migration Policy Institute, Washington, DC.

# 6 Culture, narratives and upward educational mobility

*Nicolas Legewie*

## Introduction

'To know that my parents, my grandparents came to this country with no more than primary school education, and to know what kind of opportunities I now have available, for me that meant that I wanted to make something out of these opportunities. Because otherwise it would just be a waste', Elif says. She is a university graduate in her early thirties, who made her way to higher education despite her parents having finished little more than primary school. Could the story or 'narrative' Elif formulated about her family's experiences have played a role in her way from a low-status, working-class background to a university degree?

In this chapter, I analyse how narratives can foster upward educational mobility among disadvantaged students. Narratives are people's interpretations of the world: their lives as relatively stable, coherent stories with a setting, a cast of characters, and a sequence of events (Mc Adams, 1996; Small *et al.*, 2010, p. 16f). I use the term 'disadvantaged' to refer to people whose parents have earned low educational degrees, with ten years of education or less.[1] Intergenerational upward mobility in education among this group refers to people who have entered higher education and earned a university degree.

Using narratives as an explanation of upward educational mobility speaks to two related research fields. First, it relates to research on stratification in education by contributing to a better understanding of how the rare instances of upward educational mobility occur. Second, it relates to cultural explanations of educational outcomes (such as expectations, norms, values, frames or repertoires; see Small *et al.*, 2010 for a discussion of cultural concepts) by providing a better understanding of the mechanisms that link culture and educational outcomes.

With the present exploratory analysis, I aim to contribute to these fields by (1) constructing a clear, systematic concept of 'promotive narratives', i.e. coherent stories that foster upward educational mobility; (2) further, I show how, against the expectations in current research, promotive narratives are found not only among immigrant families, but are also constructed in non-immigrant families. This finding calls for a more inclusive concept; (3) next, I use my in-depth interview data to describe the mechanism through which promotive narratives foster upward educational mobility; and (4) I use my findings to reflect on Bourdieu's notion of habitus as a prominent cultural explanation of educational outcomes.

*Table 6.1* Co-occurrence of promotive narratives and the outcome

| Educational outcome | Promotive narrative | | N |
| --- | --- | --- | --- |
| | Absent | Present | |
| Upward educational mobility | 21 | 4 | 25 |
| Replication | 11 | 0 | 11 |
| N | 32 | 4 | **36** |

The promotive narratives described in this chapter are not a universal driving force of upward educational mobility. Rather, they are relevant in a subset of cases. As Table 6.1 shows, 4 out of 25 cases with upward mobility show a relevant promotive narrative. This pattern suggests that promotive narratives are not necessary for upward educational mobility to occur, since there are several cases in which this outcome occurred without the narrative being present. But it also suggests that they play an important role in some cases of upward educational mobility, and, as I show, they allow interesting theoretical reflections in the fields of stratification and migration research.

The analysis presented in this chapter is part of a research project on the pathways to upward educational mobility among disadvantaged students.[2] For this research project, I conducted in-depth biographical interviews with 36 respondents from disadvantaged backgrounds. I used a 2 × 2 stratified case selection scheme: I selected 25 respondents with German and Turkish backgrounds who were upwardly mobile, and 11 respondents who replicated their parents' low educational attainment. Through case selection, I further ensured that half of the respondents were second-generation Germans, meaning they were born in Germany to parents who migrated to Germany from Turkey. The other half had parents solely of German descent.[3]

In the following sections, I first situate the topic of this chapter in the research literature. Second, I describe the data and methods used for the presented analysis. Third, I present my findings, before concluding with theoretical reflections and an outlook for future research.

## Upward educational mobility, cultural explanations and narratives

### Social stratification and upward mobility in education

Studying the social stratification of societies is a constant concern of sociological research. A major focus of stratification research is to explain the intergenerational reproduction of inequalities in education (e.g. Boudon, 1974; Bourdieu & Passeron, 1990; Breen & Goldthorpe, 1997; Breen & Jonsson, 2005; Coleman *et al.*, 1966; Lareau, 2003). Less attention is paid to intergenerational upward mobility in education, i.e. when disadvantaged students earn a university degree. Even in countries with very stable inequalities, such as Germany, 5 per cent of disadvantaged students manage to enter higher education (Crul, 2013, p. 6), making up around 15 per cent of the student body (Isserstedt et al., 2007; Isserstedt et al., 2010).

For a long time, studies concerned with social mobility focused on patterns of mobility at the population level. Some focused on rates of mobility within or across populations (Blau & Duncan, 1967; Bowles & Gintis, 2002; Geißler, 2006; Wright, 1997), while others tested the effect of specific factors across a population (Chan & Boliver, 2013; Goldthorpe, 1987).

Since the mid-1990s, scholars of education, stratification, and immigration are taking a closer look at mechanisms of upward educational mobility (e.g. Crul, 2013; El-Mafaalani, 2014; Jarrett, 1995; Portes & Fernández-Kelly, 2008; Raiser, 2007; Zhou et al., 2008). Research focuses on institutional arrangements (Alba et al., 2011; Crul et al., 2012), social networks (e.g. Coleman, 1988; for an overview, see Dika & Singh, 2002), and culture (Bourdieu, 1984; Fordham & Ogbu, 1986; Lareau, 2003) as causes for stratification processes. The present study aims to contribute to this ongoing effort to understand how upward mobility in education works by focusing on cultural explanations of educational inequalities.

## *Cultural explanations of educational outcomes*

Culture has long played an important part in explanations of educational attainment. Following Small et al., (2010), culture should be understood as an umbrella term for shared constructions of meaning and interpretation. The authors argue that as part of explanations, culture is best captured using concrete concepts (Small et al., 2010, p. 14). Thus, cultural explanations draw on concepts such as values, norms and motivations (Breen & Goldthorpe, 1997; Vaisey, 2010), worldviews (Young, 2006), repertoires (Swidler, 1986), frames (Young, 2010), narratives (Smith, 2014) and habitus (Bourdieu & Passeron, 1990; El-Mafaalani, 2014). Such concepts help explain educational outcomes by shedding light on why students or their parents make certain educational choices or are engaged in school (e.g. Archer et al., 2001; Breen & Goldthorpe, 1997), how the school environment can exacerbate class differences in school performance by rewarding specific behaviour and knowledge (e.g. Bourdieu & Passeron, 1990; Carter, 2003; Lareau, 2003; Valenzuela, 1999) or how teachers' grading decisions are biased through their perception of students' class backgrounds (e.g. Becker & Birkelbach, 2010, p. 115; Cortina et al., 2008, p. 221; Ditton, 2008, p. 249; Müller-Benedict, 2007, p. 635; Schneider, 2011).

The use of such concepts as explanations of social inequalities has seen varying popularity. Cultural causes have regained prominence since the mid-1990s, with researchers stressing that we should see culture not as monolithic, group-specific properties but rather as multifaceted, situational and based in social networks and interactions (DiMaggio, 1997; Smith, 2014, p. 3; for reviews of cultural explanations of inequalities, see Small et al., 2010; Small & Newman, 2001). I adopt this situational perspective on culture.

A prominent example of cultural causes in explanations of educational outcomes is the rational action model of status attainment (Breen & Goldthorpe, 1997). The main explanatory variables are perceptions of costs, benefits and the chances for success of educational options. Scholars argue that these factors contribute to the reproduction of educational inequalities between generations because disadvantaged students ascribe higher costs, lower benefits and lower chances of success to earning high educational degrees (e.g. Becker & Hecken, 2009; Breen & Goldthorpe, 1997; Stocké, 2007). Following this logic, upward educational mobility would happen if disadvantaged students and their parents perceive higher education degrees as beneficial and feasible.

While this explanation points to a potentially important piece of the puzzle, it does not reveal underlying mechanisms that lead disadvantaged students to earn higher educational degrees. Perceptions of costs, benefits and the odds for success do not form in a vacuum. The question is how perceptions of costs, benefits and odds of success are formed and internalized by students in a way that guides their educational decisions. For instance, how do parents with high educational aspirations transmit these aspirations to their children (Bengtson & Troll, 1978; Collins *et al.*, 2000, p. 227)? Furthermore, the above argument faces an empirical problem: a number of studies show that low-achieving minority students often value education and have high expectations similar to high-achieving students (Ainsworth-Darnell & Downey, 1998; Downey, 2008; Harris, 2006; Herman, 2009). Both points suggest that we need a better understanding of the mechanism through which perceptions and interpretations are formed and guide educational decisions.

Other cultural explanations provide such an in-depth analysis of underlying mechanisms. A prominent example is Bourdieu's notion of habitus (Bourdieu, 1984; Bourdieu & Passeron, 1990). Bourdieu suggests that internalized perceptions of society, social position and one's role in it lead to a stable repertoire of perceptional and behavioural patterns. These patterns affect educational choices, but also teachers' assessments in school (Bourdieu & Passeron, 1990). Upper- and middle-class students internalize perceptions that make high educational aspirations an assumption that is taken for granted, and produce behavioural patterns that teachers expect and reward in school. Working-class students, in contrast, internalize perceptions that make high educational degrees seem unattainable or not worth pursuing (Archer *et al.*, 2001; Bourdieu & Passeron, 1990; Carter, 2003; Willis, 1981).

Authors like Lareau and her colleagues (Lareau, 2003; Horvat *et al.*, 2003) describe specific habitual practices, such as parents' and children's engagement with teachers, that can be traced back to differences in parenting practices. The authors show how the practices of middle-class parents and children contribute to the reproduction of educational inequalities by affording the children decisive advantages over working-class children (Carter, 2003; Ditton, 2008, p. 252; Gomolla & Radtke, 2009, p. 274; Lareau, 2003, pp. 238ff.). In short, the congruence of practices in the family environment and expectations in school contribute to the reproduction of inequalities in educational attainment.

Thus, the habitus provides greater insight than the rational action model does in describing mechanisms of stratification. On the other hand, it has difficulties accounting for upward educational mobility as an exception to the common pattern of reproduction. Scholars drawing on the habitus concept suggest that upward mobility is only possible if disadvantaged students adopt new perceptions, appreciations and practices, thus distancing themselves from their social milieu of origin. For instance, El-Mafaalani (2014) describes how immigrant children must distance themselves from their original environment and overcome their habitus in order to become upwardly mobile (see Brake, 2006 for a similar finding).

The question, though, is whether working-class families can produce perceptions, world-views and internalized behavioural patterns that *do not* create distance to the milieu of origin, but still foster upward educational mobility.

## *Narratives as explanations of upward educational mobility*

A narrative perspective moves us in this direction. It is a promising way to approach cultural explanations of educational outcomes because, on one hand, it allows a more differentiated, mechanism-based view on how aspirations and perceptions of costs and benefits can influence students' performances. On the other hand, it simultaneously contributes to our understanding of stratification processes by showing how cultural aspects that emerge within working-class families can foster upward educational mobility.

Narratives are defined as people's interpretations and verbal construction of the world and their lives as more or less coherent stories with a setting, a cast of characters, and a sequence of events (McAdams, 1996; Raiser, 2007, p. 63; Small et al., 2010, p. 16f.). They are shared constructions that are produced through recurrent story telling within a social group or network such as the family (Somers, 1994).

The immigrant bargain (Louie, 2012; Smith, 2008) is a prominent example of a narrative that fosters upward educational mobility. The immigrant bargain describes a story of migration experiences that defines a role for students in relation to their parents and siblings: to 'redeem the parents' sacrifice through their own success' (Smith, 2008, p. 275; also see Ceballo, 2004, p. 177; Portes & Rumbaut, 2001, p. 192f.). The parents abandoned their home, family and jobs, then suffered the burdens of living in a foreign country, with poor working conditions and discrimination in daily life. Their pains are seen as instrumental in providing their children with an opportunity to achieve higher education and a well-paid job. The hope is for the children to succeed in school in order to repay their parents' sacrifice. The immigrant bargain can be understood as a 'biographical resource' (Tepecik, 2011, p. 301) because it converts the parents' experience of migration into a powerful guideline for the children's goals and conduct.

This immigrant bargain is described in various national contexts and among different migrant groups as a factor for upward educational mobility (King & Koller, 2009, p. 12; e.g. King et al., 2011; Raiser, 2007, pp. 93ff.; Smith, 2014, p. 17). It gives an example of how narratives can contribute to explanations of upward educational mobility. Like habitus-type explanations, narratives provide an understanding of *how* culture can foster upward educational mobility. Thus, they promise richer explanations than do rational action model-type explanations. But unlike the habitus, narratives, such as the immigrant bargain, help account for the fact that there are substantial numbers of students from disadvantaged backgrounds that achieve upward mobility. As the immigrant bargain shows, upward mobility can stem from working-class families themselves, not only from children distancing themselves from it.

The narrative perspective on cultural explanations of upward educational mobility can be elaborated further in a number of ways. First, as the immigrant bargain is not defined as a precise concept (King et al., 2011; Louie, 2012; Raiser, 2007; Smith, 2006, 2008), it is unclear what its main dimensions are and how they are logically connected. A clearer concept would facilitate operationalization and further theory development.

Second, the implicit expectation in the existing literature is that the immigrant bargain is a narrative exclusively constructed in immigrant families, based on their particular life histories and experiences. However, as I show in detail below, we can also find functionally equivalent narratives in non-immigrant families. While there are some hints to such narratives in the literature (Higginbotham & Weber, 1992, pp. 419, 426; Ogbu, 2003, p. 262), there is no effort to compare these narratives and analyse them as instances of the same phenomenon.

Lastly, the mechanism underlying such narratives needs to be described in more detail. How exactly does a story like the immigrant bargain become a driving force in upward educational mobility? In this chapter, I contribute to filling these three research gaps.

## Data and methods

### Case selection and data collection

For my study, the most important scope decision is low parental education: I focus my analysis on people whose parents both had at most ten years of education, excluding vocational training. I interviewed 36 students using a stratified, 2 × 2 case selection scheme.[4] I selected cases based on their educational outcome (i.e. upward educational mobility vs. replication) as well as parents' origin (foreign-born vs. native, see Table 6.2). Respondents' age was restricted to vary between 25 and 40 years in order to ensure that respondents' educational careers unfolded in comparable structural contexts.

*Table 6.2* Case selection scheme

| Educational attainment | Immigration background | | N |
|---|---|---|---|
| | Second generation | Non-immigrant | |
| Upward educational mobility | 13 | 12 | 25 |
| Replication | 5 | 6 | 11 |
| N | 18 | 18 | 36 |

Including cases with upward educational mobility as well as non-mobility provides variance on the outcome. 'Upward mobility' refers to students who earned at least a Bachelor's degree. 'Non-mobility' is defined as remaining at a comparable or lower level of education as one's parents (13 years of schooling or less).[5]

Including 'negative cases' that do not show the outcome under investigation helps avoid selection bias and facilitates inferences (King et al., 1994; Mahoney & Goertz, 2004). In this regard, the present study holds additional analytic potential compared to most studies in the field (e.g. Ceballo, 2004; Domínguez & Watkins, 2003; Higginbotham & Weber, 1992; Raiser, 2007; Smith, 2010; Tepecik, 2011; but see Crul, 2013; El-Mafaalani, 2014 for exceptions).

Regarding the main comparative dimension (parental origin), I define second-generation students as students who were born in Germany or have attended school there from first grade onwards, and whose parents grew up in Turkey. 'Non-immigrant' refers to students whose parents and grandparents were born in Germany. I only included students from German- and Turkish-born parents in order to focus the analysis.

Further scope conditions for this study were the national and local context. The study only includes respondents from Berlin, Germany, as an example of an urban area with an education system that offers comparatively few opportunities for upward mobility (Alba et al., 2011; Berkemeyer et al., 2012; Crul, 2013).[6] With this scope choice of origin group and location, I look at a least likely scenario of upward mobility. Thus, in the cases that do show upward educational mobility, the mechanisms of interest are easier to identify.

Studying the role of narratives in upward educational mobility entails certain demands on data material. First, this outcome is quite rare, limiting the pool of potential respondents. Second, to understand respondents' meaning constructions, we need to give voice to respondents' own interpretations. Third, understanding how respondents' educational careers unfold calls for life course data.

I used in-depth biographical interviews to meet these needs.[7] The in-depth biographical interviews were recorded and lasted between two and six hours. They were conducted in German,[8] in either the respondents' homes or a university office.[9] The interviews focused on relevant events in respondents' life histories and educational careers. Furthermore, respondents' family backgrounds as well as their relationships with friends, peer, and adult acquaintances were captured in detail and across the life course. The narratives analysed in this chapter arose during the respondents' accounts of their educational careers or family environments. Thus, I did not use the classic narrative interview technique (Schütze, 1983) to elicit respondents' accounts. Rather, I asked them to tell me about their school and labour market careers, and then observed whether respondents recounted a promotive narrative that was relevant for them during their educational career.

## Data analysis

In this chapter I study promotive narratives and their role in respondents' upward educational mobility. My findings are based on three analytic steps: first is the construction of a precise and operationalizable concept; second is reconstructing the respondents' educational careers; and third, analysing the link between promotive narratives and upward educational mobility. For the first step, I used qualitative data analysis software to code all 36 interviews and develop a systematic concept of promotive narratives from my data (Strauss & Corbin, 1998). For the case reconstructions, I used a case-centred analytic approach (e.g. Brady & Collier, 2004; George & Bennett, 2005; Smith, 2014, p. 8) where I treated educational careers as sequences of events and transitions. Then I used the case reconstructions to analyse how, in the cases in which they were present, promotive narratives fostered upward educational mobility.

*Analysing 'narratives of narratives' and direction of causality*

This chapter focuses on narratives that respondents and people in their personal networks constructed during the respondents' educational careers. Since in-depth biographical interviews yield data in the form of respondents' narratives of past events, interactions, perceptions, etc., in a sense I analyse 'narratives of narratives'. When I refer to a 'narrative' in this chapter, I refer to a narrative that was constructed in a respondent's personal network during a certain period in her or his life.

Since I describe narratives that fostered respondents' upward educational mobility, the question arises whether respondents construct such narratives *ex post facto*, after having successfully completed their educational careers. If so, my argument faces a problem of direction of causality (Brady, 2008, p. 224).

Two points challenge this possible critique. First, the respondents who mention a promotive narrative are able to pinpoint rather precisely when that narrative became important to them, and they give concrete examples of interactions in which network members constructed narratives (e.g. recurrent dinner-table conversations in which the parents talked about their own educational experiences).

Second, respondents also describe specific situations in which narratives influenced the decisions they made or the ways they acted. Making such a connection is harder if respondents did not really have this experience, but were constructing it *ex post facto* (Young, 2010).

The above points indicate that the narratives of interest are not constructed after the fact, but were indeed relevant *during* the respondents' educational careers, facilitating their upward educational mobility. Therefore, they strengthen my claim to validity.

## Promotive narratives and upward educational mobility

In the following sections, I present the results of my analysis. First, I describe the concept structure of promotive narratives in detail as it emerged from the data analysis. Second, I show why my findings justify the use of a new concept over existing options. Third, I scrutinize the mechanism that makes promotive narratives a driving force of upward educational mobility.

## What are promotive narratives?

In general terms, 'promotive narratives' are interactive constructions that students and members of their personal networks produce through recurrent acts of storytelling, and which foster high educational attainment. One way to contribute to existing research on narratives and upward educational mobility is to offer a clear, more specific concept that allows a clear operationalization. I constructed such a concept following Goertz's notion of 'multi-level theories' (Goertz, 2006; Goertz & Mahoney, 2005). Goertz suggests thinking of concepts as having multiple levels. The researcher breaks down abstract notions into more palpable secondary-level dimensions. One or more indicator-level dimensions serve to push each secondary-level dimension even closer to the data and operationalize them (Coppedge, 1999; Goertz, 2006, p. 240f.).

I incorporated this notion of a concept structure into my analytic procedure: I analysed what narratives respondents recounted, looked for different dimensions to these narratives and traced how these dimensions were connected in making up the narratives. Through these steps, a concept structure with connected secondary and indicator-level concepts emerged. Figure 6.1 illustrates the product of this analysis. As the essential elements of promotive narratives, I derived two secondary-level dimensions from the data: (1) The construction of education as a path to success, and (2) the construction of a family project of mobility. I expand on each dimension in turn. Table 6.3 gathers illustrative quotes from my cases for the respective indicator-level dimensions.

The first secondary-level dimension captures the role the narrative ascribes to education as the primary route to success. This dimension can take two alternative forms: success in terms of a high-paying, secure job with good work conditions; or success in terms of having the freedom to choose a job that one enjoys. Illustrating

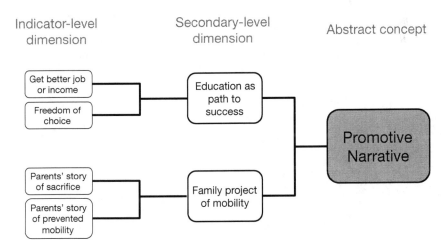

*Figure 6.1* Concept structure of the promotive narratives

the first alternative, in her quote in Table 6.3, Dilara describes how she connected her school performance directly to her future ability to secure a well-paying job, which in turn would provide more financial stability to her family. As to the second alternative, Jakob recalls his father telling him how education was the means to acquire freedom of choice regarding career options in the future, to 'do whatever you feel like doing' (see Table 6.3).

This perception of education as the path to success contrasts with alternative perceptions of education by students without a promotive narrative. Ebru, a 30-year-old law student, recalls how she perceived education during secondary school: 'I don't know, my grades weren't bad, but I wasn't interested. I didn't care what happened. Perhaps because I knew it didn't matter, there would be money anyway . . . I knew how much money the government gave you [as welfare].' Ebru

*Table 6.3* Illustrative quotes for the promotive narratives

| Secondary-level dimension | Indicator-level dimension | Example from cases |
|---|---|---|
| Education as path to success | Achieve better life | 'For me the situation [after my father's early retirement] was a spur to really focus on school, so that I could get a good job and my children wouldn't have to go through this.'<br><br>Dilara, 25, law student |
| | Freedom of choice | 'I don't quite remember what [my father] used to say exactly, but it was something along the lines of: "I really wanted to, but I couldn't" and "so you can do whatever you feel like doing . . . You go [to school] so you have all the possibilities."'<br><br>Jakob, 28, political science student |
| Life project | Parents' story as sacrifice | 'My parents, my grandparents, they didn't have the opportunities, and I get them on a silver platter. To not use them would almost be ungrateful to my family. Who have gone through so much, left their village, left everything behind, and toiled for years, so their children could have it better.'<br><br>Elif, 34, works in a public agency |
| | Parents' story as prevented success | 'My parents had a recommendation for Gymnasium, they could have gone there, but my grandparents . . . said, to both my mom and my dad: "Go to work first." And they did, and got a salary, and they didn't do more . . . My grandparents didn't make much money, one of my grandmothers was a store clerk. And my granddads didn't have such great jobs, either . . . So the idea was to stand on your own two feet as soon as possible. Going to university was completely out of the question.'<br><br>Karin, 26, law student |

describes how she came to see education as irrelevant: because of her parents' dependence on welfare subsidies, she perceived a constant flow of income was ensured regardless of one's education or occupation. In other cases, education was not constructed as irrelevant, but as less important when choosing a secondary school. Jürgen, a 31-year-old psychology student, says choosing a school was 'a pragmatic question. Here's a school, it's the closest. Done. There was no: "you should definitely get the Abitur", or anything.'[10] Jürgen recounts how his choice for a secondary school was made irrespective of the educational trajectory it would put him on. Neither he nor his parents saw the Abitur as a stepping-stone to higher education and success. Thus, both statements illustrate how students can perceive education as secondary or even superfluous.

The second dimension captures episodes from the parents' lives, around which a plot is constructed. This plot takes the form of a family project of mobility that transports a strong sense of purpose to take up the parents' story and bring it to a successful end in terms of high education and a good job. My data suggests two variations on this plot, which make up the indicator-level dimensions. The variations are not mutually exclusive and may be interwoven into the same narrative. First, parents and their child may construct the parents' life as a sacrifice for the child's opportunities. In the quote in Table 6.3, Elif describes how her parents and grandparents left their home and came to Germany, worked hard and thus afforded their children opportunities for education. She felt obliged to honour that sacrifice. Second, parents and their children may construct the parents' life as a story of prevented success. For instance, Karin, a 26-year-old law student, describes how her parents always told her about their unrealized chances to attain higher educational degrees: the financial situation and advice given by her grandparents prevented Karin's parents from accomplishing their goals; instead, they found themselves working to earn an income as early as possible.

It is helpful to contrast the described family projects with cases in which respondents did not construct a clear family project. Consider Hati, a 25-year-old education student. Hati's parents had an experience comparable to Karin's parents. They told Hati their story and placed high value on education. Thus, the parents provided the 'raw material' for a shared construction of a promotive narrative.

> '[My parents wanted] us to have a better life than they had had . . . I think my parents always saw it that way because they didn't have those opportunities themselves, or they didn't use them. My mom always wanted to go to university. But because of financial reasons, she couldn't. I think that's why she always stressed that we should do it.'

However, Hati did not join in this construction and, thus, no family project of mobility was present. An important hint to the difference in Hati's perception of her parents' story is the qualifier 'or they didn't use them [their opportunities]', which runs counter to the family life project. When the parents pointed out that getting an education was also in Hati's self-interest, she used their argument to further stress her independence: 'When they started saying "You're doing this for yourself, not for us", I said: "OK, if that's the case [I don't mind bad grades]."' Hati rejected her parents' construction and did not formulate a story that ascribed a role to herself. In short, even though the 'raw material' was present to construct a promotive narrative (i.e. the perception of education as a path to success and, in this example, the parents recounting their life story as a sacrifice), this does not mean that such a narrative was actually constructed.

## Why a new concept?

What justifies introducing yet another concept to the plethora of social science concepts? Could concepts like expectations, values or norms capture the described phenomenon just as well, and with a less complex concept? And if a narrative perspective is indeed fruitful, why not stick with the 'immigrant bargain', an existing label? As the following two statements illustrate, promotive narratives are more than mere expressions of expectations, values or norms for high educational attainment or motivations for school engagement (see King et al., 2011, p. 589 for a similar point). The first example shows expectations, values and norms. Ina, a 32-year-old artisan who dropped out of a university-track secondary school, describes her father's expectations of her performance as a demand directed toward her. These expectations are an expression of a strong norm of excellence in education and elsewhere. Neither the father nor the mother, or Ina herself constructed justifications for these expectations, nor embedded them in a coherent story.

> 'My father expected me to be at the top of the class, always. To him, there was no second place . . . At the beginning, I also really wanted to get good grades. Later, it all got way too much for me.'

Compare this statement to how Dilara, a 25-year-old law student, embeds her father's expectations in a story of her parents' migration to Germany. This story takes the form of a family project, in which the family collectively seeks upward mobility, with the parents and their children each fulfilling their part.

> 'I can remember how my father always told us that he wanted us to get a good education . . . [To come to Germany] was difficult for my parents. They didn't speak German. And to learn what's what; because they're from a small village . . . They used to tell us that story so that we know where they came from, and how they made it . . . To me that matters; it motivates me. Not to take things for granted, how we live here and that I can get an education. That I have a good life. Because had they stayed there [in Turkey], who knows what I'd be doing. I think you have all the opportunities here, and you should make the best of them.'

This coherent story is the central characteristic of promotive narratives and, as I argue below, explains why promotive narratives can foster upward educational mobility.

*Table 6.4* Distribution of narrative types over parents' origin

| Parentage group | Narrative present |
|---|---|
| Turkish | Elif |
|  | Dilara |
| German | Jakob |
|  | Karin |

Further, Table 6.4 shows that both students of Turkish and German parentage indicate promotive narratives. Thus, in contrast to most research on the topic (e.g. King *et al.*, 2011; Portes & Rumbaut, 2001, p. 192f.; Raiser, 2007; Smith, 2008; Tepecik, 2011; for exceptions, see Higginbotham & Weber, 1992, pp. 419, 426; Ogbu, 2003, p. 262), my data shows that promotive narratives similar to the 'immigrant bargain' are also present among non-immigrant students.

Through my analysis, I identify the unifying theme among promotive narratives as they were recounted by second-generation and non-immigrant respondents: the narratives' characters' decided goal was for the respondent to climb the social ladder and attain a high social status. The more general term 'promotive narratives' accommodates different kinds of narratives that are similar in fostering upward educational mobility. The immigrant bargain is thus a special case of a promotive narrative.

### *The mechanism behind the promotive narratives*

Dilara, the daughter of Turkish-born parents, grew up with five older siblings (four brothers, one sister) in the south-eastern part of Berlin. Her father was the first of the family to come to Germany. From a rural area in Turkey, he had completed four years of formal schooling. At the age of 25, he migrated to Germany and started working as unskilled labour in factories and other jobs. Dilara's mother, who finished six years of schooling in Turkey, followed later. In their neighbourhood, they were the only immigrant family until the ethnic composition started changing after 2005. In 1995, when Dilara was eight years old, the father suffered a heart attack and had to quit his job due to the resulting health issues. This put the family in a tight spot, financially. The mother became the only breadwinner of the family, until eventually Dilara's older siblings started contributing to the family income.

The surprising feature in Dilara's story is how committed she was to her school success, from a very early age. She poured all her efforts and time into achieving this goal. The question is how children and adolescents such as Dilara arrive at such commitment, and how they maintain it throughout their school careers. Consider the following quotes from Dilara's interview:

> '[My parents] came to Germany without anything, without education, no money. They didn't even have shoes back home, if they ever had meat to eat, it was maybe once a year. When my father came here, he worked hard

and earned money; he never depended on welfare . . . My parents often told me this, so that I knew where I came from.'

'For me that was really important, it motivated me. To not take things as a given, the way we live here, and that I am able to get an education. Because had they stayed there [in Turkey], who knows what I would have done. So, to have all those opportunities, and to make something of that, that's how I saw it.'

These quotes show both dimensions of the promotive narrative: (1) Dilara and her father constructed education as a path to success because performing well in school and earning a high educational degree would secure a well-paying job with good working conditions; and (2) Dilara constructs a family project based on the notion of her parents' life as a sacrifice. She evokes the circumstances under which her parents migrated to Germany: without education, financial means or even the most essential personal belongings ('They didn't even have shoes back home'). The migration to Germany and the father's work in a factory are necessary hardships in order to provide the children with the opportunity for a better life.

Such narratives are constructed through recurrent conversations in personal networks. In Dilara's case, the parents were the main participants in these conversations. In many cases, additional tools play a role in the construction, such as grade sheets showing the parents' school performances or picture books illustrating their life story. In this sense, promotive narratives are not individually held worldviews, but shared constructions.

As I show below, the family project promotive narrative is a crucial part in an answer to why Dilara and other students develop such a strong, unwavering focus on school success. In the case of family project promotive narratives, the shared story makes the child a shareholder in a collective mission, and gives it an active role to follow. Insofar as the child accepts this role, the narrative defines the broad framework of how students see the world and provides a strong guideline for her or his actions because it embodies an identity cherished by the child (Emirbayer & Goodwin, 1994, p. 1432).

More specifically, promotive narratives foster upward educational mobility by pushing the internalization of school-oriented norms and values, as well as by managing family and non-family social relations. These two aspects are two sides of the same coin, and they are intertwined: the internalization of norms and values influenced how respondents managed their social relations and social distance to different actors, and vice versa.

### *Internalizing expectations, norms, and values*

Usually, even if parents have high expectations and manage to instil the value of education in their children, there are frequent and intense conflicts around this intergenerational transmission of values, with adolescents distancing themselves from their parents and their expectations (Bengtson *et al.*, 2002; Bengtson & Troll, 1978).

The promotive narrative counteracts this tendency: it is a vehicle for the children's internalization of school-oriented norms and values by providing reasoning and a background story that legitimizes those norms and values. This finding is consistent with research on intergenerational norm transmission, which shows that children, and especially adolescents, internalize norms more readily if they are connected to reasoning (Baumrind, 1996, p. 410). Research on educational attainment suggests that children's internalization of school success norms has a positive impact on their school performance (Pomerantz et al., 2007, p. 376).

The promotive narrative's power as reasoning becomes clear by contrasting Dilara to other cases in which high parental expectations and norms of school success were not accompanied by a promotive narrative. Take Ina's case described above. Ina's father set very clear and strict norms of school engagement and sanctioned non-compliance with both open and latent rejection. But without shared constructions that embed these norms into a story that Ina has an active role in, she perceives those norms as oppressive.

> 'I probably would have liked to excel if it weren't for this pressure and no possibility of escape. If I had done everything for my own sake, I would have done all these things my father wanted me to do.'

The lack of internalization of norms is a crucial point here. Research shows that without such internalization, coercive parenting can negatively affect students' school performance (Collins et al., 2000, p. 227; King et al., 2011, p. 586). For Ina, a promotive narrative could have embedded her father's expectations into a meaningful story that could have helped in internalizing said norms; instead, she rejected these norms because they felt imposed upon her. Karin, a 25-year-old law student, faced comparably strict norms set by her parents, but they were always embedded in a promotive narrative. The narrative provided a template for making sense of the parents' views and demands, helping Karin cope with her situation (see Bettie, 2002, p. 410 for a similar finding). Thus, because the parents' norms were not treated as a given, but embedded in a story, Karin internalized those norms and adhered to them even when challenged by peers (see below for details on this aspect).

It is crucial that children internalize norms and values because parents with low educational degrees often have difficulties controlling their child's school progress due to their own lack of experience with secondary education. This pattern of parents being unable to assist their children in secondary school was pervasive among the cases in my data set (for similar findings, see Tepecik, 2011, p. 268). In most cases, parents had to rely on their children to monitor their own school performance with the start of secondary school (or even before that). Elif, a 34-year-old university graduate and government employee, recalls how her parents were unable to follow her school progress:

> 'With every passing year, that became more difficult, this supervision and help at home. Just because, as a kid you learn the language pretty fast, and

the parents, who want to supervise you, they can't keep up themselves. So pretty soon you basically supervise your education yourself.'

As a consequence of this pattern, the respondents' internalization of norms of educational success and monitoring of their own progress becomes much more important.

This issue is not exclusively caused by immigrant parents' language problems. Jutta, a 36-year old trained accountant and mother of two, notes that 'My mother wasn't really able to follow what our homework assignments were. And so I soon realized I could just show her anything when she wanted to check my homework.'

## *Managing social relations and social distance*

My in-depth analysis reveals that respondents invoked promotive narratives when managing their social relations. That is, the promotive narrative provided them with answers to questions such as: 'What people can I look to as examples for what to do or not to do? Whom should I hang out with, and whom should I avoid?'

In some cases, the respondents used the promotive narrative as a guideline for friend selection. For instance, Dilara saw it as part of her role to stay away from people going to parties, drinking alcohol or using drugs. In this way, Dilara's friendship network consisted of peers with a similar focus on education. This finding converges with what is known as 'homophily', where people are most likely to form durable social ties to others they perceive as being similar to themselves (McPherson *et al.*, 2001). Through promotive narratives, school performance and staying out of trouble become and remain the central part of the student's identity, thus becoming the major criteria for friend selection. In a similar vein, recent studies show how worldviews can shape personal networks and suggest that 'worldviews are strong predictors of changes in network composition' (Vaisey & Lizardo, 2010, p. 1).

As another important aspect of this management of social relations, promotive narratives connect family members across generations, potentially bridging intergenerational dissimilarities and conflicts. As research on intergenerational value transmission has shown, such dissimilarities and conflicts can otherwise hinder the internalization of norms by children and adolescents (Bengtson & Troll, 1978, p. 217). This issue is especially salient in low-status families with upwardly mobile children. Earning higher educational degrees creates a growing distance between the students and their original social environment in terms of social relations and sociocultural practices (Bettie, 2002, p. 410; King, 2009a, pp. 87, 96; 2009b, p. 28; Pott, 2009, p. 61; Raiser, 2007, p. 142; Wischmann, 2010, p. 280). Students start doing and thinking about things that are unfamiliar to those around them, especially their parents. They also might face diverging expectations in the different social contexts in which they move. If students are not able to negotiate successfully the differences in demands from school, the family and their peers, they might abandon their campaign for upward educational mobility (Bettie, 2002,

p. 404; Domínguez & Watkins, 2003, p. 127; Pott, 2009, p. 48; Wischmann, 2010, pp. 271, 276).

Third, promotive narratives contextualize 'role reversal'. Role reversal means that parents lose authority due to a change in the knowledge gap. Through education or acculturation (in immigrant families, e.g. language learning), the child surpasses their parents' knowledge in relevant areas of social life. This role reversal can severely disrupt family dynamics and undermine parental influence (Portes & Rumbaut, 2001, p. 53). Through promotive narratives, however, parents' authority does not stem from knowledge or ability to help, but from their life story and adversity overcome.

The relation between Jakob and his father illustrates how a promotive narrative can mitigate changes in relationships and help reframe the father–son relationship. Jakob's parents both grew up in environments with poverty and abuse. With long tenure in a public-sector job, the father eventually attained a fairly high income and was able to secure credit to buy an apartment in a middle-class neighbourhood in the south-western part of Berlin. From when Jakob was in primary school, the father stressed how important education was and how his dream was for his children to be able to attend university. While this story became more important as Jakob grew older, his father's role as a knowledgeable person of respect crumbled with Jakob's educational achievements and his father's unsuccessful venture into self-employment in construction: 'I really looked up to my father for a long time. Well, at some point you notice ... you think he knows everything. ... When you realize that his means are limited in many ways, I could tell him anything, like: "The professors in university walk around with batons." He'd say: "Oh, yeah?" So that there's a world completely alien to him. That was a shock.'

Although Jakob's respect for his father diminished in many areas, he saw him in a different light because of the promotive narrative that had been in the background for a while. It really came to the fore in late adolescence:

> 'Toward the end of Gymnasium, ... you really start to think about who my parents are ... When you realize, that [your father] was in a similar situation to you, under certain living conditions, I thought: "Wow, my father's life must have been tough!" And I always noticed, this pride in his sons, but even more, and rightfully so, in himself. That he was able to provide us with opportunities.'

The promotive narrative prevents a drastic reordering of social relations because they include the parents in the upward trajectory. The child does not surpass them and become 'something better', but continues and finishes a collective effort. Instead of being left behind, parents share in the accomplishment.

## Discussion and conclusion

In this chapter, I analyse how narratives can foster upward educational mobility among disadvantaged students. I present a systematic concept of promotive narratives with a clear inner structure, including secondary and indicator-level dimensions. My analysis further shows how, contrary to the expectations of current research, second-generation and non-immigrant students construct very similar and functionally equivalent promotive narratives, with the parents' life story as the major plot element. Lastly, my analysis teases out the mechanism underlying promotive narratives, showing how it works through two intertwined aspects: the internalization of expectations, norms and values, as well as the management of social relations and social distance.

Using narratives as part of an explanation of upward educational mobility speaks to two related research fields: first, research on stratification in education, specifically on upward educational mobility; and second, to cultural explanations of educational outcomes. My analysis shows how promotive narratives are used because they provide a rich explanation of the underlying mechanism. Further, it shows how narratives are constructed and passed from parents to children. The examples of Dilara, Karin, Jacob and Elif illuminate how expectations, norms and values gain compelling force by being embedded into a story that ascribes a clear role to the children.

From a theoretical perspective, promotive narratives call into question what is often regarded as established knowledge in research on stratification, education and second-generation integration. Some scholars argue that upwardly mobile students from Turkish immigrant families must break with family traditions, their parents' values and ties from their original social milieu in order to achieve their mobility (El-Mafaalani, 2014). Evoking Bourdieu's concept of habitus, other scholars suggest the same for upwardly mobile students from German-born parents (Brake, 2006). Examples like Dilara, Karin, Elif and Jakob show that a worldview that depicts education as a viable route to social status and promotes upward educational mobility can arise from a working-class family context. Thus, my findings suggest that the habitus might profit from a more flexible conceptualization that allows for working-class worldviews to foster upward educational mobility, and for worldviews to be less irrevocably internalized through class position and socialization. Narratives could be a useful concept in this revision. They are less rigid than the habitus, but more stable across situations and social contexts than identities (Sanders, 2002).

The presented analysis is exploratory for two reasons: first, because the main goal was to carve out a concept, describe its inner structure and explain the underlying mechanism; and second, because the data material used for this analysis does not allow for a strong claim on generalizability. Nonetheless, I claim that the described concept holds value beyond the data used or the regional context of the study. It describes a type of narrative that draws on a very common experience: parents' sacrifices for their children or obstacles that prevented their own success. Therefore, in principal promotive narratives should be a helpful analytic tool in many regional and national contexts. Studies describing similar narratives in different national contexts and for various ethnic groups buttress this claim (e.g. King et al., 2011; Raiser, 2007; Smith, 2006; Tepecik, 2011).

My analysis suggests a number of fruitful directions for future research. One step is to further elaborate the concept of 'promotive narratives' to include other, functionally equivalent life projects beyond the described family project. For instance, Frye (2012, p. 1565) describes a narrative including imagined futures and being 'one who aspires' as a vehicle for upward mobility among Malawi youth. Jarrett (1995, p. 122) shows how some families in disadvantaged neighbourhoods constructed an 'ideology of distinctiveness' that depicted their families as superior to others in their neighbourhood, and thereby helped their children maintain a strong focus on school and stay out of trouble. Bettie (2002, p. 405) describes how some working-class students profit from constructing structural rather than individual explanations of their social position. Thus, the presented concept is not exhaustive or conclusive, but a description of a narrative type detected in this study. Other types of promotive narratives can easily be incorporated into my proposed concept structure.

Another important aspect is to investigate how promotive narratives combine with other factors, such as social support or peer and neighbourhood networks, to form pathways toward upward educational mobility. Under what conditions can promotive narratives actually produce upward educational mobility, and are there circumstances under which they have a problematic rather than positive influence?

Third, to further ascertain whether promotive narratives are indeed a causal factor of upward educational mobility, longitudinal or revisit studies would provide a sound methodological basis (e.g. Smith, 2010). A longitudinal or revisit interview study would provide the best methodological basis for such an analysis because it would allow for studying respondents who construct a promotive narrative at time T1 and see whether that played a role in their educational attainment at T2.

Lastly, an open question remains regarding how pervasive promotive narratives are in a larger population, and how consistently they are linked to upward educational mobility. Thus, the present analysis comprises one step on the way to illuminate upward educational mobility and the role of cultural explanations in that process.

## Notes

1 There are further forms of disadvantage in educational systems, such as poverty or race. I focus on parental education levels because parental education has the most direct association with children's educational outcomes and accounts for much of the children's disadvantage in those other forms (Breen & Jonsson, 2005; Cortina et al., 2008, p. 215).
2 The goal of the overall study was to identify different combinations of personal network factors (such as social support, peer-group environment, role models, and narratives) that lead to upward educational mobility.
3 Gender was a further comparative dimension in the data collection; female and male respondents were selected evenly. However, this comparison is not a focus in this chapter. For findings on gender differences in paths to upward educational mobility, see Legewie (2015).
4 All respondents were vetted before the interview regarding how they fit the case selection criteria. In total, I conducted 41 interviews. In five cases, the in-depth interviews revealed that respondents did not fit the sampling scheme. These cases were excluded from the analysis.

5 Due to changes in the educational system, 13 years of education for children in 2006 is roughly equivalent to 10 years of education in the 1960s and 1970s (Becker, 2006).
6 To ensure that respondents attended school in the same education system, I only included respondents who grew up in West Berlin or who entered school in East Berlin after German reunification.
7 Survey data does not provide sufficient detail of information and lacks possibilities to give voice to respondents. Gathering ethnographic data is time and resource-consuming, making it difficult to include enough cases for systematic comparative leverage. For the purpose of this study, in-depth biographical interviews provide an optimal balance between efficient data collection and detail of information.
8 The English translations in this chapter are only for the readers' convenience; all analysis is based on the German original.
9 I used several routes to recruit respondents: referrals from acquaintances or third parties, advertisements on online websites, and calls for participation over email listservs and Facebook pages. This plurality of field access strategies helps to avoid bias in case selection.
10 The Abitur is the highest degree of the German secondary school system, granting access to university.

## References

Ainsworth-Darnell, J. W. & Downey, D. B. (1998). Assessing the oppositional culture explanation for racial/ethnic differences in school performance. *American Sociological Review*, 63(4), 536–53.

Alba, R. D., Sloan, J. & Sperling, J. (2011). The integration imperative: The children of low-status immigrants in the schools of wealthy societies. *Annual Review of Sociology*, 37, 395–415.

Archer, L., Pratt, S. D. & Phillips, D. (2001). Working-class men's constructions of masculinity and negotiations of (non)participation in higher education. *Gender and Education*, 13, 431–49.

Baumrind, D. (1996). The discipline controversy revisited. *Family Relations*, 45(4), 405.

Becker, D. & Birkelbach, K. (2010). Intelligenz und Schulleistung als Kontextmerkmale: Big-Fish-Little-Pond-oder Reflected-Glory-Effekt? Eine Mehrebenen-Analyse von Lehrerurteilen. In T. Beckers, K. Birkelbach, J. Hagenah & U. Rosar (eds), *Komparative empirische Sozialforschung* (pp. 113–41). Wiesbaden: VS Verlag für Sozialwissenschaften.

Becker, R. (2006). *Dauerhafte Bildungsungleichheiten als unerwartete Folge der Bildungsexpansion?* In A. Hadjar & R. Becker (eds), *Die Bildungsexpansion* (pp. 27–61). Wiesbaden: VS Verlag für Sozialwissenschaften.

Becker, R. & Hecken, A. E. (2009). Higher education or vocational training? *Acta Sociologica*, 52(1), 25–45.

Bengtson, V., Giarrusso, R., Mabry, J. B. & Silverstein, M. (2002). Solidarity, conflict, and ambivalence: Complementary or competing perspectives on intergenerational relationships? *Journal of Marriage and Family*, 64(3), 568–76.

Bengtson, V. L. & Troll, L. (1978). Youth and their parents: Feedback and intergenerational influence in socialization. In R. M. Lerner, G. B. Spanier & W. Aquilino (eds), *Child Influences on Marital and Family Interaction: A Life-span Perspective* (pp. 215–40). New York: Academic Press.

Berkemeyer, N., Bos, W. & Manitius, V. (2012). *Chancenspiegel: Zur Chancengerechtigkeit und Leistungsfähigkeit der deutschen Schulsysteme*. Gütersloh: Bertelsmann Stiftung, Institut für Schulentwicklungsforschung.

Bettie, J. (2002). Exceptions to the rule: Upwardly mobile white and Mexican American high school girls. *Gender & Society*, *16*(3), 403–22.

Blau, P. M. & Duncan, O. D. (1967). *The American Occupational Structure*. New York: Wiley.

Boudon, R. (1974). *Education, Opportunity, and Social Inequality: Changing Prospects in Western Society*. New York: Wiley.

Bourdieu, P. (1984). *Distinction: A Social Critique of the Judgement of Taste*. Cambridge, MA: Harvard University Press.

Bourdieu, P. & Passeron, J. C. (1990). *Reproduction in Education, Society and Culture* (2nd edn). Thousand Oaks, CA: Sage.

Bowles, S. & Gintis, H. (2002). "Schooling in capitalist America" Revisited. *Sociology of Education*, *75*(1), 1–18.

Brady, H. E. (2008). Causation and explanation in social science. In J. M. Box-Steffensmeier, H. E. Brady & D. Collier (eds), *The Oxford Handbook of Political Methodology* (pp. 217–70). Oxford: Oxford University Press.

Brady, H. E. & Collier, D. (eds). (2004). *Rethinking Social Inquiry: Diverse Tools, Shared Standards*. Berkeley, CA: Berkeley Institute of Governmental Studies Press.

Brake, A. (2006). *Das Sichtbare und das Unsichtbare: Bildungsstrategien als Strategien des Habitus*. In P. Büchner & A. Brake (eds), *Bildungsort Familie: Transmission von Bildung und Kultur im Alltag von Mehrgenerationenfamilien* (2006 edn). Wiesbaden: VS Verlag für Sozialwissenschaften.

Breen, R. & Goldthorpe, J. H. (1997). Explaining educational differentials. *Rationality and Society*, *9*(3), 275–305.

Breen, R. & Jonsson, J. O. (2005). Inequality of opportunity in comparative perspective: Recent research on educational attainment and social mobility. *Annual Review of Sociology*, *31*(1), 223–43.

Carter, P. L. (2003). Black cultural capital, status positioning, and schooling conflicts for low-income African American youth. *Social Problems*, *50*(1), 136–55.

Ceballo, R. (2004). From Barrios to Yale: The role of parenting strategies in Latino families. *Hispanic Journal of Behavioral Sciences*, *26*(2), 171 –86.

Chan, T. W. & Boliver, V. (2013). The grandparents effect in social mobility: Evidence from British birth cohort studies. *American Sociological Review*.

Coleman, J. S. (1988). Social capital in the creation of human capital. *The American Journal of Sociology*, *94*, 95–120.

Coleman, J. S., Campbell, W. Q., Hobson, C. J., McPartland, J., Mood, A. M. & Winfield, F. D. (1966). *Equality of Educational Opportunity*. Washington, DC: U.S. Government Printing Office.

Collins, W. A., Maccoby, E. E., Steinberg, L., Hetherington, E. M. & Bornstein, M. H. (2000). Contemporary research on parenting: The case for nature and nurture. *American Psychologist*, *55*(2), 218–32.

Coppedge, M. (1999). Thickening thin concepts and theories: Combining large N and small in comparative politics. *Comparative Politics*, *31*(4), 465–76.

Cortina, K. S., Maaz, K. & Baumert, J. (2008). Soziale und regionale Ungleichheit im deutschen Bildungssystem. In K. S. Cortina, J. Baumert, K. U. Mayer, L. Trommer & A. Leschinsky (eds), *Das Bildungswesen in der Bundesrepublik Deutschland: Strukturen und Entwicklungen im Überblick*. Reinbek: Rororo.

Crul, M. (2013). Snakes and ladders in educational systems: Access to higher education for second-generation Turks in Europe. *Journal of Ethnic and Migration Studies*, 1–19.

Crul, M., Schneider, J. & Lelie, F. (eds). (2012). *The European Second Generation Compared: Does the Integration Context Matter?* Amsterdam: University of Amsterdam Press.

Dika, S. L. & Singh, K. (2002). Applications of social capital in educational literature: A critical synthesis. *Review of Educational Research*, 72(1), 31–60.

DiMaggio, P. (1997). Culture and cognition. *Annual Review of Sociology*, 23(1), 263–87.

Ditton, H. (2008). Der Beitrag von Schule und Lehrern zur Reproduktion von Bildungsungleichheit. In R. Becker & W. Lauterbach (eds), *Bildung als Privileg* (pp. 247–75). Wiesbaden: VS Verlag für Sozialwissenschaften.

Domínguez, S. & Watkins, C. (2003). Creating networks for survival and mobility: Social capital among African-American and Latin-American low-income mothers. *Social Problems*, 50, 111–35.

Downey, D. B. (2008). Black/white differences in school performance: The oppositional culture explanation. *Annual Review of Sociology*, 34(1), 107–26.

El-Mafaalani, A. (2014). *Vom Arbeiterkind zum Akademiker: Über die Mühen des Aufstiegs durch Bildung*. Sankt Augustin/Berlin: Konrad-Adenauer-Stiftung.

Emirbayer, M. & Goodwin, J. (1994). Network analysis, culture, and the problem of agency. *The American Journal of Sociology*, 99(6), 1411–54.

Fordham, S. & Ogbu, J. U. (1986). Black students' school success: Coping with the burden of "acting white". *The Urban Review*, 18(3), 176–206.

Frye, M. (2012). Bright futures in Malawi's new dawn: Educational aspirations as assertions of identity. *American Journal of Sociology*, 117(6), 1565–624.

Geißler, R. (2006). *Die Sozialstruktur Deutschlands*. Wiesbaden: VS Verlag für Sozialwissenschaften.

George, A. L. & Bennett, A. (2005). *Case Studies and Theory Development in the Social Sciences*. Cambridge, MA: MIT Press.

Goertz, G. (2006). *Social Science Concepts: A User's Guide*. Princeton, NJ: Princeton University Press.

Goertz, G. & Mahoney, J. (2005). Two-level theories and fuzzy-set analysis. *Sociological Methods & Research*, 33(4), 497–538.

Goldthorpe, J. H. (1987). *Social Mobility and Class Structure in Modern Britain* (2nd edn). New York: Oxford University Press.

Gomolla, M. & Radtke, F.-O. (2009). *Institutionelle Diskriminierung: Die Herstellung ethnischer Differenz in der Schule* (3rd edn). Wiesbaden: VS Verlag für Sozialwissenschaften.

Harris, A. L. (2006). I (don't) hate school: Revisiting oppositional culture theory of blacks' resistance to schooling. *Social Forces*, 85(2), 797–833.

Herman, M. R. (2009). The black-white-other achievement gap: Testing theories of academic performance among multiracial and monoracial adolescents. *Sociology of Education*, 82(1), 20–46.

Higginbotham, E. & Weber, L. (1992). Moving up with kin and community: Upward social mobility for black and white women. *Gender & Society*, 6(3), 416–40.

Horvat, E. M., Weininger, E. B. & Lareau, A. (2003). From social ties to social capital: Class differences in the relations between schools and parent networks. *American Educational Research Journal*, 40(2), 319–51.

Isserstedt, W., Middendorff, E., Fabian, G. & Wolter, A. (2007). *Die wirtschaftliche und soziale Lage der Studierenden in der Bundesrepublik Deutschland. 18. Sozialerhebung des Deutschen Studentenwerks*. Bonn, Berlin: Bundesministerim für Bildung und Forschung.

Isserstedt, W., Middendorff, E., Kandulla, M., Borchert, L. & Leszczensky, M. (2010). *Die wirtschaftliche und soziale Lage der Studierenden in der Bundesrepublik Deutschland. 19. Sozialerhebung des Deutschen Studentenwerks*. Bonn, Berlin: Bundesministerium für Bildung und Forschung.

Jarrett, R. L. (1995). Growing up poor: The family experiences of socially mobile youth in low-income African American neighborhoods. *Journal of Adolescent Research, 10*(1), 111–35.

King, G., Keohane, R. O. & Verba, S. (1994). *Designing Social Inquiry: Scientific Inference in Qualitative Research.* Princeton, NJ: Princeton University Press.

King, V. (2009a). "... man gewöhnt sich daran, immer nur sich selber zu loben" Psychosoziale Anforderungen des Bildungsaufstiegs und der sozialen Mobilität junger Frauen. In T. Iwers-Stelljes (ed.), *Prävention, Intervention, Konfliktlösung: Pädagogisch-psychologische Förderung und Evaluation.* Wiesbaden: VS Verlag für Sozialwissenschaften.

King, V. (2009b). *Ungleiche Karrieren: Bildungsaufstieg und Adoleszenzverläufe bei jungen Männern und Frauen aus Migrantenfamilien.* In V. King & H.-C. Koller (eds), *Adoleszenz – Migration – Bildung: Bildungsprozesse Jugendlicher und junger Erwachsener mit Migrationshintergrund.* Wiesbaden: VS Verlag für Sozialwissenschaften.

King, V. & Koller, H.-C. (2009). *Adoleszenz als Möglichkeitsraum für Bildungsprozesse unter Migrationsbedingungen: Eine Einführung.* In V. King & H.-C. Koller (eds), *Adoleszenz – Migration – Bildung: Bildungsprozesse Jugendlicher und junger Erwachsener mit Migrationshintergrund.* Wiesbaden: VS Verlag für Sozialwissenschaften.

King, V., Koller, H.-C., Zölch, J. & Carnicer, J. (2011). *Bildungserfolg und adoleszente Ablösung bei Söhnen aus türkischen Migrantenfamilien.* Zeitschrift Für Erziehungswissenschaft, 14(4).

Lareau, A. (2003). *Unequal Childhoods: Class, Race, and Family Life.* Berkeley, CA: University of California Press.

Legewie, N. (2015). Puncturing inequalities: A configurational analysis of educational upward mobility (dissertation). Berlin: Humboldt University of Berlin.

Louie, V. S. (2012). *Keeping the Immigrant Bargain: The Costs and Rewards of Success in America.* New York: Russell Sage Foundation.

McAdams, D. P. (1996). Personality, modernity, and the storied self: A contemporary framework for studying persons. *Psychological Inquiry: An International Journal for the Advancement of Psychological Theory, 7*(4), 295–321.

McPherson, M., Smith-Lovin, L. & Cook, J. M. (2001). Birds of a feather: Homophily in social networks. *Annual Review of Sociology, 27*(1), 415–44.

Mahoney, J. & Goertz, G. (2004). The possibility principle: Choosing negative cases in comparative research. *American Political Science Review, 98*(4), 653–69.

Müller-Benedict, V. (2007). *Wodurch kann die soziale Ungleichheit des Schulerfolgs am stärksten verringert werden?* KZfSS Kölner Zeitschrift Für Soziologie Und Sozialpsychologie, 59(4), 615–39.

Ogbu, J. U. (2003). *Black American Students in an Affluent Suburb: A Study of Academic Disengagement.* Mahwah, NJ: Lawrence Erlbaum Associates.

Pomerantz, E. M., Moorman, E. A. & Litwack, S. D. (2007). The how, whom, and why of parents' involvement in children's academic lives: More is not always better. *Review of Educational Research, 77*(3), 373–410.

Portes, A. & Fernández-Kelly, P. (2008). No margin for error: Educational and occupational achievement among disadvantaged children of immigrants. *The ANNALS of the American Academy of Political and Social Science, 620*(1), 12–36.

Portes, A. & Rumbaut, R. G. (2001). *Legacies: The Story of the Immigrant Second Generation.* Berkeley, CA: University of California Press.

Pott, A. (2009). *Tochter und Studentin – Beobachtungen zum Bildungsaufstieg in der zweiten türkischen Migrantengeneration.* In V. King & H.-C. Koller (eds), *Adoleszenz – Migration – Bildung: Bildungsprozesse Jugendlicher und junger Erwachsener mit Migrationshintergrund.* Wiesbaden: VS Verlag für Sozialwissenschaften.

Raiser, U. (2007). *Erfolgreiche Migranten im deutschen Bildungssystem – es gibt sie doch: Lebensläufe von Bildungsaufsteigern türkischer und griechischer Herkunft*. Münster: LIT.

Sanders, J. M. (2002). Ethnic boundaries and identity in plural societies. *Annual Review of Sociology*, *28*, 327–57. Available at: http://doi.org/10.1146/annurev.soc.28.110601.140741

Schneider, T. (2011). Die Bedeutung der sozialen Herkunft und des Migrationshintergrundes für Lehrerurteile am Beispiel der Grundschulempfehlung. *Zeitschrift Für Erziehungswissenschaft*, *14*(3), 371–96.

Schütze, F. (1983). Biographieforschung und narratives Interview. *Neue Praxis*, *13*(3), 283–93.

Small, M. L. & Newman, K. (2001). Urban poverty after "The Truly Disadvantaged": The rediscovery of the family, the neighborhood, and culture. *Annual Review of Sociology*, *27*(1), 23–45.

Small, M. L., Harding, D. J. & Lamont, M. (2010). Reconsidering culture and poverty. *The Annals of The American Academy of Political and Social Science*, *629*(6), 6–27.

Smith, R. C. (2006). *Mexican New York: Transnational Lives of New Immigrants* (1st edn). Oakland, CA: University of California Press.

Smith, R. C. (2008). Horatio Alger lives in Brooklyn: Extrafamily support, intrafamily dynamics, and socially neutral operating identities in exceptional mobility among children of Mexican immigrants. *The ANNALS of the American Academy of Political and Social Science*, *620*(1), 270–90.

Smith, R. C. (2010). Strengthening qualitative research: Assimilation and the transition to early adulthood for Mexican Americans. Grant 1 2010–2012, National Science Foundation, Sociology Program.

Smith, R. C. (2014). Black Mexicans, conjunctural ethnicity, and operating identities long-term ethnographic analysis. *American Sociological Review*, 1–32.

Somers, M. R. (1994). The narrative constitution of identity: A relational and network approach. *Theory and Society*, *23*, 605–49.

Stocké, V. (2007). Explaining educational decision and effects of families' social class position: An empirical test of the Breen–Goldthorpe model of educational attainment. *European Sociological Review*, *23*(4), 505–19. Available at: http://doi.org/10.1093/esr/jcm014

Strauss, A. L. & Corbin, J. M. (1998). *Basics of Qualitative Research: Grounded Theory Procedures and Techniques* (2nd edn). Thousand Oaks, CA: Sage.

Swidler, A. (1986). Culture in action: Symbols and strategies. *American Sociological Review*, *51*(2), 273–86.

Tepecik, E. (2011). *Bildungserfolge mit Migrationshintergrund: Biographien bildungserfolgreicher MigrantInnen türkischer Herkunft*. Wiesbaden: VS Verlag für Sozialwissenschaften.

Vaisey, S. (2010). What people want: Rethinking poverty, culture, and educational attainment. *The ANNALS of the American Academy of Political and Social Science*, *629*(1), 75–101.

Vaisey, S. & Lizardo, O. (2010). Can cultural worldviews influence network composition? *Social Forces*, *88*(4), 1595–618. Available at: http://doi.org/10.1353/sof.2010.0009

Valenzuela, A. (1999). *Subtractive Schooling: US-Mexican Youth and the Politics of Caring*. Albany, NY: SUNY Press.

Willis, P. (1981). *Learning to Labor: How Working Class Kids Get Working Class Jobs* (Morningside Books). New York: Columbia University Press.

Wischmann, A. (2010). *Adoleszenz – Bildung – Anerkennung: Adoleszente Bildungsprozesse im Kontext sozialer Benachteiligung*. Wiesbaden: VS Verlag für Sozialwissenschaften.

Wright, E. O. (1997). *Class Counts: Comparative Studies in Class Analysis.* Cambridge: Cambridge University Press.

Young, A. A. (2006). *The Minds of Marginalized Black Men: Making Sense of Mobility, Opportunity, and Future Life Chances.* Princeton, NJ: Princeton University Press.

Young, A. A. (2010). New life for an old concept: Frame analysis and the reinvigoration of studies in culture and poverty. *The ANNALS of the American Academy of Political and Social Science, 629*(1), 53–74.

Zhou, M., Lee, J., Vallejo, J. A., Tafoya-Estrada, R. & Yang Sao Xiong (2008). Success attained, deterred, and denied: Divergent pathways to social mobility in Los Angeles's new second generation. *The ANNALS of the American Academy of Political and Social Science, 620*(1), 37–61.

# Part 3
# Peers, family and community

# 7 Parents, schools and diversity

## Challenges and opportunities for parental involvement in a changing global context

*Gill Crozier*

This chapter focuses on the role of parents' and families' relationships with schools in the development of participative and socially just engagement. The engagement with 'diversity', will be discussed as an important part of that process. The term 'diversity' is problematic in that it can mean many things but here I am using it to denote non-hegemonic, minority value positions and ways of being. Primarily, I will focus on ethnic minorities while recognizing that White working-class parents are also marginalized and frequently ignored by their children's schools. Drawing on the literature I will explore ways parents and families who are perceived as diverse are constructed and analyse how the embodiment of difference serves as a barrier to addressing the richness of the multi-ethnic school. I will locate this discussion within the context of the educational neoliberal market where a construction of the parent as consumer and the parent as compliant is key, and within a global context, which has given rise to transnationalism on a scale in Britain and Western Europe much larger than hitherto.

The impact of globalization in terms of migration has thus presented one of the greatest challenges to nation states and to their sense of identity. Global flows and transnationalism disrupt the security of the implied set of dominant values implicit in this statement, which historically have been ethnocentric: White, male and middle-class. These changes raise the question of how education systems should engage with ethnic diversity and this in turn poses the question of what set of values and whose values will be acknowledged, respected and given expression. Multiculturalism has been criticized by European governments and cited as responsible for riots and youth antagonisms (Wright & Taylor, 2011; Weaver, 2010). There has therefore been a shift towards the down-playing of difference and the reproduction of sameness. In Britain this has been manifested as a commitment to 'citizenship' as a homogeneous, hegemonic 'type'. For over a decade in Britain in the light of security threats from 'terrorist' attack and an emphasis on homogeneity, the focus on 'British values' has become a political mantra. The requirement for schools to teach what are promoted as 'British values', now defined as 'respect, tolerance, democracy, fairness and individual liberty' (DfE, 2011), has become an explicit curriculum requirement; the emphasis on 'British' seems to set them apart even though they are indeed universal values and indistinguishable from modern-day human values. In the summer of 2014 alarm was raised and accusations made that extremist Muslim community representatives were infiltrating school governing bodies with the aim of inculcating 'Islamist values/perspectives' in schools with a predominant Muslim school population (Wintour, 2014). The wars in the Middle East and the development of right-wing Islamic groups intent on asserting an Islamic State appear to be encroaching on the perceptions of the urban centres of Birmingham, Leeds, and so on. The hyperbolic reaction that has ensued has fuelled the climate of Islamophobia (Stone, 2004) and distorts the debate on diverse values. It constructs diversity as embodying the Other and feeds into the negative discourse on immigration as a problem and undesirable (Tomlinson, 2008). However, these current issues emphasize the importance for the engagement with value differences and debate over what this might be and point to a role for parents and schools.

Therefore, in this chapter I want to challenge the hysteria around 'values' and focus on the role of parents[1] and families in school to support their children's educational progress. Central to this is the development of mutual respect for all parents and the professionals and, as part of that, the development of civic engagement and participatory democracy, or communities of participation (Sahlberg, 2011). The chapter focuses on the role of parents' and families' relationships with schools in the development of these kinds of engagement.

The chapter therefore comprises consideration of:

- Issues of difference: engaging with diversity in schools.
- The importance of the role of minority ethnic and working-class parents as advocates for the educational well-being of young people.
- Addressing the obstacles to and constraints on parental involvement.
- Developing democratic communities of practice.

## Issues of difference, engaging with diversity

Before discussing the significance of diversity and how it can be engaged with, I want to consider what is meant by this term and to discuss the problems with it, together with the concept of 'culture' which is implicit in notions of diversity.

Diversity is manifested through physical differences in terms of colour, for example, and also ethnicity: cultural differences, manifested sometimes via, for example, language, dress, religion. Failure to recognize cultural, ethnic, racial diversity is to devalue the richness of society and to privilege White middle-class domination: the White norm. Anyone who does not fit into that norm is marginalized and disadvantaged. Specifically, this can lead to the alienation of Black and Minority Ethnic people, as well as White working-class, disabled people, and so on.

However, in many ways the use of the term 'diversity' has become meaningless (Ahmed, 2007). It is often used to give an appearance of recognizing different needs but it can be used to obfuscate what might be regarded as challenging issues.

*Parents, schools and diversity* 141

This can contribute to a hierarchy of oppression. In terms of race and ethnicity, in Britain, there has been and continues to be a move to eliminate these issues from the political and policy agenda. In Britain, the introduction of the Equality Act (2010), which has subsumed the Race Relations Amendment Act (2000), Disability and Gender Equality provision under a very broad umbrella is a clear example of this. By subsuming these forms of oppression under the generic banner of 'equality' it serves to diminish their significance and the possibilities for challenge. Each of these forms of oppression, discrimination and disadvantage need to be addressed in particular ways, and there are times when we need to foreground specific concerns and in this instance race, ethnicity and anti-racism (Hall, 1992).

When referring to diversity, people are often talking about difference and this usually means different from the White norm. Difference can carry with it a sense of inadequacy: if it is 'different', then it is different from something else – something which is implied as more permanent, more established, normative, accepted. Difference can be constructed as, or suggest that it is, something someone else 'brought to the nation' (Stratton & Ang, 1994). If so, how much do we want to draw attention to difference? To our own difference? To the difference of others? Therefore, is it relevant and/or appropriate to identify difference in the school and the classroom? The answer depends on why the identification is being made. In identifying difference, it is important that the difference is positive and celebrated as such. In doing so, it is the beginning of 'decentring'. That is to say that the world is not just White; White values are only a part of a whole. Whiteness frequently goes unrecognized and taken for granted (Leonardo, 2004). Hence, identifying difference is as much a recognition of Whiteness as it is of Black, or other minority ethnic differences and heritages (Garner, 2007). Therefore, in recognizing difference we have to critique and analyse the notion of Whiteness and White dominance. In a White dominated society, this is challenging for White people since it questions White identity and the centrality of this identity: it questions and disrupts White privilege. There is a clear need to address the invisibility of White privilege and White normalization, but this has to be part of a critical challenge to racism and a challenge to hegemonic culture and values. Sara Ahmed (2004) for example, has warned against making visible something which is already clearly visible and dominant, and unintentionally reifying and recentring rather than decentring Whiteness. As she says, it is necessary to make what can already be seen, visible in a different way.

Difference in educational discourses is frequently attributed to cultural differences. Culture, however, is a fluid concept and a problem with the term is that it tends to essentialize people. People, and Black and Minority Ethnic people in particular, are often described via cultural traits or ascribed a particular manifestation of culture as though that is their absolute identity. Black and Minority Ethnic people then come to be fixed by some often fairly arbitrary, putative cultural signifier. Any engagement with 'diversity' must recognize that culture is organic, evolutionary and reinterpreted by individuals. The term 'culture' is also used extremely loosely in the sense, for example, of talking about people of 'different cultures' when they often mean of different colour or ethnic or national heritage. 'Different culture' is used, I suggest, as a shorthand for identifying some perception of 'difference' often difference of skin colour or physiology, but it is often meaningless since it is based on a subjective perception.

Often a key criticism of multicultural education is the issue of representing 'all cultures' in the curriculum, for instance; this criticism is based on an incorrect premise. It is rather about having and generating respect, and about developing critical thinking and engagement with ideas. It is about decentring from the dominant White norm and recognizing the colour and ethnic diversity in society as a whole. It is not about recognizing a particular cultural facet and generalizing or attributing this to all minority groups. Likewise and following this logic, engaging with difference and diversity in an all-White school/classroom is also very important and relevant. On the basis of my argument all classrooms are diverse in a range of ways and not all ethnicities are visible. Moreover, part of addressing diversity, as I have said, is making Whiteness visible, raising consciousness about the ways Whiteness is hegemonic and overriding and, in so doing, addressing diversity as an act of decentring (Marx, 2006).

At the present time in Europe we seem to be a long way off decentring Whiteness. In fact, the developments around multiculturalism and anti-racism are being undermined not just by financial cutbacks, but also by changing attitudes. Currently, there is the view – as already stated – that multiculturalism in Europe has not worked. Consequently, there is pressure, once again, towards assimilation and sameness in the belief that this will lead to harmonious relations. The dominant desire for sameness and uniformity, and an ignoring of difference and diversity, is a central challenge to the debate on participatory democracy. Difference or differences as Stuart Hall (2000) has argued, are not stable phenomena and therefore organizing around difference in itself is problematic. Ethnic minority groups are not homogeneous, and are themselves intersected by factors and experiences affecting their expressions of ethnicity. How this is dealt with in terms of group participation is one of the key challenges. Anne Phillips (2000) also argues that instead of just being concerned with 'validating difference' (p. 40), our starting point should be an acceptance and understanding of difference as being the norm. Yet, in order to have a say in your child's education, you are obliged to adopt practices and behaviours that correspond to the 'norm'. She argues that parents who are perceived as 'different': 'will be accepted into the fold [. . .] only on condition that they highlight similarities, cover their differences, make themselves more like those who are already full citizens in order to be welcomed as their equals' (Phillips, 2000, p. 40).

This is the same for White working-class parents as well as those from ethnic minority groups but for ethnic minority group parents there is the additional oppression of racism to contend with. Nevertheless, an acceptance of difference is only part of it. Unless inequalities of opportunity and power relations are tackled, equal participation will be impossible. Equitable and democratic involvement of parents is an essential part of the process of achieving educational opportunities for young people, their own but also those of the community, but the basis upon which this can be achieved needs to be reappraised and reoriented. In order to do this the starting point has to be foregrounding the views and the experiences of Black and Minority Ethnic people themselves. Developing the right conditions for ensuring parental voice and involvement requires respect and the need to challenge power imbalances, challenge racism, and challenge structural and systemic barriers.

## Parents and families and school involvement: what, when and why?

The role of parents takes on different forms in relation to different constituencies: government; school/teacher; other parents; the student and at different historical moments according to policy shifts. Within educational policy internationally, parents have become very important in the eyes of governments, for a variety of reasons. At a time when greater social cohesion is seen to be needed (Cantle, 2001) parent–school relationships are seen by governments as one means of arresting the decline of parental/family influence on young people, a means of binding in parents to facilitate government agendas. In Britain, for example, parents are seen as essential to the operationalization of neoliberal policies of the marketization of education primarily through school choice (Crozier, 1998). The process of school choice involves schools competing for pupils (they receive payment on the basis of pupil numbers) and also parents competing against other parents for school places in the apparently high-status schools; this has made some parents favoured and quite powerful while marginalizing others (Butler & Hamnett, 2010). It has therefore often led to or exacerbated individualistic behaviours (Reay et al., 2011) which conflict with the attempts to develop collective practices.

From the school and teachers' perspectives, parental involvement has tended to be regarded as an adjunct to the teacher and the requirements of the school (Crozier, 2000). Parents of primary children are expected to support their child's key skills' development, get their child to school on time and support fund-raising activities; at the high school level the focus is more on exam preparation, completing homework and ensuring 'good' behaviour. The emphasis has been on 'assimilation' rather than on sharing or discussing values. Schools want and indeed need harmonious relations but they want these on their terms. Given the competition between schools, the schools seek to build up a reputation, produce excellent exam results, and maintain their reputation and position in the league tables. This is one of their chief motivations for parent–school relationships; they need parents to support them in this endeavour and, moreover, they need parents to endorse this and identify with it. Not all schools can do this where they have more diverse families, in that not all families want to fit in, in the sense of relinquishing their identities. Parents are frequently constructed as a homogeneous group in the image of the White, middle-class parent. Those who fail to fit that model are often problematized as recalcitrant and thereby ignored and silenced (see, for example, Bhopal, 2011). Over ten years ago Levitas (1998) wrote of the policy initiatives to bind in parents in the bid to achieve what were termed 'common purposes'. Certain parents were seen as a threat to the neoliberal policies of the stakeholder and the development of the 'active citizen'. Levitas (2012) today writes of similar themes critiquing the policies targeted at the so-called 'troubled families'.

The notion of the 'good' parent, as Carol Vincent coined it, (1996) seems to prevail. The active parent who chooses her or his child's school is regarded as good and it is most likely White and middle-class parents who have the requisite capitals – cultural, social and economic to make effective and appropriate school choices (Ball, 2003). These types of 'acceptable and desirable' parents are not, however, always 'good' for the teacher. Schools and teachers do like middle-class parents because they are more likely to be 'like them', to share the same values and have the same expectations and ambitions for their children (Crozier, 2000). However, these parents are also most likely to be powerful, confident and demanding of teachers. Not only do powerful middle-class parents call schools and teachers to account and may threaten the position of the teacher, they are also competing with less powerful and influential parents for scarce resources, such as the teachers' time (see Crozier, 2000), the top sets/tracks, and the specialist opportunities such as the Gifted and Talented scheme (Reay *et al.*, 2011). For middle-class parents, the school experience and the home experience are frequently seamless (Edwards & Alldred, 2000). They engage in the process of concerted cultivation enhancing and reinforcing school practices, ideas, the curriculum: underpinning the dominant, hegemonic values (Crozier *et al.*, 2011; Lareau, 2003). White middle-class parents are therefore advantaged in their influence on school values and they are most likely to contribute to the social reproduction of hegemonic values (see Crozier *et al.*, 2009 and Reay *et al.*, 2011). These powerful positions of White middle-class parents therefore have implications for Black and Minority Ethnic parents asserting their perspectives.

Engaging with the education system whether it is at the level of school choice or supporting their child's academic progress, requires both knowledge of the education system, how the market operates and what exactly is involved in the educational process that would support their child. Social class and ethnicity, in particular, are highly significant in parent–school engagement (Bourdieu & Passeron, 1977; Rollock *et al.*, 2011). Both of these social identities ensure that school relationships and levels of involvement are experienced differently and differentially. The involvement of parents which lends itself to the further empowerment of the already influential and privileged parent, exposes a number of contradictions with respect to the alleged desire for civic engagement and active parental involvement. The promotion of individualized parental practice and the homogenization and thus deracialization of parents, are two of the most stark (Crozier, 2001).

Research into classed and raced parent–school relationships has shown that Black and Minority Ethnic parents are generally not perceived as the 'good' or particularly 'desirable', parent. Indeed, research demonstrates a series of negative and stereotypical views of ethnic minority parents held by teachers (see, for example, Bhatti, 1999; Cork, 2005). Moreover, more recent research demonstrates that race is disadvantaging irrespective of social class (Archer, 2010; Rollock *et al.*, 2011; Vincent *et al.*, 2012), which adds a further dimension to the concept of social reproduction.

## Barriers to involvement

Much has been written about Black and Minority Ethnic parents and indeed White working-class parents not being involved in their children's school. However, substantial research has shown that this is often the result of exclusionary and discriminatory attitudes on the part of teachers, together with unhelpful administrative arrangements of events and either unrealistic expectations of involvement or lack of communication about involvement. Minority Ethnic parents may not be fully respected; their values and cultural heritage may not be regarded as relevant or important; the parents may feel inhibited to meet teachers, and so on. In a project involving the professional development of teachers and their work with Roma families, as part of the INSETRoM project funded by the Comenius European Commission Lifelong Learning Programme (2007–2009) conducted in the North East of England, there was a clear lack of communication and understanding between the parents and the teachers. While language issues due to the parents' lack of English language (and teachers' Czech) and a lack of interpreters was obviously central to this, parents' behaviours were misunderstood or misrecognized. For example, parents or family members brought their children to the classroom door each morning and congregated there. Teachers reported that they saw this as a hindrance rather than as an opportunity to draw the parents in and get to know the families better (Crozier et al., 2009). Parental involvement in schools is based upon teachers' or the schools' definitions of involvement, partnership, cooperation and trust. Some minority ethnic parents may not be in a position to relate to this, where they are not sufficiently confident to participate. The lack of the 'right kind of' cultural capital (Bourdieu & Passeron, 1977) may hamper Black and Minority Ethnic parents' ability to make their voices heard, but it is overwhelmingly clear that the prevalence of racism is a key obstacle. This becomes particularly clear where the Black and Minority Ethnic parents are themselves middle class and endowed with the necessary capitals and yet still find they are silenced, marginalized and disempowered, as referred to above (Rollock et al., 2011).

The opportunities, therefore, for Black and Minority Ethnic parents to intervene successfully on behalf of their children, or at least to be involved on their own terms, seem limited. Additionally, this scenario is likely to be compounded by other boundaries and barriers for some parents such as lack of knowledge of the education system, limited English language, limited education, lack of confidence (Crozier & Davies, 2007). As Gillborn and Youdell (2000) point out, schools select pupils for different destinations and do so increasingly in order to maintain their positions in the league tables. With the high visibility of school performance and the intensive competition between schools they are, for example, unlikely to allow the disempowered Black parent to interfere if they decide to put a child in a low set.

The research evidence suggests that many schools are not sufficiently welcoming to help the parents overcome their own apprehensions or lack of confidence, or even anxiety about how they will be received as an ethnic minority. The schools have also failed to address racist abuse towards their children (see Crozier & Davies, 2007), which undermines parents' confidence. These scenarios indicate exclusion, embedded with negative classed and raced stereotypes, and resistance to change. Parents are likely to be reluctant to enter schools which seem hostile, albeit unintentionally (Hong, 2011). The evidence therefore points to the urgent need to reconsider parent–school relationships, and seek ways of achieving more equitable and meaningful involvement.

## Doing parental involvement differently: developing dialogic and communities of practice

In this final section of the chapter, I want to redress the balance of this argument around parental involvement, away from the negative deficit model of Black and Minority Ethnic parents, to assert the contribution that those seemingly 'less visible' parents actually play and could play. It is the recognition of these parents and their contribution that relates to the issue of 'diversity'. My chief concern around parent–school 'involvement' is that parents can develop their role as advocates for and supporters of their children's education. Research has shown that this is the type of role that secondary/high school aged young people wish their parents to play; as they say, 'they want them to be there for them' (Crozier, 2000) as and when necessary. Parental involvement should be about parents having a voice in what they want for their children and for the school, and, as Warren and Hong (2009) have argued, parental involvement is about helping other children and not just one's own. If we recognize the school as an important element of the local community, then parents' role in this is even more salient or could be; it could become transformative involving social consciousness development and democratic engagement for change for the common good.

However, in order to achieve this it will be necessary to engage with and address the range of issues that I have discussed and that act as barriers to this kind of participation. Also, schools and teachers often forget to see the child and the family as individuals who have their own sets of beliefs and values, desires and responsibilities. Many parents have talked about the burden of school requests when they have their own family affairs to attend to (Crozier, 2000). A further example of this is the tension between, for example, Muslim families and their religious practices (such as children's attendance at the mosque after school) and the demands of the school (such as homework clubs and so on) (Bhatti, 1999; Crozier, 2004). By contrast, teachers often focus on Black and Minority Ethnic families' 'culture' as something negative, and interfering with the child's educational opportunities and progress: something Other rather than as a part of the school and local community. In our INSETRoM project referred to above, for example, this led to teachers' insistence of the need for 'cultural background' knowledge of the families, making the mistake of viewing culture as fixed and monolithic. The problematics of this and its danger of tokenism have been well rehearsed by others (e.g. Troyna, 1993). It is notable, however, how such erroneous beliefs prevail, but also indicates their importance and significance of the need to challenge these in order to forge change of practice.

Although much has been written about some parents' non-involvement in school, there is also substantial research about parents' attempts to 'have a say' in representing the interests of their children. Rollock *et al.*'s (2011) research already cited is a recent example, Archer's work (2010) is another, Cork (2005) demonstrates a range of parent and community group support initiatives, and Vincent (2000) discusses parent grass-roots initiatives and the display of active citizenship by parents attempting to make significant contributions to their children's school experience. Crozier's (2005) research with Black British Caribbean heritage parents, showed the concerted work and emotional labour expended by the parents who were marked out as troublesome parents with troublesome children. These parents not only tried to engage teachers in dialogue, they paid for private tuition for their children and even attended evening classes with their children to support their academic achievement, albeit frequently to no avail. The studies just mentioned challenge the misrecognition (Fraser, 1997) of Black and Minority Ethnic parents as being indifferent towards their children's education and school, or indeed unwilling and unable to contribute. They do, however, demonstrate further the challenges of exclusion these parents face as well as the diverse possibilities and manifestations of 'doing parental involvement differently'.

In his account of the journey towards a relatively successful Finnish Education system, Sahlberg (2011) outlines a number of important conditions, which have to be addressed if this is to be achieved – inequality of wealth and social capital are two central factors. However, part of the success is also attributed to the involvement of parents and the creation of school, parent and community organization which facilitates equitable and democratic participation. In their studies Warren and Hong (2009) and Hong *et al.* (2009) present analyses of an extensive school–family–community initiative in North West Chicago (Logan Square neighbourhoods) which they argue has established parent initiatives that have transformed parent leadership and participation on an equitable basis with teachers and other education professionals in the neighbourhood schools. The on-going programme of school–family and community engagement is based on principles of equity and a programme of training for parents. Although the focus is on parents working with teachers in the classroom, the emphasis is on working alongside the teacher and teaching assistants in relation to, for example, supporting children with their reading. Through the various initiatives and training opportunities parents are supported to meet together to get to know each other and build a strong sense of community (Hong *et al.*, 2009). The interrelationship between the importance of educational issues and those of the community was also recognized and generated. A strong sense of trust was developed and parents were enabled to develop as leaders and thus exercise their voice. The emphasis here is clearly on developing equity and shifting the balance of power.

## Concluding comments

Teacher professionalism has been used as a defence from parental 'interference' or criticism, and as a mechanism for reinforcing the boundaries between home and school. Perceived parental interference in the professional's domain is a major tension for schools wanting to encourage parental involvement. Many parents, particularly less powerful parents and those from minority ethnic backgrounds, in fact recognize and respect the teacher as expert (Denessen *et al.*, 2001). They trust the teacher and the professional educator but seek a more dialogic relationship.

As I have already argued, a major obstacle to Black and Minority Ethnic parents' productive school involvement is racism and stereotypical perceptions and expectations. In Britain, policies to challenge racist discrimination and stereotypical attitudes have been significantly diminished and debates around race issues in policy and school education developments are now virtually non-existent. Pre-service and in-service teachers are therefore given little if any support in addressing diversity and developing their own positive attitudes towards difference. The ideas suggested above around collective action may seem inadequate in the face of these structural obstacles. However, it is essential to hold on to the idea of the power of the subject to transform and change structural conditions and, as Freire (1972) said, to recognize that no conditions are absolute or static and closed. There is no given reality but, as Shaull said (1972), 'it is rather a problem to be worked on and solved' (p. 12). Individuals cannot do this alone. It is necessary to organize and work collectively but again, as Freire showed, individuals need to be supported and given preparation to enable her/him to engage in these ways. Indeed, Freire recognized the importance of the relationship between the individual and society/the world.

While no system is perfect and needs to be continually generated and reappraised, the Logan Square initiative seems to offer exciting and progressive possibilities for parent and family participative and democratic engagement with school and community. It suggests possibilities for empowerment without which parents will remain in a subjugated position and recognition of their beliefs and values will remain marginalized or ignored. This type of democratic participation provides an opportunity for educational professionals and parents and families to develop mutual understanding and insights, and benefit from this sharing of perspectives. Of course, this suggestion challenges White hegemonic norms and requires the decentring of Whiteness argued for earlier. However, the proposal is not about an absolute acceptance of anything and everything but rather, it is about exploring difference and diversity with a view to generating more informed and enriched perspectives.

## Note

1   I am using the term 'parents' to denote not only parents but also carer or guardian and also would like to note that parental involvement in many cultural groups is a family relationship/enterprise, rather than simply mother or father (Crozier & Davies, 2006).

# References

Ahmed, S. (2004). Declarations of whiteness: The non-performativity of anti-racism. *Borderlands e-journal*, *3*(2). Retrieved from: www.borderlands.net.au/vol3no2.2004.

Ahmed, S. (2007). The language of diversity. *Ethnic and Racial Studies*, *30*(2), 235–56.

Archer, L. (2010). 'We raised it with the Head': The educational practices of minority ethnic middle-class families. *British Journal of Sociology of Education*, *31*(4), 449–69.

Ball, S. J. (2003). *Class Strategies and the Education Market*. London and New York: RoutledgeFalmer.

Bhatti, G. (1999). *Asian Children at Home and at School*. London and New York: Routledge.

Bhopal, K. (2011). 'This is a school, it's not a site': Teacher's attitudes towards gypsy and traveller pupils in schools in the UK. *British Educational Research Journal*, *33*(3), 465–83.

Bourdieu, P. & Passeron, J. C. (1977). *Reproduction in Education, Society and Culture*. London, California and New Delhi: Sage Publications.

Butler, T. & Hamnett, C. (2010). *Ethnicity, Class and Aspiration: Understanding London's New Eastend*. Cambridge: Polity Press.

Cantle, T. (2001). The community cohesion report. London: The Stationery Office.

Cork, L. (2005). *Supporting Black Parents and Children*. London and New York: Routledge.

Crozier, G. (1998). Parents and schools: Partnership or surveillance? *Journal of Educational Policy*, *13*(1), 185–95.

Crozier, G. (2000). *Parents and Schools: Partners or Protagonists?* Stoke-on-Trent and Sterling, VA: Stylus Publishing/Trentham Books.

Crozier, G. (2001). Excluded parents: The deracialization of parental involvement. *Race Ethnicity and Education*, *4*(4), 329–41.

Crozier, G. (2004). ESRC End of Award report: Parents, children and schools: Asian families' perspectives (R000239671).

Crozier, G. (2005). 'Beyond the call of duty': The impact of racism on black parents' involvement in their children's education. In G. Crozier & D. Reay (eds), *Activating Participation: Parents and Teachers Working Towards Partnership*. Stoke-on-Trent and Sterling, VA: Stylus Publishing/Trentham Books.

Crozier, G. & Davies, J. (2006). Family matters: A discussion of the role of the extended family in supporting the children's education, with specific reference to families of Bangladeshi and Pakistani heritage, in the UK. *The Sociological Review*, *54*(4), 677–94.

Crozier, G. & Davies, J. (2007). Hard to reach parents or hard to reach schools? A discussion of home-school relations, with particular reference to Bangladeshi and Pakistani parents. *British Educational Research Journal*, *33*(3), 295–313.

Crozier, G., Davies, J. & Szymanski, K. (2009). Education, identity and Roma families: Teachers' perspectives and engagement with INSETRoM training. *Intercultural Education*, *20*(6), 537–48.

Crozier, G., Reay, D. & James, D. (2011). Making it work for them: White middle-class families and working-class schools. *International Studies in Sociology of Education*, *21*(3), 199–216.

Denessen, E., Driessen, G., Smit, F. & Sleegers, P. (2001). Culture differences in education: Implications for parental involvement and educational policies. In F. Smit, K. van der Wolf & P. Sleegers (eds), *A Bridge to the Future: Collaboration Between Parents, Schools and Communities* (pp. 55–65). Nijmegen: ITS.

DfE (Department for Education). (2011). PREVENT Strategy. Cm8092. London: The Stationery Office. Retrieved from: www.communities.gov.uk/publications/communities/preventstrategy.

Edwards, R. & Alldred, P. (2000). A typology of parental involvement in education centring on children and young people: Negotiating familialisation, institutionalisation and individualism. *British Journal of Sociology of Education*, *21*(3), 435–55.

Fraser, N. (1997). *Justice Interruptus: Critical Reflections on the "Postsocialist" Condition*. London and New York: Routledge.

Freire, P. (1972). *Pedagogy of the Oppressed*. London: Penguin Books.

Garner, S. (2007). *Whiteness*. London and New York: Routledge.

Gillborn, D. & Youdell, D. (2000). *Rationing Education*. Buckingham and Philadelphia, PA: Open University Press.

Hall, S. (1992). New ethnicities. In J. Donald & A. Rattansi (eds), *Race, Culture and Difference*. London, Thousand Oaks, CA and New Delhi: Sage Publications, in association with the Open University.

Hall, S. (2000). Multicultural citizens, monocultural citizenship? In N. Pearce & J. Hallgarten (eds), *Tomorrow's Citizens: Critical Debates in Citizenship Education*. London: Institute for Public Policy Research.

Hong, S. (2011). *A Cord of Three Strands: A New Approach to Parent Engagement in Schools*. Cambridge, MA: Harvard Educational Publishing Group.

Hong, S., Warren, M. R. & Mapp, K. L. (2009). *Building Parent Leadership Through Community Organizing: The Logan Square neighbourhood Association's Parent Mentor Program in Chicago*. Harvard, MA: Harvard Education Press.

INSETRoM (In-service Training for Roma Inclusion). (2007–2009). Comenius European Commission Lifelong Learning Programme (134018-LLP-1-CY-COMENIUS-CMP).

Lareau, A. (2003). *Unequal Childhoods*. Berkeley, Los Angeles, CA and London: University of California Press.

Leonardo, Z. (2004). Whiteness studies. In G. Ladson Billings & D. Gillborn (eds), *Multicultural Education*. London and New York: RoutledgeFalmer.

Levitas, R. (1998). *The Inclusive Society? Social Exclusion and New Labour*. London: Macmillan.

Levitas, R. (2012). There may be trouble ahead: What we know about the 120,000 'troubled' families. Parents and social exclusion in the UK. Working Paper 3: Swindon: Economic and Social Research Council.

Marx, S. (2006). *Revealing the Invisible*. New York, London: Routledge.

Phillips, A. (2000). Second class citizenship. In N. Pearce & J. Hallgarted (eds), *Tomorrow's Citizens: Critical Debates in Citizenship Education*. London Institute for Public Policy Research.

Reay, D., Crozier, G. & James, D. (2011). *White middle-class identities and urban schooling*. Hampshire: Palgrave Macmillan.

Rollock, N., Vincent, C., Gillborn, D. & Ball, S. J. (2011). The public identities of the black middle classes: Managing race in public spaces. *Sociology*, *45*(6), 1078–93.

Sahlberg, P. (2011). *Finnish Lessons*. New York & London: Teachers College Press and Columbia University.

Shaull, R. (1972). Foreword. In P. Freire. *Pedagogy of the Oppressed*. London: Penguin Books.

Stone, R. (2004). *Islamophobia, Issues, Challenges and Action*. Stoke-on-Trent and Sterling, VA: Trentham Books.

Stratton, J. & Ang, I. (1994). Multicultural imagined communities: Cultural difference and national identity in Australia and the USA. *Journal of Media & Cultural Studies*, *8*(2), 124–58.

Tomlinson, S. (2008). *Race and Education: Policy and Politics in Britain*. Berkshire: Open University Press/McGraw-Hill.

Troyna, B. (1993). *Racism and Education*. Buckingham and Philadelphia, PA: Open University Press.

Vincent, C. (1996). *Parents and Teacher: Power and Participation*. London: Falmer Press.

Vincent, C. (2000). *Including Parents?* Buckingham and Philadelphia, PA: Open University Press.

Vincent, C., Rollock, N., Ball, S. & Gillborn, D. (2012). Being strategic, being watchful, being determined: Black middle-class parents and schooling. *British Journal of Sociology of Education*, 33(3), 337–54.

Warren, M. R. & Hong, S. (2009). More than services: Community organising and community schools. In R. Deslandes (ed.), *International Perspectives on Contexts, Communities and evaluated Innovative Practices*. London and New York: Routledge.

Weaver, M. (2010). Angela Merkel: German multiculturalism has 'utterly failed'. *The Guardian*, 17 October.

Wintour, P. (2014). Trojan horse inquiry: 'A coordinated agenda to impose hardline Sunni Islam'. Retrieved from: www.guardian.com/news-uk/j2014/uly/birmingham-schools-inquiry.

Wright, O. & Taylor, J. (2011). Cameron: My war on multiculturalism. *The Independent*, 5 February.

# 8 Aspirations disclosed

The case of Turkish-Belgian parents in Brussels

*Fatma Zehra Çolak*

## Introduction

Migration demands adaptation to the culture and socio-structural conditions of the country the migrant settles in – to the extent that s/he desires to participate in the society of destination. This affects men, women and children in divergent ways, since they usually experience acculturation processes in different milieus, with specific roles ascribed to them by different actors. The process of adaptation intensively impacts their feelings, aspirations, dreams and ideals. Migration research is a dynamic domain of study that includes quantitative and macro-level research on the economic and political aspects of migration, involving, among other factors, labour markets, housing and education (Beck, *et al.*, 2012; Zimmermann & Constant, 2013), as well as qualitative research focusing on the personal dimensions of migration, dealing with the subjective feelings and contextualized experiences of people and analysing the interactions that take place between the meso- and micro-levels (Catalano, 2013; Kloppenburg & Peters, 2012; McFadden *et al.*, 2014; Thulin & Vilhelmson, 2014; Timmerman *et al.*, 2014). Belgium, where this study is based, has also shown strong advances in migration research in recent years, with considerable interest in marriage and partner choice, different forms of identities and ethnic relations, empowerment, educational pathways and school experiences (Casier *et al.*, 2013; Dierckx & Van Dam, 2014; Kochuyt, 2012; Piot *et al.*, 2010). Still, there is a continuous need to approach the topic of migration from diverse perspectives, using original concepts that offer new perspectives on the lives of our interlocutors. This study not only aims to take such a new approach, but also fills a gap in the research by focusing on Brussels; there are still to date very few studies using Brussels as a case study, particularly studies investigating the aspirations of parents with different ethnic backgrounds.

In this chapter, I develop a theoretical approach that is 'sensitive to issues of people's outlook to the world, their sense of expectation and their lived experience' as Graw & Schielke (2012, p. 12–13) inspire scholars to do. They suggest to 'turn towards more existentially sensitive ways of researching', in order to better comprehend the lives of those who have been influenced by the migration processes (2012, p. 9). They elaborate on the notion of *horizon* to theorize immigration as an act that goes beyond moving from one place to another, thereby shedding light on the 'need for theoretical directions that help to make sense of the processes of imagination and expectation' (2012, p. 13). Having chosen the concept of *aspiration* as the theoretical framework for the very same reason, I aim to examine the personal experiences, expectations and dreams of parents in relation to their children's education and elucidate how such a sensitive concept can be utilized in analysis.

Aspiration as a concept offers a useful framework to analyse the dreams and prospects of parents, while simultaneously framing their actual views about the education of their children. As a concept, aspiration also offers a dynamic approach to the views and feelings of parents, seeing them as elements in flux, open to be shaped by a variety of interactions, experiences, encounters and opportunities (Hlalele, 2012). This reveals the subjective and anti-essentialist nature of aspiration; it is an intricate helix of the individual's interconnected perspectives, expectations and views entwined with a number of structural and personal factors (Hlalele, 2012; Macleod, 2009). This study distinguishes long-term aspirations from short-term aspirations of mothers. Long-term aspirations are broad wishes informed primarily by metaphysical and cultural norms and values, while short-term aspirations pertain to *choices* made in order to realize the long-term aspirations (Appadurai, 2004).

## Why study the aspirations of migrant parents?

The literature on educational expectations and aspirations often focuses on children of immigrants (Minello & Barban, 2012). Research on aspirations, specifically within the educational, sociological and economical spheres (Sellar & Gale, 2011), has mostly focused on educational and parental aspirations in relation to the children's level of achievement, social class, age, ethnicity, gender, equity and peer influences (Beck *et al.*, 2012; Carpenter, 2008; Genicot & Ray, 2009; Jacob & Wilder, 2010; Portes *et al.*, 2010). On the other hand, investigating parents' aspirations using a conceptual and theoretical lens that would provide a closer and more sensitive look into their personal stories, experiences, dreams, lives and thoughts has not evoked much interest.

Aspirations act as 'a conceptual link between structure and agency in that they are firmly rooted in individual proclivity (agency), but also are acutely sensitive to perceived societal constraints (structure)' (Macleod, 2009, p. 139). The relationship between habitus and opportunity structure is not direct. In fact, the way in which structures are internalized by individuals is personal, and the internalization process itself is impacted by other factors (Macleod, 2009). In his research, Macleod builds a direct relation between aspirations and opportunities on one hand, and the migrant-individual's perceptions on the other. He states that aspirations provide a mediating platform between the 'individual desires' and 'what society can offer' (2009, p. 7). Accordingly, there is an intimate relationship between aspirations and available options. Furthermore, the role of the individual capacity in relation to 'functioning of aspiring' should not be ignored (Hart, 2012, p. 99). The question of whether objective structures outweigh the individual capacity to aspire has led to several discussions. Following Bourdieu & Passeron, one may consider the dual role the school environment can play; on one hand, it allows dominant classes to achieve higher academic levels and acquire more economic capital, while on the other hand, it prevents lower classes from gaining those same standards. Bourdieu & Passeron further claim that students from lower classes are rooted in a particular habitus, shaped by their lived experiences in their own social world, which strengthen and reproduce inequality by making them develop a conventional response to objective structures (1977). However, Bourdieu & Passeron's emphasis on objective structures and their limiting consequences has been criticized. For instance, Macleod's critique was that Bourdieu and Passeron's theory lacked space for 'opposition, challenge, delegitimation, diversity and nonconformity' (2009, p. 14).

## Aspirations: a theoretical tool

Aspirations, according to Macleod, are a reflection of the individual's view of his/her 'own chances for getting ahead', and result from the 'internalization of objective probabilities' (2009, p. 15). He argues that 'they are not the product of a rational analysis but acquired in the habitus of the individual' (Macleod, 2009, p. 15). From another perspective, the habitus as evoked by Hlalele is informed by socialization and acculturation processes taking place within the societal structure; it is neither the 'result of free will, nor determined by structures', but created by the complex interplay of several feedback processes or 'dispositions'. These dispositions, he adds, condition one's intentions and perceptions, since they are both 'shaped by past events and structures' and 'shape current practices and structures' (2012, p. 269).

From another angle, Appadurai claims aspirations to be related to 'wants, preferences, choices and calculations' (2004, p. 83). He argues that aspirations can never be seen as separate from the social life, since it is not possible to imagine an individual existing in a vacuum outside a societal sphere. Aspirations remain 'part of some sort of system of ideas which locates them in a larger map of local ideas and beliefs' (2004, p. 84). They are simultaneously transformed into the immediate choices in relation to the norms, which appear as part of metaphysical systems, cultural values and structural realities.

Undoubtedly, aspirations provide a flexible transition between the past and the future. Being shaped by past experiences and cultural norms, aspirations become a form of projection that informs future orientations (Appadurai, 2004). Thus, researching the formation of aspirations makes it possible to develop a future-oriented approach that is not isolated from the past, but rather informed by it.

Furthermore, Appadurai emphasizes a link of proportionality between high levels of aspirations and high economic status, in the sense that high resources increase one's awareness of 'objects of aspiration'. He links the capacity to aspire to 'a dense combination of nodes and pathways' on which there is a flow back and forth between abstract values and concrete choices (2004, p. 85). It is, however, important to note that the relationship between aspirations and choices is not direct. Different aspirations may lead to the same choices, while the same aspirations may result in different choices, depending on available objective structures in the society and how these aspirations are being realized by the individual in the real world depending on his or her capabilities (Hart, 2012). Aspirations are thus not only fed by

156   F. Z. Çolak

desires, wants and capacity but also by structural factors, background characteristics and social networks (Appadurai, 2004; Genicot & Ray, 2009).

Having outlined the theoretical framework of the study, I will now proceed to the empirical sections to demonstrate how aspirations are intertwined with various dynamics and how mothers, gathered around one school space, develop their aspirations for their children's education in relation to diverse determinants.

## L'Ecole des Etoiles

My first encounter with l'Ecole des Etoiles came about unexpectedly in a conference on education organized by Fedactio[1] (Federation of Active Associations in Belgium) in 2012. It was an ideal place to look closer into issues like education of migrants' children since the school had a high percentage of students with non-Belgian (or rather immigrant) background.

L'Ecole des Etoiles is a primary school established in 2005 in the municipality of Schaerbeek, in Brussels. The school has 60 working personnel, 380 students in its primary section and 180 students in its secondary one. Enrolment data shows that 8 per cent of students are Belgian, 58 per cent are Turkish-Belgian, 32 per cent are Moroccan-Belgian and 2 per cent from other nationalities.

It is a private/non-state, non-confessional school (*enseignement libre non-confessionnel*) subsidized by the French Community. At l'Ecole des Etoiles education is based on principles of free enquiry or specific educational theories, such as Freinet and Decroly schools. This category of schools is characteristically private, grant-aided and non-denominational (Eurydice 2009/2010). A member of FELSI (*La Fédération des Etablissements Libres Subventionnés Indépendants*), l'Ecole des Etoiles stands alone as the only *libre non-confessionel* school in Brussels. Other regional schools are *libre confessionel* (mostly Catholic).

L'Ecole des Etoiles is a member of Fedactio, a Turkish-Belgian association founded in Brussels in 2010. The school is known to be founded by people inspired by the Hizmet Movement, which is a voluntary, faith-inspired, transnational civil society movement founded on the principles and ideas of Fethullah Gulen, a renowned Turkish-Muslim preacher and scholar (Cetin, 2009; Ebaugh, 2010; Khan, 2011; Yavuz & Esposito, 2003). People inspired by the ideas of Gulen have supported the foundation of four Lucerna schools in the Dutch-speaking part of Belgium, with a total of 1,230 enrolled students, and one in Brussels with 340 enrolled students. L'Ecole des Etoiles is the only French school founded with the support of those inspired people.

There is often an emphasis by directors and by some parents on the idea that L'Ecole des Etoiles is open to everyone and does not belong to the Turkish or any other community. According to them, it has a philosophical base which is open to all religious and philosophical convictions. It is implied that the school is subsidized by the French community, meaning Turkish-Belgian parents, civil society organizations, entrepreneurs and common people. Mr Demir, the director of the primary school, only admits he is inspired by the ideas of Gulen when I ask him if there is any connection between his school and the movement, adding that his affiliation does not necessarily have any effect on the way the school is run. While it is true that one does not find the books or the pictures of Gulen being shown in the school, one would be hard pressed to deny the existence of a particular ethos in the school. Mr Demir says that the goal of bringing *conscience morale* (moral conscience) back into the educational sphere lies at the foundation of his school, explaining further that this refers to infusing the relationships between teachers, parents and students with qualities of caring, sacrifice, respect, tolerance and understanding.

Although he is clearly inspired by the books and ideas of Gulen, he says there is no intention or desire to implant an Islamic ideology into the school; the focus is rather on moral cultivation and representation – we can infer here that he believes these qualities to go beyond specific religious and cultural expression. He explained during the interview that the definition of the moral in that context encompasses the universally acknowledged human values:

> 'Gulen talks about unconditional love and affection towards other people. He mentions the significance of altruism. We are motivated by the desire to gain the approval of God. We may be motivated by a religious desire but the purpose is not the transmission of religion. We focus on loving people, and providing peaceful spaces for them, in a way addressing the needs of their conscience, too. This gives peace to people.'

According to Mr Demir, Gulen offers a new and unique interpretation of Islam, and this allows them to live together and get on well with everyone. In this regard, he gives a Gulen-inspired school in Australia as an example that as the school was awarded a prize for its diversity – the students represented a total of 38 different ethnic groups.

At l'Ecole des Etoiles, Catholic, Protestant and Islam religion lessons begin in primary classes. Alternatively, lessons about secular values have been specially designed for secular students. Some of the teachers have Swedish, Spanish, Haitian, Portuguese, Moroccan and Turkish backgrounds. There are three Turkish-Belgian teachers in the primary school and four in the secondary section. The rest is of Belgian origin.

## Methodological implications

I began fieldwork in September 2012 and finished in February 2013. During this period, I commuted between my city of residence and the case-study location. I met parents at their houses or school depending on their preference. In total I carried out 13 semi-structured interviews (with one male and 12 female) as well as two in-depth interviews with the school directors. Although it was not my initial goal to focus on mothers, they were more available during the day and willing to participate in the research. More than half of the parents had bachelor's degrees. Since my access to parents happened either through snowballing or introducing myself to them when they came to school to pick up their children or to talk to their teachers, I happened to meet educated parents for the most part. Also, the fact that these parents were, in general, more open to talking about their schooling experiences and how this led them to look into the range of choices concerning the education of their children helped further the development of the research. Interviews lasted between one and three hours. They were all in Turkish, except for one in French with a mother of Moroccan origin. All interviews were then translated to English by me. Due to certain limitations I indicate below, it was not possible to include parents with other backgrounds.

The school directors at l'Ecole des Etoiles facilitated my contact with prospective parents by introducing me to the parents' committee, whose help proved to be useful in arranging meetings. However, upon my second visit I opted for more independence in my moves. On one hand, I feared that parents from the committee might be regarded as school staff by my informants, which could eventually hinder or shift the flow and fluidity, as well as the reliability of the data they provided. On the other hand, I was keen on developing a warm thread of trust between myself and my potential target community. Unfortunately, the level of intimacy that might have been afforded by taking part in the daily lives of my group of study, in the sense of observing relationships between parents and their children, was not obtainable within the school context.

At the onset of my research, conversations and interviews were mainly open-ended. Once concrete concepts emerged, I accordingly developed a question list through which I sought some new horizons (Charmaz, 2006). A semi-structured interview approach led to in-depth exploration and interpretation of parents' diverse views and experiences regarding their children's education.

Sharing the same ethnic background and common values with my informants paved the way to a mutual understanding and a stronger grasp of their approach in dealing with certain matters. To the eyes of most informants, I counted as an insider. Being a female Muslim researcher from Turkey certainly impacted the way my informants recounted and expressed their perspectives. For instance, one participant openly criticized a teacher's negative attitude towards her daughter after she decided to wear a veil. The ease and relief with which she expressed her views made me wonder whether or not being veiled myself had 'automatically' opened up such a comfort zone.

I have developed some initial 'sensitizing concepts' (Blumer, 1969) to illuminate my direction and to give 'a loose frame' (Charmaz, 2006, p. 16) to my research. For instance, concepts like educational conceptualizations, experiences, practices and the perspectives of parents regarding the future of their children served as an *entrée* into the field, helping to formulate questions and categories (Charmaz, 2006, p. 17).

My research questions aimed first to understand why aspirations are formed and which factors go into their formation, and second, to understand the content of the parents' aspirations concerning the education of their children, which in a sense act as an empirical evidence for the former. The questions then revolved around what parents wanted for their children and what strategies they employed towards their education. It was not until my informants voluntarily and repeatedly affiliated particular experiences from their past with their choices and wishes regarding their children's education that my theoretical framework was clarified.

One of the biggest challenges was what Glaser and Strauss call the 'maximization of differences among groups' (1974, p. 62). I tried to deepen the saturation of my categories by choosing parents from different socioeconomic and educational backgrounds; still, the majority of my informants had quite similar opinions and aspirations about certain matters.

## Aspirations as long-distance norms

More than half of my informants reflected not only about their particular choices and strategies about their children's education but also made strong references to what they wanted their children to be like when they grew up.

My informants expressed their long-term aspirations about their children's education in reference to their cultural and ethical norms, which require them to situate education in a secular environment in such a way that it will serve their metaphysical interests and concerns. They reflected those aspirations and dreams through the choices they have made, such as the choice of l'Ecole des Etoiles. As Appadurai writes, the aspirations are formed in interaction with the social life and what societal structures can (not) offer has a defining role in shaping the specific choices (2004). Some of my informants highlighted this during the interviews, referring to the fact that their current school choice is not satisfactory to the utmost degree, especially due to the large number of immigrant-origin children, but it is the best they have right now. While parents talk about what they aspire for their children in the future, most emphasize that they want their children to be good, morally cultivated people first, while the educational or occupational success comes in the second place.

Parents showed a high degree of aspiration in terms of differentiating themselves and their children from their co-ethnics (Belgian-Turks), expressing that they do not want their children to act in such 'stereotypical' ways. Some of the parents also referred to the significance of being part of a multicultural society in which they believe they themselves and their children should play an active role, striving to make it equal for everyone. They wished for their children to learn respect for people from other cultures and expected their school to cultivate this quality in their children. However, they were also aware of the fact that l'Ecole des Etoiles still has a long way to go to achieve this by way of providing a diverse student population, simply because it is not [yet] very multicultural: it caters primarily to Turkish and Moroccan Belgian families, as families from other cultural backgrounds are – as of now – not attracted to the school.

In the following sections, I first elaborate the ways with which parents aspire for the combination of education with moral values and then move on to their aspirations to raise their children in a more mixed and multicultural environment rather than a monocultural one.

### 'First, I want them to be good Muslims – and then comes education'

Among the many factors that have an impact on the aspirations of my respondents, moral values play a significant role. Most of the parents felt the need to talk about the importance of having brought up their children to be morally sensitive about how their own values might differ from others. According to them, while it is essential to maintain their core values, it is also essential to have a balanced and open view towards those who do not share the same values, a view which should not prevent them to become friends with people from different backgrounds. The comment below is from Erkan, who is the father of three children, aged 17, 10 and 3. Erkan received a high school degree and works for a Turkish-Belgian newspaper in Brussels. In this comment, there is a great emphasis on moral cultivation, which is expected to characterize the attitude of his children towards others from different backgrounds. He said:

> 'The priority for me is that they will be good human beings, connected with their religion, and useful to humanity. Regardless of their religion, what matters is the happiness of humanity. If you are a good person, people know that when they look at your face. Even if you do not speak, you will be influential if you are a good person. First, I want them to be good, nice Muslims and then education comes. Get your diploma and become a Muslim who can stand on his feet. They must bring religion and science together.'

The aspiration Erkan has for his children is informed by the religious and cultural norms within which he was raised and came to internalize. Erkan's interpretation of his values requires him to be a good person, which is only possible by becoming a good Muslim and then getting a diploma. He believes that achieving this will make it possible for his children to be open and tolerant towards others and respect their values.

Erkan's aspirations are also determined by the attitudes of other Turkish-Belgians. He believes they have lost their moral basis and he wants to distinguish himself and his children from them. He argues that education will help his children to realize their duties so that they will not have an inferiority complex like other Turkish-Belgians:

> 'Turkish-origin people have an inferiority complex, and they keep saying they are seen as the foreigners and are thus treated as second-class citizens. However, I have the same citizenship and the same rights. We must not see everyone as an enemy of the foreigner. There are a lot of people with goodwill. I did not have many Turkish friends, but European friends. This is what I want for my children as well. They must be aware of their rights and responsibilities to the society and contribute to it as well-educated people. This awareness can be achieved only through a good education. It will make the difference.'

Erkan believes that the failure of integration was only due to the fact that the first immigrants were not conscious about their values and were thus not motivated enough to educate themselves. Thus, Erkan's aspirations for his children are created both by referring to his cultural, moral and religious values, and by comparing himself to other Turkish-Belgians who do not feel like a part of the society mainly due to, in his words, the lack of a consolidated moral life and education. Obviously, his understanding and perception of values were shaped not only by the culture in which he was brought up at home but also by the norms in the society, as illustrated well by the emphasis on getting educated in order to do well and contribute to society. Other parents, who had the same opinion as Erkan, usually shared a similar social environment of friends or acquaintances and their aspirations followed a parallel trajectory.

In conclusion, the long-term aspirations of the parents were primarily centred on a form of education that would provide their children not only with the ways of being responsible and useful citizens but that would also develop moral awareness and sensitivity. The following section discloses an analysis of parents' aspirations which were mainly focused on providing the opportunity for their children to live in an open and diverse society before anything else.

### *'We cannot stay within our own ethnic borders'*

The impact of the educational background on the formation of aspirations cannot be ignored. There were significant differences between parents in that regard. Parents with a bachelor's degree, constituting more than half of the informants, had strong aspirations for their children to have Belgian-origin friends and to attend activities with them. Parents had serious concerns about the future of their children in that their children would not be able to integrate into the diverse nature of the society if they did not come up with alternative ways to mingle with native Belgian children. They appreciated that the school had an open philosophy and tried to attract students from all segments of society, even if it was not yet successful in that regard. Their sociocultural and educational background as well as the social environment they were raised in influenced the way they approached the question of multiculturalism, diversity and openness.

One such example is Seda. Seda came to Belgium when she was five years old after her father was appointed as an imam in Charleroi. She grew up in Brussels and completed her undergraduate studies in Sociology. She is working as an Islamic teacher in six different schools in Schaerbeek now. Her sons, aged 5 and 8, are going to l'Ecole des Etoiles. Due to the fact that Seda's parents had a different motivation for immigrating to Belgium from others, from the beginning her identity was shaped distinctly and she always had close relations with diverse groups of friends.

When talking about her long-term aspirations for her children, unlike Erkan and some other parents, she does not mention the importance of moral cultivation and when I ask her about it, she states that she considers it as something very personal and an issue to be dealt with in the private sphere. She mainly talks about the importance of adapting to the multicultural society and developing oneself in line with that. She attributes this aspiration to the fact her parents were very open-minded. They had Italian, Greek and Moroccan neighbours. She always had friends from several backgrounds. She believes this has been very useful in her relationship with her children, because she considers herself as having learnt how to understand people without judging and criticizing. She says she can easily communicate with people, and she wishes that for her children, as well:

> 'I completed my education at ULB, where there were many people from different ethnic backgrounds and ideologies, including the most extreme liberals and communists. I have always been together with very different people, not with those who have specific patterns. In ULB, there are atheists, believers, all types of people.'

Deniz is a fervent proponent of the need for a diverse educational environment and society. Her background in languages and the interactions with all different types of people in her profession as a translator have been influential in the development of her perspectives. To define her aspirations for a mixed society, she also refers to Turkish-Belgians who were not able to adapt. She believes they are too nationalistic, not open to other languages, and unable to cross the borders between their closed communities and the world outside of them. She passionately argues that it is no longer possible to stay within prescribed ethnic borders.

It was clear that she made a serious effort to increase the cultural capital of her sons and channel their interests towards the mainstream culture. She regularly took them to museums and said she was planning to send one of them to art academy. She was trying to find alternative mechanisms herself to integrate her children through cultural appropriation of the values which she deemed to be more 'Belgian-like'. Her emphasis on building bridges between her own moral and cultural values and the mainstream values of Belgian society suggests that her aspirations are oriented towards a combination of elements from both cultures.

Deniz's main concern about the future of her children seems to be triggered by the lack of cultural capital and interest among Turkish-Belgians. This, she believes, is one of the primary reasons for the boundaries between them and mainstream culture, and is a consequence of the fears and doubts they have about losing their identity and essence. According to Deniz, this cannot and should not be an obstacle to learn more about the cultural paradigms of the country one lives in as long as one has consolidated his/her own values. Her aspirations in that sense are well illustrated by her choice of a non-ghetto neighbourhood:

> 'After you provide your children with a stable and steady value system of your own, they should be able to distinguish between what is good and what is bad for them. This is how it has been for me. No matter what the risks may be, the solution is not to stay within your community. I do not really enjoy living in ghetto neighbourhoods. We easily tend to forget we are living in Belgium, Brussels, and we make a world of our own. I am afraid of that. This is generally the way it works in these neighbourhoods. I grew up in one of them and I had difficulties later on, especially when I started

university. It was the first time I met so many people from different backgrounds and I was overwhelmed.'

The aspirations that Deniz has for her children are strongly interrelated with her personal interpretation of what she has been through, as are her ideas as to what is best for them and for the society in general.

In conclusion, while the parents who had higher educational degrees developed aspirations in line with that, not all of the aspirations took the same shape. The majority of the parents placed great importance on a future society and educational system more embracing of diversity and heterogeneity, and accordingly produced strategies to find environments where their children could meet and become friends with Belgian children.

In the following section, I discuss the relationship between experiences and aspirations, and indicate how aspirations are being shaped and challenged by a number of structural and personal variables.

## Aspirations inspired by parents' experiences

The data from the interviews revealed that the relationship between experiences and aspirations is more explicitly associated with the choices people make to reach their long-term aspirations. It does not necessarily suggest that there is a direct relationship between experience and aspirations. When parents refer to their educational aspirations for their children, they tend to compare their own past experience to their children's current circumstances/situation. Their choices are not only informed by their values and capabilities, but also by their life experience, which is in turn influenced by societal conditions. The parents expressed their aspirations and priorities for the education of their children within the context of their relationship with cultural and ethical norms. Those norms inform specific choices they make to meet their aspirations, such as choosing l'Ecole des Etoiles, in this case.

Just as Appadurai points out, the aspirations are formed in interaction with the social life; societal structures play a defining role in shaping the specific choices, if not the general aspirations as well (2004). Although Macleod sees aspirations as coming from the habitus and not as the product of rational analysis, the role of the structures and the dialectical relationship between the agent and structure should not be underestimated. It is important to keep in mind that the response of the 'active and creative' individual to the same structures may diverge widely from that of the group praxis, depending on a great number of factors that have an impact on the development and realization of aspirations (Macleod, 2009, p. 139). As I will explore further in detail below, parents use their agency to realize their aspirations, while at the same time being challenged and shaped by the structural conditions. It still refers to the capability of human beings to change the social world they inhabit, albeit not wholly. In the following part, I will look in particular into the parents' experience in order to understand its relationship with the choices they make in order to achieve their long-term aims.

## 'Suddenly it was all like a flashback to me!'

The life experiences of parents were one of the strongest determinants for the particular choices they made. These choices were limited: they could not always send their children to the school they wanted, due to a number of reasons such as the long waiting lists for high-quality schools, or the fear of rejection. Melike is one of the parents whose experience at school played a striking role in her decision to make a particular choice for her children's schooling:

> 'I took my son to school to register him for kindergarten. He has an introvert personality and after some time they told me that he needs to have special education. This moment took me back to years ago when I was not allowed to pass the class. I immediately decided to take him out of this school.'

Her biggest motivation to send her sons to another school is her negative experience with respect to her own childhood education. This drives her to aspire for a school which she says may be labelled as a 'ghetto' but which will provide a safe environment for her children to complete their educational process without being psychologically hurt. She seems to be regretting the fact that she was never able to express her opinions and feelings in class, both because of the fear that she was going to be mocked and because of her father's advice to keep quiet. Those parents with more negative experiences from the past were more sensitive about how their children were treated and received in school.

The experiences of Elif were not the same as Melike's, however. They made the same choice for their children's education, which can either be explained through their common long-term aspirations or not having another alternative. Elif was the only Turkish-Belgian in the Catholic school she went to. She had difficulties because her parents came from a village in Turkey and therefore did not have modern clothes and did not speak any Dutch/Flemish. She always had to translate when there were parent–teacher meetings:

> 'I was kind of ashamed of my mother. As a kid, I thought, my [Belgian] friends had modern mothers and they went out together, did things, you know. I remember my [Turkish] friends who [were also ashamed of their mothers, like me, and] introduced their brother's wives as their mothers, because they were more modern-looking.'

Elif explained that it was basically the headscarf which differentiated her mother from her friends' mothers. She felt humiliated and left out due to the lack of cultural capital in her family, when she compared it with mainstream culture. The differences in the lifestyles of her friends made her feel as if she were falling behind. This was the main motivation for her to look for a solution and an alternative where her children would not feel the same, because she was also wearing the headscarf, like her mother. The fact that she came to be more conscious of her religious values later on in her life was one of the primary reasons that drove her to search for a particular situation for her children. Her foremost desire was that her children would not feel the same as she did, and she saw the solution in a more grounded and solid approach to teaching certain values – namely, those of their ethnocultural background. She herself had had a mixed education where values were concerned; she emphasized that she knew more about Christianity than Islam as a child. Her parents could not teach them much, as they themselves had been brought up in a village without adequate religious education, so Elif and her siblings had learned Christian stories, values and traditions through school. She therefore aspired to find a school where her kids would be offered better opportunities and would not be ashamed of their cultural, religious roots. However, at the same time, she hoped to send them to a school with a diverse student population. She believed that sending them to an immigrant-majority school would hinder them from learning good French and deprive them in general of a high-quality education. Again here, we see her own experiences in a non-ghetto school interfering in her aspirations. She was the only one in her family who achieved a university diploma and this, according to her, was a consequence of the schooling she received.

Elif was very clear about what she expected from her children's school. While she was looking for a school that would meet her criteria, her husband told her they could move back to Turkey. This made her quit her search and send her daughter to l'Ecole des Etoiles, because she had friends there and she was pregnant. Although the school perhaps did not meet all her criteria, she at least knew she could trust them to take care of her daughter if she had any problems. It was basically the practical matters that first motivated Elif to choose the school, not the fact that the school was the ideal educational space she was looking for. However, when their plans changed and they decided to stay in Belgium, Elif became stressed about it again:

'When we decided to stay here in Belgium, I regretted my decision, because the quality of education [at L'Ecole des Etoiles] was not that high two, three years ago. There were many Turkish-Belgians in her class and they were mainly speaking Turkish. She was having a hard time understanding the texts when she was in the first year of primary school. If she had been in school among Belgians, she would not have had trouble understanding. I sent her to kiddy classes for additional language education and this helped her a lot. I started to think [that by sending her to this school] I was preventing my daughter from having a brighter career in the future.'

The process she went through clearly reveals the complexity and ambiguity of the development of her aspiration and choice. She cannot access the precise schooling environment to which she aspires for her children, but has not given up hope that it may be a future possibility. As mentioned before, however, the structural limitations along with specific preferences and choices create a more complex picture. The interplay of experiences, particular choices and what is available in the society defines Elif's aspirations.

## Concluding remarks

The contribution of this research involves the subjective experiences and aspirations of parents about the education of their children. I chose to employ 'aspirations' as a framing concept for several reasons. First of all, it helped to grasp the views, feelings, and ideas of the Turkish-Belgian parents about education and to find a balanced approach between structure and agency, taking into account the interaction between both. Furthermore, the concept facilitated an understanding of the past and future implications of the parents' interpretations of their experiences.

The long-term aspirations of Turkish-Belgian parents, informed in general by cultural and religious ideas, norms and values, mainly revolved around a dream of a future which would be less compartmentalized and more welcoming of multiculturalism. Their reflections about the future of their children mainly focused on the moral cultivation accompanied with a well-informed education. Several of them made specific references to the negative image of the Turkish-Belgian community and emphasized the differentiated future image for their children. The negative image of the ethnic group to which they belong was a strong factor in the development of their aspirations.

For the majority of my informants, the primary aspirations for their children included being a good human being and doing good deeds, doing no harm, and contributing positively to society. Having a high-quality education and profession was either secondary to those or not mentioned at all. Their aspirations were basically fed by what they valued most in a human being and accordingly how they wished their children to be when they grew up. These aspirations are morally loaded with specific values inspired by parents' own cultural baggage, background characteristics and social environment, all of which help to create a certain habitus. It is not, however, possible to assume a direct relationship between habitus and aspirations, since parents with a similar habitus also made different choices and vice versa.

The long-term aspirations parents had about their children's education and future were satisfied to a large extent by the short-term aspirations. The factors behind the choices of parents that emerged from their stories vis-à-vis their choices for their children was an interwoven picture of their deeply-ingrained personal life experiences (habitus) and the limitations and possibilities shaped by societal structures. However, their ideals were not always attainable in terms of what was available in educational spaces, and this encouraged them to look further for alternatives. As discussed earlier, the complicated interplay of various processes shape the way aspirations are constructed and informed by the dialectical relationship between free will and structures, both of which are influential on the formation of intentions, choices and dreams to various degrees. Also, it was noted that over-emphasizing certain limitations of objective structures ignores the capacity and capability of human beings to develop atypical, diverse and challenging responses to them.

L'Ecole des Etoiles responds to a certain degree to the wishes of my respondents. In general, parents seemed especially content with the level of caring in the school environment, with the visits by teachers, and with the individual-oriented education. The school has its deficiencies in terms of creating the diverse environment desired by some parents. This has motivated some parents to search for clubs, courses and summer camps organized by communes or private associations, through which their children can interact with more Belgians. This is an indication of the strength of the desire parents have to not remain confined by existing ethnic boundaries. Those who had experiences in other schools were able to make better comparisons and presented their aspirations in line with their experiences. This shows that past experiences interpreted along the lines of cultural and societal values, individual desires and structural factors play a definite role in the building of aspirations, thereby informing the way the actor determines her future orientation.

As has been illustrated, the development of aspirations and choices is a complicated process, which makes it hard to be able to answer the question regarding the relevance of anthropological research on aspiration. The scope of this research does not allow for a deeper analysis of the incentives, outcomes and transitions; what is needed is a longer period of fieldwork, along with a more diverse group of informants.

However, as I endeavoured to reveal, aspirations can help to dissolve the meanings and implications of past experiences and act as a mediator between the structural factors and agency. It allows the understandings, experiences, voices and dreams of parents to enter into the research domain of immigration and education. New theories and concepts that are sensitive to the issues discussed above will help clarify the nuances of the intensely personal stories, revealing in turn the complexity, ambiguity and diversity of the processes of developing certain aspirations and making certain choices.

## Note

1   Fedactio is an umbrella organization of 25 associations located in three different administrative regions of Belgium. It was founded in May 2010 mainly with the support of the Turkish-Belgian community. For more information, see www.fedactio.be/en/

## References

Appadurai, A. (2004). The capacity to aspire: Culture and terms of recognition. In V. Rao & M. Walton (eds), *Culture and Public Action* (pp.59–84). Stanford, CA: Stanford University Press.

Beck, A., Corak, M. & Tienda, M. (2012). Age at immigration and the adult attainments of child migrants to the United States. *Annals of the American Academy of Political and Social Science*, 643, 134–59.

Blumer, H. (1969). *Symbolic Interactionism*. Oakland, CA: University of California Press.

Bourdieu, P. & Passeron, J. C. (1977). *Reproduction in Education, Society and Culture*. London: Sage Publications.

Carpenter, D. (2008). Expectations, aspirations, and achievement among Latino students of immigrant families. *Marriage & Family Review*, 43(1–2), 164–85.

Casier, M., Heyse, P., Clycq, N., Zemni, S. & Timmerman, C. (2013). Breaking the in-group out-group: Shifting boundaries in transnational partner choice processes of individuals of Moroccan, Tunisian, Algerian Turkish, Punjabi Sikh, Pakistani and Albanian descent in Belgium. *The Sociological Review*, *61*(3), 460–78.

Catalano, T. (2013). Anti-immigrant ideology in U.S. crime reports: Effects on the education of Latino children. *Journal of Latinos and Education*, *12*(4), 254–70.

Cetin, M. (2009). *The Gulen Movement: Civic Service Without Borders*. New York: Blue Dome Press.

Charmaz, K. (2006). *Constructing Grounded Theory: A Practical Guide Through Qualitative Analysis*. London: Sage.

Dierckx, D. & Van Dam, S. (2014). Redefining empowerment interventions of migrants experiencing poverty: The case of Antwerp, Belgium. *British Journal of Social Work*, *44*(1), 105–22.

Ebaugh, H. R. (2010). *The Gulen Movement: A Sociological Analysis of a Civic Movement Rooted in Moderate Islam*. Houston, TX: Springer.

Eurydice. (2009/2010). Organization of the education system in the French Community of Belgium. Brussels: Education, Audiovisual & Culture Executive Agency. Retrieved from: http://eacea.ec.europa.eu/education/eurydice/thematic_reports_en.php.

Genicot, G. & Ray, D. (2009). Aspirations, inequality, investment and mobility. Retrieved from: www.nyu.edu/econ/user/debraj/Courses/Readings/GenicotRayAspirations.pdf.

Glaser, B. G. & Strauss, A. L. (1974). *The Discovery of Grounded Theory: Strategies for Qualitative Research*. Chicago: Aldine Publishing Company.

Graw, K. & Schielke S. (eds). (2012). *The Global Horizon: Expectations of Migration in Africa and the Middle East*. Leuven: Leuven University Press.

Hart, C. S. (2012). *Aspirations, Education and Social Justice: Applying Sen and Bourdieu*. London: Bloomsbury Academic Press.

Hlalele, D. (2012). Exploring rural high school learners' experience of mathematics anxiety in academic settings. *South African Journal of Education*, *32*(3), 267–78.

Jacob, B. A. & Wilder, T. (2010). Educational expectations and attainment. National Bureau of Economic Research Working Paper 15683. Retrieved from: www.nber.org/papers/w15683.

Khan, M. A. (2011). *The Vision and Impact of Fethullah Gulen: A New Paradigm for Social Activism*. New York: Blue Dome Press.

Kloppenburg, S. & Peters, P. (2012). Confined mobilities: Following Indonesian migrant workers on their way home. *Wiley Online Library*, *103*(5), 530–41.

Kochuyt, T. (2012). Making money, marking identities: On the economic, social and cultural functions of Moroccan weddings in Brussels. *Journal of Ethnic and Migration Studies*, *38*(10), 1625–41.

McFadden, A., Atkin, K. & Renfrew, M. J. (2014). The impact of transnational migration on intergenerational transmission of knowledge and practice related to breast feeding. *Science Direct*, *30*(4), 439–46.

Macleod, J. (2009). *Ain't No Makin' It: Aspirations and Attainment in a Low-income Neighborhood*. Philadelphia, PA: Westview Press.

Minello, A. & Barban N. (2012). The educational expectations of children of immigrants in Italy. *The ANNALS of the American Academy of Political and Social Science*, *643*(1), 78–103.

Piot, L., Kelchtermans, G. & Ballet, K. (2010). Beginning teachers' job experiences in multi-ethnic schools. *Teachers and Teaching*, *16*(2), 259–76.

Portes, A., Aparicio, R., Haller, W. & Vickstrom, E. (2010). Moving ahead in Madrid: Aspirations and expectations in the Spanish second generation. *International Migration Review*, *44*(4), 767–801.

Sellar, S. & Gale, T. (2011). Mobility, aspiration, voice: A new structure of feeling for student equity in higher education. *Critical Studies in Education*, *52*(2), 115–34.

Thulin, E. & Vilhelmson, B. (2014). Virtual practices and migration plans: A qualitative study of urban young adults. *Population, Space and Place*, *20*(5), 389–401.

Timmerman, C., Hemmerechts, K. & De Clerck, H. M. (2014). The relevance of a 'culture of migration' in understanding migration aspirations in contemporary Turkey. *Turkish Studies*, *15*(3), 496–518.

Yavuz, H. & Esposito, J. (2003). *Turkish Islam and the Secular State: The Gulen Movement*. Syracuse: Syracuse University Press.

Zimmermann, K. F. & Constant, A. (eds). (2013). *International Handbook on the Economics of Migration*. Northampton, MA: Edward Elgar Publishing.

# 9 The Polish community school in Flanders

Bridging the gap between school and home environment

*Edith Piqueray, Noel Clycq and Christiane Timmerman*

## Introduction

Even though the Flemish educational system is rated as one of the best in the world (De Meyer & Warlop, 2010) and the participation rate is high, the gap between the results of the best and the worst performing pupils is much higher than in Belgium's neighbouring countries (Danhier *et al.*, 2014). Compared to native Flemish youngsters, recently migrated pupils[1] as well as second- or third-generation pupils with an immigrant background receive poorer grades, experience more grade retention and leave education without an ISCED level 3 qualification. Some research even indicates that the educational systems increase these differences rather than decrease them (Groenez *et al.*, 2009). Already in the first year of secondary education, pupils with an immigrant and/or a lower socioeconomic background are overrepresented in (part-time) vocational education (Duquet *et al.*, 2006), which are tracks with the highest early school leaving rates (Groenez *et al.*, 2009). These same groups are also overrepresented in (youth) unemployment rates (VDAB, 2014) which stresses the dramatic impact of educational tracking on the future of these pupils.

Academic scholars have pointed out that minorities are often driven by 'community forces' to ensure a certain amount of internal continuity and cohesion, while at the same time focusing on upward social mobility. Communities often develop strategies and depend on specific social and cultural resources to improve their overall educational situation (González *et al.*, 1995; Moll *et al.*, 1992). In Flanders, the Polish community schools,[2] where pupils are taught the Polish language and culture on Wednesday afternoons and/or Saturday mornings, can be seen as an example of such a strategy. As their importance, in particular in quantitative terms, has increased during the last decennium, they become a relevant site for research on education. Within the ethnically and socially stratified Flemish educational context, Polish community schools are gaining significance as they can offer social, cultural and linguistic capital absent in mainstream education but sought after by parents and children (Archer *et al.*, 2010; Creese *et al.*, 2006; Francis *et al.*, 2009; Reay & Mirza, 1997; Zhou & Kim, 2006).

Using both quantitative and qualitative data, this chapter gives an overview of the educational trajectories of Polish pupils in Flemish secondary education and focuses on the obstacles experienced by Polish parents and pupils when making educational track choices. The main research questions it tries to answer are: What is the role of the Polish community schools in the school trajectories of Polish pupils in Flemish mainstream education? And what are the critical success factors of the Polish schools?

As research on the educational situation of youngsters with an immigrant background in Flanders usually refers to people of Turkish or Moroccan origin (for example Duquet et al., 2006; Timmerman et al., 2002), we focus on the Polish community. In contrast to the Turkish and Moroccan Muslim communities, the Polish minority group closely resembles the majority in terms of skin colour, culture, religion, sociocultural praxis and EU membership. We might suggest that the educational situation of Polish youngsters differs from the most investigated communities regarding education, considering that several international and national academic studies have pointed out that the socioeconomic status of pupils' parents and family (Glick & Hohmann-Marriott, 2007; Kao & Thompson, 2003) and the ethnic background play an important part in pupil's educational trajectories (Duquet et al., 2006; Latuheru & Hessels, 1996; Roosens, 1998; Timmerman, 1999).

Before explaining the results, we give an overview of the structure of the Flemish educational system, which is characterized by social and ethnic stratification. Then we present some theoretical perspectives that shed light on the different roles of community schools. These theoretical perspectives help to navigate the findings and form the basis for the discussion.

## Social and ethnic stratification within the Flemish educational system

Secondary education in Flanders is not comprehensive but characterized as an early tracking system with three main distinct pathways: general education (ASO) leading to (academically oriented) higher education, technical education (TSO) leading to (professionally oriented) higher education and vocational education (BSO) leading more directly to specific professions on the labour market. The PISA reports 2003 and 2006 show a strong correlation between school type and mathematics performance in Flanders. For example, ASO-type schools perform above average, TSO-type schools or BSO-type schools perform below average. In turn, the PISA results show that school type (general, technical and vocational track) and student SES are highly linked. In contrast to most of the OECD countries, in Flanders, the impact of SES on student performance did not change significantly between PISA 2000 and PISA 2012 (De Meyer & Warlop, 2010; Danhier et al., 2014).

A clear hierarchy of social appreciation exists between the educational tracks (ASO, TSO and BSO), with general secondary education at the top and vocational secondary education at the bottom (Clycq et al., 2014; Van Houtte et al., 2012). In the beginning of secondary education, parents and students often opt for general secondary education, without taking the talents, competences and interests of the students sufficiently into account. As a result, many students do not perform to their potential and soon 'go down the waterfall' from general to vocational education, eventually through technical education (Duquet *et al.*, 2006). Students in vocational education are either trained for unskilled or low-skilled labour. Part-time vocational education is even more negatively perceived and often a last step down the waterfall of educational tracks, right before leaving education early, and is often not a positive choice (Creten *et al.*, 2004). Dropping out and leaving secondary education without qualification is too often the final result of this 'waterfall system' (Duquet *et al.*, 2006).

Lucas (2001) argues that 'curricular tracking' is an instrument to continue inequalities in society. The hierarchy of social appreciation between the different educational tracks is caused by the extreme specialization of the tracks within technical and vocational education and, more importantly, because of the poor level of the theoretical courses in (part-time) vocational education (Hirtt *et al.*, 2007). Several studies demonstrate indeed that students from higher 'tracks' – even weak students – can learn more because they have access to better curricula and better education (Hallinan, 2001; Oakes *et al.*, 2000).

Already in the first year of secondary education, students with an immigrant background are overrepresented in technical, vocational and part-time vocational education. For example, recent figures show that almost 50 per cent of the Turkish and North African girls start secondary education in the vocational track. Grade-retention rates of Turkish and Moroccan origin youngsters are higher than grade-retention rates of native youngsters. The other immigrant youth (East European immigrants included) take an intermediate position. Grade retention and following the B-track[3] decrease the chances of qualified outflow strongly (Duquet *et al.*, 2006; Lamote *et al.*, 2013). In 2003, about 50 per cent of the Turkish and North African pupils and 20 per cent of the other immigrant youth left secondary education without any qualification. This contrasted strongly with the group of native youngsters, which had an early school leaving rate of 10 per cent (Duquet *et al.*, 2006). Unfortunately, this situation did not improve after a few years. In 2010, 40 per cent of male pupils with a lowly educated mother and without Dutch as their mother tongue left school early, compared to 8 per cent of male pupils speaking Dutch as their mother tongue and having a highly educated mother (Lamote *et al.*, 2013).

Within the group of immigrant youngsters, newcomers are most vulnerable within early tracking systems. Furthermore, many Polish youngsters follow OKAN courses (Reception Classes for Foreign-speaking Newcomers), which are mandatory one-year courses that non-Dutch-speaking newcomers aged 12–18 attend before being admitted to regular secondary education. Research demonstrates that pupils who finished the OKAN class experience numerous difficulties in the transition to mainstream secondary education. Many former OKAN pupils are enrolled in vocational secondary education, half-time vocational secondary education and special secondary education (Sterckx & Gysen, 2006; Vlaams Parlement, Commissie vergadering nr. C203, 7 April 2011). Moreover, pupils entering Flemish secondary education with a grade retention have less chance of leaving school with a diploma.

Every year of grade retention cuts the chances of qualified outflow in half (Duquet et al., 2006).

The overview above points out the complexity of the Flemish educational system as well as the current difficulties the system struggles with.

## Community schools as bonding and bridging actions

Community schooling is a global phenomenon. Since the first waves of migration in the 19th century, immigrants have set up schools to socialize their children in the language and culture of their country of origin (Anderson & Boyer, 1970; Creese, 2009; Malakoff & Hakuta, 1990). Community schools have taken various forms. An important distinction is the one between full-time and part-time education. Full-time education established by minorities often refers to Afro-Carribean schools, religious schools (Creese, 2009) and bilingual schools which are established in many different types ranging from a focus on learning two different languages to the use of the native language to learn the dominant language (Anderson & Boyer, 1970; August & Garcia, 1988 in Malakoff & Hakuta, 1990). Part-time education, which is the subject of this chapter, offers courses outside the mainstream school hours, often on Wednesday afternoon or during the weekends. In international scientific literature many different names are given to this kind of education, such as 'heritage education' in the North American context, 'community schools' or 'ethnic schools' in the Australian context, and 'complementary schools' or 'supplementary education' in the UK (Creese, 2009). The choice between establishing full-time or part-time education is often related to the financial resources of an ethnic minority, the main purposes of those schools and the laws, and the political climate of the immigration country (Kifano, 1996; Malakoff & Hakuta, 1990). The main reason for the existence of part-time schools set up by immigrant groups is the teaching of the language and customs/traditions, which is linked to the desire to preserve the cultural/ethnic identities and/or faith/traditions (Creese et al., 2006). One common feature of all those different kinds of schools is that they offer a curriculum that is insufficiently (or in some cases not at all) developed in mainstream education and for which there is a demand on the part of minority families (Li, 2006). Consequently, the establishment of community schools – similar to all formal schooling – can be understood as situated social actions through which individuals and groups work together with specific intentions (Myers & Grosvenor, 2011). Therefore, one should take into account the context wherein these schools have been developed and analyse the discourses and actions of the stakeholders directly involved in order to gain deeper insight in these processes.

The cultural emblems of the majority are omnipresent in mainstream education, considering it was established decades ago by 'representatives', such as policy makers, of this dominant group. Approximately 65 per cent of all secondary school pupils in Flanders are enrolled in 'Catholic schools', Dutch is the main language of instruction, and educational policy aims first and foremost to teach all minority pupils sufficient proficiency in Dutch (Clycq, 2009). Flemish cultural emblems are self-evident and central in mainstream education in such a way that parents of Flemish origin generally feel supported by a system that to a large extent shares their emblems and ethnocultural background. This institutional support for family socialization processes strengthens the congruence between the home and school environment. Minority parents, on the other hand, have to develop different strategies to ensure this ethnocultural continuity (Hughes et al., 2006).

Attention for and transmission of 'home language and culture' provides children (and their parents) with a significant amount of support in a society where they are identified as different and sometimes even problematized (Clycq et al., 2014; Gibson, 1988; Roosens, 1998). Knowledge and a positive perception of 'the culture of origin' provides important social, cultural and emotional resources to support young people through the educational system (Suárez-Orozco & Suárez-Orozco, 1995; Valenzuela & Dornbusch, 1994). A crucial role is attributed to language in these processes. Earlier research has shown that bilingual children have better access to the social and cultural capital of their (grand)parents than children who do not acquire the language of their parents (Antrop-Gonzalez et al., 2010; Clycq, 2009). Knowledge of the 'home language' gives young people the opportunity not only to tap into the social and cultural capital of their (grand)parents, but also to enter into relevant and information-rich community, institutional and even transnational networks (Stanton-Salazar & Dornbusch, 1995).

However, community schools set by immigrant groups not only reinforce social networks within their own ethnic community, but might also function as a tie with the dominant community. Teachers working in community schools with social networks in both communities can function as important 'bridge ties', which means that they can facilitate the exchange of relevant information and connections between minority and majority communities (Zhou & Kim, 2006). Research has pointed out that in comparison with mainstream education, teachers in community schools can be important resources of social and cultural capital as they share the same language and culture with the pupils and parents. Moreover, pupils in Chinese community schools in the UK were of the opinion that teachers in these schools have a very strong 'intrinsic love' of teaching and of working with the children, considering they work on a voluntarily basis. This intrinsic commitment leads to intense involvement of these teachers with the pupils (Archer et al., 2009).

While perceiving community schools as important spaces of different resources, it is also important to study the explicit and implicit intentions that underlie the establishment of community schools (Myers & Grosvenor, 2011). Community schools are set up with certain intentions and have, like any organization, their own political agenda through which they attempt 'to define the boundaries of culture and identity' which make them 'inherently (and inevitably) political acts' (Archer et al., 2010). In some contexts, for example in the case of certain community schools in the UK, they can be identified as 'resistance schooling', fighting the racist or discriminatory processes in mainstream education (Dove, 1993; Hall et al., 2002; Reay & Mirza, 1997). Other scholars stress that individuals (or communities) investing too much in bonding networks miss out on opportunities or resources present in networks only tapped into through bridging relations (Zhou

& Kim, 2006). Furthermore, not every minority parent and/or pupil considers these schools useful or relevant to their situation (Francis et al., 2009). All these criticisms apply more to full-time than to part-time community schools. As the latter are often small, grassroots, local, community-based schools, they are not considered in the same light as the religious 'ethnic' full time schools arguing for separate provision. Part-time community schools support a philosophy of inclusion rather than segregation and promote a sense of community cohesion[4] (Creese, 2009; Issa & Williams, 2009; Reay & Mirza, 1997).

Based on these theoretical perspectives about the structure of the Flemish educational system and the Polish schools as important community resources, we might suggest good communication processes and solid relationships between Flemish mainstream schools and Polish parents/pupils are needed to ensure the latter will be well informed and able to make adequate school trajectory and educational tracking choices. Moreover, deep insights into pupils' competences and interests are required on the part of the Flemish schoolteachers, parents and pupils themselves. We will explore whether these conditions are fulfilled and which role the Polish schools can play in supporting Polish parents and pupils with their educational trajectory issues and in overcoming the limitations of the Flemish school system.

## Polish community schools in Flanders

The history of Polish schools in Belgium stretches back to 1926. Over the years, the system occurred in various forms: as full-time education, as a supplement to regular school hours, and as additional courses integrated into the Belgian educational system (Caestecker, 1990, 2003; Goddeeris, 2003). Nowadays, Polish youngsters can learn the Polish language and culture in community schools that usually offer classes on Wednesday afternoons and Saturday mornings. Two of these schools are managed, controlled and funded by the Ministry of Education in Poland. One is located in Antwerp; the other school, which has three different locations, is headquartered in Brussels. They belong to ORPEG (Ośrodek Rozwoju Polskiej Edukacji za Granicą), the Polish institution for the education of children of Polish citizens who temporarily live abroad. The latter was established in 1973 for children of Polish diplomats and currently counts about 74 institutions around the world. On top of that, Belgium also has a private Polish school in Brussels and several schools organized by the Polish Catholic Mission, which are usually limited in scope in comparison to the other Polish schools. The mission schools are primarily located in the former mining regions (Liège, Limburg, Charleroi). This chapter focuses on the situation of Polish schools organized by the Ministry of Education in Poland.

Polish education was established to protect migrants from becoming alienated from their native country. During the last decade, it aimed in particular at the (re)integration of pupils into the Polish educational system upon their return to Poland. Eventually, it became a comprehensive programme geared towards the Polish educational system. During classes on Wednesday afternoons and Saturday mornings, pupils are taught the Polish language, history, geography and socio-political sciences. In some schools, the study of Catholicism is included in the curriculum; in others, this is an optional class. All the courses are taught in Polish. The programme consists of six years of primary education and three to six years of secondary education. Pupils receive a certificate for every year they complete, which allows them, in combination with a certificate from mainstream education in Flanders, to join the Polish educational system without having to repeat a year.

Although nowadays fewer pupils follow the Polish school with the aim of being able to reintegrate in the educational system in Poland, and notwithstanding the increasing importance of succeeding in mainstream education, the number of pupils in the Polish schools has increased considerably during the last 15 years. This means that the Polish community feels the need to keep their 'own' language and culture by transmitting it to the next generations (Levrau et al., 2014). Although Polish schools have been growing, the Ministry of Education in Poland reformed the Polish schools in the Diaspora in the last few years by reducing the curriculum and replacing some traditional classroom courses with Internet courses. They decided to reform the schools because of the changes in the educational system in Poland and because many Polish migrants remain in the diaspora for a longer time period (Piqueray, 2011).

## Methodology, research population and setting

In order to answer our research questions, we relied on a multi-method design encompassing (1) a review of the academic literature, (2) documents obtained within the different schools, (3) qualitative and quantitative research in one Polish community school and (4) qualitative and quantitative research within mainstream education in Flanders. The qualitative research consisted of observations, informal conversations, semi-structured interviews and focus-group discussions with different respondents within the mainstream and community school context, and within the after-school (home) context during a two-year period, from 2010 to 2012. We studied pupils (n=31), parents (n=15) and school staff (1 Polish school: n=10). The school staff consisted of principals, teachers and care supervisors.

The data were transcribed literally and coded in thematic topics and analysed using the software program NVivo 9. This software program allowed us to generate recurring themes from testimonies of the informants and from the observations in the field.

The pupils were aged between 12 and 18. Of the 31 Polish pupils, 12 were boys and 19 were girls. Most Polish youngsters were born in Poland and came to Belgium at different ages. Importantly, we only selected children from ethnically homogeneous marriages to avoid the question of which ethnocultural group a youngster belongs to when coming from an ethnically mixed family. In terms of social class, the majority of the Polish parents were low-skilled and employed in the housekeeping or construction industry. A qualitative research among 25 key informants within the Polish community in Flanders has shown that these characteristics are common to Polish migrants who migrated after the 1990s (Levrau et al., 2011).

Table 9.1 Research population and methodology

| | Observations/ informal conversations | Semi-structured interviews (40 to 60 minutes) | Focus group discussions |
|---|---|---|---|
| 31 pupils | Several informal conversations in the school and home context | 1 to 3 per pupil | 1 focus group discussion with the peer group of 4 pupils and 3 focus group discussions with pupils at Polish school |
| 15 parents (mostly mothers) | Several informal conversations in the home context | 1 to 3 per parent | – |
| 10 school staff members in Polish school | Several informal conversations in the staffroom and during breaks | 1 to 3 per school staff member | – |
| Classes in Polish school | 4 Wednesday afternoons | | – |

In contrast to the parents, the Polish teachers were highly skilled, as they were selected on the basis of their Polish diploma. The majority of the teachers only worked at the Polish school because they experienced a lot of difficulties finding a job in the Belgian labour market that was suitable to their diploma. Due to numerous efforts to obtain a Belgian diploma and to learn the languages of the country (French and/or Dutch) some of them had a job – suited to their diploma level – besides their job at the Polish school.

Taking into account the specificity of the Flemish educational system, we selected pupils in different educational tracks[5] and schools with different governing bodies. The Flemish educational system is divided into three networks: first, public education organized by the Flemish government, second, subsidized public education organized by provinces and municipalities and finally, subsidized free education that is mainly affiliated with and organized by the Catholic pillar. This study focuses on the only Polish community school in Flanders partially organized by the Ministry of Education in Poland. This Polish school is established in Antwerp, a Flemish city and province in Belgium, and it counted 547 pupils in 2012. According to national statistics, in 2011 Antwerp as a province counted the largest number of officially registered Poles (10.081) in Flanders. These numbers are based on nationality, which means we can expect that the real number of immigrants from Poland staying in Antwerp is higher. Some of our Polish pupils were enrolled at a Polish school; others had quit the Polish school or have never been enrolled in community education.

The language of the interviews depended on the language proficiency of the respondents. The interviews were mainly conducted in Dutch, English or French, complemented with a basic knowledge of Polish. Occasionally we made use of Polish interpreters.

The quantitative research at the Polish school consisted of a survey on the pupils' background (age, sex, birthplace, migration history, etc.), language (skills, preferences, etc.), ethnic identity and social networks. The objective of the survey was to get an overview of the pupil's identity and his/her perceptions of the latter-mentioned themes. All pupils (n=34, missings=7) in secondary education at the Polish school – except the pupils who followed Internet classes at home – were questioned. The questionnaires consisted mostly of closed-answer categories and were analysed in IBM SPSS Statistics. As almost all questions were on nominal or ordinal scale, the analyses were merely descriptive analyses.

The research presented here forms part of a larger interuniversity research project (BET YOU!)[6] on the school careers of adolescents in Flanders. A survey aimed at questioning the entire student population of the second grade of secondary education in three Flemish cities. The final database constitutes 11,015 unique non-blank records, representing about 50 per cent of the foreseen population; 43 per cent of these pupils has at least one grandparent born abroad. The pupils were given a written questionnaire in Dutch during school hours, asking about a broad set of background variables, their school career, ambitions, psychological characteristics, etc. The survey was set up to provide deeper information on the factors within the school and the home contexts which might influence the school careers of immigrant youngsters.

## Findings

### *School trajectories of Polish pupils*

Quantitative data on the educational trajectories of Polish pupils in Flemish education are scarce. Nevertheless, it is generally assumed that these trajectories are less 'problematic' than those of Moroccan or Turkish origin youth, but 'more' problematic than those of native youngsters. The BET YOU! project was one of the first to collect this information. However, only a glimpse of their trajectories can be found, as only a small sample of pupils can be constructed. Only 89 pupils have both grandmothers born in Poland. Even though the numbers are small, some general trends seem to emerge in line with international findings. The descriptive analysis shows that indeed a smaller percentage of Polish pupils experienced at least one year of grade retention – 42 per cent of the Polish pupils – in comparison with Moroccan (64 per cent) or Turkish (61 per cent) pupils. Native pupils experienced even less grade retention (30 per cent).

Similar results occur when considering and comparing the percentages of pupils per ethnic community in the ASO (the general track, perceived as the most prestigious track) and BSO (the vocational track, perceived as the 'least prestigious' track). The following table demonstrates the number of Flemish/Turkish/Moroccan/Polish pupils – with both grandmothers born in the country of origin – in each study track in the third year of secondary education in 2010. We might

*Table 9.2* The percentage of ethnic minorities within different educational tracks

|  | ASO % | TSO % | BSO % | BUSO % | KSO % |
| --- | --- | --- | --- | --- | --- |
| Flemish (n= 5775) | 52 | 24.8 | 14.5 | 2.0 | 6.5 |
| Turkish (n= 780) | 25.3 | 22.9 | 45.5 | 3.6 | 1.0 |
| Moroccan (n= 862) | 22.3 | 26.8 | 46.1 | 3.7 | 0.3 |
| Polish (n= 89) | 47.2 | 19.1 | 23.6 | 2.2 | 6.7 |

conclude that Polish pupils perform better or have more chances to follow the general track than Turkish and Moroccan pupils do. Opposite results emerge when comparing Polish pupils with Flemish pupils.

The qualitative fieldwork data show that 10 of the 17 Polish pupils had to repeat at least one school year during their school career. Some 7 of the 17 pupils had smooth school trajectories without grade retention. It is striking that while the pupils without grade retention all started their school career in Flemish education from the first year of primary education, many pupils with grade retention started Flemish education at a later age. This is in line with national research pointing out that newcomers experience numerous difficulties in the transition to mainstream (secondary) education (Sterckx & Gysen, 2006; Vlaams Parlement, Commissie vergadering nr. C203, 7 April 2011). When studying the school trajectories of the 17 pupils during the first three years of secondary education, some aspects come to the forefront. While almost all pupils started secondary education in the A-track, a considerable amount of pupils, who followed a technical or vocational track, went down 'the waterfall'. While, in general, less than 5 per cent of the pupils who started in the B-track changed to the A-track (Groenez *et al.*, 2009), we observed that in our small sample of 17 pupils, 4 Polish pupils 'streamed up' from the B to the A-track. These results stress the importance within the Polish community to follow an educational track as high as possible, according to their perception (see below).

In the following sections we study how Polish schools can support parents and pupils with their school trajectory choices in mainstream schools. We do this based on various obstacles and problems that Polish parents and pupils put forward regarding their school trajectories in mainstream schools. First, we focus on parents' poor knowledge of the Flemish educational system and on the communication problems between parents and mainstream schools. Second, we explain issues emerging from parents' negative perception of technical and vocational educational track. Then we concentrate on the Polish school's facilities to estimate Polish pupil's competences and talents. In the last part, we shed light on the role of the Polish school as a safety net.

### Knowledge of the Flemish educational system

Because of a lack of knowledge about the Flemish educational system some parents (and pupils) experienced some misunderstandings about school trajectory choices.

Parents (and pupils) are used to the Polish educational system which has some important differences compared with the Flemish system. For example, contrary to the situation in Flanders, in Poland it is only possible to choose between different educational tracks and subjects at the transition from the 3th to the 4th year of secondary education.[7] While grade retention rates are high and commonly found in Flemish schools (*Statistisch Jaarboek van het Vlaams Onderwijs 2008–2009*), these rates are low in the Polish educational system (Eurydice, 2011). Unsurprisingly, one of the Polish mothers in Antwerp was very upset at the end of the school year when her 17-year-old daughter received the advice to repeat her school year again.

> 'At the end we bought flowers although we were the only ones. And it turned out that she [her daughter] had failed, she had to repeat the school year. That was just terrible. I did not expect it. (. . .) Here in Belgium, it seems to me that it is rather normal to repeat a school year. I think it is better to repeat the school year immediately than to delay it, but in Poland, we know that pupils who have to repeat the school year are weak students and . . . in Poland it [repeating a school year] is considered differently, . . . I began to cry, it was really a shock, at the last day of the school year. (. . .) Formerly it was not so obvious to us that repeating a school year is considered as normal here, but after that experience we learned it.'

This example shows the need of some parents to get more information about the Flemish educational system, but they miss a common language to communicate with the teachers in mainstream education. Although many parents have been living in Belgium for more or less 10 years, most of them do not speak Dutch or know only the basics, and only learned Russian as a second language during their school years in Poland. As such, many parents do not have access to important information about the Flemish school system and do not feel 'at ease' within the mainstream school context. In worst cases parents take decisions 'blindly' and/or do not understand decisions or advice of the school staff in mainstream education. At this point it becomes clear that the Polish community school is an information-rich network for these parents. Because of the common language between the different actors in the Polish school, this community school can play an important role. A teacher at the Polish school in Antwerp argues:

> 'Here [at the Polish school] the parents are at ease. They are even moaners, they come here to moan, euh/(. . .) Yes, they are very self-confident here [at the Polish school]. We know that the same parents have less self-confidence in Belgian schools; they follow all the rules and are very obedient because they feel uncomfortable.'

Several parents share this feeling. The answer of one of them to the question whether her relationships with teachers in mainstream and community schools differ, is:

'Yes, for me it is better at the Polish school, because of the language, . . . As I speak Polish, I do not have communication problems at the Polish school and maybe I ask more there [Polish school] as the communication is easier. At the Belgian Dutch [mainstream] school, I do not always ask everything I would like to, because of my insufficient Dutch skills.'

The interviews with the teachers and parents demonstrate that some teachers of the Polish school succeed to fill in the need to get better informed on the Flemish educational system, especially the teachers who work in mainstream and in community schools. However, various teachers mentioned not having the time to help the parents because of the workload at the Polish school. The teachers linked the high workload to the comprehensive programme and the implications of the current reorganization (structurally as well as curriculum-wise) of the Polish schools. However, not all teachers can take up this role. It became obvious during the fieldwork that some teachers have a lack of knowledge of and even less experience within Flemish mainstream education. Therefore, and because of their poor knowledge of Dutch and/or French, they could not function as bridge ties between the mainstream schools and the Polish schools.

However, in many cases and mainly due to the common language, the Polish school not only strengthens the relationships between teachers and parents, but this school is also a meeting place between parents. They meet each other at the school gate, parent committee and during activities such as traditional Polish celebrations. For some parents those meetings are opportunities to get information and support with respect to their children's school trajectories. Similar to the situation in mainstream education, parents' involvement at the Polish school is stronger in primary education than in secondary education. Some parents become close friends and meet also after school. For example, the mothers of two Polish girls became friends at the Polish school, and supported each other by sharing the costs of tutoring in English language when their girls had language problems. It can be assumed that such examples also occur with respect to educational track choices.

### *Perception of the different educational tracks*

Track choice is often influenced by the personal interests of the pupils and of the parents, but also by the dominant perception of the prestige of tracks in broader society. This is also the case for our respondents. The case pupils choose their educational track themselves, as their parents believe this way the educational track matches their child(ren)'s interests and future perspectives best. However, at the same time various parents stimulate or even push their child(ren) to follow an educational track as high as possible – according to their perception – with the general track and the subject 'Latin' on the top of the hierarchy. Almost all pupils of the qualitative research once followed the A-track, which stresses the importance that parents attach to general education. Some parents did not even take into account the talents and competences of their children. One of the pupils (a 16-year-old girl), who had problems succeeding at school explained: 'Although the school already had advised me several times to follow a lower track, my mother obliged me from the first year of secondary school to follow Latin.' Consequently, the school careers of different interviewed youngsters were similar to the 'waterfall system'; they ended up in the vocational track after failing in the general track.

What is interesting and something wherein the Polish school differs completely from mainstream schools, is that the hierarchies between pupils of different educational tracks in mainstream education and the negative stigma on pupils in the vocational track tend to disappear in the community schools, in part because pupils are grouped together differently. In contrast to the Flemish educational system, all classes in the Polish schools are composed of pupils from different mainstream educational tracks. One of the possible consequences is that the strong educational segregation in mainstream education, with its different appreciation of the various tracks, can be altered in the Polish school. Our fieldwork has shown different examples of pupils (and parents) who changed their views on the different educational tracks as a result of community schools being meeting places between pupils (and parents) of different educational tracks. For example, one of the pupils (a 17-year-old boy) did not feel comfortable in the general track and changed to the technical track after being informed about it by some friends of the Polish school who were following the technical track. He learned to appreciate the technical track, which was more suited to his competences and interests, and he succeeded. Another pupil (an 18-year-old boy) with a similar story, argued: 'I always had a lot of friends [in mainstream and in Polish school] who followed the technical track, or the vocational track, and they told me that the technical track could sometimes be more difficult than the general track.' He said that, contrary to what his mother told him, 'They informed me that the technical track can lead to higher studies.'

Up until now we have focused on the role and importance of information about the Flemish educational system in helping pupils to make an adequate study choice. However, next to this, a good estimation of pupils' competences by the pupils themselves, the teachers and parents is equally important. In the section below, we will study the role of the Polish school on this issue.

### *Estimation of pupils' competences and behaviour*

As mentioned above, many newcomer pupils, Polish pupils included, end up in vocational, part-time and special secondary education (Sterckx & Gijsen, 2006; Vlaams Parlement, Commissie vergadering nr. C203, 7 April 2011). According to the teachers at the Polish school, the teachers in mainstream education recommend these educational tracks without (sufficiently) taking into account or without having a good view of pupils' competences and interests. Flemish teachers have difficulties estimating pupils' competences and intelligence supposedly because of the pupil's lack of Dutch proficiency; they tend to construct an image of the pupil primarily based on this proficiency. Another important reason – especially in the case of Polish pupils – is their older age, because primary education in Poland only starts at the age of 7. Consequently, at the transition from primary to secondary education teachers in Flemish education often advise Polish pupils to skip one school year by going to the B-track, which leads mostly to vocational, part-time or special secondary education. The link between educational grade retention and the educational tracking system has been confirmed by previous research (Groenez et al., 2009). The group of pupils in the B-track – on average 11 per cent of all the pupils in Flemish schools – consists of 9 per cent of pupils without an educational grade retention, and 36 per cent of pupils with a grade retention in primary education. Therefore, Polish schoolteachers try to intervene by informing, sensitizing and supporting parents and pupils in their study track choices. One of the teachers at the Polish school in Antwerp stated:

> 'The ones who are successful at the Polish school, I am sure they will be well placed, but with some errors. It happened that one of my brilliant pupils had to go to the vocational track. (. . .) Yes, so (. . .) I informed the mother that she had to enrol her girl in another study track. The girl changed and has been following the technical track since that intervention.'

The principal of the Polish school mentioned that Polish teachers have more facilities and collect more information and resources to get a view of Polish pupils' competences than Flemish school teachers do:

> 'we've got really much more information about the Polish students than the Belgian teachers even after a few years because we speak [in their] own language and we know their families. I think we are important partners for them [mainstream school teachers] just for using our knowledge about uh those cultural differences and many other things. They [mainstream school teachers] sometimes do not understand them [Polish pupils].'

Our qualitative fieldwork has pointed out that especially newcomer parents and pupils confirm the importance of Polish schoolteachers in their educational track choice. This can easily be understood as resulting from their lack of Dutch proficiency. However, newcomers are not the largest group within secondary education of the Polish school; most Polish pupils were newcomers once. The survey at the Polish school demonstrates that only one third of the pupils (10/34) have stayed in Belgium for almost their entire lives.

Polish teachers working in mainstream as well as in Polish community education can function as important bridge ties between both types of education. One of the teachers who teaches in a mainstream as well as in the Polish school, explains:

> 'I am also a teacher at a French mainstream school, and for example, I had four Polish pupils in my class. Two of them did not belong there. I saw them talking and reading in Polish. They [teachers of the French mainstream school] told me that one of those two Polish pupils had dysphasia. I saw that he did not have dysphasia. Dysphasia is a language disorder. He had a language disorder

in French but not in Polish, and they [teachers of the French mainstream school] were going to recommend him to go to the vocational track. So I helped him.'

The teacher helped by explaining to the teachers in mainstream education that the Polish boy did not have a language disorder in his mother tongue. As a result, the perception of teachers in mainstream education on the pupil's competences changed, which prevented them from advising him to follow a 'lower' educational track. This testimony shows the value of Polish teachers who work in mainstream as well as in Polish community education. However, teachers with this double function and relationships between both types of education are scarce.

The common Polish language enables not only the teachers at the Polish school, but also the parents to support the Polish pupils in their educational track choices in mainstream education. Polish schools offer tools to pupils which can strengthen intergenerational communication by focusing on an elaborate Polish curriculum with courses such as maths and geography. While parents stress that they often experience difficulties helping their children with school work in mainstream education, they can and do take up this role with respect to similar tasks in the community schools. As pupils learn to translate the Dutch texts or tasks into Polish, in-depth communication on educational issues between parents and pupils emerges. Through this interaction, parents get a better view on their children's competences and interests, which in turn improves appropriate study track choices.

## *The Polish school as a safety net*

Our fieldwork data have shown that Polish schools not only support Polish parents and/or pupils with their educational track choices in mainstream education, but that these community schools also have a remedial function.

Polish pupils from different educational tracks in mainstream education attend the Polish school. The population survey at the Polish school (n=34) shows that 42 per cent of the youngsters in the second and third year of secondary education follow ASO (the general track) in Flemish mainstream education. The other 55 per cent of the pupils at the Polish school follow technical, (part-time) vocational, OKAN or artistic secondary education in Flemish schools. As mentioned before, a significant number of Polish youngsters, especially newcomers, end up in these tracks – tracks which often lead to less attractive or simply fewer future possibilities – because of their low proficiency in Dutch and their higher age when entering mainstream education. The qualitative fieldwork data have demonstrated that Polish school staff members, parents and pupils consider the Polish school as a safety net for those pupils because the community school gives them opportunities to return and to take their chances on the Polish labour markong these lines, the Polish school principal argues:

> 'There is one group of students who are smart enough, and they are perfect enough in the [Polish] language to finish [succeed] in Polish [educational]

system, but in the Belgian [educational] system they will never attain the same level. So their parents are deciding: "OK, I will maintain your [Polish] language at such a level, (. . .) that you know the books, you know the Polish literature, you can speak without any faults, you can write mostly without any mistakes. Then you can always go back to Poland." They are making them safe [they want to be sure their children do not lose their labour market opportunities in Poland]. Most of these students came here very late [at a higher age] and they aren't successful in [the] Belgian [educational] system. But they are smart enough to go to ASO here if their Dutch proficiency were better.'

In the quotation below, the mother of a 15-year-old Polish boy confirms that while she attaches a lot of importance to succeeding in mainstream education, at the same time she wants her son to be taught the Polish language and culture to give him the opportunity to return to Poland.

'But yes, in my opinion, we live in Belgium, so we have to respect the rules of this country and I want him [her son] to succeed well here [in Flemish mainstream education]. But I also want him to have a basic knowledge of the Polish language and culture, because, as I said, you never know what will happen. So, he has the opportunity to choose to go back to Poland for his work if he would like to.'

## Discussion

This chapter studies the role of the Polish community school as a space providing (alternative) social, cultural and linguistic resources regarding the school trajectory choices of Polish pupils within mainstream education. While numerous (inter)national studies point out that the overall performance level of pupils is very high in Flanders, the PISA findings support the idea that social inequalities are still strongly reproduced by the Flemish school system and over the last few decades stratification related to SES and ethnicity remains largely unchanged (De Meyer & Warlop, 2010). Recently migrated pupils or youngsters with a different socioethnic background from the dominant majority and middle class seem to be confronted with numerous difficulties in this school system (Groenez et al., 2009).

This research has demonstrated that Polish parents and pupils experience several obstacles in mainstream education. Because they are used to a different educational system and due to language barriers between Polish parents (and pupils) and teachers in mainstream education, misunderstandings take place. In the worst case scenarios, as they do not understand each other, school staff in mainstream schools have difficulties adequately understanding pupils' competences, and parents are unable to make the right decisions regarding their children's school trajectories. This results in pupils following educational tracks where they do not belong with respect to their interests and competences. As a result, a significant number of pupils, especially newcomer pupils, have to repeat a school year and/or end up in (half-time) vocational or special secondary education through the 'waterfall system'.

At first sight it could seem that Polish community schools are focused on creating bonding social networks within the Polish community, as pupils are taught the Polish language and 'culture' and enhance the opportunity to take their chances on the Polish labour market. Next to realizing bonding social networks, the qualitative fieldwork data have shown that the Polish community school tries to be a bridge between the Polish community and the Flemish mainstream schools. These community schools are important meeting places between teachers, parents and pupils, where they share information on the Flemish educational system and on pupils' talents. The common Polish language and 'culture' between the different actors in the Polish school, the absence of educational tracks at the Polish schools, and the teachers who are related to both types of schools (mainstream as well as community) are critical success factors. Moreover, the Polish school fills the lack of opportunities for a specific group of immigrant youth within mainstream education by serving as a kind of a safety net. However, Polish schools also have their bottlenecks; teachers with a high Dutch or French proficiency and experience and sufficient knowledge of the Flemish educational system are scarce.

These results can be translated into several policy recommendations. It would be favourable to strengthen the ties between Flemish mainstream education and Polish community schools. A well-organized exchange of information between both types of schools could improve the school trajectories of Polish pupils. Furthermore, this chapter has shown the importance of employing more teachers of ethnic minorities within mainstream education, as they can serve as 'bridge ties'. However, most teachers within Flemish mainstream education are highly educated people of Belgian-Flemish origin who belong to the middle class (Clycq, 2012).

Polish schools have been transforming in fundamental ways in the past few years; the bonding, social networking opportunities created by bringing Polish pupils together in a physical space as well as the broad and in-depth curriculum in the Polish language are changing. Their curriculum is slimmed down and Internet courses are increasingly replacing traditional classroom courses. This chapter shows that the consequences of these current transformations for pupils, parents and teachers with respect to the resources available in their (new) social networks and the different ethnic socialization strategies can be far-reaching. This leads us to the question 'What will the consequences of the reformations of the Polish schools be on the social capital of Polish parents and pupils?' Or, in other words, 'Will Polish schools be able to maintain their function as social resources in the future?' It would be interesting to study these questions in further research.

## Notes

1 Our respondents are pupils with both parents born in Poland.
2 In international scientific literature, many different names are given to this kind of education. In this chapter we opt for the name 'community' schools, as we want to stress that the Polish schools in Belgium are established by and for the Polish ethnic communities themselves and do not form part of mainstream education.
3 The first two years of Flemish secondary education are divided into an A-track, leading to general and technical education, and a B-track, mostly leading to vocational education (www.ond.vlaanderen.be).

4   For a definition of the term 'community cohesion', we refer to Ofsted (2008, p. 3): 'working towards a society in which there is a common vision and sense of belonging by all communities; a society in which the diversity of people's backgrounds and circumstances is appreciated and valued; a society in which similar life opportunities are available to all (. . .).'
5   As mentioned before, secondary education in Flanders is subdivided into four types: ASO (General Secondary Education), TSO (Technical Secondary Education), KSO (Art Secondary Education) and BSO (Vocational Training). In theory, the choice for a specific track solely depends on the capacities and interests of the individual student. In reality, however, there exists a strong hierarchical differentiation between the different types, with ASO at the top and BSO at the bottom (Van Avermaet & Sierens, 2012).
6   Our research is part of the interuniversity research project BET YOU! – Boosting the Educational Trajectories of Youth in Flanders, in which the school careers of pupils of Moroccan, Turkish, Polish, Chinese origin as well as native Flemish pupils in secondary education were examined. For more information on the project 'BET YOU!', see www.oprit14.be.
7   In the Polish educational system there is no differentiation in educational tracks and subjects during the first three years of secondary education (Mikiewicz, 2011).

## References

Anderson, T. & Boyer, M. (1970). *Bilingual Schooling in the United States*. Austin, TX: Southwest Educational Laboratory.

Antrop-Gonzalez, R., Garrett, T. & Vélez, W. (2010). Examining the success factors of high achieving Puerto Rican male high-school students. *Roeper Review*, 2(32), 106–15.

Archer, L., Francis, B. & Mau, A. (2009). 'Boring and stressful' or 'ideal' learning spaces? Pupils' constructions of teaching and learning in Chinese supplementary schools. *Research Papers in Education*, 24(4), 477–97.

Archer, L., Francis, B. & Mau, A. (2010). The Culture Project: Diasporic negotiations of ethnicity, identity and culture among teachers, pupils and parents in Chinese language schools. *Oxford Review of Education*, 36(4), 407–26.

Caestecker, F. (1990). Le multiculturalisme de la Belgique: Une analyse de la politique de scolarisation des enfants polonais en Belgique 1923–1940. *Belgisch tijdschrift voor nieuwste geschiedenis*, 21(3/4), 535–73.

Caestecker, F. (2003). Polish migrants' children in interwar Belgium and the Netherlands: The choice for ethnic education. In J. Belchem & K. Tenfelde (eds), *Polish and Irish Migration in Comparative Perspective* (pp. 169–81). Essen: Klartext.

Clycq, N. (2009). *Van keukentafel tot 'God': Belgische, Italiaanse en Marokkaanse ouders over identiteit en opvoeding*. Antwerpen: Garant.

Clycq, N. (2012). Het onderwijs als monoculturele context? Vanzelfsprekendheden ter discussie. In C. Timmerman, N. Clycq & B. Segaert (eds), *Cultuuroverdracht en onderwijs in een multiculturele context* (pp. 128–55). Gent: Academia Press.

Clycq, N., Nouwen, W. & Vandenbroucke, L. (2014). Meritocracy, deficit thinking and the invisibility of the system: Discourses on educational success and failure. *British Educational Research Journal*, 40(5), 796–819.

Creese, A. (2009). Building on young people's linguistic and cultural continuity: Complementary schools in the United Kingdom. *Theory Into Practice*, 48, 267–73.

Creese, A., Bhatt, A., Bhojani, N. & Martin, P. (2006). Multicultural, heritage and learner identities in complementary schools. *Language and Education*, 20, 23–43.

Creten, H., Van de Velde, V., Van Damme, J. & Verhaest, D. (2004). *De transitie van het initieel beroepsonderwijs naar de arbeidsmarkt met speciale aandacht voor de onderwijsverlaters.* Leuven: HIVA, KU Leuven.

Danhier, J., Jacobs, D., Devleeshouwer, P., Martin, E. & Alarcon, A. (2014). *Naar kwaliteitsscholen voor iedereen? Analyse van de resultaten van het PISA 2012-onderzoek in Vlaanderen en in de Federatie Wallonië-Brussel. Een uitgave van de Koning Boudewijnstichting.* Brussel: Manufast-ABP vzw.

De Meyer, I. & Warlop, N. (2010). *PISA. Leesvaardigheid van 15-jarigen in Vlaanderen: De eerste resultaten van PISA 2009* (UGent: Vakgroep Onderwijskunde/Brussel: Departement Onderwijs en Vorming, Afdeling Strategische Beleidsondersteuning).

Dove, N. (1993). The emergence of black supplementary schools: Resistance to racism in the United Kingdom. *Urban Education, 27*(4), 430–47.

Duquet, N., Glorieux, I., Laurijssen, I. & Van Dorsselaer, Y. (2006). *Wit krijt schrijft beter: Schoolloopbanen van allochtone jongeren in beeld.* Antwerpen: Garant.

European Commission – Eurydice. (2011). *Grade retention during compulsory education in Europe: Regulations and statistics. Education, Audiovisual and Culture Executive Agency – Eurydice:* Brussels.

Francis, B., Archer, L. & Mau, A. (2009). Language as capital, or language as identity? Chinese complementary school pupils' perspectives on the purposes and benefits of complementary schools. *British Educational Research Journal, 35*(4), 519–38.

Gibson, M. (1988). *Accommodation Without Assimilation: Sikh Immigrants in an American High School.* Ithaca, NY: Cornell University Press.

Glick, E. & Hohmann-Marriott, B. (2007). Academic performance of young children in immigrant families: The significance of race, ethnicity, and national origins. *International Migration Review, 41*(2), 371–402.

Goddeeris, I. (2003). De Poolse schoolstrijd in België (1945-ca. 1955): Een schoolvoorbeeld van de strijd tussen Poolse communisten en Londenaars. *Brood en rozen: Tijdschrift voor de geschiedenis van sociale bewegingen, 8*(1), 27–47.

González, N., Moll, L. C., Tenery, M. F., Rivera, A., Rendon, P., Gonzales, R. & Amanti, C. (1995). Funds of knowledge for teaching in Latino households. *Urban Education, 29*(4), 443–70.

Groenez, S., Nicaise, I. & De Rick, K. (2009). *De ongelijke weg door het onderwijs.* In L. Vanderleyden, M. Callens & J. Noppe (eds), *De sociale staat van Vlaanderen 2009* (pp. 33–68). Sint-Niklaas: Drukkerij Room.

Hall, K. A., Özerk, K., Zulfiqar, M. & Tan, J. E. C. (2002). 'This is our school': Provision, purpose and pedagogy of supplementary schooling in Leeds and Oslo. *British Educational Research Journal, 28*(3), 399–418.

Hallinan, T. M. (2001). Sociological perspectives on black-white inequalities in American schooling. *Sociology of Education, 74,* 50–70.

Hirtt, N., Nicaise, I. & de Zutter, D. (2007). *De school van ongelijkheid.* Antwerpen: Epo.

Hughes, D., Rodriguez, J., Smith, E. P., Johnson, D. J., Stevenson, H. C. & Spicer, P., (2006). Parents' ethnic–racial socialization practices: A review of research and directions for future study. *Developmental Psychology, 42*(5), 747–70.

Issa, T. & Williams, C. (2009). *Realising Potential: Complementary Schools in the UK.* Stoke-on-Trent: Trentham Books.

Kao, G. & Thompson, J. (2003). Racial and ethnic stratification in educational achievement and attainment. *Annual Review of Sociology, 29,* 417–42.

Kifano, S. (1996). Afrocentric education in supplementary schools: Paradigm and practice at the Mary McLeod Bethune Institute. *The Journal of Negro Education, 65*(2), 209–18.

Lamote, C., Van Landeghem, G., Blommaert, M., Nicaise, I., De Fraine, B. & Van Damme, J. (2013). *Voortijdig schoolverlaten in Vlaanderen: Een stand van zaken en een voorstel tot aanpak.* In M. Callens, J. Noppe & L. Vanderleyden (eds), *De sociale staat van Vlaanderen 2013* (pp. 13–60). Peer: Drukkerij Hendrikx.

Latuheru, E. & Hessels, M. (1996). Schoolprestaties en de invloed van etnische en sociaaleconomische herkomst. *Tijdschrift voor Onderwijsresearch, 19*(3), 227–39.

Levrau, F., Piqueray, E. & Vancluysen, K. (2011). Een verkenning van de migratie, integratie en participatie van de Poolse minderheidsgroep in Antwerpen. In F. Levrau, P. Loobuyck & C. Timmerman (eds), *Pluriforme integratie. Een verkenning van de migratie, integratie en participatie van de Poolse, Senegalese en Turkse minderheidsgroep in Antwerpen* (pp. 23–130). Antwerp: Steunpunt Gelijkekansenbeleid, University of Antwerp.

Levrau, F., Piqueray, E., Goddeeris, I. & Timmerman, C. (2014). Polish migration in Belgium since 2004: New migration and integration dynamics? *Ethnicities, 14*(2), 303–23.

Li, W. (2006). Complementary schools, past, present and future. *Language and Education, 20*(1), 76–83.

Lucas, S. R. (2001). Effectively maintained inequality: Education transitions, track mobility, and social background effects. *American Journal of Sociology, 106*(6), 1642–90.

Malakoff, M. & Hakuta, K. (1990). History of language minority education in the United States. In A. Padilla, H. Fairchild & C. Valadez (eds), *Advances in Language Education: Theory, Research, and Practice* (pp. 27–45). New York: Sage Publications.

Mikiewicz, P. (2011). School dropout in secondary education: The case of Poland. In S. Lamb et al. (eds), *School Dropout and Completion: International Comparative Studies in Theory and Practice* (pp. 173–90). Poland: Springer.

Moll, L., Amanti, C., Neff, D. & González, N. (1992). Funds of knowledge for teaching: Using a qualitative approach to connect homes and classrooms. *Theory Into Practice, 31*(2), 132–41.

Myers, K. & Grosvenor, I. (2011). Exploring supplementary education: Margins, theories and methods. *History of Education: Journal of the History of Education Society, 40*(4), 501–21.

Oakes, J., Muir, K. & Joseph, R. (2000). Course taking and achievement in math and science: Inequalities that endure. Paper presented at the National Institute for Science Education Conference, May, Detroit, MI.

Ofsted (The Office for Standards in Education, Children's Services and Skills). (2008). *Every language matters.* London: Ofsted.

Piqueray, E. (2011). Recent developments within the Polish community and the Polish schools in Belgium. *The Poland-Polonia Review, 2*, 150–67.

Reay, D. & Mirza, H. (1997). Uncovering genealogies of the margins: Black supplementary schooling. *British Journal of Sociology of Education, 18*, 477–99.

Roosens, E. (1998). *Eigen grond eerst? Primordiale autochtonie: Dilemma van de multiculturele samenleving.* Leuven: Acco.

Stanton-Salazar, R. & Dornbusch, S. (1995). Social capital and the social reproduction of inequality: The formation of informational networks among Mexican-origin high school students. *Sociology of Education, 68*(2), 116–35.

Sterckx, M. & Gijsen, S. (2006). De voornaamste vaststellingen en conclusies uit het onderzoek naar de doorstroming van ex-onthaalklassers in het secundair onderwijs in het eerste en tweede jaar na het onthaaljaar. In T. Koole, J. Nortier & B. Tahitu (eds), *Artikelen van de vijfde sociolinguïstische conferentie* (pp. 417–28). Delft: Eburon.

Suárez-Orozco, C. & Suárez-Orozco, M. (1995). *Transformations: Family Life, and Achievement Motivation Among Latino Youth.* Palo Alto, CA: Stanford University Press.

Timmerman, C. (1999). *Onderwijs maakt het verschil: Socio-culturele praxis en etniciteitsbeleving bij Turkse jonge vrouwen*. Leuven: Acco.

Timmerman, C., Hermans, P. & Hoornaert, I. (2002). *Allochtone jongeren in het onderwijs: Een multidisciplinair perspectief*. Leuven – Apeldoorn: Garant.

Valenzuela, A. & Dornbusch, S. (1994). Familism and social capital in the academic achievement of Mexican-origin and Anglo high school adolescents. *Social Science Quarterly*, 75(1), 18–36.

Van Avermaet, P. & Sierens, S. (2012). Van periferie naar de kern: Omgaan met diversiteit in het onderwijs. In C. Timmerman, N. Clycq & B. Segaert (eds), *Cultuuroverdracht en onderwijs in een multiculturele context* (pp. 16–50). Gent: Academia Press.

Van Houtte, M., Demanet, J. & Stevens, P. A. J. (2012). Self-esteem of academic and vocational students: Does within-school tracking sharpen the difference? *Acta Sociologica*, 55(1), 73–89.

VDAB studiedienst. (2014). *Werkzoekende schoolverlaters 2014, 27e editie: Zet je talenten aan het werk*. Brussels.

Vlaams Ministerie van Onderwijs en Vorming (2009). *Statistisch jaarboek van het Vlaams Onderwijs 2008–2009*. Brussels. Retrieved from: www.ond.vlaanderen.be.

Vlaams Parlement, Commissie voor Onderwijs en Gelijke kansen: Commissie vergadering nr. C203 (7 April 2011). Retrieved from: https://docs.vlaamsparlement.be/docs/handelingen_commissies/2010–2011/c0m203ond22–07042011.pdf.

Zhou, M. & Kim, S. S. (2006). Community forces, social capital, and educational achievement: The case of supplementary education in the Chinese and Korean immigrant communities. *Harvard Educational Review*, 76(1), 1–29.

# Part 4
# Social, systemic and school dynamics

# 10 Aspirations and stigmatization as factors of school success[1]

*Noel Clycq, Ward Nouwen and Marjolein Braspenningx*

## Introduction

Education is one of the most valued social domains in society (Steele *et al.*, 2002). Being successful in this field is often seen as a necessary condition for success in the subsequent transitions into the labour market and family life (Clycq *et al.*, 2013). In this light, it seems reassuring that recent research shows the Flemish educational system to be one of the most highly trusted social institutions in Flanders: 76 per cent of the 'Flemings' had (very) deep trust in education (Studiedienst van de Vlaamse Regering, 2012, p. 35). Moreover, international comparative research such as the PISA-assessments clarify that Flemish education is indeed in the top tiers with respect to performance in mathematics, reading and science subjects (De Meyer & Warlop, 2010). Last but not least, the Flemish government itself expresses its high regard for education by according it the highest budget of all domains it is politically responsible for (Turtelboom, 2014). Suffice to say that education is of the utmost importance to political leaders, and Flemish citizens in general seem to agree.

However, despite these enviable 'results', one wonders why education was one of the most heavily and emotionally debated topics in recent years, especially during the recent elections in May 2014. If Flanders is already at the top, why is there such a great concern with respect to the performance of its educational system? Two main trends can be discerned from the PISA data, which are increasingly perceived as the most important benchmarks not only for educational actors but especially for policy makers (Danhier *et al.*, 2014). One trend is that Flanders' position at the top seems to be threatened. Of course, this generates great anxiety in an era of the so-called knowledge society. While part of the debate focuses on this issue, there seems to be a more urgent matter to address, which manifests as the second trend visible in the PISA results: Flanders is at the top also in terms of social stratification between the highest and lowest performing students. Moreover, important socioethnic segregation processes are apparent throughout Flemish education and have an important influence on the educational trajectories of students. The trajectories of youth with an immigration background[2] in particular are negatively affected. It is an important finding that these differences have not seemed to decrease over the past decade (Jacobs *et al.*, 2009; Wouters & Groenez, 2013).

In this chapter, we try to dig deeper into the underlying mechanisms which could to some extent clarify the general patterns we see reproduced over time. We use the qualitative interview data and focus in particular on how educational success and failure is explained by teachers in 'multiethnic and multicultural' schools and more in particular on how the individual student and his cultural background is represented as a central determinant for educational success and failure. However, not all students with an immigration background are perceived the same way, and their cultural background is not always problematized. In a final paragraph, we take these dominant narratives on the relation between ethnocultural diversity and educational success as a basis to relate them to the survey data. This allows us to test to what extent stigmatized groups of pupils are affected by these negative stereotypes, which in turn contributes to the literature on stereotype threat effects.

## Explaining stratification processes through the social reproduction of inequality

Scholars have long been studying the reproduction and continuity of social phenomena (Giroux, 1980; Hannerz, 1992). The question remains why – given that human beings are 'assumed' by many to be predominantly rational and possess free will – many social patterns persist over time in such a way that human life is to a large extent predictable (Bourdieu, 1990). This is also the case when focusing on the reproduction of inequality and the socioethnic stratification in educational systems around the world. There is no question that many educational outcomes can be predicted beforehand: focusing on the Flemish educational system, the chance is greater that students from families with a lower socioeconomic status, with an immigrant background and/or another home language (than the official language Dutch) will experience difficulties in school (Duquet *et al.*, 2006; Hirtt *et al.*, 2007). A recent report on early school leaving even revealed that variables such as gender, socioeconomic status and home language are strongly correlated to early school leaving: boys, pupils from families with a lower SES and pupils who speak a language other than Dutch at home all have higher risks for leaving school early. Moreover, having a more lowly educated mother puts boys as well as girls at a higher risk, irrespective of the home language (although the risk is higher if your home language is not Dutch). Moreover, an intersectional approach shows how strong the impacts of the combination of gender, class and home language variables can be: 40 per cent of the boys with a lower educated mother and not Dutch as a home language left school before attaining an ISCED 3 level qualification, while this is only the case for 4 per cent of the girls with a higher educated mother and Dutch as a home language (Van Landeghem *et al.*, 2013). European comparative reports show similar results across various countries with different student compositions, with only a few exceptions such as the UK and Portugal (RESL.eu, 2014). Similar results are also found in the United States (Alba & Holdaway, 2013).

As many educational outcomes seem quite predictable, we need to understand why certain negative trends are so difficult to change. In the early 1960s and 1970s, comprehensive analyses and theoretical frameworks were developed to clarify these reproduction mechanisms. Bourdieu and Passeron focused on the importance of one's background and capital accumulation to explain educational outcomes. Working-class students in particular were (and still are) 'failing' in education and theories focusing on their limited intelligence as an explanation were dismissed over time, with the exception of the 1994 publication of *The Bell Curve* (Herrnstein & Murray, 1994). A more common perspective on group differences in educational outcomes is that these differences are related to contextual and certain psycho-social differences between social classes and/or ethnic groups.

A very short overview of some of the most important scholars in this field shows that in different national and educational contexts, these scholars came to rather similar conclusions. For Bourdieu and Passeron (1977), it was clear that working-class students did not fit into the middle-class school environment and that this mismatch was the reason for their 'underperformance'. Similar to this approach, Bernstein (1971) focused more concretely on language use and the linguistic codes of students, parents and educational actors. The differences in these codes, often related to differences in social class, could to some extent explain the differences in educational outcomes. Freire (1970), on the other hand, studied the practice of teaching and developed the metaphor of 'banking education', where students are primarily seen as passive recipients wherein teachers deposit knowledge. These different theoretical approaches of educational policy and practice to some extent share the idea of the importance of power differences in explaining educational outcomes (Applebaum, 2005; Valencia & Black, 2002).

Elaborating on these issues, different scholars have approached schools as essentially contested cultural sites (Levinson & Pollock, 2011). In a similar vein, González et al., (2005) argue that individuals and communities with an immigration background (or minority status, as they call it) often have various resources they can make use of, but these resources – in particular the student's mother tongue when it differs from the main instruction language at school – are often not appreciated by mainstream educators as being useful or important resources. More in particular, Banks and Banks (2010) argue that school curricula are often contested phenomena, and in schools various tensions arise on the design and implementation of 'schooling'. Sometimes mainstream schools adapt to these differing views on the 'content' and practice of schooling, while in other cases, minority communities develop alternative schools, a process sometimes called 'resistance schooling' (Dove, 1993; Hall et al., 2002; Reay & Mirza, 1997). In Chapter 9, Piqueray et al. discuss the process of 'community or complementary' schools as a community force engaging with the limitations set out by mainstream schools (Francis et al., 2009). These findings show how formal schooling is not a neutral process and that minority communities can challenge the way schooling is designed and implemented. However, the findings that communities often develop new ways of schooling outside of formal schooling, or that the challenging and revision of the curriculum is often a difficult process, also show that minorities – often those with a lower socioeconomic status – do not always have the opportunity to adapt mainstream education to their needs.

Mainstream educational systems still tend to reflect the ideas and perspectives of the dominant group in society, and it is this group in their roles as policy makers, principals and teachers that has more power to design and implement the educational policy and practice than subordinate groups such as ethnic minorities and/or socioeconomically vulnerable groups (see, for example, Chapter 7 in this book). These powerful differences often lead to the idea that the dominant perspective is presented as neutral, objective and unproblematic, and that adaptation to this perspective is the best path to educational success (Lukes, 2005). This relates strongly to the idea of subtractive schooling, a term/concept coined by Gibson (1988) and developed by different scholars.

## Subtractive schooling in a meritocratic school environment

Education systems are set up to socialize children into becoming useful and adapted citizens who participate in, help to sustain, as well as improve society (Reay, 2010). From this perspective, education is similar to the civic integration courses designed and implemented to teach new migrants how to become adapted citizens in Flemish society (Bourgeois, 2009, 2013; Smet, 2011). Both are based upon a perspective that new knowledge, behaviour, attitudes and values need to be internalized in order for the individuals to become productive and good citizens (or students). However, as will be argued below, in Flanders the curriculum and representation of society is primarily based upon the perspectives of the society's dominant majority group. This is apparent in Flanders where most students are enrolled in Catholic schools, where Dutch is the omnipresent language of instruction, and the headscarf and 'the home language' is banned in secondary schools. A diversity of individuals is obliged to participate in an educational system which is designed and implemented by the ethnic and cultural majority group in Flanders.[3]

This resembles the discussion between a subtractive or an additive educational approach (Gibson, 1988; Roosens, 1995; Valenzuela, 1999). In the former case, one general and dominant perspective on education (and more broadly on society) is put forward. In the case of Flanders, this is apparent when one looks at the role of identity and related cultural features. In many cases but in particular with respect to minority languages, the Flemish educational system is characterized by a subtractive approach. In different schools, signs are put up saying 'Here we speak Dutch' and our own research has shown that many schools sanction the use of the home or native language on the school premises (Clycq et al., 2014). This reflects the dominant perspective in Flanders, especially on policy level, on the centrality of Dutch as *the* language of Flemish society, and consequently the road to success in this society. Various (mostly social-democratic) ministers of education throughout the decades have signalled that proficiency in Dutch is the only way to become successful and is as such a prerequisite for entering the educational system and not something to be mastered over the years. One of the ministers even adhered to the motto: multilingualism leads to zerolingualism (Blommaert & Van Avermaet, 2008). However, this negative representation of multilingualism is not directed towards all languages, considering that implicit and sometimes very explicit reference is made to 'good' multilingualism versus 'bad' multilingualism. Underlying this categorization is an economic rationale: the previous minister of education stated that as a society, Flanders should value its multilingualism and needs to think about incorporating the main languages of the BRIC-countries (Brasil, Russia, India and China), as economic opportunities can open up in the future, given their 'booming economies' (Smet, 2011). The reasons for implementing a subtractive or an additive approach towards diversity and multilingualism seem to be inspired by an economic approach, rather than a humanistic or multiculturalist approach.

This is in line with another mechanism underlying many educational systems, that of meritocracy. Research shows that the dominant group that designs the educational system tends to represent this system as democratic and meritocratic (Valencia, 2010; Weis et al., 2006). As a consequence, inequalities appearing in education are explained in individualistic terms and causes are sought outside this system. While in the past, mainly working-class families were represented as deficient and ill-adapted to the educational system (Bourdieu & Passeron, 1977), in recent decades, the scope has broadened to include ethnic minorities. As societies and schools are diversifying, existing differences become salient and new boundaries are constructed. In many European countries, as is shown by consecutive comparative research projects such as the PISA-data or the data from the European Labour Force survey, strong educational inequalities emerged between ethnic minority groups and ethnic majority groups (Danhier et al., 2014; De Meyer & Warlop, 2010). Whereas in the past working-class values and behaviours were problematized and said to be the cause of educational failure, this has now shifted towards the problematization of ethnic minority families who are assumed to hold on too strongly to their language, to be unmotivated, and less or simply not interested in education (Alba & Holdaway, 2013; Clycq et al., 2013; Gibson et al., 2013). These families are mainly represented and approached as lacking the right features to be successful in education and are told that they should adapt better to the requirements of the educational system and broader society. A difficult question to answer – as always – is, what are the effects of such stigmatization processes related to ethnicity and/or study track, in particular in an educational system that is strongly stratified and segregated (Nouwen & Mahieu, 2012; Wouters & Groenez, 2013)?

## Representation of the other and the influence of stigmatization processes

An abundance of research has focused on stigmatization in educational settings and the stereotype threat literature in particular has shown some interesting insights. In that line of research, the important question has arisen regarding how students in stigmatized groups respond to the negative stereotypes in education that threaten their (academic) self-concept. A prerequisite to experiencing a 'stigmatization threat' is that the stigma be related to a relevant social group identity that exists in a domain valued by the individual (Aronson et al., 1999; Steele et al.,

2002). If the individual did not care about a stereotype, it would probably not influence him. Nonetheless, it is not necessary that an individual be convinced that the stereotype will impede success in this domain; it is sufficient that the individual be conscious of the stereotype with respect to 'his group' and that he value the domain sufficiently to invest in disproving the stereotype (Aronson et al., 1999). The importance of the educational domain seems clear, as it is universally valued in society and success in education is represented as a necessary condition for success on the labour market and in family life (Clycq et al., 2014; Steele et al., 2002). Consequently, a stereotyped student is likely to reduce the negative effects of this stereotype with respect to their social and personal identity (Aronson et al., 1999; Steele & Aronson, 1995; Steele et al., 2002). Various strategies are possible, ranging from more chronic responses such as disidentification from the educational domain, to more acute reactions – like discounting negative feedback from teachers for being dishonest and disengaging one's academic self-concept from actual school performances – which could lead up to more chronic strategies. All-in-all, most strategies serve the protection of a student's (academic) self-concept (Régner & Loose, 2006; Steele et al., 2002).

While schools can be environments that threaten pupils' (and parents') identity, they can also be spaces that individuals perceive as 'identity safe' (Antrop-González, 2006). Through well-thought of and broadly supported programmes, schools can foster ethnic, cultural and religious diversity (and so much more) in such a way that actors in these schools feel appreciated (Banks & Banks, 2010). The educational and school policy, the curriculum and the composition of the staff in such schools are not solely designed according to the perspectives of the dominant group in society, but incorporate the perspectives of parents and students from diverse backgrounds.

Given the insights from the current literature and the data gathered via our qualitative and quantitative fieldwork, we aim to answer the following research questions. How is educational success and failure defined and explained by teachers in schools with many students possessing an immigration background? What weight is given in this explanation to the role of the different actors involved? Is ethnic and/or cultural diversity (or concentration of specific ethnic groups) as defined by school staff used as an explanatory variable in these discourses? If stigmatization of specific minority pupils and parents is present, to what extent is this stigmatization related to pupils' identification with education?

## Research context, methodology and sample

This chapter is based upon a research project focusing on the educational trajectories of students with an immigrant background in Flemish secondary education. To gain sufficient descriptive and in-depth data on these trajectories, different methodologies were applied. In this chapter we focus on the qualitative (9 schools) and quantitative fieldwork (90 schools) within the school environment across 3 cities, but do not incorporate the findings from the fieldwork executed outside of the school (for some specific findings on this, see Chapter 9). The selected schools are situated in one of three Flemish cities: Antwerp, Ghent and Genk. The first two are Flanders' largest cities and boast a large amount of ethnic and cultural diversity, and are therefore most suited for research on urban multicultural education. Genk, a city with only roughly 65,000 inhabitants, is included in the study because it provides us a different profile of immigration. The specific history of immigration to Genk is closely linked to its previous function as an important mining area up until the 1980s, and the city still has a large, although less diverse, immigrant population. In the three cities mentioned above, we conducted a survey resulting in a database composed of 11,015 unique, non-blank records, representing just about 50 per cent of the foreseen population (third and fourth year of secondary education). Around 43 per cent of these students has at least one grandparent who was born abroad. For the analysis presented in this chapter we rely on two databases, one of a qualitative nature and one of a quantitative nature. In the former, the research team interviewed 110 pupils and over 80 school staff linked to a total of 10 schools. The quantitative database survey consists of data from 6,244 students. As said, the ethnographic fieldwork collected in-depth data on 114 focus students[4] in their school and community environment.

For the ethnographic fieldwork within the selected cities, we focused on pupils with a Chinese, Moroccan, Polish and Turkish immigration background, based upon our condition that at least all their grandparents were born in mainland China, Morocco, Poland or Turkey, respectively. As we wanted to disentangle the influence of SES and that of immigration background, and as there were no similar data available for those students without an immigration background (for whom all grandparents had been born in Belgium), ten focus students without immigration background were included in the analysis as well. The focus schools were selected on the basis of their school population (socioethnic composition), curriculum (tracks) and governing body (public/private). These schools were supplemented with a few additional schools in order to study more specifically the widely dispersed Chinese community. The selection of the 114 focus students was based on four central variables: ethnic background, sex, study track and school career. It is important to notice that regarding these selection criteria, we were not striving for a representative sample, but rather for a group of students with significant variation with respect to these variables.

Next to the quantitative–qualitative triangulation, the ethnographic fieldwork also applied extensive triangulation of different qualitative methods: in-depth interviewing, autobiographical interviewing, focus group discussions, and participant observation in communities and schools (Miles & Huberman, 1994). A year in advance of the fieldwork, a first information meeting was organized for the total student body of the second grade of each focus school. Subsequently, focus group discussions with students were organized in a class context. The selected focus students were then interviewed extensively by both the school and community research teams throughout the remainder of the two-year fieldwork period. The school researchers – who only did fieldwork within the school – also interviewed the school principals and a range of teachers, and by doing so, made some observations in the focus schools. Meanwhile, community researchers – who only did fieldwork in the home or community environment of students – interviewed the focus students' parents and peers.

Evidently, the ethnographic fieldwork delivered a wide range of complementary data, all related to the direct environment of at least one of the focus students. To be able to comprehensively address these qualitative data, interviews were fully transcribed, coded and analysed using NVivo 9 software. By use of a uniform and detailed coding scheme (both thematic and case-related), different discourses on educational success and/or failure of students were revealed, thereby broadening and deepening our understanding of the statistical findings.

To test the quantitative hypothesis, we rely on a database that contains 6,244 pupils in the third or fourth year of Flemish secondary education in the cities Antwerp, Genk and Ghent.[5] With respect to the survey data, the SES variable was constructed by running an exploratory factor analysis on a series of variables connected to the pupils' SES. The final factor was determined by the labour market situation of both parents, their educational attainment, as well as the availability of a quiet room, a computer and Internet at home. To determine the pupil's ethnic background, we took into account the student's place of birth, as well as the country of birth of their father, mother and two grandmothers. As we addressed in the description of our sample, the 'ethnic' background is applied as a dichotomous variable distinguishing pupils with no immigration background and those with non-mixed Turkish or Moroccan immigration backgrounds. It is important to emphasize that we do not argue that there are no ethnic group related differences within the Moroccan/Turkish and 'other' categories. However, as will be argued below, in terms of stigmatization within Flemish education and in statistics on education, pupils in the Turkish/Moroccan ethnic groups find themselves in a similar negatively stigmatized position.

In order to test our disidentification hypothesis, we used Shavelson and Marsh's (1986) measurement of a general academic self-concept to construct the *pupil's academic self-concept*. Since previous research has shown that academic achievement is more correlated with academic self-concept than with general self-esteem (Marsh, 1987; Van Houtte et al., 2012), we argue to test the psychological disengagement hypotheses using this scale rather than a global self-esteem scale (Régner & Loose, 2006). Thus, we will test if and how psychological disengagement manifests itself. The other main variable in these analyses is the pupil's academic performance level, measured through their grade point average (GPA) at the end of the second grade of secondary education. This GPA value is based on a self-reported scale and categorizes the pupil's GPA as follows: less than 50 per cent, 50–60 per cent, 60–70 per cent, 70–80 per cent and more than 80 per cent. Yet, the five-point scale in the survey data did not limit us to working with a categorical variable. Normality testing encouraged us to use the self-reported GPA as a proxy for a continuous variable in the analyses.

# Results

## *The educational situation in the research areas: Antwerp, Genk and Ghent*

Before focusing on the qualitative data, we use the survey data to illustrate the educational situation in the three cities where data were collected. This picture relates important sociodemographic variables such as immigration background and socioeconomic status to educational variables such as grade retention and educational track. The strong stratification processes discussed in the theoretical framework are immediately and clearly revealed in this picture via correspondence analysis[6] (Figure 10.1). Students not having experienced grade retention tend to be the no-immigration background students (BEL), students with a high SES and students in the general track. At the other end of the figure, a group of students can be found with two years or more of grade retention. Here we can find a strong correspondence with students of Moroccan or Turkish immigration background (MTM) and students in the vocational track. Students with an immigration background other than Moroccan and Turkish can be found to take a position in between natives and students with a Moroccan or Turkish background. Consequently, the educational trajectories of social groups can differ strongly according

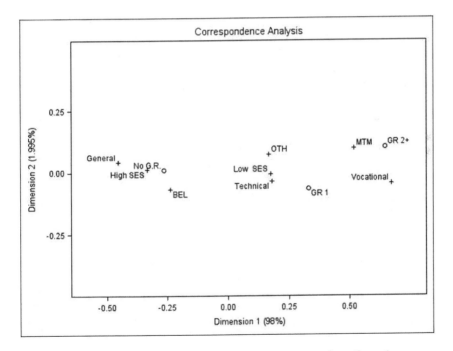

*Figure 10.1* Correspondence analysis representing the association of specific student characteristics in our sample[1]

to their SES and ethnic background. More specifically, the relation between both variables shows important socioethnic stratification processes.

It is within this educational context that actors such as teachers, principals but also students and parents construct meaning and represent 'the other' with respect to successful versus failing educational trajectories. The analyses below show that these stratification processes are discussed in hierarchical terms wherein stigmatization processes are omnipresent.

### Narratives on the unmotivated and unwilling student

When explaining differences in educational outcomes, specific groups of failing students are easily singled out by school personnel, of which Turkish and Moroccan students are the most problematic in their eyes. While research has incessantly shown that an explanation of differences in educational outcomes is inherently complex, it is clear that school personnel focus on two specific elements: on the microlevel, the role of the students and on the mesolevel, the role of the family. Absent or only rarely touched upon in these discourses is the role of the school, teachers or policy makers – even though they design and/or implement educational policy, whereas students and parents are simply subject to these policies and practices. However, when looking for explanations of the aforementioned phenomena, the problems and deficiencies are placed outside the school and educational environment.

The first crucial element in explaining outcomes is the role of the student himself. School outcomes depend first and foremost upon this individual student, who has to be motivated, interested and make the right choices (with respect to track or subject) if he wants to succeed. It seems an undeniable logic in a meritocratic discourse: if you want it, you can do it. The school (and its staff) is presented as the facilitator, offering all the necessary help but more often than not, not being accepted by the students (and parents). As a teacher in a Genk school explained:

> 'So the school is really trying its best to bring students to the same level as other students. But the responsibility is also to a large extent on the part of the students themselves. And that's where the shoe pinches sometimes.'

Some teachers become demotivated themselves when they feel the students are not accepting help or are not willing to take the necessary steps, as one explained:

> 'Sometimes I try. I try my best, but if that really accomplishes something? Usually not, no. But I'm talking about students at the beginning of the school year, then you can motivate them, but for example in this period now. Someone who has given up because he has such bad marks so he says "I'm not doing anything any more". That's really difficult.'

Some teachers reported a similar problem, in that students do not even understand why the help is offered – they do not see themselves as needing any help. According to these teachers, this phenomenon is in part related to the parents, who do not understand the importance of extra help, either. One teacher said:

> 'If you offer some extra support, they do not perceive it as very important and they see it as an additional load and not as an extra favour, what they are offered. It is very difficult motivating them with that and they also do not understand why the hell should I do anything extra. Why me and not the others? And you have to try to explain that to them, and that works better only as they get older. But first- and second-year students are very sensitive to that. (. . .) Also, the parents do not understand it quite well. Why is my son or daughter like that again? When I ask an non-migrant student, it is considered more like "okay, it's nice that you (. . .)". So that will probably be a bit of cultural difference.'

The last narrative above shows that the parents, the home situation and even the cultural background are brought into the picture to explain why certain groups in society do not understand the importance of education. So, while the individual student is often singled out as the most important actor on the microlevel, the focus also shifts towards the family environment at the mesolevel. A dominant narrative among school staff is that students cannot do everything alone and need the support of their parents to become successful. However, if these parents are not interested in education, are not willing to invest and to be involved, and – most importantly – do not want to learn the dominant language 'Dutch', then that student is a 'lost cause'.

### Narratives on the deficient home environment

As mentioned before, in a multiethnic and multicultural (school) environment and with such strong educational inequalities correlating with variables such as ethnicity, it is to be expected that processes of subtractive schooling are emerging (Roosens, 1998; Valenzuela, 1999). A second dominant narrative is revealed when school staff discuss the role of the home environment. The latter is often represented as problematic and an important obstacle for students in their educational trajectories, as a teacher from a school in Genk explained:

> 'At home, there is practically no education, leaving aside if they are even followed up [by their parents]. So the school diaries are rarely or never checked [. . .] Honestly, I think they're all, quote unquote, 'poor souls' [. . .] there are some abuses, believe me. It all comes down to what I call language deficiencies. There is no education. The boys don't even stand a chance, they aren't educated, they are abandoned.'

Home language is often singled out as the most important indicator of a deficient upbringing and of parents unwilling to integrate and participate in society. A teacher from a school in Antwerp said:

'It might be something stupid, but watching television, they continue watching television [programmes from their country of origin] – OK, that might be a connection with their country. That's the first thing they all have, satellite connection and they continue to watch all those programmes . . . While I think that is so important to watch all that in Dutch, movies – subtitle them in Dutch! At parent-teacher conferences I always say that to parents, but if that really happens?'

Some teachers even report confronting parents directly with their deficient parental practices. A teacher from a school in Antwerp explained:

'At one parent evening I meet a father of a girl from the fifth-year Care Course. "Hey, I have bad results [for your daughter]" and then he starts to me like "You see, yes, and she and she and she" and then I say, "Sir, have you already thought of it being your mistake?, that your daughter who was born here in Belgium has a language deficiency, and that because of your failing she has to clean together with you in the same company you work for?"'

Although research abundantly showed that socioeconomic status remains one of the most important variables related to educational differences, this is seldom touched upon by school staff. Students' and parents' ethnic, cultural, linguistic and religious features become the most important explanatory variables, thus enabling actors 'representing' the dominant educational system to remain unproblematized themselves. The deficiencies are placed outside the school environment, while the latter is presented as democratic, meritocratic and neutral when it comes to equal educational opportunities.

## Narratives on successful and unsuccessful minorities

However, the representation of minorities is more complex than discussed until now. What was implicit in all the narratives shown above is that especially Turkish- and Moroccan-origin students and parents are problematized and stigmatized. But this is not the case for all students and families with an ethnic minority background. In Flanders, Chinese, Polish or Italian minorities are represented much more positively based upon a presumed cultural and ethnic closeness with the Flemish native population, or, in the case of Chinese students, with a strong motivation to perform well. This representation of minorities is thus also a categorization of minorities in a hierarchical order. The principal of a school in Genk said:

'The Polish people and Italians have never really been experienced the way the Turks and Moroccans have been, huh. They were also with less [the idea that Polish and Italian migration was much smaller in absolute numbers]. They look similar [to us], which is also a difference, eh.'

As said, especially Moroccan (and Turkish) students are represented in quite negative terms:

'X she's a real Moroccan. She has 85 faces (. . .). She lies and lies and lies and lies and lies with a grin on her face and you have no idea that that child is lying to you.'

While Chinese-origin students are also stereotyped, it is clear that this happens in more positive terms, in line with the model minority theory (Archer, Francis, & Mau, 2010). A teacher in Antwerp discussed:

R: 'Yeah, and it was clear from the first week he [Chinese student] was here, he was someone who was very focused on 'I have to do this' and 'I want that'. Also very strict with himself.'
I: 'Who had discipline?'
R: 'Yeah, who really had discipline as they in China often have [. . .]. So, if you see, Olympics, training and sport. But that is someone who calls himself that and I think that is actually really great.'

The analysis above shows that quite a few dominant and stigmatizing narratives are present among the teachers we interviewed. Especially Moroccan- and Turkish origin students are represented in negative terms, not only in relation to the dominant ethnic majority, but also in relation to other, supposedly more integrated minorities.

## Psychological disengagement as a stigmatized group's reaction to stereotype threat

In this section we relate the findings regarding the Flemish urban educational context and its narratives on the explanations for educational success and failure to the survey data. As the 'ethnic minorities' problematized and stigmatized (mainly) in the teacher discourses presented above are Moroccans and Turks, we focused on those groups in the statistical analyses, testing effects of stigmatization. Moreover, in contrast to the group of pupils within the group of other ethnic backgrounds, these groups were sufficiently large and homogeneous to allow for more in-depth statistical analysis.

As discussed in the theoretical sections, research shows that stigmatized individuals react to certain stigmatization processes and deploy specific strategies to protect their self-concept. We therefore start from the finding that students in vocational education and those with Turkish or Moroccan backgrounds – and especially this particular combination of ethnicity and track – can be considered to belong to a stigmatized group in Flemish education (Clycq et al., 2014; Van Houtte et al., 2012). One of the main strategies found in stereotype threat effect literature is that such individuals disengage their academic self-concept from their achievements in education to protect their self-concept (Aronson et al., 1999; Steele et al., 2002). As Turkish and Moroccan students in vocational education are subjected to this double stigmatization, we tested the relation between students' GPA and academic self-concept separately per subgroup, defined by both their educational track and ethnic background. Per subgroup we engaged in a regression analysis, controlling for gender and SES. It is important to acknowledge that no causal relations can be tested, since the direction of the relations between students' GPA and academic self-concept is not clear.

We start by reporting the influence of the control variables gender and SES on students' academic self-concept for the different subgroups. Since both control variables can be defined as exogenous variables, the direction of the effects are clear. The pupil's SES does not yield significant effects in most analyses – that is, when controlling for at least gender and GPA. Only native students in technical education experience a small, positive effect from SES ($\beta$=0.06363; p<.05) on their academic self-concept. Gender mainly affects students' academic self-concept for native students, for the students with a minority background, the results only show a (albeit rather strong) negative effect in general education. For all significant effects of gender, we can report that female students report a lower academic self-concept than boys.

Next, we report on the relation between students' GPA and academic self-concept. When exploring the results, we can confirm our psychological disengagement hypothesis: for students in the least stigmatized group – i.e. students in general education, especially for those without an immigration background –

Table 10.1 Standardized regression parameter estimates for the regression analyses on relation between GPA and academic self-concept ($\star$ = p<.05)

|  | Native pupils in general education | Native pupils in technical education | Native pupils in vocational education |
|---|---|---|---|
| Gender | −0.17116$\star$ | −0.07766$\star$ | −0.07871$\star$ |
|  | 0.02999 | 0.04893 | 0.07058 |
| SES | 0.02770 | 0.06363$\star$ | −0.00293 |
|  | 0.03205 | 0.04901 | 0.06810 |
| GPA | 0.44057$\star$ | 0.23623$\star$ | 0.20552$\star$ |
|  | 0.01900 | 0.02912 | 0.03301 |
| Adj. $R^2$ | 0.21 | 0.07 | 0.04 |
| N used | 2778 | 1260 | 643 |
|  | MTM[1] Pupils in general education | MTM pupils in technical education | MTM pupils in vocational education |
| Gender | −0.28032$\star$ | −0.10366 | −0.05351 |
|  | 0.08887 | 0.09722 | 0.08067 |
| SES | −0.05910 | 0.01586 | 0.06731 |
|  | 0.08631 | 0.09339 | 0.07405 |
| GPA | 0.27641$\star$ | 0.14577$\star$ | 0.15055$\star$ |
|  | 0.05468 | 0.05426 | 0.03809 |
| Adj. $R^2$ | 0.14 | 0.02 | 0.02 |
| N used | 328 | 314 | 519 |

1 Students of Moroccan or Turkish origin.

the results show a strong relation between their GPA and academic self-concept (native: β=0.44057, p<.05; minority: β=0.27641, p<.05). This strong positive correlation is significantly lower when considering the parameters for students in technical and vocational education. The lowest correlations are found for students in the most stigmatized group – i.e. students with a Turkish or Moroccan immigrant background in technical and vocational education. We can therefore state that those students in the most stigmatized groups indeed disengage their GPA from their academic self-concept as theorized by the stereotype threat literature. This could be interpreted as a (not necessarily conscious) protection mechanism to maintain a positive self-concept in a (educational) domain wherein success for them seems difficult to achieve. However, more research is needed to understand the underlying processes and to gain more insights into the long-term effects of this psychological disengagement strategy.

## Discussion: identity-safe and identity-dangerous schools

In the introduction to this chapter, the Flemish educational system was described as a system with strong stratification processes related to the socioeconomic and ethnic background of students. Despite important financial input by the Flemish government and the efforts of various actors involved, the social reproduction of inequality is one of the main characteristics of the Flemish educational system. In such an educational environment, socially vulnerable students are especially at risk. In few countries is the social determination of performance differences between the 'best' and the 'worst' students this strong (Danhier et al., 2014). Specific groups of students, those with a lower socioeconomic background and/or with an immigration background, remain overrepresented in the category of students at-risk. They are predominantly enrolled in the vocational track or in part-time vocational education, they experience more grade retention and they leave secondary school without a degree more often than native Flemish students. This chapter relates this structural environment to the interactions between students and teachers, and more in particular to the narratives of school staff on the ethnocultural diversity present in their classrooms.

The findings show that specific dominant narratives emerge, mainly in the school staff discourses. School success is often defined in individualistic and meritocratic terms: individual students need to make the right choices, need to be motivated and will then become successful. This implies that if they are not successful, it is their own fault, and – here, a second narrative emerges – their deficient home environment. Minority parents are insufficiently interested, hold on to their culture and language too much, and are therefore an obstacle in the educational trajectories of their children. The third dominant narrative nuances this dichotomy between the majority versus a cluster of minority groups, as mainly Turkish- and Moroccan-origin students and parents are seen as problematic while others such as Chinese, Polish or Italian families are represented as much more similar to the dominant group in terms of motivation, interest in education and overall cultural outlook. This could be perceived as a counterintuitive finding, in particular with respect to the Polish and Chinese families, as these have a much more recent immigration background than the Turkish and Moroccan families, who have been part of established communities already for some decades. However, research on the intersection of identity, culture and class shows these processes are found across different countries (Leonardo, 2009). With respect to the context of Flanders and the Flemish education system, Piqueray et al. discuss the case of the Polish families more elaborately in another chapter of this book. The case of the Chinese families is often found in international research and captured with the concept of 'model minority' (Min, 2006; Song & Wang, 2003). In Clycq et al. (2014) teacher and school staff discourses on Polish and Chinese students and families are indeed more positive than those on Turkish or Moroccan students. It is shown that this is mainly due to the representation of the 'culture' and religion of the latter two groups as obstructing (educational) success, while in particular 'Chinese culture' is represented as synonymous for hard work, discipline and success, even though this is disputed in research (Min, 2006). The case of the Italian families is seldom discussed in the domain of education – they are in that domain not a particularly successful or model minority in Flanders – but research on family socialization processes shows how strong the assumption that Italians are much closer to Belgians than Moroccans or Turks is felt in everyday life (Clycq, 2012, 2015; Clycq et al., 2014). The creation of a common European identity of which Polish and Italians are part and Turkish and Moroccans are not, is often argued as one of the main reasons these minorities are perceived more positively in Flanders (Roosens, 1995, 1998).

Returning to our main argument, research, and stereotype threat literature in particular, has shown that negative stigmatization processes such as those directed towards students with a Turkish and Moroccan immigration background can have negative effects on the academic self-concept and educational performance of students. In our own research we could only study these effects very limitedly. Nevertheless, it was shown that stigmatized groups are indeed more inclined to disengage their academic self-concept from their actual test results than groups with a more positive image in the educational domain, as well as to develop strategies to protect their self-concept from this stigmatization, as was hypothesized based on the main findings within the stereotype threat literature.

These are important findings, insofar as schools to a large extent can be identified as 'identity safe' or 'identity dangerous'. In the former the school is a positive and safe environment to experience and practice your identity, wherein differences with respect to language, religion or other cultural elements are not problematized (Antrop-González, 2006). However, this is not always the case and socially vulnerable minorities in particular are victim of harsh stigmatization processes and subjected to subtractive schooling processes (Gibson, 1988; Gibson et al., 2013; Roosens, 1995; Valenzuela, 1999). For these minorities, schools are not identity-safe environments, considering that their language and often also their religion (in particular Islam) is strongly problematized.

When explaining continuing differences in educational outcomes and stratification processes, the scope needs to be broadened in order to study the role and effect of stigmatization. Schools are not neutral spaces where only formal relations between students and teachers are performed, but are reflections of broader social processes present in Flemish society. A broader scope is necessary to gain more insight into the reproduction of these negative differences between social categories.

## Notes

1 This chapter elaborates on the main findings of two articles: 'Meritocracy, deficit thinking and the invisibility of the system: Discourses on educational success and failure' (Clycq et al., 2013) and 'The role of feeling respected by teachers in pupils' psychological disengagement and disidentification in Flemish secondary education' (Nouwen & Clycq, in review).
2 A general definition that is often used in Flemish research and also in this chapter is that youngsters with an immigration background are those youngsters who themselves have migrated to Belgium or those who have at least one parent or grandparent that migrated to Belgium.
3 In Flanders there is a 'compulsory learning age' until age 18, and a very small number of students are educated by their parents, for example, until they are 18. However, they too have to follow a general curriculum similar to that of mainstream education.
4 Initially, there were 90 focus pupils (4 minority communities × 20 pupils + 1 native group × 10 pupils) selected, extra pupils were introduced to the fieldwork to compensate for attrition.
5 Age 14–16 in case of no grade retention.
6 Correspondence analysis (CA) is a technique for exploring and describing tables of categorical data (see Blasius & Greenacre, 1994; Greenacre, 1984; Watts, 1997). We produced the CA of the pupil-by-background variables to explore whether the picture of a socio-ethnic achievement gap can be found in our dataset. In Figure 10.1, the CA expresses the relationships between these variables as points in a bi-plot (see Weller and Romney, 1990).

## References

Alba, R. & Holdaway, J. (2013). *The Children of Immigrants at School: A Comparative Look at Integration in the United States and Western Europe*. New York: New York University Press.
Antrop-González, R. (2006). Toward the school as sanctuary concept in multicultural small school urban education: Implications for small high school reform. *Curriculum Inquiry*, 36(3), 273–301.
Applebaum, B. (2005). In the name of morality: Moral responsibility, whiteness and social justice education, *Journal of Moral Education*, 34(3), 277–90.
Archer, L., Francis, B. & Mau, A. (2010). The culture project: Diasporic negotiations of ethnicity, identity and culture among teachers, pupils and parents in Chinese language schools. *Oxford Review of Education*, 36(4), 407–26.
Aronson, J., Lustina, M. J., Good, C., Keough, K., Steele, C. M. & Brown, J. (1999). When white men can't do math: Necessary and sufficient factors in stereotype threat. *Journal of Experimental Social Psychology*, 35, 29–46.
Banks, A. J. & Banks, C. A. M. (2010). *Multicultural Education: Issues and Perspectives*. Hoboken, NJ: Wiley-Blackwell.
Bernstein, B. (1971). *Class, Code and Control: Volume 1 – Theoretical Studies Towards a Sociology of Language*. London: Routledge.

Blasius, J. & Greenacre, M. J. (1994). Computation of correspondence analysis. In M. J. Greenacre & J. Blasius (eds), *Correspondence Analysis in the Social Sciences* (pp. 3–78). San Diego, CA, Academic Press.

Blommaert, J. & Van Avermaet, P. (2008). *Taal, onderwijs, en de samenleving: De kloof tussen beleid en realiteit.* Berchem: EPO.

Bourdieu, P. (1990). *The Logic of Practice.* Cambridge: Polity Press.

Bourdieu, P. & Passeron, J. C. (1977). *Reproduction in Education, Society and Culture.* London: Sage Publications.

Bourgeois, G. (2009). Policy document civic integration (*Beleidsnota inburgering en integratie*). Flemish Government. Retrieved from: www.inburgering.be/inburgering/sites/www.inburgering.be.inburgering/files/Beleidsnota_Inburgering_Integratie_2009-2014.pdf.

Bourgeois, G. (2013). Policy document civic integration (*Beleidsnota inburgering en integratie*). Flemish Government. Retrieved from: www.integratiebeleid.be/vlaams-integratiebeleid/beleidsbrieven-en-beleidsnotas.

Clycq, N. (2012). 'My daughter is a free woman, so she can't marry a Muslim': The gendering of ethno-religious boundaries. *European Journal of Women's Studies*, 19(2), 157–71.

Clycq, N. (2015). From 'people just like us' to the 'fundamentally other' in an era of antiracism: The instrumental use of religion to exclude the other while avoiding stigma. *Current Sociology*, 1–18. DOI: 10.1177/0011392115583679.

Clycq, N., Nouwen, W. & Vandenbroucke, A. (2013). Meritocracy, deficit thinking and the invisibility of the system: Discourses on educational success and failure. *British Educational Research Journal* (early view).

Clycq, N., Timmerman, C., Van Avermaet, P., Wets, J. & Hermans, P. (2014). *Oprit 14: Naar een schooltraject zonder snelheidsbeperkingen.* Gent: Academia Press.

Danhier, J., Jacobs, D., Devleeshouwer, P., Martin, É. & Alarcon, A. (2014). *Naar kwaliteitsscholen voor iedereen? Analyse van de resultaten van het PISA 2012-onderzoek in Vlaanderen en in de Federatie Wallonië-Brussel.* Brussel: Koning Boudewijnstichting.

De Meyer, I. & Warlop, N. (2010). *PISA. Leesvaardigheid van 15-jarigen in Vlaanderen: De eerste resultaten van PISA 2009.* Gent: Universiteit Gent, Vakgroep Onderwijskunde/Brussel: Departement Onderwijs en Vorming, Afdeling Strategische Beleidsondersteuning.

Dove, N. D. E. (1993). The emergence of black supplementary schools: Resistance to racism in the United Kingdom. *Urban Education*, 27, 430–47.

Duquet, N., Glorieux, I., Laurijssen, I. & Van Dorsselaer, Y. (2006). *Wit krijt schrijft beter: Schoolloopbanen van allochtone jongeren in beeld.* Antwerpen/Apeldoorn: Garant.

Francis, B., Archer, L. & Mau, A. (2009). Language as capital, or language as identity? Chinese complementary school pupils' perspectives on the purposes and benefits of complementary schools. *British Educational Research Journal*, 35(4), 519–38.

Freire, P. (1970). *Pedagogy of the Oppressed.* New York: Continuum.

Gibson, M. (1988). *Accommodation without Assimilation: Sikh Immigrants in an American High School.* Ithaca, NY: Cornell University Press.

Gibson, M., Carrasco, S., Pàmies, J., Ponferrada, M. & Ríos-Rojas, A. (2013). Different systems, similar results: Youth of immigrant origin at school in California and Catalonia. In R. Alba & J. Holdaway (eds), *The Children of Immigrants at School: A Comparative Look at Integration in the United States and Western Europe* (pp. 84–119). New York: New York University Press.

Giroux, H. A. (1980). Beyond the correspondence theory: Notes on the dynamics of educational reproduction and transformation. *Curriculum Inquiry*, 10(3), 225–47.

González, N., Moll, L. C. & Amanti, C. (2005). *Funds of knowledge: Theorizing practices in households and classrooms.* Mahwah, NJ: Erlbaum.

Greenacre, M. J. (1984). *Theory and Applications of Correspondence Analysis*. London: Academic Press.
Hall, K. A., Özerk, K., Zulfiqar, M. & Tan, J. E. C. (2002). 'This is our school': Provision, purpose and pedagogy of supplementary schooling in Leeds and Oslo. *British Educational Research Journal*, 28(3), 399–418.
Hannerz, U. (1992). *Cultural Complexity: Studies in the Social Organization of Meaning*. California: Columbia University Press.
Herrnstein, R. & Murray, C. (1994). *The Bell Curve: Intelligence and Class Structure in America*. New York: Freepress.
Hirtt, N., Nicaise, I. & De Zutter, D. (2007). *De school van de ongelijkheid*. Berchem: EPO.
Jacobs, D., Rea, A., Teney, C., Callier, L. & Lothaire, S. (2009). *De sociale lift blijft steken: De prestaties van allochtone leerlingen in de Vlaamse Gemeenschap en de Franse Gemeenschap*. Brussels: Koning Boudewijnstichting.
Leonardo, Z. (2009). *Race, Whiteness and Education*. New York: Routledge.
Levinson, B. A. U. & Pollock, M. (2011). *A Companion to the Anthropology of Education*. Hoboken, NJ: Wiley-Blackwell.
Lukes, S. (2005). *Power: A Radical View*. New York: Palgrave Macmillan.
Marsh, H. W. (1987). The big-fish-little-pond effect on academic self-concept. *Journal of Educational Psychology*, 79(3), 280–95.
Miles, M. B. & Huberman, A. M. (1994). *Qualitative Data Analysis: An Expanded Sourcebook*. Thousand Oaks, CA: Sage Publications.
Min, P. G. (2006). *Asian Americans: Contemporary Trends and Issues* (2nd edn). Thousand Oaks, CA: Pine Forge Press.
Nouwen, W. & Mahieu, P. (2012). Omvang van segregatie in het basisonderwijs: Ongelijke spreiding, concentratie en relatieve aanwezigheid. In O. Agirdag, W. Nouwen, P. Mahieu, P. Van Avermaet, A. Vandenbroucke & M. Van Houtte (eds), *Segregatie in het basisonderwijs: Geen zwart-wit verhaal* (pp. 16–29). Antwerpen: Garant.
Reay, D. (2010). Identity making in schools and classrooms. In M. Wetherell & C. Talpade Mohanty (eds), *The SAGE Handbook of Identities* (pp. 277–95). London: SAGE Publications.
Reay, D. & Mirza, H. S. (1997). Uncovering genealogies of the margins: Black supplementary schooling. *British Journal of Sociology of Education*, 18, 477–99.
Régner, I. & Loose, F. (2006). Relationship of sociocultural factors and academic self-esteem to school grades and school disengagement in North African French adolescents. *British Journal of Social Psychology*, 45, 777–97.
RESL.eu. (2014). *Policies on Early School Leaving in Nine European countries: A Comparative Analysis*. Antwerp: University of Antwerp.
Roosens, E. (1995). *Rethinking Culture, 'Multicultural Society' and the School*. Oxford: Pergamon.
Roosens, E. (1998). *Eigen grond eerst? Primordiale autochtonie: Dilemma van de multiculturele samenleving*. Leuven: Acco.
Shavelson, R. J. & Marsh, H. W. (1986). On the structure of self–concept. In R. Schwarzer (ed.), *Anxiety and Cognitions*. Hillsdale, NJ: Erlbaum.
Smet, P. (2011). *Conceptnota: Samen taalgrenzen verleggen*. Retrieved from: www.ond.vlaanderen.be/nieuws/2011/doc/talennota_2011.pdf
Song, D. W. & Wang, J. T. (2003). *Modelling the Model Minority: Educational Investment and Returns for Asian Americans*. Durham, NC: Duke University.
Steele, C. M. & Aronson, J. (1995). Stereotype threat and the intellectual test performance of African Americans. *Journal of Personality and Social Psychology*, 69, 797–811.

Steele, C. M., Spencer S. J. & Aronson, J. (2002). Contending with group image: The psychology of stereotype and social identity threat. In M. P. Zanna (ed.), *Advances in Experimental Social Psychology* (pp. 379–440). San Diego, CA: Academic Press.

Studiedienst van de Vlaamse Regering. (2012). *VRIND 2012: Vlaamse regionale indicatoren*. Brussel: Studiedienst van de Vlaamse Regering.

Turtelboom, A. (2014). *De Vlaamse Begroting 2015*. Brussel: Departement Financiën en Begroting.

Valencia, R. R. (2010). *Dismantling Contemporary Deficit Thinking: Educational Thought and Practice*. New York: Routledge.

Valencia, R. & Black, M. (2002). Mexican Americans don't value education! – On the basis of myth, mythmaking and debunking. *Journal of Latinos and Education*, 1(2), 81–103.

Valenzuela, A. (1999). *Subtractive Schooling: U.S. Mexican Youth and the Politics of Caring*. Albany, NY: State University of New York Press.

Van Houtte, M., Demanet, Y. & Stevens, P. A. J. (2012). Self-esteem of academic and vocational students: Does within-school tracking sharpen the difference? *Acta Sociologica*, 55(1), 73–89.

Van Landeghem, G., De Fraine, B., Gielen, S. & Van Damme, J. (2013). *Vroege schoolverlaters in Vlaanderen in 2010. Indeling volgens locatie, opleidingsniveau van de moeder en moedertaal*. Leuven: Steunpunt Studie-en Schoolloopbanen, rapport nr. SL/2013.05/1.2.0.

Watts, D. D. (1997). Correspondence analysis: A graphical technique for examining categorical data. *Nursing Research*, 46(4), 235–9.

Weis, L., McCarthy, C. & Dimitriadis, G. (2006) *Ideology, Curriculum, and the New Sociology of Education: Revisiting the Work of Michael Apple*. New York: Routledge.

Weller, S. C. & Romney, A. K. (1990). *Metric Scaling: Correspondence Analysis: Sage University Paper Series on Quantitative Applications in the Social Sciences 07–075*. Newbury Park: Sage.

Wouters, T. & Groenez, S. (2013). *De evolutie van schoolse segregatie in Vlaanderen. Een analyse voor de schooljaren 2001–2002 tot 2011–2012*. Leuven: Steunpunt Studie-en Schoolloopbanen.

# 11 Partnership between schools and immigrant families and communities

*Geneviève Audet, Marie Mc Andrew and Michèle Vatz Laaroussi*

## Introduction

Research in Quebec as well as elsewhere in the world clearly shows that family and community play a central role in the educational success of students, regardless of their ethnic origin. Among other things, it points to the close link existing between school performance and various characteristics, attitudes and behaviour associated with the family. In this chapter, we distinguish two main groups: a general positive ethos towards education and learning in the family, and targeted practices of support in the schooling of children. Among the first type of characteristics, some are linked to the socioeconomic condition of families, such as having healthy eating and living habits, enjoying sufficient rooms in the family house in order that the students can carry out tasks related to learning (such as doing their homework), as well as access to computer and cultural resources that are often needed in this regard (Harker, 2006; US Department of Health and Human Services, Centers for Disease Control and Prevention, 2011). Other characteristics are related to what the literature has deemed the cultural capital of families (Bourdieu, 1970), which, in some instances, is closely linked with their socioeconomic condition, but in others can be rather different from it. Cultural capital, among other things, refers to valuing education and holding high expectations for one's children's mobility; engaging, in daily family life, in various literacy practices and in activities supporting cognitive development; and adopting a democratic style of parenting (Chamberland *et al.*, 2007; Hoghughi, 1998).

With regard to parental behaviours that are directly linked to school success (Epstein, 2001; Deslandes, 2004), many authors stress the importance of regular communication with children about their school experience, as well as proper management of homework, which does not necessarily imply direct support from the parents. Other important aspects include the capacity of parents to understand the school system and follow closely the trajectories of their children within it, as well as the quality of their relation and communication with the school staff, more specifically, with teachers. These later elements are influenced by the socioeconomic conditions and the cultural capital of families, but also by their social capital (e.g. the access of parents to networks of support, their knowledge of the complexity of institutions and of the schooling 'game'), as well as their capacity to be recognized by schools as legitimate partners (Canisius *et al.*, 2007; Putnam, 2000).

These characteristics, attitudes and behaviours are extremely relevant in explaining the educational experience of immigrant-origin students, whether they are from first- or second-generation (let's remember here that the second-generation children have immigrant parents). But, in addition, many elements are specific to immigrant families, which present at the same time more risk factors and more protection factors than families whose roots in the country can be traced back many generations (Booth *et al.*,1997; Bouteyre, 2004; Suárez-Orozco & Carhill, 2008; Vatz Laaroussi, 2009).

On one hand, for example, migration and settlement in the host country carried out in negative circumstances can represent significant obstacles to the practice of parental skills. When migration stems from a catastrophic situation in the host country, the family structure, as well as the positive climate towards education which might have existed before within the family, are deemed to be affected (Smith *et al.*, 2004). But even when immigration is planned, the family dynamic is usually transformed, and the period of adaptation to these changes may be difficult. The negative impact of a long separation between the mother and the father, or between them and children is also largely documented (Legault *et al.*, 2000; Moreau *et al.*, 1999).

After settling in the host country, the hard socioeconomic condition experienced by many immigrant parents can affect access to material and cultural resources needed for their children to succeed in school (Rumbaut, 2005; Zhou & Kim, 2007). The fact that many parents do not possess a proper mastery of the school language also impedes both the exercise of parental skills linked to supporting the children's at-home learning, as well as the development of an egalitarian relationship with the school milieu (Schmidt, 1994; Suárez-Orozco *et al.*, 2008). Regarding communication with schools, more specifically, many misunderstandings can emerge due to divergent conceptions of education and learning, of discipline and of corporal punishment, as well as of gender roles (Cohen-Emerique & Hohl, 2004; Eurydice, 2009; Zhou, 2012). Finally, the involvement of immigrant parents in the labour market, albeit important, is a major challenge to their participation in various school activities, as they often accumulate many jobs with irregular hours (Pratt, 2008; Tyyskä, 2008). These difficulties do not affect the immigrant families in a homogeneous manner, but are mitigated by their socioeconomic status, their cultural capital as well as by their knowledge of the host language. Nevertheless, all are at risk to experience a loss of status in their relation with educational institutions, in comparison with the position they may have benefited from in their country of origin.

On the other hand, immigrant families also exhibit many characteristics supportive of the school success of their children, which can act as protective factors in the relationship with schools. First, there is high consensus in the literature on the central role that access to education plays in family strategies related to migration and settlement. Regardless of the level of education of parents themselves, social promotion of their children via a more accessible and egalitarian schooling often constitutes the main factor in their decision to migrate to a new country (Kao, 2004; Krahn & Taylor, 2005; Suárez-Orozco et al., 2008). When compared with families whose roots in the host country can be traced back many generations, immigrant families generally bear higher expectations regarding access to post-secondary education for their children, especially highly schooled families experiencing downward social mobility following their migration. Nevertheless, the degree of cultural and linguistic capital held by different families, as well as their actual socioeconomic conditions, influence the extent to which these aspirations can be transformed into actual practices (Kim, 2002; Krahn & Taylor, 2005). Other research explains the paradoxical school success of many immigrant children by the similarity of specific ethnic cultural characteristics with the requirements of school culture. These include the capacity of the child to control his/her body, the value put on effort and on deferred reward, the importance given to the written word, the respect for authority, the high social status of teachers, as well as the close link between school success and the family's honor (Valdés, 1996; Zhong, 2011). Some analyses go as far as using these traits to explain the differences between different communities in school performance. Nevertheless, some qualification is needed here. On one hand, it is not values that influence school success, but the extent to which families are able to transform them into actual practices of support to their children, and, most of all, to give priority to this issue over other needs that may be more immediately pressing (Li, 2003; Yan, 1999). On the other hand, the more or less conflictual relationship that some communities have developed with the dominant culture and schooling, whether in the country of origin or in the new society, also has a clear impact on the extent to which families will mobilize those characteristics (Ogbu & Simmons, 1998; Zhou & Logan, 2003).

Even if, until now, we have stressed factors linked to family, one must not forget the central role that proper institutional response plays in reinforcing protective factors within immigrant families and in responding to some of the deficits associated with risk factors. For example, government and community policies and programmes ensuring some financial security to families, as well as specific aid to those who went through traumatic situations can contribute significantly to the school success of children (Eurydice, 2009; Inglis, 2008). In school, such roles are filled by psychologists, social workers and various professionals involved in the relationship with parents and/or the community.

This brief literature review points to many issues linked to the development of collaborations between immigrant families, schools and the broader community, which this chapter aims to discuss more thoroughly in the Quebec context. We will put forward five important goals for educational decision-makers with regard to the relationship between schools and immigrant families and communities:

1  Developing a proper knowledge among the school staff on the multi-dimensionality of the experience and trajectory of immigrant families.
2  Being open to a variety of models of relationship with the parents.

3   Granting a central role to issues linked to equity and school success within strategies aiming at fostering school/family/community relationships.
4   Benefiting fully from the resources available in the wider community.
5   Implementing initiatives supporting the transformation of attitudes and practices within schools.

## Issues and challenges: a Quebec perspective

*Developing a proper knowledge among the school staff on the multidimensionality of the experience and trajectory of immigrant families, especially the significant strengths they present*

Lack of knowledge often leads educators to view relations between immigrant families and schools as problematic. The Department of Education stresses the need for collaboration between schools, families and communities, with particular focus on parental involvement in the academic progress of children. It affirms that 'school alone cannot assume the entire responsibility for improving student performance and retention rates [. . .] and no progress shall be made without close collaboration between parents, community and work environment' (MELS, 2009, p.3). Nonetheless, as seen before, these collaborations still pose a challenge, notably in the case of immigrant families, or at least some of them. Indeed, financial hardship and cultural differences prevalent in underprivileged communities can be intensified among immigrant families, especially among the refugees. There are also other challenges, intercultural and migration-related, that are faced by immigrant families in particular.

The school milieu has a rather paradoxical vision of immigrant families. On one hand, teachers and staff often hold a general but rather vague positive attitude towards immigrant students, but, on the other hand, they are often more able to identify in a precise manner their shortcomings as well as the problems linked to their presence in the school milieu. Educators often have a pessimistic outlook on potential collaborations, and ethnocentric representations of immigrant families do not help in establishing trust (Vatz Laaroussi, 2009). Research on the immigrant family-school relations often points to the difficulties faced by schools upon initiating contact with families. It also tends to emphasize conflicts that can develop within the family as children become involved in school culture, while their parents often remain imbued with the traditional culture of their country of origin (Bérubé, 2004; Hohl, 1996).

Due to the selection of the immigration in Quebec, between 1980 and 2010, over 80 per cent of newcomers fell into either the 'independent immigrant' or the 'family reunification' categories. Among those, between 1980 and 2010, 70 per cent were selected as independents – candidates with a promising socio-professional profile and a higher education diploma (ISQ, 2013a; MICC, 2012a). Another 15 per cent of families who had arrived in Quebec in that period held the status of refugees or asylum seekers; in comparison with other immigrant families, their status is less favourable. Usually, they do not speak French and often have known a life of insecurity, violence and exile (Vatz Laaroussi *et al.*, 2005).

Over the past decade, 60 per cent of received immigrants spoke French upon arrival. Between 1992 and 2011, 54 per cent of newcomers to Quebec were university graduates, whereas in Quebec's general population that number amounts to 25 per cent (ISQ, 2010, 2012a, 2012b, 2013b, 2013c; MICC, 2011, 2012b). That is to say, upon arrival, the majority of immigrant families possess a significant cultural capital which, as will be shown further on, inevitably influences their relations with educational institutions and with the community. What is more, in the Quebec context, the knowledge of French, the common language, impacts the ways in which families can contact schools and how frequently they do so, as well as their capacity to show support to their children and supervise their schoolwork.

As seen above, immigrant families certainly bring not only risk factors with them, but also protective factors, which teachers and the rest of the school staff must then reinforce. According to immigrant parents in Quebec (Kanouté *et al.*, 2008; Vatz Laaroussi *et al.*, 2008), and to the first-generation youth themselves (Potvin *et al.*, 2010), the success of a migration project is often intimately linked to the academic success of children in the host country. Families, therefore, especially those who used to enjoy high status in their country of origin and who live in situational poverty as a result of migration, hold high, 'middle-class' expectations regarding schools and school performance (Audet *et al.*, 2010; Potvin *et al.*, 2010). A recent study (Archambault *et al.*, 2015) has shown that the level of education obtained by parents predicts children's chances for staying in school better than the socioeconomic conditions they encounter in the host country.

Therefore, the challenge to educators collaborating with immigrant families is to remain mindful of their social and cultural capital, and to be particularly sensitive to the way in which migration might have affected, and might still be affecting, their potential to mobilize in support of their children. This angle should not be neglected by educators. We will see later on that there are many possible ways for families to 'authorize success', and that the role of educators is to acknowledge the legitimacy of these diverse manifestations of support and cooperation.

## *Being open to a variety of models of relationship with the parents, especially those based on a full recognition of the legitimacy of families*

Collaboration, or even a willingness to collaborate, can be understood in different ways by the actors involved. A family's idea of their role in the education of their children may differ from the role the school wants to assign them, and vice versa. Research done by Vatz Laaroussi *et al.* (2008) has shown that several types of collaboration among immigrant families, schools and communities exist. In a case study of immigrant students who attained academic success, the authors met with parents, teachers and pupils in order to identify their winning strategies. They found that several types of collaboration could be effective, depending on the distribution of functions of socialization, education and instruction among parents, communities and schools. Cultural, religious and intercultural communities can provide an important mediation space for families and schools; in those neighbourhoods or regions where this space was barely present due to a lack of structured ethnic communities, the gap between strategies employed by families and schools could be larger.

Thus, six types of immigrant family-school collaborations were identified as conducive to supporting student success, provided that they are recognized and accepted by families and other stakeholders involved (Vatz Laaroussi et al., 2008). In the *mandatory involvement* model, parents become involved in school life in institutionally defined ways, i.e. by attending meetings with teachers, assisting with homework or participating in extracurricular activities. The school assumes the responsibility for integrating immigrant families, perceived as culturally foreign, thus building an asymmetrical relationship in which the school holds a monopoly on the meaning of collaboration. Even though it is often presented in literature as an ideal model, the study found that it was not the most prevalent one.

The *partnership model of collaboration* is characterized by mutual recognition and a relationship of equality. The mission of educating, socializing and instructing is shared between the school and the family, turning them into partners. However, for such partnership to be established, parents must feel that they are on equal footing with the school system, and the school needs to recognize them as such. In this model, parents' and teachers' mutual appreciation of each others' competencies is necessary for establishing a symmetrical collaboration, as stated by Audet (2008) in her study of the narratives of intercultural educational practices.

*Fusional collaboration* arises somewhat differently. Indeed, in such cases, it is the school that steps out of its institutional function and reaches out to the families. In this model, it is the personalized relationships, maintained outside of school, that make collaboration possible by allowing families to form a bond of trust with the school. More specifically, these are the cases of teachers or school principals who visit students' homes or communities in order to connect with the parents.

The fourth model, *collaboration with mediation space*, can be found particularly in multicultural neighbourhoods. It is a type of relationship that requires the presence of a third party, a 'space' where two systems can mediate and connect. Here, not only community organizations, but also ethnic and religious communities pull together to facilitate young people's academic success. Parents' knowledge of French and socioeconomic status influence their choice of using this mediation space and workers in their contacts with the school. We will see later on that, from the outset, certain Quebec schools have chosen to appoint or to use the services of mediators in school–family–community relations.

Where families have trouble being recognized as equals with schools because of socioeconomic, linguistic or cultural reasons, an *'assumed distance' collaboration* is more likely to be established, with all actors keeping their distance. Here, the ethnic or religious community takes it upon itself to support the family in its mission of education and socialization, leaving instruction to schools. Direct contact is rare. However, if the school accepts and recognizes the potential role of an ethnic and religious community in its relationship with parents and in the academic success of children, it could find that the other actors might be aiding the child's progress, instead of seeing them as obstacles to integration or promoters of isolationism, and establish a positive collaboration, with the ultimate goal of encouraging academic success. It must be remembered that, for some families, ethnic or religious communities may be the only source of validation of their social and cultural capital (Frideres, 2005).

When the support lent to immigrant families by community, ethnic or religious spaces is not recognized as legitimate, a model of *collaboration in search of visibility* is often adopted. Especially in the case of families that have not yet been fully accepted into their host society, the influence of these communities must be recognized and legitimized; if it is ignored, students' academic success might be compromised.

Studies like this highlight the importance, and the challenge, of developing links between families and schools, 'recognizing [family] competence' (Audet, 2006, 2008), and considering families as legitimate partners. In certain cases, this could mean opening schools to families in a variety of ways, whether physically or symbolically. In others, it would entail decentralization and acceptance of the fact that learning continuity can be provided through other channels as well, as long as students' success remains a central concern. Studies also point out the necessity of including communities in the collaborative effort, as for some families, their engagement is essential not only to their integration, but also to their children's academic success. Indeed, even if strategies of 'authorizing success' might differ from family to family, they all eventually contribute to students' academic success through building resiliency and recognition, as well as developing intercultural competencies of families, pupils and school staff alike.

### *Granting a central role to issues linked to equity and to school success within strategies fostering school/family/community relationship, and not only to issues related to linguistic, cultural or social integration of newcomers*

Understanding family migration patterns and their social and intercultural consequences is not done for the sake of collaboration only. These connections must be made and maintained within a larger framework, fulfilling the threefold mission of the Quebec school system: to instruct, to socialize and to provide qualifications – that is, to ensure student success.

A study of initiatives promoting school–family–community collaborations, undertaken in four of Montreal's most ethnically diverse and underprivileged neighbourhoods (Bilodeau et al., 2011), has shown that these are usually related to sports, culture, recreation and skills development. They mostly take the form of extracurricular activities, i.e. they happen outside school hours and out of the classroom, mainly at primary school level. Whether in the case of immigrant families or of underprivileged communities, few existing initiatives aim at reducing the cultural and social distance between school and the community; rather, they focus almost exclusively on troubled youth and are generally corrective and compensatory in nature.

Typical examples of collaboration with communities include homework assistance in primary schools and dropout prevention and integration into the job market programmes at a high school level. Regarding the school–family relations, allophone parents are offered the 'francization' courses, where they can learn about the Quebec school system; there are also workers dedicated to fostering relations between families, school and the community. Generally, it seems, then, that there is particular interest in supporting the social integration of families for the sake of harmony within the society, while the family–school–community collaborations mostly focus on circulating information. Essentially, schools view these collaborations as a means of socializing and integrating families and parents (Bilodeau et al., 2011), and are predominantly concerned with methods of legitimizing the school system with families. At the same time, young people's success at school and the measures that could promote it seem to be put aside, as if in the case of immigrants and ethnic minorities integration replaced success. And while integration is by no means harmful to school success, it is not sufficient in itself.

In this context, one study distinguished three different situations of academic success experienced by immigrant-background students, relative to their family profile, thus highlighting the link between a family's social capital and a child's schooling (Kanouté et al., 2008). The three revealingly labelled categories are: 'school success embedded in family continuity', 'school success as social advancement' and 'school success for the family'. Even though they share certain characteristics, such as dependence on the family in pursuit of success and the eventual achievement of academic success, students who fall into these different types have distinct profiles.

Thus, the *success-and-continuity* pupils typically have a strong desire to uphold the family tradition of academic success, frequently pre-established in their country of origin. In their quest to succeed, they do not hesitate to use any resources at their disposal, often identifying with successful role models within their own nuclear families. Their parents accumulated high levels of academic capital, reflected in either diplomas or a valued professional status, and so these students plan their future in response to their parents' high expectations, often extended to the teachers.

In contrast, those who fall into the *success-and-advancement* category view success more as a facilitator of integration and a chance for a new beginning. The need to persevere is clearly present in the discourse of families and their youngsters, who resolutely strive to find their place in the host society. Even if these families do not necessarily possess high cultural or social capital, students learn to mobilize other individuals in their broader environment, such as teachers or neighbours, to help them progress.

Finally, those who succeed '*for the family*' are, in a way, invested in a project larger than themselves; in some cases, they uphold the honour of the entire family. While they maintain strong links with their country of origin, whether symbolic or actual, these families see their children's academic success as a chance to stand out, individually and with the entire family. Organizing themselves around a highly structured, *familial 'us'* (Vatz Laaroussi, 2006), these students and their families make more use of the resources available in their ethnic or religious communities than other types.

This perspective highlights the need for educators to learn about the various family migration patterns, as they can shape and adapt the immigrant-background students' paths to success. Acknowledging this variety of experiences can also encourage suitable responses from educators and sensitize them to the existence of different methods of collaborating with concerned families and communities – ways of collaborating that contribute to their integration, but also to success.

### *Benefiting fully from the resources available in the wider community, including those within specific ethnic communities*

Regardless of the ethnic origin of students, schools cannot succeed alone in ensuring their educational success. Many other institutions have indeed developed a complementary expertise in informal education and in the support of children and families. International and national literature show that extracurricular programmes and activities represent spaces of liberty less regulated and less focused on school performance than school activities. Thus, they allow youth to value themselves as individuals and as learners and to develop new competencies (Bauthier & Rayou, 2009; Delgado, 2002; Eccles & Templeton, 2002; Gouvernement du Québec, 2005). In this regard, for example, the impact of programmes aiming at developing positive attitudes in girls towards science or in underprivileged boys towards literacy is well documented (Casey *et al.*, 2005). Other research stresses the central role of various NGOs in the development and the exercise of parenting skills or in giving direct support for academic learning to children, especially in socioeconomically challenged milieu (Lemieux *et al.*, 2005; Tseng & Pinderhughes, 2006).

Given the socioeconomic, linguistic and cultural challenges they encounter, immigrant families and their children are especially deemed to benefit from the positive impact of resources, programmes and activities available in the community. On one hand, international and national studies (Bérubé, 2004; Vatz Laaroussi, 2009; Zhou, 1995) have confirmed the essential role played by some institutions in helping parents better understand the new society and its school system, and helping them better interact with school. The community sector also supports the school staff, and especially school principals, towards a better communication with immigrant families and towards the development of strategies to increase their participation. On the other hand, in addition to the development of a positive relationship to learning, which is common to all students as noted above, community programmes represent – for immigrant-origin youth – spaces where they can take a break and develop their independence in the face of the contradictory pressures they often experience from their family and from the school milieu (Glasman, 2001). These activities, thus, contribute to the strengthening of complex strategies of identity construction, based on an equilibrium between the heritage culture and the host culture.

Many initiatives target entire neighbourhoods, providing livelihood and resources to youth and their families; other projects focus on particular ethnic groups – for example, Haitian or Latin-American. The many types of existing collaborations depend on a given community's structure and its approach to school and education. For instance, in Quebec, South Asian communities are less institutionally organized in their support for pupils (Bakhshaei, 2013; Bakhshaei et al., 2012), whereas others, such as the Chinese community, place a lot of importance on the perseverance and academic success of their youth. The latter exerts a positive impact, but can also lead to isolationism and, consequently, undermine the social integration of youth coming from this community (Sun, 2014). Forging collaborations with ethnic, cultural or linguistic communities legitimizes them as spaces of belonging for the youth and their families. By doing so, we recognize that these spaces might be conducive to promoting the academic success of the young people they support, either by providing assistance with homework or through extracurricular activities. Moreover, some of these organizations and projects create a link between families and schools, especially by circulating information and inviting parents to participate in community meetings. To be more specific, it is the emphasis put on school and education-related issues within the scope of collaborative activities that is most likely to promote success among students coming from immigrant backgrounds (Mc Andrew et al., 2015).

However, some groups are still seemingly absent from this partnership debate. For example, we could consider certain religious communities which tend to avoid involvement with the school system because of its staunch secularism but which, nevertheless, constitute an essential place of belonging, socialization and integration to many families. As a case in point, the Ismaili community in Quebec is very well organized around a joint promotion of religious belonging and school success. It could also be useful to focus more on transnational family networks as transmitters of resiliency and vehicles for academic success, as they seem to be heavily relied upon for material and emotional support, yet for the most part ignored by the educators (Vatz Laaroussi, 2009).

Indeed, drawing on the three types of student success listed earlier on (continuity, advancement and family – Kanouté et al., 2008), we can see that these strategies correspond to different ways in which families approach 'communities'. Thus, students whose success is an expression of family continuity tend not to rely on their community of origin too much; families who perceive academic success as an opportunity for social advancement tend to seek out mainstream community organizations well rooted in the host society, while students who seek success for their family often maintain very strong links with their own community and are more likely to join religious or ethnic organizations. The challenge, therefore, is to recognize and include all communities and networks as potential partners, taking into account how crucial they might be to youth and their families at these very important times in their lives.

## Implementing initiatives supporting the transformation of attitudes and practices within schools, and not only compensatory measures aiming at responding to the deficits of families

Several instances of action research and other promising initiatives have been carried out in Quebec over the last few years. For instance, Françoise Armand has been introducing activities promoting language awareness and openness to linguistic diversity in schools by means of the Élodil program,[1] representing an original form of connecting family, community of origin, and school through a dialogue of languages (Armand & Maraillet, 2013). Cécile Rousseau, in collaboration with community organizations and schools, engaged art therapy and storytelling in action-research with young refugees who had lived through multiple traumas (Armand et al., 2011). In this unique approach, the school connects not only with the student's family, but also with her trajectory, as well as her cultural and social circumstances. Lilyane Rachédi teamed up with the Third Avenue Resource Centre to have youth develop their tales of dignity, based on the aforementioned concepts of recognition and resiliency. In becoming aware of these students' stories, schools can see their strengths, instead of just focusing on their shortcomings and difficulties[2] (La Troisième Avenue, 2012). The *Table de concertation des organismes au service des personnes réfugiées et immigrantes* (TCRI, 2011a, 2012) has also developed video materials, notably with the SERY organization, using testimonies to illustrate the rapprochement process between schools and immigrant families as it was mediated by a provincial community organization.

In the same vein, Vatz Laaroussi and her team (2013) developed an action-research project in which family histories of immigrant allophone children were used in schools to stimulate their motivation to learn to write in French. It asked the youth enrolled in welcome classes, or in regular classes offering language support, to write a book on their family history. The book could feature passages written by family members and include texts written in the student's language of origin. The experiment has shown that the more concerned and involved the students felt in their written output, in this case consisting of telling their family stories, the more they enjoyed writing and showed readiness to develop the necessary competencies to write well in French. The project allowed families and schools to come together through pride felt by everyone involved in the creation of this book, with families participating and committing to the project in a variety of ways.

This experiment strengthened the young people's motivation to write and to learn, encouraged them to interact with other pupils and with their own families, inspired confidence in their teachers and in themselves, as well as improved their French learning and written competencies. With regard to parents, the project helped them better understand their children, see them experience success and pride, and participate in their learning. According to both teachers and parents, this experiment has enabled students to make progress in writing and in French, to find motivation to study, and to like school.

Teachers, on the other hand, also had an opportunity to learn more about their students, their talents, their families and stories, while fostering collaboration with community organizations and building up their pedagogical competencies. We have identified the dimensions of a meaningful context that boosts young people's motivation, perseverance and French writing skills: a chance to talk about themselves, interest in their history and family, permission to use the mother tongue, producing a 'real' book, shared pride, acknowledgement of knowledge and talents (of youth and their families alike), writing freedom, creativity, personalization and aesthetics.

Four major principles have emerged from this research as cornerstones of future initiatives strengthening student motivation at school and creating collaborations between school, diverse communities, and families: creation of meaningful learning contexts, appreciation for the dialogue between students' mother tongue and French, innovation in family-school interactions and daring to be creative. Indeed, attitudes toward writing and language vary depending on the different trajectories of migration (Vatz Laaroussi et al., 2013).

Lastly, we will present an overview study documenting an innovative project involving 'community-school workers' (CSWs) *(intervenants communautaires-scolaires)*, carried out in underprivileged and multiethnic neighbourhoods of the Island of Montreal (Audet & Potvin, 2013). Over the last decade, three such neighbourhoods have made use of 'field workers', now called the community-school workers. Based in primary and secondary schools, they develop a network of community organizations and schools in order to meet the needs of students and their families, whether from immigrant background or not. The main goal of these initiatives is promoting student success, but a larger vision, shared by the three school districts in question, has emerged and been clarified over the years: to promote children's social and academic success by supporting the integration of their parents.

Diverse activities are offered to pupils within the project's framework. Some of them, especially at the primary level, may involve the participation of parents and community organizations. Thus, there are several types of activities carried out or supported by the CSWs: continuous activities (cooking workshops for parents and children, choir practice, soccer), one-time activities (annual picnic, handing out school reports), inter-school activities (student newspaper, talent show) and summer activities (camping trips, summer camps) (Bilodeau et al., 2010). In one district, the CSWs' offer largely consists of activities related to parents' employment.

The interviewed workers estimated that being 'recognized' by the direction, by other staff, teachers and parents had an extremely positive impact on the exercise of their functions. A sense of belonging in schools and having other actors acknowledge their credibility unquestionably drove the initiative of community-school workers across the three districts. They also appreciated the feeling of contributing to and participating in the rapprochement of schools, families and communities (Montgomery et al., 2010). Most workers agreed that the precariousness of funding available for such initiatives was a major challenge.

A similar practice of intercultural community-school workers (ICSWs) was introduced in several Quebec regions, mainly outside of Montreal. Employed by community organizations specifically devoted to refugee and immigrant families, these workers are especially active in towns selected by the Ministry of Immigration and Cultural Communities as part of a strategy for regionalizing immigration. Their role is similar to that of the CSWs, described above, but the ICSW mandate requires them to 'exemplify the community-centred approach and intercultural expertise' (TCRI, 2013). Having developed an 'intercultural' expertise, their actions focus on immigrant populations, and refugees in particular. They also advocate a 'family approach' (different from focusing on parents only), reaching out to a broader population than just the youth. According to a TCRI assessment, the ICSW 'facilitator' and 'mediator' mandate benefits four different groups: young refugees and immigrants, refugee and immigrant families, educators and various community actors (TCRI, 2013).

A survey conducted among the Quebec ICSWs (TCRI, 2011b) highlighted a number of positive effects related to the presence of such workers, recognized by both schools and families. Thus, on one hand, there was a broad consensus within schools about the following eight positive outcomes of the ICSW activity: improving motivation and retention rates, reducing tension in the school environment, contributing to preventing violence and delinquency, facilitating communication and collaboration with parents, decreasing a sense of isolation and lightening the workload of teachers 'dedicated to immigrant pupils', reassuring and informing teachers, raising awareness among teachers and other school staff of the need for greater involvement in assisting immigrant students, and contributing to the adoption of practices that accommodate the specific needs of students. On the other hand, the ICSW's activity among families facilitated or allowed parents to assimilate the rules and norms of educating children in the Quebec school system, participate in their children's schooling, gain access to programmes and resources available to them according to their specific needs, maintain parental authority and implement preventive measures in case of family conflicts. It can therefore be concluded that their actions had largely beneficial effects in those environments that needed them most.

Clearly, then, it is possible to rise to the challenges presented in Quebec, as elsewhere, by the immigrant family–school–community relations, while recognizing everybody's legitimacy within that conversation. In this sense, the above-mentioned initiatives are particularly promising and hold tremendous potential for being transferred into other contexts.

## Research, training and transformation as the way forward

The above-listed projects and initiatives permit a vision of developments which would address the challenges of multiple family–school–community collaborations while establishing new, creative and innovative spaces supporting the academic success of young people from immigrant backgrounds. The many different avenues and strategies implemented by schools should continue to be explored, analysed and evaluated. The paths charted by open schools, community schools and inclusive education come to mind. To achieve this, research and training strategies for various education and community workers are indispensable; however, they must be accompanied by transformations in institutional practices and policies. Finally, let it be remembered that any collaboration must involve the participation of all actors, with reciprocity in terms of mutual recognition and decentralization.

## Notes

1 See: www.elodil.umontreal.ca.
2 See: www.imagineeducationquebec.org/les-recits-de-dignite/.

## References

Archambault, I., Brault, M.-C., Mc Andrew, M., Janosz, M., Ledent, J., Dupéré, V. & Tardif-Grenier, K. (2015). *Impact des facteurs psychosociaux, familiaux et des caractéristiques de l'environnement scolaire sur la persévérance des élèves issus de l'immigration en milieu défavorisé. GRÈS/GRIÉS. Rapport soumis à la Direction des services aux communautés culturelles du MELS.*

Armand, F. & Maraillet, E. (2013). *Éducation interculturelle et diversité linguistique.* Retrieved from: www.elodil.umontreal.ca.

Armand, F., Rousseau, C., Lory, M.-P. & Machouf, A. (2011). *Les ateliers d'expression théâtrale plurilingue en classe d'accueil.* In F. Kanouté & G. Lafortune (eds), *Familles québécoises d'origine immigrante: Les dynamiques d'établissements.* Montréal: Presses de l'Université de Montréal, pp. 97–111.

Audet, G. (2006). *Pour une 'altérité en acte': Reconstruction et théorisation de récits de pratique d'éducation interculturelle en maternelle.* Thèse de doctorat inédite. Québec: Université Laval.

Audet, G. (2008). La relation enseignant-parents d'un enfant « d'une autre culture» sous l'angle du rapport à l'altérité. *Revue des sciences de l'éducation,* 24(2), 333–50.

Audet, G. & Potvin, M. (2013). *Les intervenants communautaires-scolaires dans trois quartiers pluriethniques et défavorisés de Montréal. Synthèse comparée de deux initiatives et état de la situation.* Partenariat ARIMA et Centre de recherche et de partage de savoirs InterActions, CSSS de Bordeaux-Cartierville-Saint-Laurent-CAU, Montréal.

Audet, G., Potvin, M., Carignan, N. & Bilodeau, A. (2010). *Famille et expérience sociocolaire d'élèves d'origine immigrée en contexte de défavorisation socioéconomique à Montréal: La parole aux jeunes.* In G. Pronovost, *Familles et réussite éducative. Actes du 10e symposium québécois de recherche sur la famille* (pp. 55–71). Québec: Presses de l'Université du Québec.

Bakhshaei, M. (2013). *L'expérience sociocolaire d'élèves montréalais originaires de l'Asie du Sud: Dynamiques familiales, communautaires et systémiques.* Thèse inédite de doctorat. Montréal: Université de Montréal, Faculté des sciences de l'éducation.

Bakhshaei, M., Mc Andrew, M. & Georgiou, T. (2012). *Le vécu scolaire des élèves montréalais originaires de l'Asie du Sud au secondaire: État de situation et prospective pour une intervention en faveur de leur réussite.* Rapport déposé à la Direction des services aux communautés culturelles.

Bauthier, E. & Rayou, P. (2009). *Les inégalités d'apprentissage: Programmes, pratiques et malentendus scolaires.* Paris: PUF.

Bérubé, L. (2004). *Parents d'ailleurs, enfants d'ici: Dynamique d'adaptation du rôle parental chez les immigrants.* Sainte-Foy, Québec: Presses de l'Université du Québec.

Bilodeau, A., Lefebvre, C., Couturier, Y., Paradis, C. & Bastien, R. (2010). *Modélisation de la pratique de l'intervenant communautaire scolaire dans l'initiative "Un milieu ouvert sur ses écoles" de Bordeaux-Cartierville à Montréal.* Montréal: Rapport de recherche, CSSS-Bordeaux-Cartierville-St-Laurent-CAU.

Bilodeau, A., Lefebvre, C., Deshaies, S., Gagnon, F, Bastien, R., Bélanger, J., Couturier, Y., Potvin, M. & Carignan, N. (2011). *Les interventions issues de la collaboration école-communauté dans quatre territoires montréalais pluriethniques et défavorisés. Service social*, 57(2), 37–54.

Booth, A., Crouter, A. C. & Landale, S. N. (eds). (1997). *Immigration and the Family: Research and Policy on US Immigrants* (pp. 3–46). Mahwah, NJ: Lawrence Erlbaum Associates.

Bourdieu, P. (1970). *La reproduction*. Paris: Minuit.

Bouteyre, E. (2004). *Réussite et résilience scolaires chez l'enfant de migrants*. Paris, France: Dunod.

Canisius, K., Zhang, X.Y., Deblois, L. & Deniger, M. A. (2007). L'influence du capital social sur la formation du capital humain chez les élèves résilients de milieux socioéconomiques défavorisés. *Revue des sciences de l'éducation*, 33(1), 127–45.

Casey, D. M., Ripke, M. N. & Huston, A. C. (2005). Activity participation and the well-being of children and adolescents in the context of welfare reform. In J. L. Mahoney, R. W. Larson & J. S. Eccles (eds), *Organized Activities as Contexts of Development: Extracurricular Activities, After-school and Community Programs* (pp. 65–84). Mahwah, NJ: Erlbaum.

Chamberland, C., Léveillé, S. & Trocmé, N. (2007). *Enfants à protéger: Parents à aider*. Québec: PUQ.

Cohen-Emerique, M. & Hohl, J. (2004). Les réactions défensives à la menace identitaire chez les professionnelles en situation interculturelle. *Les Cahiers Internationaux de Psychologie Sociale*, 61, 21–34.

Delgado, M. (2002). *New Frontiers for Youth Development in the Twenty-first Century: Revitalizing and Broadening Youth Development*. New York: Columbia University Press.

Deslandes, R. (2004). Collaboration famille-école-communauté: Pour une inclusion réussie. In N. Rousseau (ed.), *La pédagogie de l'inclusion scolaire* (pp. 326–46). Québec: Presses de l'Université du Québec.

Eccles, J. S. & Templeton, J. (2002). Extracurricular and other after-school activities for youth. *Review of Research in Education*, 26, 113–80.

Epstein, J. L. (2001). *School, Family, and Community Partnerships: Preparing Educators and Improving Schools*. Boulder, CO: Westview Press.

Eurydice. (2009). *L'intégration scolaire des enfants immigrants en Europe: Dispositifs en faveur de la communication avec les familles immigrantes et de l'enseignement de la langue d'origine des enfants immigrants*. Bruxelles: Commission Européenne.

Frideres, J. S. (2005). Ethnogenèse: L'origine ethnique des immigrants et le développement des clivages sociaux qui y sont associés. *Canadian Issues-Thèmes canadiens*, Printemps, 65–8.

Glasman, D. (2001). *L'accompagnement scolaire: Sociologie d'une marge de l'école*. Paris: PUF.

Gouvernement du Québec. (2005). *Et si la participation faisait la différence: Les activités para-scolaires des élèves du secondaire et la réussite éducative. Rapport d'enquête. Version abrégée*. Québec: Ministère de l'Éducation.

Harker, L. (2006). *Chance of a Lifetime: The Impact of Bad Housing on Children's Lives*. London: Shelter.

Hoghughi, M. (1998). The importance of parenting in child health. *British Medical Journal*, 316, 1545–50.

Hohl, J. (1996). Qui sont "les parents"? Le rapport de parents analphabètes à l'école. *Lien social et politiques-RIAC*, 35, 51–62.

Inglis, C. (2008). *Planning for cultural diversity*. Paris: UNESCO: International Institute for Educational Planning.

Institut de la statistique du Québec (ISQ). (2010). *Population de 25 ans et plus, selon le plus haut degré de scolarité atteint, le sexe et le groupe d'âge*, Québec, 2006.

Institut de la statistique du Québec (ISQ). (2012a). *Immigrants actifs admis au Québec selon la profession projetée, 2007–2011 et 2011*.

Institut de la statistique du Québec (ISQ). (2012b). *Taux d'activité, taux d'emploi et taux de chômage des personnes nées au Canada et des immigrants*, Québec, 2006–2009.

Institut de la statistique du Québec (ISQ). (2013a). *Immigrants selon la catégorie d'immigrants, Québec, 1980–2012*. Institut de la statistique du Québec: Statistiques et publications, Population et démographie, Migration.

Institut de la statistique du Québec (ISQ). (2013b). *Immigrants selon la connaissance du français et de l'anglais*, Québec, 1980–2012.

Institut de la statistique du Québec (ISQ). (2013c). *Immigrants selon la langue maternelle*, Québec, 1980–2012.

Kanouté, F., Vatz Laaroussi, M., Rachédi, L., & Tchimou-Doffouchi, M. (2008). Familles et réussite scolaire d'élèves immigrants du secondaire. *Revue des sciences de l'éducation*, 34(2), 265–89.

Kao, G. (2004). Social capital and its relevance to minority and immigrant populations. *Sociology of Education*, 77(2), 172–5.

Kim, E. (2002). The relationship between parental involvement and children's educational achievement in the Korean immigrant family. *Journal of Comparative Family Studies*, 33(4), 529–40.

Krahn, H. & Taylor, A. (2005). Resilient teenagers: Explaining the high educational aspirations of visible-minority youth in Canada. *Revue de l'intégration et de la migration internationale*, 6(3–4), 405–34.

La Troisième Avenue avec la collaboration de Lilyane Rachédi. (2012). *Imagine Éducation*. Retrieved from: www.imagineeducationquebec.org/les-recits-de-dignite/.

Legault, G., Oxman-Martinez, J., Guzman, P., Gravel, S. & Turcotte, G. (2000). La séparation familiale en contexte migratoire: Conflits parents-enfants. *Interactions*, 4(1), 60–76.

Lemieux, D., Charbonneau, J. & Comeau, M. (2005). *La parentalité dans les organismes communautaires famille. Rapport final présenté dans le cadre d'une Action concertée du FQRSC: Famille et responsabilité parentale; 2002–2005*.

Li, G. (2003). Literacy, culture, and politics of schooling: Counter-narratives of Chinese Canadian family. *Anthropology and Education Quarterly*, 34(2), 182–204.

Mc Andrew, M., Balde, A., Bakhshaei, M., Tardif-Grenier, K., Audet, G., Armand, F., Guyon, S., Ledent, J., Lemieux, G., Potvin, M., Rahm, J., Vatz Laaroussi, M., Carpentier, A. & Rousseau, C. (2015). *La réussite éducative des élèves issus de l'immigration: Dix ans de recherche et d'intervention au Québec*. Montréal: Presses de l'Université de Montréal.

Ministère de l'Éducation, du Loisir et du Sport (2009). *L'école j'y tiens: Tous ensemble pour la réussite scolaire*. Québec: Gouvernement du Québec.

Ministère de l'Immigration et des Communautés culturelles (MICC). (2011). *La planification de l'immigration au Québec pour la période 2012–2015*. Document de consultation. Québec: MICC.

Ministère de l'Immigration et des Communautés culturelles (MICC). (2012a). *Immigrants âgés de 15 ans et plus admis au Québec, selon le nombre d'années de scolarité et le sexe, par période d'immigration, 1992–2011*. Québec: MICC.

Ministère de l'Immigration et des Communautés culturelles (MICCz). (2012b). *Présence en 2012 des immigrants admis au Québec de 2001 à 2010*. Québec: MICC.

Montgomery, C., Xenocostas, S., Kanouté, F., Rachédi, L., Audet, G. & Brémont, S. (2010). *Bilan du projet-pilote intervenantes communautaires scolaires: Évaluation participative*. Montréal: CSSS de la Montagne et Table de concertation jeunesse Côte-des-Neiges.

Moreau, S., Rousseau, C. & Mekki-Berrada, A. (1999). Politiques d'immigration et santé mentale des réfugiés: Profil et impact des séparations familiales. *Nouvelles pratiques sociales*, 12(1), 177–96.

Ogbu, J. U. & Simmons, H. (1998). Voluntary and involuntary minorities: A cultural-ecological theory of school performance with some implications for education. *Anthropology and Educational Quarterly*, 29, 155–88.
Potvin, M., Carignan, N., Audet, G., Bilodeau, A. & Deshaies, S. (2010). *L'expérience scolaire et sociale des jeunes d'origine immigrante dans trois écoles de milieux pluriethniques et défavorisés de Montréal*. CSSS de Bordeaux–Cartierville–Saint-Laurent: Direction de la qualité et de la mission universitaire.
Pratt, G. (2008). Deskilling across the generations: Reunification among transnational Filipino families in Vancouver. Metropolis BC Working Paper No. 08–06, 42.
Putnam, R. (2000). *Bowling Alone: The Collapse and Revival of American Community*. New York: Simon & Schuster.
Rumbaut, R. G. (2005). Children of immigrants and their achievement: The roles of family, acculturation, social class, gender, ethnicity, and school context. In R. D. Taylor (ed.), *Addressing the Achievement Gap: Theory Informing Practice* (pp. 23–59). Series on Research in Educational Productivity. Greenwich, CT: Information Age Publishing.
Schmidt, P. R. (1994). Home/school connection: The vital factor in bilingual ethnic-minority literacy learning. Paper presented at the annual meeting of the National Reading Conference, San Diego, CA.
Smith, A., Lalonde, R. & Johnson, S. (2004). Serial migration and its implications for the parent-child relationship: A retrospective analysis of the experiences of the children of Caribbean immigrants. *Cultural Diversity and Mental Health*, 10(2), 107–22.
Suárez-Orozco, C. & Carhill, A. (2008). Afterword: New directions in research with immigrant families and their children. *New Direction in Child and Adolescence Development*, 121, 87–104.
Suárez-Orozco, C., Suárez-Orozco, M. & Todorova, I. (2008). *Learning a New Land: Immigrant Students in American Society*. Cambridge, MA: Belknap Press of Harvard University Press.
Sun, M. (2014). The educational success of Chinese origin students in a French-speaking context: The role of school, family, and community. Thèse de doctorat. Montréal: Université de Montréal.
Table de concertation des organismes au service des personnes réfugiées et immigrantes (TCRI). (2011a). *L'intégration scolaire des jeunes réfugiés: Granby se mobilise. Série de sept capsules documentaire d'une durée totale 30 minutes*.
Table de concertation des organismes au service des personnes réfugiées et immigrantes (TCRI). (2011b). *Une initiative québécoise porteuse d'inclusion. L'intégration scolaire des jeunes réfugiés: Contribution de l'intervenant communautaire scolaire interculturel*. Montréal: TCRI.
Table de concertation des organismes au service des personnes réfugiées et immigrantes (TCRI). (2012). *Soutien aux apprentissages des jeunes immigrants: Contribution des organismes au service des nouveaux arrivants*.
Table de concertation des organismes au service des personnes réfugiées et immigrantes (TCRI). (2013). *Rencontre nationale des intervenants communautaires scolaires interculturels (ICSI). Vous avez dit ICSI? Actes de la journée d'échange du 27 février 2013*. Montréal: TCRI.
Tseng, W. & Pinderhughes, H. (2006). Restricted incorporation: Chinese and Vietnamese community service organizations in the San Francisco Bay Area. Paper presented at ISTR Seventh International Conference, Bangkok, Thailand, 9–12 July.
Tyyskä, V. (2008). Parents and teens in immigrant families: Cultural influences and material pressures. *Canadian Diversity/Diversité canadienne*, 6(2).
US Department of Health and Human Services, Centers for Disease Control and Prevention. (2011). Health risk behaviours and academic achievement. Retrieved from: www.cdc.gov/HealthyYouth.

Valdés, G. (1996). *Con Respeto: Bridging the Distances between Culturally Diverse Families and Schools*. New York: Teachers College Press.

Vatz Laaroussi, M. (2006). Le nous familial comme vecteur d'insertion pour les familles immigrantes. *Canadian Issues – Thèmes canadiens*, 72–5.

Vatz Laaroussi, M. (2009). *Mobilités, réseaux et résilience: Le cas des familles immigrantes et réfugiées au Québec*. PUQ, Coll. Problèmes sociaux et intervention sociale.

Vatz Laaroussi, M., Armand, F., Kanouté, F., Rachédi, L., Steinbach, M., Stoica, A. & Rousseau, C. (2013). *Écriture et histoires familiales de migration: Une recherche action pour promouvoir les compétences à écrire des élèves allophones immigrants et réfugiés dans les écoles primaires et secondaires du Québec*. Rapport final produit pour le FQRSC/Action concertée.

Vatz Laaroussi, M., Kanouté, F. & Rachédi, L. (2008). Les divers modèles de collaboration familles immigrantes/école. De l'implication assignée au partenariat. *Revue des sciences de l'éducation*, 34(2), 265–89.

Vatz Laaroussi, M., Rachédi, L., Kanouté, F. & Duchesne, K. (2005). *Favoriser les collaborations familles immigrantes-écoles: Soutenir la réussite scolaire*. Sherbrooke, Québec: Université de Sherbrooke.

Yan, W. (1999). Successful African American students: The role of parental involvement. *Journal of Negro Education*, 68(1), 5–22.

Zhong, L. (2011). Chinese immigrant parents involvement in the education of their elementary school children in Windsor, Ontario: Perceptions and practices. Thèse de doctorat inédite. Windsor, Ontario: University of Windsor.

Zhou, G. (2012). Chinese immigrant parents' communication with school teachers: Patterns, disputes, and suggestions for improvement. *Rapport final remis au CERI*.

Zhou, M. (1995). Chinatown revisited: Community-based organizations, immigrant families, and the younger generation. Working Papers no 67. Russell Sage Foundation.

Zhou, M. & Kim, S. (2007). After-school institutions in Chinese and Korean immigrant communities: A model for others? Migration Information. Available at: www.migration information.org/. Washington, DC: Migration Policy Institute.

Zhou, M. & Logan, J. R. (2003). Increasing diversity and persistent segregation: The challenges of educating minority and immigrant children in Urban America. In S. J. Caldas & C. L. Bankston (eds), *The End of Desegregation*. New York: Nova Science Publishers.

# 12 Rethinking values and schooling in white working-class neighbourhoods

*Ruth Lupton*

## Introduction

Many of the chapters in this book deal with the question of increasing ethnic diversity in Western societies which were formerly ethnically homogeneous (white). In many European countries, children of migrants do less well at school than children of indigenous parents. Educators, scholars and policy-makers are looking for ways in which schools could better value and engage young people from minority backgrounds, thus reducing or eliminating inequalities in educational experiences and achievements between ethnic groups.

In England, the pattern, and the current policy emphasis, is rather different (DfE, 2015). Overall, children of Chinese and Indian heritage achieve the most by the end of compulsory schooling. Black African and Bangladeshi children, on average, also achieve more than the majority group (white British children), while black Caribbean and Pakistani children achieve less on average. Children who are eligible for Free School Meals (FSM) – a benefit available to families whose parents are not working, or working less than sixteen hours per week, and who have very low incomes, do less well than children who are not eligible, in every ethnic group. However FSM-eligible children from all the major minority ethnic groups do better on average than white British FSM-eligible children. Among the larger ethnic groups,[1] the lowest attaining group of pupils/students is white British FSM-eligible children. In 2014, 28.2 per cent of such students achieved five higher grade passes (including English and mathematics) in national tests taken at age 16, compared with 56.6 per cent overall (DfE, 2015), and, by way of example, 41.9 per cent and 56.1 per cent for Pakistani and Bangladeshi children eligible for FSM. Schools and local authority areas where the majority of children are white British and where there are high levels of poverty tend to have the lowest academic results. These are situated in deindustrialized cities, former mining and seaside towns. White British children living in London perform better on average than those elsewhere.

These patterns were recently documented and explored in a parliamentary enquiry which identified a range of explanatory factors including low aspirations and expectations, access to social capital, parental engagement and skill, and issues relating to the relevance of the curriculum in the context of changing labour markets. The relatively higher absence and exclusion of white British young people was also noted, suggesting their lower engagement with schooling (House of Commons Education Committee, 2014). Much evidence given to the enquiry touched on issues of values. Some expert witnesses expressed views that white working-class culture was associated with negative attitudes towards schooling and low aspirations, while others cited research showing similar aspirations among different social class groups (St Clair & Benjamin, 2010), and noted that young people became disaffected and disillusioned when it became clear that their aspirations would be hard to reach given labour market conditions and relative disadvantage. Evidence was given of 'culture clashes' around expected behaviour (Evans, 2006) and around different levels of interest and engagement in school choice between middle and working classes (Francis & Hutchings, 2013), although this same report also found working-class parents who were actively choosing schools to advance their children's education.

There are other important factors that affect the achievement of white working-class children, not least family poverty (Cooper & Stewart, 2013) and the failure of governments to fund and organize disadvantaged schools adequately (Lupton, 2004). The position that values are the explanation for low achievement among white working-class children is therefore not the point of departure for this chapter. However, in the context of this book, it is interesting to observe that perceived value dissonance between the school system and a substantial part of the majority ethnic group in the country plays a prominent part in education policy discussions. This chapter explores the issue in more detail.

In the first part, I give an extended descriptive account of economic change, identity, values and schooling in a particular deindustrialized white working-class neighbourhood in Northern England – named 'Steeltown' here – which exemplifies the problems that policy is trying to address. The case draws on four different research projects conducted between 1998 and 2010, and from the work of other researchers who have worked there and in similar neighbourhoods.[2] In the second part of the chapter, I explore ways in which the problem in this area and others like it might be rethought in ways which might contribute to more successful school practices. Like Bright (2011), I argue for a more historically and spatially situated account of value formation, with a greater emphasis on economic values and economic opportunities. A particular contribution of this chapter, therefore, is its call for a better understanding of working-class neighbourhoods. I locate this within a critique of recent research on 'neighbourhood effects'. I also suggest how such an account might lead to different and more equitable practices in schools, although the chapter is far from a set of recommendations for practice and much more research would be needed in that direction.

## Work and identity in 'Steeltown'

'Steeltown' was established in the late 19th century to provide housing for workers in the growing steel and shipbuilding industries. As such, it has been, since its inception, a working-class neighbourhood and a relatively poor one. Small, low value, Victorian-era terraced houses open straight on to the pavement, and the steelworks overshadows the town. However, for long periods during the 19th and 20th centuries, the area enjoyed high employment levels, characterized by local employment in large firms, manual and physically hard (male) labour. For parents and grandparents of today's Steeltown youth, decently paid regular employment, in the form of waged labour, could be expected without formal academic qualifications.

This changed very dramatically from the 1980s onwards. Extremely rapid industrial decline led to very high unemployment, deep poverty, associated social problems and major population loss, as well as environmental decay (in the form of abandoned housing, rubbish dumping and arson) and a loss of community stability and efficacy. The neighbourhood stabilized to a certain extent during the 2000s, with the demolition of large numbers of abandoned properties, and investments in new facilities and neighbourhood management, but remains a desolate relic of its former self, with very little in the way of replacement employment. There is local demand for small numbers of highly skilled workers in industries such as offshore technologies, but the majority of work in the area is in low-skilled, low-waged occupations – factory work, distribution, packing, contract cleaning or catering. Many workers experience a 'low-pay, no-pay cycle', with a series of temporary jobs, high insecurity, and lack of progression (Shildrick *et al.*, 2010).

Interviews with young people, teachers and community members suggest that this is a context of 'Peripheral Youth' (Pilkington & Johnson, 2003). Globalization accounted for both the growth and decline of Steeltown's industries, but its location leaves it isolated to a large extent from global flows of people, capital and consumption. The predominant forms of employment, although now in different industries, remain 'waged labour' rather than 'knowledge work', thus creating little demand for high educational qualifications. Identities remain largely locally situated – shaped by the historical employment structures and labour relations of a few large industries rather than the diversity, ebb and flow and reinvention of more mixed economies. Transitions to adulthood continue, for many young people, to be imagined through the frame of the social structures of modernity (class, gender and racial identities) rather than the more fluid, less place-specific, forms of postmodernity. MacDonald *et al.* (2005), for example, interviewing young people in Steeltown and nearby neighbourhoods, observed strongly embedded patterns of neighbourhood-based sociality and mutuality, including reliance on informal job searches through family and friends, and unwillingness to move away from the area because of what one respondent described as the 'security blanket' provided by knowing people locally. More recent interviews with young unemployed men in Steeltown revealed hopes for relatively well-paid work but an unwillingness to market themselves, lamenting lost labour market conditions in which one could 'just walk straight in (to a job)' – in contrast to the accounts of young people in a southern English city who seemed to accept the necessity of building their own biographies and acquiring work via active self-promotion in a competitive labour market.[3]

## Values and schooling

In terms of its educational outcomes, Steeltown exemplifies the problem of white working-class underachievement that currently concerns policy-makers and educators across the country. Average attainment throughout and at the end of compulsory schooling is consistently very much below the national average. In 2014, the proportion of students passing five higher grade GCSEs including English and maths ranged from less than half the national average in the lowest attaining secondary school to approximately ten percentage points below it in the highest attaining school.[4]

I observed some of the challenges of schooling in Steeltown through the lens of one of its secondary schools. By the end of fieldwork in the early 2000s, this school was rated an 'outstanding school' and was popular and fully subscribed, although this had not always been the case. Key features of its improvement were a relentless drive by the new head teacher in setting the highest expectations, with scrutiny and pressure on teacher performance and a sustained effort to recruit teachers who were experts in their subjects. In order to focus on teaching and learning, elaborate systems were established for setting behaviour standards and following up on infringements. Nevertheless, there was a caring rather than a punitive ethos. The head teacher personally, and the school as a whole, placed a very strong emphasis on emotional and social support, particularly to children who struggled with more problematic behaviours. Substantial efforts were devoted to creating belonging and a supportive social structure through a 'house' system and personal tutoring. There were also considerable attempts to compensate for material poverty – for example, in providing breakfast, subsidies for uniforms and school trips, and places to study after school. Thus, in many respects this school was an excellent example of what would be expected of a school in a disadvantaged area and its results had visibly improved, albeit remaining well below the national average.

However, it was also evident that the school was involved in a situation of value conflict with some of the students and their families.[5] The head teacher of this school described an anti-intellectual culture in the area, which clashed with the values of the school. One example was the unwillingness of children to bring a bag to school – bringing a bag signified the intention to take work home and therefore to identify oneself as an intellectual, a 'boffin', a cultural outcast. Teachers described a culture of 'low aspirations', and also of parents who 'simply do not think that education is important because it won't make any difference to anybody' (Steeltown teacher). Low attendance and disruption of lessons was a persistent challenge, and the school also reported a significant minority of parents who did not participate in parents' evenings/progress meetings or who did not support the school on matters concerning behaviour, attendance and coursework.

Clashes over values extended not only to academic work but to expectations around behaviour and culture. In one particular example, a teacher described a dispute over the wearing of a tongue stud to exemplify the clash of values between the school and a parent: the school representing the importance of education, qualifications and conformity to 'professional' appearances, and the parent, representing the importance of conformity to local gendered appearance norms, with the parent in the role of supporting early transition to adulthood rather than investing in qualifications for the future. Describing the behaviour of the mother, he remarked that:

> 'The 37-year-old women I know have briefcases and you know, little machines like that to tape their research project on. They're not being photographed on the front page of [the local newspaper] fighting for her daughter's right to make a total prat[6] of herself. . . . Now if I go round to someone's house to talk about GCSE[7] and expectations and grades that I anticipate their daughter to get, it's much easier to be able to go talk to someone who knows what GCSE is about and what I'm talking about, than someone who's interested in whether she's going to get a tongue stud.'

Like some of the witnesses to the aforementioned House of Commons Education Committee, these accounts clearly placed the school as the keeper and promoter of legitimate values and positioned local parents and children as being 'in deficit' – from families or communities where people dress, speak or behave improperly and whose cultural values and labour market aspirations are 'low' and in need of transformation. The response of the school was to try to attempt to inculcate a different set of values and behaviours, insisting on the importance of attendance, academic work and qualifications, and on the 'correct' clothing, language and behaviour. The head teacher described the school as 'a haven away from the community', a phrase also used in similar circumstances by head teachers interviewed by Crowther *et al.* (2003). While this referred in part to the school being a place of protection from violence, it was also a clear reference to isolating the students from the 'negative' culture, language and aspirations perceived to be present in their homes and neighbourhood. Notably, none of my interviews with teachers in Steeltown revealed any positive accounts of the culture of the area or any mention of assets or strengths. Neither the curriculum nor the pedagogy of the school were adapted to draw on the experiences or knowledge of the students.

I have not interviewed students at this school about how they experienced this. Other research has tended to show that the sense of being in deficit is quickly picked up by working-class children and young people who feel that teachers do not understand or care about them (Bright, 2011), as is the recognition that the school is trying to get them to perform an identity which may not feel authentic and is therefore resisted (Stahl, 2014b). Reay and others have also illuminated the ways in which working-class children can find themselves positioned as 'unknowing' at early ages, because, in contrast to middle-class children, their knowledge and experiences are not recognized or called upon in the classroom and they quickly come to recognize that what they implicitly value is of no value (Lupton & Hempel-Jorgensen, 2012; Reay, 2006).

At the same time as researching this school in Steeltown, I also made close studies of three others – another in a white working-class area in a seaside town where many of the same difficulties with disengagement and disaffection arose, and two in ethnically diverse neighbourhoods in large cities (Lupton, 2004). The latter two reported less resistance and greater participation and also achieved higher levels of attainment. In these schools, three reasons were put forward for this. One was that families with a recent history of migration (forced or chosen) were more likely to subscribe to the notion that education could be transformative in their lives. Another was that more recently arrived families, while possibly sharing the same current socioeconomic status as indigenous working-class families, do not share an identity with past modes of labour or social relations and are therefore not constrained by these. A third was that migrant families were often from more authoritarian cultures and/or religious codes, in which parent/child authority relations are more aligned with those experienced at school than they are in British working-class families, where young people tend to enjoy a high level of independence. Some of these factors were also noted by the House of Commons Education Committee (2014) in describing a possible 'immigrant paradigm'.

No doubt these explanations understate the complexities and tensions in the lives of young people from low-income families coming to and living in multiracial inner urban neighbourhoods, and the identity work that they also do to negotiate relationships with education and school (see, for example, Dillabough *et al.*, 2007). As Kulz (2014) points out, there may also be much more to these accounts than meets the eye: teachers who find it more acceptable to denigrate the English working class to a researcher than they would members of ethnic minorities, and a rhetoric of happy multiculturalism obscuring practices that pathologize the local area and enforce (white) middle-class norms in much the same way as in Steeltown. However, there appears at least the possibility that in these circumstances, schools could embrace a concept of 'value plurality' without necessarily 'value conflict'. Differences in background, religion, language and culture could be seen as assets to the learning endeavours of the school. Crucially, they could allow children of low socioeconomic status (and their families) to be acknowledged as 'knowers', because they had different experiences to bring to the table. In both of the schools I studied, some of the curriculum, especially in the arts and humanities, was organized around the experiences and knowledge of children from different cultures, and the schools made very visible celebration of the different languages spoken and the different religions represented.

This observation, and the conference which led to this book, suggested to me the possibility of rethinking Steeltown's educational difficulties from the perspective of 'value plurality'. What would it mean to think of Steeltown as a site of legitimate value formation rather than as a place with a deficit of values? What would be the implications for schools? In the rest of this chapter, I explore some of these possibilities.

## Understanding white working-class neighbourhoods as sites of value formation

Central to the approach of this chapter is the claim that an understanding of *neighbourhood* is critical to more equitable and productive schooling in deindustrialized working-class neighbourhoods. I share with Bright (2011) a sense that policy discussions of 'white working-class underachievement', in looking for general fixes, fail to situate youth disengagement and aspiration in particular local settings. In so doing, they can contribute to an account that reads this disaffection as a 'near pathological – even congenital – intellectual *and* moral deficit extending to the white working class as a whole' (p. 68), missing the general connection with working-class politics and history, as well as its specific locally situated forms. Bright's own study (2011), in a village in the Derbyshire coalfield, identifies a 'resistant aspiration' for traditional working-class lives (regular manual employment, marriage, family, a local friendship group and community life) infused with a particular resistance to authority shaped by the cultural memory of the protracted miners' strike, police brutality and the forced closure of the mine by the Thatcher government in the 1980s.

Such localized understandings of social class have not been helped, in my view, by the fact that much recent thinking about the ways in which place affects education has taken place within the 'neighbourhood effects' paradigm. Interest in neighbourhood effects on many facets of life has burgeoned in the last twenty-five years (see van Ham *et al.*, 2012 for a useful review). Indeed, it was a request to address the question of neighbourhood effects which prompted my involvement in the project that led to this book. In education, the importance of neighbourhood as a context for child development has increasingly been recognized by scholars working with Urie Bronfenbrenner's 'ecological approach', in which the neighbourhood provides one micro- or meso-level context (depending on the interpretation) interacting with other contexts – home, wider family, school, other institutions, parents' work, societal culture, and so on (Bronfenbrenner, 1979). However, a typical 'neighbourhood effects' approach has some serious limitations when thinking about the ways in which neighbourhoods like Steeltown operate as sites of value formation. Most of this research is quantitative and thus limited by the data available. It tends therefore to focus on temporally current features of neighbourhoods rather than their historical evolution, on neighbourhoods in isolation rather than in relation to others, and on characteristics of neighbourhood residents (such as poverty or employment status) rather than broader economic and social processes. Galster (2012) points to these limitations and others in his within-paradigm critique.

An alternative and, I believe, more helpful set of thinking tools for understanding the values of the inhabitants of Steeltown comes from the discipline of geography, particularly the work of Doreen Massey. In education, Massey is best known for her challenge to the notion of places as bounded and static – containers in which people are gathered. Instead, she argues that places are dynamic, unbounded, subjective and relational. The identities of places are always 'unfixed, contested and multiple' (1994, p. 5) and space cannot be separated from time – we should always try to think of space-time. Thus, any given place is a particular moment in the interaction of multiple 'nets' of social relations, some contained within the place, others stretching beyond. However, another aspect of Massey's work is particularly salient when considering places like Steeltown. Massey started her career as an economic geographer studying patterns of regional economic development in the UK. In the 1980s she was noting the uneven spatial consequences of industrial decline, and subsequently, in her book *World City* (2007), of post-industrial economic growth. Critically, she points to the structural origins of spatial patterns and to the interdependent trajectories of different places. Commenting on what appears a paradoxical situation that London has high levels of poverty *despite* its wealth, she notes that, on the contrary, London is poor *because* it is rich. London's investment in the financial and service sectors creates the conditions both for rapid accumulation of wealth and for low wages, low job quality, high competition and low housing affordability. The economic logic of late capitalism demands low wages and insecurity at the bottom of the labour market in order to generate shareholder profit. New spatial inequalities also emerge, as neighbourhoods where industrial jobs were concentrated (especially those which are peripheral and have no appeal in the terms of agglomeration economics) have been pushed down the economic ladder, and those whose connectivity and human capital have enabled them to capture knowledge jobs, have in turn become increasingly prosperous. Thus, the characteristics of poor neighbourhoods are not accidents, nor are they created by the people who live in them. They are the spatial consequence of the wider dynamics of the post-industrial economic order. In encouraging us to think of places as overlapping webs of social relations, Massey also reminds us to think of space as 'relations of domination and subordination, of solidarity and co-operation . . . a kind of power-geometry' (1994, p. 265).

This approach has profound consequences for understanding neighbourhood dynamics and the emergence of values different to those of schools and educators. First, we are able to see working-class neighbourhoods in terms of their economic history and past structures of industrial organization and economic relations, and the differing expectations of gendered roles and geographical, occupational or social mobility that came with these. Second, particular focus is given to the economic power relations that have made the neighbourhood marginalized rather than the deficits of the people within it – as Thomson (2010) says, 'neighbourhoods made poor'. In a generic sense, this is important because it draws attention to the fact that it is the economic system of deregulated global markets and the privileging of knowledge (the values and practices of which schools are attempting to inculcate) which has made redundant the labour and values of people in places like Steeltown. More specifically, it allows us to understand how these forces have played out in specific neighbourhoods, at specific times. Industrial neighbourhoods in England have undergone widely different processes of change in the last thirty to forty years, depending largely on their location. Many Inner London neighbourhoods, for example, have gentrified rapidly, as well as become much more ethnically mixed, and surrounded by areas of visible economic opportunity, while peripheral towns such as Steeltown have seen decline without these rapid processes of resettlement and re-creation (Lupton, 2003). We can move from the afflictions of the working class to the effects of specific processes in specific places. Bright's (2011) coalfield study is a particular example. Two other (non-UK) examples also spring to mind, illustrating different contexts and processes of local change. One is Wilson's (1997) case study of inner city neighbourhoods in Chicago, in which he argued that the spatial mismatch caused by the disappearance of work not only depleted the social networks of young men of working people (and their norms and values) but presented young women with 'unmarriageable' partners, influencing rates of young lone motherhood. Another is Dillabough et al.'s study of a deindustrialized inner urban neighbourhood in a Canadian city. The researchers illuminate how global economic forces (gentrification by capital) and social forces (immigration) combine with local political economies of education with inner urban youth becoming 'warehoused' in 'demonized' schools abandoned by more advantaged families. In this context, school and neighbourhood become sites for intra-class and racial conflict in young people's attempts to reclaim meaningful symbolic territory. The authors report a complex picture – girls taking on working-class resistance to school norms, while also resisting the traditional 'good girl' norms of their local communities, through extra-conformity to established definitions of femininity and heterosexuality (Dillabough et al., 2007).

The scope of this chapter does not allow for a full exposition of how these issues play out in Steeltown. However, the implication is that less attention might be paid to the 'low aspirations' that characterize the Steeltown culture, and more both to the values and aspirations associated with social and economic life in these communities (for example, hard work, pride in the making of products, values of family, staying local and community support) and the consequences of the violence done to the area through rapid industrial decline, depopulation and public disinvestment.

Narratives of violent destruction and hopelessness were particularly prominent in the accounts of adults whom I interviewed in Steeltown. They recalled that 'The place got torn to shreds. Everything's gone, the houses, the shops, everything ... the heart's been knocked out of it.' A young person from Steeltown recounted the sense that 'people look at you funny when you say where you live' and others talked about the effect of people with no other housing choice being 'dumped' in the neighbourhood because of the abundance of empty housing.

A Steeltown teacher explained:

'the whole place kind of reflects that. A lot of the people that live there kind of feel that this is a dump and they kind of feel a bit like rejects themselves, you know. I don't think they have anything like the kind of self-esteem that somebody who's arrived at (market town) has got, nothing like it. I mean, you know, you've got to apologize for living in Steeltown, don't you, whereas you wouldn't apologize for living in Harrogate, say, would you? You wouldn't feel embarrassed about putting it on a form for credit, would you, whereas Steeltown people would, because that could easily be a reason for being refused.'

The clear implication of this kind of thinking is that 'low aspirations' or a lack of interest in education was perceived not as a deficit of the individual or family, something that needs to be corrected, but the product of wider economic and political forces. The dissonance between the official narrative of contemporary

English education (that success is made through the acquisition of qualifications and labour market progression) and the reality of economic life and futures comes into stark relief. While individualized accounts of working-class values may be more useful in socially mixed areas, place-based accounts provide powerful insight for teachers working in predominantly working-class neighbourhoods.

## Implications for school practice

I want to close by thinking what schools might do differently, given an historical, spatial and economic understanding of the origins of students' values. Given the economic realities that students will face when they leave school, teachers find themselves with no obvious alternatives. Success at school may well not lead to labour market opportunities for Steeltown youth, but failure at school will almost certainly lead to fewer opportunities. Commitments to more equal educational outcomes and life chances therefore leave teachers with little choice but to continue to valorize certain kinds of knowledge and behaviours over others (for example, academic knowledge, a flexible approach, good physical presentation and emotional 'literacy' over mutual loyalty and physical labour), and certain kinds of aspirations over others (for example, higher education over raising a family). Implicitly, they must also valorize certain places over others – places of opportunity over places of decline – and encourage strategies of 'getting out' in order to 'get on'.

One way forward, then, is to rethink what would constitute equitable or just education in such circumstances. In the Steeltown case, it would appear that equity in education is being conceived in terms of the equal distribution of educational outcomes and the ensuing labour market chances. Distributive justice is being privileged over 'relational justice' (Gewirtz, 1998), a situation which arises to a lesser extent, perhaps, in middle-class neighbourhoods or neighbourhoods of recent migration.

But what would 'relationally just practices' look like in these settings? There may be a danger here of becoming sidetracked into a politics of cultural identity ending up in a nostalgic reification of white working-class culture. I do not want to argue that cultural representations are unimportant. Fraser's (1996, p. 7) examples of misrecognition are certainly recognizable in accounts of working-class young people's experiences of school in England (Bright, 2011; Reay, 2001; Stahl, 2014a):

> Examples include cultural domination (being subjected to patterns of interpretation and communication that associated with another culture and are alien and/or hostile to one's own); nonrecognition (being rendered invisible via authoritative representational, communicative, and interpretative practices of one's culture); and disrespect (being routinely maligned or disparaged in stereotypic public cultural representations and/or in everyday life interactions).
> (Fraser, 1996, p. 7)

However, questions of economic power must also be kept in mind. As Gewirtz (1998, p. 471) puts it, 'relations' include micro, face-to-face interactions and 'macro social and economic relations which are mediated by institutions such as the state and the market'. Indeed, in her later essay, 'Rethinking recognition', Fraser argues that seeing recognition in terms of identity politics is not enough (Fraser, 2000). First, she argues, valorizing group identities does nothing to change economic injustices. There is no point in a naive celebration of white working-class machismo, for example. Second, group identities cannot in any case be separated from economic injustices. The meaning of being young, white and working class in Steeltown is largely configured by the historic relations of capital and labour and, to return to Massey's work, the ways in which these have been played out spatially. Fraser articulates a more sophisticated version of justice as recognition, which postulates that recognition is not just about valorization of existing values, but about according members of all groups the same status as participants in society. She exemplifies this by reference to institutional practices such as welfare regimes that grant greater benefits to couple-headed than single-headed households. In this case, recognitive justice would require equal status in institutional practice – i.e. one kind of household should not be more generously recognized in terms of welfare payments than another.

Clearly institutions other than schools need to be involved in this kind of recognitive justice. A key site of action must be the economic, fiscal and regulatory policies which shape labour market structures. But this reading of justice as recognition does invite us to consider not only how the add-on activities of schools can support white working-class educational achievement (for example, providing subsidies for uniforms and school trips) but how their core practices (curriculum and pedagogy) might be rethought. Recall that in Steeltown the efforts being made by the school were to encourage students to participate in the standard curriculum, not to review its content and how it was being taught, nor to review the established roles of school, students, parents and community.

To explore what this might mean in practice would take much more than one chapter of one book, but examples can be drawn from existing studies. Thomson (2010) identifies three core principles. One is the idea that schools need to identify the 'funds of knowledge' residing in the labour relations, and family and community practices in which their pupils/students are enculturated, and not only to affirm these but to work out how they can form a bridge to the kind of learning that counts as school success. Another is the idea that all children have 'virtual school bags' (knowledge, experiences and dispositions that they bring with them). Schools should aim to start by opening *all* children's virtual school bags, working from what is in there towards what counts as valuable knowledge. A third idea is that of place-based curriculum – drawing on local phenomena for at least part of children's learning experiences, so that they can understand the systems and processes that underpin social systems (and natural systems) and the ways in which they are positioned within them.

Munns *et al.* (2013) extend these ideas, focusing in more detail on the pedagogies that are effective in stimulating educational engagement. They argue that starting from an understanding of economic power relations enables teachers to reflect whether their pedagogy offers the same 'discourses of power' to students from these kinds of neighbourhoods as from those more privileged backgrounds. Economically advantaged children, they suggest, are more likely to come to the classroom with a confidence in their ability and the place they come from, an understanding of the connection between the formal curriculum and their own lives and futures, and an expectation of helping to direct their own learning. Young people in marginalized areas may well expect to be looked down upon and fail to see the relevance of school knowledge for their current and future lives. Classroom activities must therefore extend them the same opportunities to connect with learning, feel good about the places where they live and have some choices and control. In practice, this means lessons that are not only, in Munns et al.'s terms, 'high cognitive' (with strong academic content) but also 'high affective' (valuing students participation and with students and teachers negotiating learning situations) and 'high operative' (with children as active participants in learning experiences that enable them to become more competent and empowered). Curriculum activities based around local neighbourhoods and starting from the students' existing knowledge and questions are common in the examples in Munns et al.'s work.

Raffo (2014) takes a broader view: an 'educational equity toolkit' covering classroom, school and neighbourhood levels, as well wider policies. Similarly, he raises issues of curriculum choices and bridges from these to 'appropriately codified powerful knowledge', as well as the engagement of young people in the development of school policy and practice, particularly in relation to pedagogy, curriculum and behaviour policies. He also proposes that families and communities need to be invited into schools as partners in learning and that each school should see itself as an asset base in the community, building social capital and engaging in local enterprise that supports families and local communities economically. This is a very different stance from the idea of creating a haven away from the community that I witnessed in the Steeltown school.

I draw attention to these examples not because they are the only things that schools could or should do. Schools in white working-class neighbourhoods must also have in place all the normal practices of effective schooling and additional activities such as practical support and financial subsidies for low-income families. They may need to do more than this – for example, to work closely with agencies concerned with children's well-being (for example, health and housing organizations). Nor am I arguing that these practices on their own will make a significant impact on the size of attainment gaps or social mobility, since these are ultimately determined by the state of the labour market, not by the practices of schools. In the context of this book, I offer them as ways in which schools might make a contribution by allowing white working-class young people to develop a 'self of value' (Stahl, 2014b) in neoliberal times.

## Conclusion

My hope is that this chapter has illuminated some of the ways in which we might think about neighbourhoods as sites of value formation – providing a spatialized perspective on the theme of this book – and demonstrating some of the possible implications for schools. In particular, I have argued that questions not just of cultural geography but in particular of economic geography are important, and that they suggest a different set of challenges for schools in economically marginal areas than those in major employment centres. I have tried to offer some ways to think about what it might mean for schools to take on ideas of recognitive as well as redistributive justice in these contexts, emphasizing the central role of curriculum and pedagogy.

I should add that the situation in England is not conducive to such approaches. England's strong central accountability regime in the form of school league tables and associated naming, shaming and closing of schools means that any departure from standard pedagogies is a highly risky business: an option typically only available to head teachers in very successful schools with strong local reputations and market positions, as well as outstanding results. Schools in neighbourhoods like Steeltown, which are constantly under pressure to raise attainment, tend to have little room to depart from standard approaches. Responding to local neighbourhoods therefore tends to occur at the margins of school activities, in the form of extended services and multi-agency engagement, rather than at their core, dealing explicitly with value conflicts and congruences in the classroom.

Since the election of the Coalition government in 2010, there has been a very rapid 'liberalization' of the school system in England, with more than half of secondary schools now outside local authority control (Lupton & Thomson, 2015). Networks of 'Teaching Schools' are taking on responsibility for initial teacher training. Schools are also now accountable for their performance in closing the gap between children eligible for Free School Meals and others. These developments arguably create conditions in which schools could potentially be more closely connected to local neighbourhoods and integrated with employers and other agencies. On the other hand, another rapidly emerging model is the development of multi-school Academy chains, running schools according to their particular values and models in numerous geographically disparate locations. This would tend to make schools potentially less locally orientated than under the former local education authority model. More importantly, the overarching performative system has not changed. Indeed, under the Coalition government, the inspection system has been made tougher, a wider range of performance information is published, and the baseline targets for school attainment have been increased. Thus, the problem of low achievement in white working-class neighbourhoods remains politically prominent; it remains to be seen whether schools are able to tackle it in the ways suggested here.

## Notes

1   Three much smaller ethnic/social groups do worse, white Irish pupils eligible for FSM score slightly less well than white British pupils on average (27.5 per cent reach five higher grade passes including English and maths), and travellers of Irish origin along with Gipsy/Roma pupils score substantially less well (11.0 per cent and 4.7 per cent respectively).

2  Brief details are as follows. My first encounter with the neighbourhood came through its inclusion in a mixed methods study of the dynamics of low income neighbourhoods, in the late 1990s and early 2000s (Lupton, 2003). I collected statistical, documentary and interview data about the history of the area and the current dynamics of its labour and housing markets, community and social life. Semi-structured interviews were conducted with 15–20 local residents, activists and professionals (including headteachers) on repeated occasions over a four year period. In the late 2000s I had the opportunity to update some of this data as part of a government study which I do not cite here for reasons of neighbourhood anonymity. The neighbourhood was also included in a study of postcode discrimination in employment (Tunstall et al., 2014) which involved interviews with young people about their employment expectations and experiences. Between 1999 and 2003 I also carried out research for my doctoral thesis in one of the local secondary schools, examining the relationship between the local socio-economic context and the schools' organization and processes through observations and interviews with teaching and support staff (Lupton, 2004). It will be clear that none of these studies were themselves studies of youth values and identities, and that I have interviewed only a small number of young people directly, which is why I supplement my own studies by drawing on other local research.
3  These interviews were conducted as part of Tunstall et al. (2014), but were not written up in that publication.
4  I have deliberately not supplied exact figures in order to avoid identification of the schools.
5  As always, there is a risk of implying that characteristics prevalent in an area apply to everyone in the area. The headteacher also described children and parents who were aspirational and supportive of the school. However, it remains the case that those who were thought not to be were much more abundant in this area than in middle-class areas, where such issues are rarely commented upon by headteachers (Thrupp & Lupton, 2011).
6  'Prat' is an English slang word meaning 'idiot'.
7  GCSE (General Certificate of Secondary Education) is the examination taken at the end of compulsory schooling in England at 16, the 'national test' referred to in the introduction.

## References

Bright, N. G. (2011). "Off the Model": Resistant spaces, school disaffection and "aspiration" in a former coal-mining community. *Children's Geographies*, 9(1), 63–78. doi:10.1080/14733285.2011.540440.

Bronfenbrenner, U. (1979). *The Ecology of Human Development: Experiments by Nature and Design*. Cambridge, MA: Harvard University Press.

Cooper, K. & Stewart, K. (2013). Does money affect children's outcomes?: A systematic review. York: Joseph Rowntree Foundation.

Crowther, D., Cummings, C., Dyson, A. & Millward, A. (2003). Schools and area regeneration. Bristol: Policy Press for the Joseph Rowntree Foundation.

DfE. (2015). Revised GCSE and equivalents results in England, 2013 to 2014. Statistical First Release SFR 02/2015. London: Department for Education.

Dillabough, J., Kennelly, J. & Wang, E. (2007). Warehousing young people in urban Canadian schools: Gender, peer rivalry and spatial containment. In K. Gulson & C. Symes, *Spatial Theories of Education: Policy and Geography Matters*. New York and London: Routledge.

Evans, G. (2006). *Educational Failure and Working-class White Children in Britain*. London: Palgrave Macmillan.

Francis, B. & Hutchings, M. (2013). Parent power? Using money and information to boost children's chances of educational success. London: The Sutton Trust.

Fraser, N. (1996). Social justice in the age of identity politics: Redistribution, recognition and participation. The Tanner Lectures on Human Values. Stanford University.

Fraser, N. (2000). Rethinking recognition. *New Left Review*, II, 3 (June), 107–20.

Galster, G. (2012). The mechanism(s) of neighbourhood effects: Theory, evidence and policy implications. In M. van Ham, D. Manley, N. Bailey, L. Simpson & D. Maclennan (eds), *Neighbourhood Effects Research: New Perspectives* (pp. 23–56). Dordrecht: Springer.

Gewirtz, S. (1998). Conceptualising social justice in education: Mapping the territory. *Journal of Education Policy*, 13(4), 469–84.

House of Commons Education Committee. (2014). Underachievement in education by white working-class children. London: TSO.

Kulz, C. (2014). "Structure liberates?": Mixing for mobility and the cultural transformation of "urban children" in a London academy. *Ethnic and Racial Studies*, 37(4), 685–701. doi:10.1080/01419870.2013.808760.

Lupton, R. (2003). *Poverty Street: The Dynamics of Neighbourhood Decline and Renewal*. Bristol: The Policy Press.

Lupton, R. (2004). School in disadvantaged areas: Recognising context and raising quality. CASEpaper 76. London: CASE, LSE.

Lupton, R. & Hempel-Jorgensen, A. (2012). The importance of teaching: Pedagogical constraints and possibilities in working-class schools. *Journal of Education Policy*, 27(5), 601–20. doi:10.1080/02680939.2012.710016.

Lupton, R. & Thomson, S. (2015). The coalition's record on schools: Policy, spending and outcomes 2010-2015. Social Policy in a Cold Climate Working Paper 13. London: Centre for Analysis of Social Exclusion.

MacDonald, R., Shildrick, T., Webster, C. & Simpson, D. (2005). Growing up in poor neighbourhoods: The significance of class and place in the extended transitions of "socially excluded" young adults. *Sociology*, 39(5), 873–91.

Massey, D. (1994). *Space, Place and Gender*. Cambridge: Polity Press.

Massey, D. (2007). *World City*. Cambridge: Polity Press.

Munns, G., Sawyer, W. & Cole, B. (eds). (2013). *Exemplary Teachers of Students in Poverty*. London and New York: Routledge.

Pilkington, H. & Johnson, R. (2003). Peripheral youth: Relations of identity and power in global/local context. *European Journal of Cultural Studies*, 6(3), 259–83.

Raffo, C. (2014). *Improving Educational Equity in Urban Contexts*. Abingdon; New York: Routledge.

Reay, D. (2001). Finding or losing yourself?: Working-class relationships to education. *Journal of Education Policy*, 16(4), 333–46. doi:10.1080/02680930110054335.

Reay, D. (2006). The zombie stalking English schools: Social class and educational inequality. *British Journal of Sociology of Education*, 54(3), 288–307.

St Clair, R, & Benjamin, A. (2010). Performing desires: The dilemma of aspirations and educational attainment. *British Educational Research Journal*, iFirst article, 1–17.

Shildrick, T., MacDonald, R., Webster, C., & Garthwaite, K. (2010). *The low-pay, no-pay cycle: Understanding recurrent poverty*. York: Joseph Rowntree Foundation.

Stahl, G. (2014a). The affront of the aspiration agenda: White working-class male narratives of "ordinariness" in neoliberal times. *Masculinities & Social Change*, 3(2), 88–118.

Stahl, G. (2014b). White working-class male narratives of "loyalty to self" in discourses of aspiration. *British Journal of Sociology of Education*, December, 1–21. doi:10.1080/01425692.2014.982859.

Thomson, P. (2010). A critical pedagogy of global place: Regeneration in and as action. In C. Raffo, A. Dyson, H. Gunter, D. Hall, L. Jones & A. Kalambouka (eds), *Education and Poverty in Affluent Countries* (pp. 124–34). New York and Abingdon: Routledge.

Thrupp, M. & Lupton, R. (2011). Variations on a middle-class theme: English primary schools in socially advantaged contexts. *Journal of Education Policy*, 26(2), 289–312.

Tunstall, R., Green, A., Lupton, R., Watmough, S. & Bates, K. (2014). Does poor neighbourhood reputation create a neighbourhood effect on employment? The results of a field experiment in the UK. *Urban Studies*, 51(4), 763–80. doi:10.1177/0042098013492230.

van Ham, M., Manley, D., Bailey, N., Simpson, L. & Maclennan, D. (eds). (2012). *Neighbourhood Effects Research, New Perspectives*. Dordrecht, Heidelberg, London, New York: Springer.

Wilson, W. J. (1997). *When Work Disappears: The World of the New Urban Poor*. New York: Vintage Books.

# Major contributions of the book and the complementarity of its chapters
## A critical reflection

*Alhassane Balde and Marie Mc Andrew*

Behind our reflection on youth and ethnocultural diversity lies the core issue of complex educational situations, where relationships between institutions and various actors involved are being played out. This interplay of actors and institutions manifests itself in a number of ways. Without necessarily adopting a comparative perspective on situations observed in Europe and in Canada, our work nevertheless offers an overview of what is happening in both of these geographical areas. The division of the book into four parts allows the reader to get immediately acquainted with the different sociogeographical and historical contexts it deals with, as well as the various strategies employed by actors directly or indirectly involved in young people's education. The reader will also be able to identify factors that allow for comprehending and locating these different relations.

As even an overview of the present work testifies to its richness, we clearly cannot elaborate on all its contributions in this limited space. This is why we chose to focus on four main issues: (1) the variety of disciplines and methodological approaches; (2) the complementary levels of analysis; (3) the diversity of social and political contexts, and (4) the identification of best practices and interventions. It is worth noting that most chapters could be used to illustrate all of these issues, but for the sake of brevity we will make use of only a few examples.

## The variety of disciplines and methodological approaches

The texts presented in this book have been authored by researchers coming from diverse disciplinary backgrounds (education sciences, demography, sociology, psychology, anthropology), and therefore propose a new research perspective on the questions of education and youth identity in the context of ethnocultural diversity. This kind of openness becomes necessary when trying to grasp the complexity of relations and situations at stake, since the behaviour of actors goes well beyond the educational dynamics alone and extends to the economic, social, cultural and political dimensions. There is no discipline that can serve as one unique reference here, and so it becomes necessary to turn to others, equally relevant and recognized in the field, in order to capture the studied phenomenon in its totality.

Jean-Luc Guyot and Sébastien Brunet (2014) adopt this position in their discussion of the 'scientific community': far from being monolithic, it consists of subsets defined by disciplinary affiliation, each subset characterized by its own subculture and its own field of study, the authors assert.

The diversity of disciplines represented by the authors of this book accounts for a remarkable richness of its methodological approaches, with the robust combination of qualitative and quantitative methodologies producing relevant and significant data. These analyses of the dynamics and issues at work in educational institutions, as well as of the place and role of the many actors involved show the need to go well beyond disciplinary boundaries and isolated methodological expertise of individual researchers in order to better grasp these complex phenomena.

Thus, for instance, Fatma Zehra Çolak's reflection (Chapter 8) on the aspirations of Turkish-Belgian parents for the future and education of their children is approached in terms of an anthropological analysis of aspirations. The author leads us on a quest in search of understanding the points of view, feelings and ideas of Turkish-Belgian parents, structured around the dream of a better social integration for their children. This chapter demonstrates how parental aspirations are conditioned by personal life experience. Several interviewees specifically refer to the negative image associated with the Turkish-Belgian community and admit wishing for a different picture in the future for their children.

Addressing a similar issue from a sociological point of view, Nicolas Legewie (Chapter 6) opts for the analysis of 'success stories'. Defying the concept of 'habitus', he demonstrates how, in rather unfavourable circumstances, success stories produce educational mobility among the second-generation Turkish youth. Legewie's research shows how, based on their own life experience, parents develop a discourse around school and education that induces upward educational mobility in their children.

## The complementary levels of analysis

In their diverse approaches, texts published in this book illustrate the need for multiple entry points in the analysis of complex situations concerning youth and education in a context of diversity. They also examine the interplay of various spheres. In this light, we have identified three levels of analysis: micro, meso and macro (Mc Andrew et al., 2015; Piché, 2013). *The micro level* concerns mostly individual approaches and corresponds to what could be called personal factors, such as the attributes, characteristics and attitudes of the student. *The meso* (intermediate) *level* refers to the mediating dynamics between the structural or systemic (macro) and the individual factors (micro). It focuses on the interactions taking place within families and communities, as well as the relations between them and other social or institutional spaces. It takes into account the baseline characteristics of a family, the scale of community organization, and the strategies the two deploy in their relations with educational institutions, for instance. *The macro level* includes both structural factors and a systemic perspective. It concerns the organizational and/or the decision-making sphere, as well as institutions and politics. Indeed, the context in which decisions concerning youth and ethnocultural diversity in education are made determines the introduction and implementation of structural measures.

A multidimensional approach taking into account these macro, meso and micro levels of analysis allows for a greater understanding of social phenomena, as well as of their multiple ramifications and complexities (Arcand, 2012). Similarly, such conceptual approach is needed when exploring ethnocultural diversity in education.

The first perspective, adopted in the body of work presented in this book, is based on two levels of analysis. For example, Klaus Boehnke and David Schiefer (Chapter 2) contrast the micro and the macro levels to address the issue of the horizontal transmission of values – that is to say, peer-to-peer transmission within a social space shared by youth: the school. In this study, the classroom is a place where value transmission among peers is introduced and negotiated. Naturally, classrooms are not the only microsystems providing interaction space for horizontal transmission, the authors are quick to point out. Neighbourhoods, friend groups on social media, sports teams, etc. can also constitute such spaces.

On the other hand, the explanatory approach adopted by Gisela Trommsdorff (Chapter 1) focuses on the first two levels – micro and meso. Her study looks at intergenerational relations in diverse cultural contexts, focusing first on the demographic changes and the evolution of values in various cultures, then on the intergenerational transmission of these values, and finally on mutual support within families across generations. The author explains that these relations are asymmetrical and bidirectional, and that they usually involve a long-term commitment based on trust and reciprocity.

The second perspective, adopted in the remaining texts, emphasizes the association of all three levels of analysis: micro, meso and macro. The following two complementary texts on the academic progress of students with an immigrant background illustrate this approach.

Jacques Ledent and Marie Mc Andrew (Chapter 5) argue that even though Quebec students with an immigrant background score lower on measures of personal, familial and schooling-related characteristics, their educational trajectories are more positive than expected, especially among the second generation. What is more, when controlling for baseline characteristics, second-generation immigrant students are more likely to graduate than students of third or any further generation, which illustrates their significant resilience.

On the other hand, Christiane Timmerman, Noel Clycq, Kenneth Hemmerechts and Johan Wets (Chapter 4) show, in the example of Flanders, that students' outcomes are influenced by a whole complex of elements located at different, yet overlapping levels. They emphasize the importance of systemic constraints (institutions and policies), of such socialization networks as family (socioeconomic status), school, community and peer groups (with particular emphasis on the processes occurring in these networks), and of personal characteristics, such as attributes and attitudes. These factors very likely induce poor academic performance among students from immigrant families, especially those from disadvantaged socioeconomic backgrounds.

## The diversity of social and political contexts

Out of the twelve texts presented in this book, three focus on North America, specifically Quebec, while the remaining nine deal with Europe: four coming from Flanders, three from Germany and two from Great Britain. Nation building in these different countries has been a long process, and is still being pursued today, even though the stakes have changed as societies saw their populations diversify in terms of ethnicity, religion and culture (Bauboeck & Rundell, 1996). With globalization and increased migration flows, a classical division has arisen between countries realizing a selective immigration plan (North America, Australia and New Zealand) and European states, where immigration is more likely to be 'put up with'.

In North America, and particularly in Canada, legal immigrants constitute the majority of the immigration flow. Illegal immigration in this case is limited, to a large degree due to the geographic situation. Migration policies in place are selective, planned and aim at permanent settlement into a nation in development; immigrants are chosen on the basis of objective criteria, including degrees and qualifications (Pellerin, 2011). Such policies certainly create populations less at risk with regard to education (Payet & Henriot-Van Zanten, 1996), which might explain the differences of results in the two above-cited studies. Nevertheless, youth with an immigrant background, and especially those from racialized minorities, still face multiple challenges in such contexts (Mc Andrew et al., 2015). Thus, in her comparative analysis (Chapter 3), Marie Mc Andrew concludes that, despite the real impact of specific contexts on migration and school policies, the main debates concerning schooling segregation and social marginalization of certain groups, legitimacy of multilingualism in education, and the recognition of cultural and religious diversity in schools still present more similarities than differences on both sides of the Atlantic.

In Europe, where the process of constructing national identities began much earlier, immigrants (particularly non-Europeans) bear the effects of integration policies favouring national values and identities over multiple identities, which are nevertheless a reality on the continent (Schlenker-Fischer, 2011). Noel Clycq, Ward Nouwen and Marjolein Braspenningx (Chapter 10) indicate that the accounts of school staff regarding ethnocultural diversity in the classroom and interactions between students and teachers are stereotypical, and tend to relieve educational institutions of their responsibility to support these students. Academic success is defined mostly in individualistic and meritocratic terms. It is up to students as individuals to make good choices and be motivated to succeed, and it is up to their families to create a supportive environment, favourable to academic success.

The Flemish situation seems to mirror that of other European countries studied in this book, with the notable exception of Great Britain, where, as we are reminded by Gill Crozier (Chapter 7), the ideas of multiculturalism and antiracism have been actively implemented for more than three decades now. Consequently, the general attitude of authorities towards diversity in this context has resulted in the development of numerous initiatives encouraging the participation of marginalized parents in school life and aiming to improve the quality of school/family/ community relations. However, Gill Crozier also documents the limitations of such approaches and of their effects. Once again, it shows that the common challenges arising in the field of educational integration of minority youth are largely shared throughout the host countries.

Indeed, as we have shown in the preceding section, policies are just one of the factors influencing these dynamics. Administrative resistance, as well as attitudes of school staff towards diversity, can create a significant gap between reality and the official normative positions, as illustrated by Geneviève Audet, Marie Mc Andrew and Michèle Vatz Laaroussi (Chapter 11) on the example of relations between Quebec schools and immigrant families.

## The identification of best practices

Last but not least, it is worth mentioning that, although it was not its explicit objective, this book has allowed us to identify possible interventions and best practices in the field. They can be used to support school communities in shifting their perspective on ethnic minority youth education from what we have identified as a *subtractive* approach towards an *additive* one, which considers the linguistic, migratory, cultural and religious capital of immigrant students to be an asset, and not an obstacle to academic success and future participation in the constantly transforming society (Gibson et al., 2014; Roosens, 1995).

Thus, Gill Crozier (Chapter 7) emphasizes that it is up to schools to create conditions favourable to communication, participation, partnership, cooperation and trust for ethnic minority families. Indeed, parents who feel that they are not being fully respected or that their values or cultures are not recognized as relevant will be reluctant to visit schools, which may have a negative impact on their children's integration. Among the possible ways of dealing with this issue, proposed by Geneviève Audet, Marie Mc Andrew and Michèle Vatz Laaroussi (Chapter 11), three seem especially pertinent: sensitizing teachers to the complexity of lived experiences and trajectories of immigrant families; promoting openness to a variety of models for establishing relations with parents; finally, introducing changes which will support the transformation of school staff attitudes and practices.

The role of the community at large, and more specifically of organizations created by immigrant groups themselves in educational success of minority youth, is also not sufficiently acknowledged, according to Edith Piqueray, Noel Clycq and Christiane Timmerman (Chapter 9). While decision makers and school workers often view such organizations as promoters of pedagogical approaches alien to those of the host country, the authors have observed significant transformations take place in Polish schools in Flanders over the recent years. Increasingly, these institutions have become a vehicle for social cohesion by gathering Polish students in a physical location. Moreover, their program has been reviewed in depth and streamlined, making it largely complementary with that of Flemish schools.

Finally, Ruth Lupton (Chapter 12), seeking to understand the difficulties experienced by white British students from low-income families, especially those living in formerly industrial areas, illustrates the gap between school culture and family and personal culture of these young people. Arguing that ethnocultural diversity is often more openly acknowledged than social diversity, she insists that schools should be more attuned to the values and experiences of marginalized students, whether they belong to ethnic minorities or not. In order to do that, she emphasizes, it is necessary that policy makers and educators rethink the context of their neighbourhood and the values they promote in structural rather than individual terms.

Lupton's findings largely coincide with those presented in chapters concerning students with an immigrant background. In the end, it provides solid evidence that socioeconomic and ethnocultural diversity, explored extensively in the present book, is a promising entry point to a greater understanding of the lived experience of young people, and especially of the differences and inequalities which affect them in school and in the society at large.

## References

Arcand, S. (ed.). (2012). *Migration et marché du travail au Québec. Recherches sociographiques,* 53(2), 281–86. doi: 10.7202/1012401ar

Bauboeck, R. & Rundell, J. (ed.). (1996). *Blurred Boundaries.* Avery: The European Center.

Gibson, M., Carrasco, S., Pàmies, J., Ponferrada, M. & Ríos-Rojas, A. (2014). Different systems, similar results: Youth of immigrant origin at school in California and Catalonia. In R. Alba & J. Holdaway (eds), *The Children of Immigrants at School: A Comparative Look at Integration in the United States and Western Europe* (pp. 84–119). New York: New York University Press.

Guyot, J.-L. & Brunet, S. (2014). *Construire les futurs: Contributions épistémologiques et méthodologiques à la démarche prospective.* Namur: Presses Universitaires de Namur.

Mc Andrew, M., Balde, A., Bakhshaei, M., Tardif-Grenier, K., Audet, G., Armand, F., Guyon, S., Ledent, J., Lemieux, G., Potvin, M., Rahm, J., Vatz Laaroussi, M., Carpentier, A. & Rousseau, C. (2015). *La réussite éducative des élèves issus de l'immigration: Dix ans de recherche et d'intervention au Québec.* Montréal: Presses de l'Université de Montréal.

Payet, J.-P. & Henriot-Van Zanten, A. (1996). Note de synthèse [L'école, les enfants de l'immigration et des minorités ethniques – Une revue de la littérature française, américaine et britannique]. *Revue française de pédagogie, 117* (L'école et la question de l'immigration), 87–149. doi: 10.3406/rfp.1996.1186

Pellerin, H. (2011). De la migration à la mobilité: Changement de paradigme dans la gestion migratoire. Le cas du Canada. *Revue Européenne des Migrations Internationales,* 27(2), 57–75.

Piché, V. (2013). Les fondements des théories migratoires contemporaines. In V. Piché (ed.), *Les théories de la migration* (pp. 19–60). Paris: INED (Collection Les Manuels, Série des Textes Fondamentaux).

Roosens, E. (1995). *Rethinking Culture, "Multicultural Society" and the School.* Oxford: Pergamon.

Schlenker-Fischer, A. (2011). Multiple identities in Europe: A conceptual and empirical analysis. In D. Fuchs & H.-D. Klingemann (eds), *Cultural Diversity, European Identity and the Legitimacy of the EU* (pp. 86–122). Cheltenham, Northhampton (MA): Edward Elgar.

# Index

*Italics* are used to refer to figures and tables. US spelling is used throughout.

Aboriginal communities 46, 47, 49, 52, 56
academic performance: *see* performance
accommodation, lens of 17
accountability, schools 245
acculturation 2–4, 69, 127, 153, 155
acculturative stress 3
achievement: *see* performance
action research 225
activism: Language Awareness Movement 53; race 48
adaptation process, immigrants 153
additive pluralism 57
additive schooling 3, 198, 253
adolescents: horizontal value transmission 31–41; intergenerational relations 11–12, 15, 19, 21–22
adult education 93, *97*, 97–98, 104
adulthood transition 2, 235
African Americans 50
agency (individual proclivity) 154–155
Ahmed, Sara 141
altruism 157
Amanti, C. 197
ANOVAs 38, *39–40*
anthropology 250
anti-intellectual culture 236
antiracist constructivists 59
Antwerp: community schools 176, 178, 181; stigmatization 201–211
Appadurai, A. 155–156, 159, 163
Armand, Françoise 225
artistic track 76, 77, 78
Asia *see also individually named countries;* intergenerational relations 14, 19–20
ASO (general education), Flanders 172–174, 179, 182–183

aspirations 5, 166–167, 195–196, 250; and culture 114–122, *120*, 129; immigrants 121–127, 153–155, 217; l'Ecole des Etoiles 156–159, 250; narratives 121–127, 129; norms 159–163; parents 121–127, 154, 158–165; theoretical tool 155–156; working class 234, 236–237, 241, 242
assimilation theory 3
'assumed distance' collaboration model 220–221
asylum seekers 218
atmosphere, school 72
attachment relationships 11, 16
attainment: *see* performance
attendance rates 236
attitudes: home-school partnerships 225–227; teachers 72, 92, 226, 227, 252, 253
Audet, G. 6, 215, 220, 253
Australia, language 54
authoritarian parenting 16
Azuma, H. 17

Baier, D. 28–29
Balde, A. 249
banking education 197
Banks, A. J. 197
Banks, C. A. M. 197
Baumrind, D. 16
behaviors 12, 183–185, 199, 215–216, 234, 236–237
Belgium 5, 67–68, 153, 156–166, 201–211, 250; *see also* Flanders
*Bell Curve* (Herrnstein & Murray) 197
belonging, sense of 3

Bengtson, V. L. 13, 19, 21
Bernstein, B. 197
best practice 6, 253–254; attitudes 225–227; culture 71, 197–198; curriculum 45, 55–59; parental involvement 114–115, 142, 146–147; training 227–228; working class 242–244
BET YOU! project 179
bidirectional influences, values 16–17
bilingualism 52–55
bilingual schools, Flanders 174
biographical resources 115
blacks: *bourgeoisie* 47; home language 89–90; parental involvement 145, 147; performance 233
Boehnke, K. 4, 27, 28, 251
Bourdieu, P.: culture 70, 111; habitus 111, 114, 128, 154–155; performance 197; social networks 72
*bourgeoisie*, blacks 47
Braspenningx, M. 5, 195, 252
BRIC countries 198
Bright, N. G. 234, 239, 240
Britain 5, 6, 252–253; and diversity 139–140; values 139–142, 236–242; working class 233–235, 242–245
Bronfenbrenner, U. 11, 15, 239
Brunet, S. 250
Brussels: community schools 176; Turkish-Belgian immigrants 5, 153, 156–166, 250
BSO (vocational education), Flanders 172–174, 179, 183, 185

California, language 54
Canada 3, 5, 252; ethnic minority groups 47; language 53, 54, 92–95; policies 3, 5, 105; *see also* Quebec
capital, cultural: *see* cultural capital
capitalism 240
capital, social 2, 105, 147, 222
careers 117–118, 119–120, 179, 187
Catholicism, Flanders 174–175, 177
causality, direction of 118, 129
Chicago 241
children: cultural capital 162, 164–165; infancy 16, 17; intergenerational relations 4, 11, 13, 15–17, *18*; narratives 121–127, 129; value of 15, 18–19; value transmission 28, 29
Chinese immigrants 175, 201–211, 210, 224, 233

choices: aspirations 154, 155; school choice 143, 163, 164
Christianity, culture 165
citizenship 1; and diversity 139–140; educational institutions 49; parents 147; preferred citizenship model 57–58
civil society, Hizmet movement 156–157
class: *see* social class
classical assimilation theory 3
classical liberal models 57–58
Clycq, N. 1, 4–5, 67, 79, 171, 195, 210, 251–252, 253
Coalition government, UK 245
coercion, norms 125
Çolak, F. Z. 5, 153, 250
collaboration 219–223; *see also* partnerships, home/school
collaboration in search of visibility model 221
collaboration with mediation space model 220
collectivism 18–19, 31
colonialism 91
common socialization 50
communitarians 58
community, involvement in education 5, 49–50, 147, 252–253
community programmes 223–224
community schools, Polish immigrants 171, 174–187
community-school workers (CSWs) 226–227
competencies 2; home-school partnerships 221; tracking systems 183–185
complementary analyses 250–251
complementary (community) schools 171, 174–187
concept structure 119, *119*
congruence, school/home 4–5, 67–83; *see also* partnerships, home/school
*conscience morale* 157
constructivism 47–48
context: diversity of 252–253; individuals 69; intergenerational relations 11, 13–16, 17; values 27, 29–31; *see also* structures, education
Crowther, D. 237
Crozier, G. 5, 139, 147, 252–253
CSWs (community-school workers) 226–227

cultural capital 2; home-school partnerships 215–217, 222; immigrants 92, 162, 164–165
cultural markers 3
cultural relativists 58
cultural reproduction 48, 50
culture: data 116–118; and diversity 1, 55–59, 140–142; Flanders 174–175, 187; home-school partnerships 223–224; immigrants 73, 218; integration 251; intergenerational relations 11, 13; narratives 111–116, 118–129; parents 146; religion 164–165; stigmatization 206–207; and success 196, 198, 205, 210; values 14–15, 35; working class 236–237
culture clashes 234, 236–237
curricular tracking 173
curriculum 4, 45; culture 56–57, 59; diversity 142; Flanders 174–175, 176–177; language 51–55; place-based 243–244; and success 197

data: educational mobility 5, 111, 116–118; horizontal transmission 28, 29, 31–41; intergenerational relations 18, 20; Quebec immigrants 92–96, *94*, 104; school/home congruence 74–75
daughters, intergenerational relations 19, 21
Davidov, M. 16
decision-making, Quebec 217–218
de facto segregation 49, 50–51
definitions, success 68
deindustrialization 6, 235, 238–239, 240–241, 254
democracy: diversity 58–59, 140; ethnic minority groups 46; participatory 140, 142
democratization 1; Flanders 67; parental involvement 142, 146–147, 148; and success 199
demographics 1, 12, 14–15, 46
difference, maximization of 159
difference, meaning of 141–142
Dillabough, J. 241
disabilities, discrimination 141
disciplinary background (academia) 249–250
discipline, Chinese immigrants 207
discrimination: and diversity 141–142; parents 115, 145–146; race 148, 175

disengagement 237–238, 239
distributive justice 242
diversity 1–4, 6, 250–251, 252; as aspiration 159, 161–162, 167; of context 252–253; education structures 45, 46–48, 49, 60; ethnic minority groups 46–48; legitimacy 55–59; and parents 139, 140–143, 148; values 35, 140
domain-specific approach, parenting 16
drop-out rates, Quebec immigrants 96–98
Dutch language 174–175, 183–185, 186, 196, 198
dysphasia 184–185

early child development 16, 17
ecocultural perspectives 11
ecological approaches 69, 239; embedded context approach 68–79, *80–81*; see also embedded context approach
ecosystems approach 15
educational institutions 1, 4, 249; structure 45, 48–51, 59–60
educational mobility: data 116–118; narratives 111–116, 118–129; see also social mobility
educational pathways: see pathways
education structures: see structures, education
efficient citizens 1
elderly 12, 14, 15, 19–20
El-Mafaalani, A. 115
embedded context approach 68–79, *80–81*
employment: see labour market
epistemological realists 59
Equality Act, UK 141
equalization of opportunities 50, 242
equity: home-school partnerships 221–223; race 141–142; working class 244
essentialism 47
ethics, diversity 58–59
ethnic minority groups 1–3; aspirations 159–162; diversity 46–48, 140–142; education structures 45, 48–51, 59–60; inequality 67–68; parental involvement 144–146, 147–148; performance 68, 69–70, 171–172, 233; policies 48–59; Polish immigrants 177–178; and success 206–207; see also blacks; immigrants; whites
ethnic schools 174; see also community schools

ethnic stratification: *see also* socioethnic stratification
ethnic stratification, Flanders 172–174, *203*, 203–204
ethnocentrism 59
ethnocultural diversity 4, 196, 209, 249, 252, 254
ethos, school 72
Europe 252; education structures 45, 51–55, 60; immigrants 91; *see also individually named countries*
European Labour Force survey 199
European Social Survey (ESS) 30, 35, 37
European Union: membership 47; migration 67
exosystems, school type 34, 37, 38, *39*
expectations: Flanders school system 181, 182; immigrants 91, 92, 217, 219, 222; narratives 124–126; teachers 236–237
extracurricular activities 220, 221, 223, 224

failure/success: *see* success
fairness 140
families 1, 5; home-school partnerships 215–218, 220–221; intergenerational relations 11, 13, 27; narratives 111, 121–127, *123*, 129; and success 204–205, 222–223, 224; value of 18–19; *see also* parents
family reunification 218
family solidarity model 13, 19
Fedactio, Brussels 156
Fernandez-Kelly, P. 3
fertility rates 14, 15
field workers (community-school workers) 226–227
filial anxiety 20
filial piety 14, 20
finances, immigrants 218
Finland, socioethnic stratification 67
first-generation immigrants, Quebec 90–101, *94*, 104, 219
Flanders 251; aspirations 195–196, 198, 200–211; Polish immigrants 5, 171–187; school/home congruence 67–69, 73–82
formal schooling 197
francization courses 222
Fraser, N. 242–243
freedom of conscience 48
Free Schools Meals (FSM) 233, 245
Freire, P. 148, 197

friendships, and performance 72, 76–77, 77, 79
fundamentalism 55
'funds of knowledge' 243
fusional collaboration model 220

Galster, G. 239
GCSEs 236, 237
gender: diversity 141; intergenerational relations 21; over-performance 91; performance 70, 71, 76, 77, 78, 82
general education (ASO), Flanders 172–174, 179, 182–183
general track 76, 77, 78
generations: *see* first-generation immigrants; intergenerational relations; second-generation immigrants; third-generation immigrants
genetic makeup, values 28
Genk, Flanders 201–211
Geography classes 56
geography, working classes 239–240, 245
Germany 5; immigrants 117, 128, 250; narratives 112, 123; value transmission 35–37, 40–42
Gewirtz, S. 242–243
Ghent, stigmatization 201–211
ghettos 162–163, 164, 165
Gibson, M. 198
Glaser, B. G. 159
globalization 1, 5; diversity 139; intergenerational relations 12; migration 252
Goertz, G. 119
González, N. 197
the 'good parent' 144
government, Flanders 195
grade point average (GPA) 202, *208*, 208–209
grade retention rates: Belgium 203; Flanders 173–174, 181, 184; parents 71; *see also* performance
graduation rates, Quebec 90, 95, 96–103, *99, 102–103*
grass-roots initiatives 147, 176
Graw, K. 153
Great Britain: *see* Britain
Greece 67
gross drop-out rate 98
group identity 243
Grusec, J. E. 16
Gulen, F. H 156–157

Guyot, J. -L. 250
*Gymnasium* schools 36

habitus 111, 114, 128, 155, 250
Hadjar, A. 21
Hall, S. 142
headteachers: Britain 236–237; Flanders school system 184, 185–186
hegemony, diversity 139, 141, 142, 144, 148
Hemmerechts, K. 4, 67, 251
heritage education 174; *see also* community schools
Heritage Language Programme 53
heritage languages 52–55
heterogeneity, values 31–33, 36, 37
'high affective' practices 244
'high cognitive' practices 244
higher education 2; educational mobility 111, 126; Flanders 67, 172–174
'high operative' practices 244
History classes 56, 59
history of migration 46–47
Hizmet movement 156–157
Hlalele, D. 155
Hofstede, G. 31
home: congruence with school 4–5, 67–83; partnerships with school 5–6, 215–228; and success 205–206
home language: Flanders 175; and success 196, 205–206
home-school partnerships 5–6, 215–228; Quebec 215, 218–227
homework, assistance with 71, 215, 220, 222, 224
homogeniety: intergenerational relations 21; Quebec immigrants 95, 97; values 31–41, 139–140
homogenization of culture 1
Hong, S. 146, 147
horizon, immigration 153–154
horizontal transmission 4, 15, 29, 31–41, 251
House of Commons Education Committee 234, 237, 238
housing, working classes 241
Human Development Index (HDI) 19

identity: community programmes 223–224; diversity 139; Europe 252; intergenerational relations 11; language 53; places 239–240; safety of 209–211;

schooling 45; and success 199–200; working class 237, 242; *see also* self-concept
identity safe 200
immigrant bargain 115, 116, 122, 123
immigrant paradigm 238
immigrants 2–5; aspirations 121–127, 153–155, 156–159; community schools 175; context 252; curriculum 51–55; educational institutions 46–48, 49, 50–51; home-school partnerships 215–228; inequality 67; intergenerational relations 21–22; narratives 111, 115–116; performance 71, 73, 78–79, 90–91; Quebec 89–105, *94, 97, 102–103*, 251; religion 55–56; school/home congruence 71, 73, 75, 77, 78–79, 82; and success 196, 198, 200–211; values 35, 36–37, 40; working class 238; *see also* ethnic minority groups
independence, intergenerational relations 17
independent immigrants 218
Indian immigrants 233
individual context 69, 250
individualism 252; intergenerational relations 17, 19, 20; school choice 143; values 31
individuation 17
industrial decline 6, 235, 238–239, 240–241, 254
inequality 1–2; and culture 113; diversity 58, 142; Flanders 171, 172–174; immigrants 67; post-industrialism 240; school/home congruence 82; social mobility 112–115; structures 155; and success 196–198, 199
infancy 16, 17
inferiority complex 160
informal education 223
Inglehart, R. 30
INSETRoM project 145, 146
inspection system, schools 245
institutions: *see* educational institutions
integration, immigrants: and aspirations 160–161, 162; educational institutions 49–50; home-school partnerships 220–221
intelligence 183–184
intercultural community-school workers (ICSWs) 226–227

intercultural expertise 227
interdependence, intergenerational relations 17
intergenerational relations 4, 11–14, 251; demographics 14–15; narratives 121–128, 125; values 15–20, 28
interlingua 48
internalization: norms 5, 124–126; structures 154–155
interruption, school career 71–73, 75–78, 81–82
interviews: aspirations 157–163; educational mobility 117–118; Flanders school system 182; stigmatization 201–202; working class 235, 237, 241
involuntary minorities 46, 47, 91
ISCED level 3 qualifications 67, 196
Islam: and British values 140; educational institutions 48; legitimacy 56–57; morality 156–157, 160
Islamophobia 55, 140
Island of Montreal 226–227
Ismaili immigrants 224
isolationism 220, 224
Israel 36
Italian immigrants 210
Ittel, A. 28–29

Japan, demographics 14
jobs/careers 117–118, 119–120, 179, 187
justice 242–243, 245
justice as distribution 6
justice as recognition 6

Kagitcibasi, C. 21
Kluckhohn, C. 30
knowledge 4; diversity 57, 59; 'funds of knowledge' 243; of immigrant experiences 218–219; labour market 235; schooling 45
knowledge gap 67
knowledge society, Flanders 195
Kulz, C. 238
Kymlicka, W. 57

labour market: careers 117–118, 119–120, 179, 187; immigrants 216; post-industrialism 240; socioethnic stratification 67; working class 235, 242–243

language 3–4; aspirations 162, 165; Canada 53, 54, 92–95, 218–219; curriculum 51; Flanders 174–175, 178–179, 181–182, 183–187; home-school partnerships 225–226; interlingua 48; legitimacy 47; parental involvement 145, 216–217; and success 196, 205–206
Language Awareness Movement 53
Latin lessons 182–183
layers (values) 4
league tables 143, 245
leaving certificates 36
l'Ecole des Etoiles, aspirations 156–159
Ledent, J. 5, 89, 92, 251
Legewie, N. 5, 111, 250
legitimacy: diversity 55–59; home-school partnerships 221, 222; immigrants 46–48, 219–221
Levitas 143
liberalization, UK 245
liberty 140
life expectancy 12, 14
Logan Square initiative 148
London 233, 240
loneliness 14
long-distance norms 159–163
love (altruism) 157
Lucas, S. R. 173
Lupton, R. 6, 233, 253–254

Mc Andrew, M. 4–6, 45, 89, 92, 215, 249, 251–253
Macleod, J. 154–155, 163
macrosystems 242–243, 250; see also structures, education
mainstream education: Flanders 171–172, 174–175, 177, 181–187; and success 197–198
majority supremacists 58–59
mandatory involvement model 220
marginalization 3, 252–253, 254; diversity 58; religion 56
marriage 241
Marsh, H. W. 202
Maslow, A. 30
Massey, D. 239–240, 243
Mathematics classes 56, 59
maximization of differences 159
meritocratic schools 198–199, 252
mesosystems 250, 251; school 34, 37; and success 204–205
methodological approaches 249–250

metropolitan areas 1
microsystems 250, 251; and success 204–205; values 34, 41; working class 242–243
middle class: aspirations 114; interaction with school 69; parents 144; success 197; values 238
migration 1; adaptation 153; ethnic minority groups 46–47; globalization 252; reasons for 216–217; *see also* immigrants
minimalist democrats 58
Ministry of Education: Poland 176, 177, 178; Quebec 89, 218
Ministry of Immigration and Cultural Communities, Quebec 227
minority groups: and diversity 139; religion 55–59; *see also* ethnic minority groups
Miyake, K. 17
mobility: *see* educational mobility; social mobility
model minority theory 70, 210
Moll L. C. 197
Montreal 6, 221, 226–227
moral conscience 157
morality, Islam 157, 160
Moroccan immigrants 201–211
mothers: attachment relationships 16; cultural capital 164–165; working class 241
motivation: learning home language 225–226; narratives 121–126; performance 113; prosocial 20; and success 204–205
multiculturalism 3; as aspiration 159, 161–162; British values 139–142; home-school partnerships 220; success 196; values 238
multiethnic schools 196
multi-level theories 119
multilingualism 52–55, 198–199
Munns, G. 243–244
Muslims: *see* Islam

narratives 5; data 116–118; and educational mobility 111–116, 127–129; promotive 111–112, *112*, 118–127, *119–120*, 128–129; stigmatization 204–211
national minorities 46–47
nation building 252
neighbourhood effects 6, 234–235, 238–242

neighbourhoods, integration 162–163, 164, 165
neoliberalism 5, 139, 143, 244
net drop-out rate 98
networks: community schools 175–176; promotive narratives 119, 126; social 51, 69, 72, 82, 175, 187
New World countries, education structures 60
NGOs (non-governmental organizations) 223
non-EU citizens, inequality 67–68
non-governmental organizations (NGOs) 223
non-mobility 117
norms 5; aspirations 159–163; and difference 142; narratives 124–126
North African immigrants 68
North America 45, 51–55, 252; *see also individually named countries*
Nouwen, W. 5, 79, 195, 252
NVivo 9 (software) 177, 202

oblique transmission 27, 29
odds ratios (OR) 100–101
Ogbu, J. U. 91
OKAN courses, Flanders 173
older people 12, 14, 15, 19–20
Old Europe 60; *see also* Europe
openness, values *30*, 34, 37, *38*
outcomes: *see* performance
over-performance, immigrants 91

parent–child relationships 4; intergenerational relations 11, 13, 15–17, *18*; values 28, 29
parents 5, 127; aspirations 121–127, 154, 158–165, 236–237, 250; barriers to involvement 144–146; diversity 139, 140–143; education level 116–117, 121–122; expectations 91; Flanders school system 181–182; the good parent 144; home-school partnerships 215–216, 219–221; intergenerational relations 11; narratives 121–127, *123*, 129; relationship with school 139–140, 143–144, 146–148; school/home congruence 71, 76, 77, 82–83
participatory democracy 140, 142
partnership model of collaboration 220
partnerships, home/school 5–6, 215–228; *see also* congruence, school/home

part-time education, Flanders 174, 176
Passeron, J. C. 154–155, 197
pathways 90; Flanders 172–174, 178, 195; Quebec immigrants 92–93, 96–98, *97*; school-home congruence 4–5, 67–83; tracking systems 172–174, 178–185, *180*, 209
peers 5; horizontal transmission 4, 15, 29, 31–41, 251; and performance 72–73, 76, 77, 79; values 31
performance: aspirations 154–155; and culture 113–122; ethnic minority groups 68, 69–70; gender 70, 71, 76, 77, 78, 82, 91; graduation rates 90, 95, 96–103, *99*, *102–103*; immigrants 90, 222–223; school/home congruence 70–73, 75–83, *77*, *80–81*; stigmatization 202–211; track choices 171, 172–174, 186; working class 234, 236, 238, 245; *see also* grade retention rates; success
Phillips, A. 142
Piqueray, E. 5, 171, 197, 210, 253
PISA data 195, 199
place-based curriculum 243
pluralism 2, 3–4; educational institutions 45, 49, 57, 60; Quebec 89; values 238
pluralistic integration 49
Poland 177
policies 253; Britain 143, 148; Canada 3, 5, 105, 252; ethnic minority groups 48–59, 148; Flanders 187; immigration 105, 252; parents 143, 148; working class 244
Polish immigrants 5, 171–187, 201–211, 253
political science 30
politics, Flanders 195
population 1, 12, 14–15, 46
Portes, A. 3
Portrait Value Questionnaire (PVQ) 31, *32–33*
post-industrialism 240
post-materialism 19
Pott, M. 17
poverty: performance 90; socioethnic stratification 67; working class 233, 234, 236
power relations 69, 243–244
practices 6, 253–254; attitudes 225–227; culture 71, 197–198; curriculum 45, 55–59; parental involvement 114–115, 142, 146–147; training 227–228; working class 242–244

preferred citizenship model 57–58
principals: Britain 236–237; Flanders school system 184, 185–186
private schools: Canada 93; l'Ecole des Etoiles 156
private tuition 147
professionalism, teachers 147–148
programmes: diversity 55–59; heritage languages 53
promotive narratives 111–112, *112*, 118–127, *119–120*, 128–129
proportionality, aspirations 155–156
prosocial motivation 20
psychology 3; intergenerational relations 11, 13; stigmatization 207–209; values 30
public schools, Canada 93
pupil's academic self-concept 202

qualifications 67, 236; *see also* performance; success
qualitative approaches 250; Flanders 177, 179, 180, 184, 200–211; Quebec 89
quantitative approaches 4, 250; Britain 239; Flanders 177, 179, 200–211; Quebec 89
Quebec 5, 6; home-school partnerships 217–227; immigrants 89–105, *94*, *97*, *102–103*, 251
questionnaires, school/home congruence 74

race: *see* ethnic minority groups
Race Relations Amendment Act, UK 141
Rachédi, L. 225
radical pluralism 49
Raffo, C. 244
rational action model 114–115
Reception Classes for Foreign-speaking Newcomers (OKAN) 173
recognition, identity 243
refugees 218
regionalization, immigration 227
relatedness, intergenerational relations 17
relational justice 242–243
relationships 4; *see also* intergenerational relations
religion: culture 164–165, 210; diversity 55–59; educational institutions 48, 49, 55–59; home-school partnerships 224; *see also* Islam
remedial schooling 185

repeating years 181
reproduction of inequality 196–198
resiliency 221, 224, 225
resistance schooling 175, 197
resources, access to 155, 223–224
respect: British values 139–140; at school 72, 76, 77, 82–83
results 5
retention rates: *see* grade retention rates
reward, performance 113
Roberts, R. E. L. 13, 21
Rokeach, M. 30
role reversal, promotive narratives 127
Roma families 145
Rothbaum, F. 17, 20
Rousseau, C. 225

safety, identity 209–211
Sawyer, W. 243–244
Schiefer, D. 4, 27, 251
Schielke, S. 153
school: aspirations 154–155; congruence with home 4–5, 67–83; ethos 72; graduation rates 101; partnerships with home 5–6, 215–228; pluralism 45; relationship to parents 139–140, 143–144, 146–148; stigmatization 199–200; value transmission 34; and working class 242–244; *see also* educational institutions
school choice: aspirations 163, 164, 165; individualism 143
school types 34, 37, 38, *39*
school uniforms 57
Schwartz, S. 12, *30*, 30, 33, *38*
second-generation immigrants: Germany 117, 128, 250; Quebec 90–101, *94*, 104, 251
segmented assimilation 90–91
segmented assimilation theory 3
segregation 49, 50–51, 195, 252
self-concept 199–200, 202, 207–209, *208*
self-enhancement *30*, 37, *38*
self-esteem 72, 202
'self of value' 244
self-transcendence *30*, 37, *38*
sense of belonging 3
sensitizing concepts 158
sexual education 57
Shaull, R. 148
Shavelson, R. J. 202
similarity, values 28, 31–33, 41

slavery 46, 91
social advancement, by schools 222, 224
social capital 2, 105, 147, 222
social class: aspirations 114–116; and failure 197; immigrants 51, 90; parents 144; upper class 114; *see also* middle class; working class
social cohesion 1, 49, 60, 143, 253
social distance 5, 126–127, 128, 221
social entities 27
socialization 1, 4; education structures 45, 50, 60, 155; home-school partnerships 222; intergenerational relations 11, 15; stigmatization 210
social mobility 5; educational mobility 111–129; immigrants 91
social movements: Language Awareness Movement 53; race 48
social networks 51, 69, 72, 82, 175, 187
social relations 5, 126–127
social science: minority groups 56, 59; narratives 122; values 27, 29–31
social stratification 112–115; Flanders 67–68, 172–174, *203*, 203–204, 209; success 196–198
sociocultural perspectives 11
socioeconomic status: Flanders 172–174; home-school partnerships 215–216; immigrants 91, 93, 101, 104, 201–202; performance 70–71, 76–77, 77, 82; and success 196, 208, 222; working class 238
socioethnic stratification 112–115; Flanders 67–68, 172–174, *203*, 203–204, 209; success 196–198
sociology 250
solidarity, intergenerational relations 13, 19, 21–22
South Asia, drop-out rates 98
space 239–240
Spain, language 54
spatial injustices 6
staff: *see* principals; teachers
status-quo, values *30*, *38*
'Steeltown' 234–235, 237–238, 240–241, 243, 245
stereotype threat effects. 196
stereotyping: aspirations 159; ethnic minority groups 144–146, 148; and success 196, 199–211
stigmatization 5; race 48; school 199–200; and success 196, 199–211
stigmatization threat 199

stratification: *see* socioethnic stratification
Strauss, A. L. 159
structural perspectives, intergenerational relations 11
structures, education 4, 250; ethnic minority groups 45, 48–51, 59–60; school/home congruence 70–71, 82; socialization 45, 50, 60, 155
structure (societal constraints) 154–155
student's academic self-concept 202
subjectivity, aspirations 166
substantive democrats 58
subtractive acculturation 2–3, 69
subtractive pluralism 57
subtractive schooling 3, 198–199, 205, 253
success 5, 195–196, 200–211, 250; criteria for 68; home-school partnerships 215–217, 219–223; narratives 119–120, 206–207; social stratification 196–198; stigmatization 199–200; subtractive schooling 198–199; *see also* performance
supplementary (community) education 171, 174–187
symbiotic harmony, intergenerational relations 17

TCRI assessments 227
teachers: attitudes 72, 92, 226, 227, 252, 253; expectations 236–237; Flanders school system 181–182, 184, 187; home-school partnerships 215–216, 218–219; and parents 144–145, 147–148; and success 196, 204–205
teacher training 245
'Teaching Schools', UK 245
technical education (TSO), Flanders 172–174, 183
technical track, Flanders 76, 77, 78
terrorism, and diversity 139–140
Thatcher government, UK 239
'thick' culture 57
'thin' culture 57
Third Avenue Resource Centre 225
third-generation immigrants 90, 100, 104, 171, 251
Thomson, S. 240, 243
Timmerman, C. 1, 4–5, 171, 251, 253
tolerance 140
tracking systems, Flanders 172–174, 178–185, *180*, 209
tracks (students) 76, 77, 78, 79
tradition, Flanders 174–175

training 227–228, 245
trajectories: *see* pathways
transmission of values 4, 15–16, 21–22, 27–29; horizontal transmission 15, 29, 31–41, 251; vertical transmission 15–16, 27, 29
Triandis, H. C. 31
Trommsdorff, G. 4, 11, 15, 251
troubled families 143
TSO (technical education), Flanders 172–174, 183
Turkey, narratives 112, 123
Turkish-Belgian immigrants 5, 68, 153, 156–166, 201–211, 250

UK: *see* Britain
unconditional love 157
underperformance 197
unemployment 171, 235
uniforms, school 57
universality 12, 13, 59
upper class aspirations 114
upward mobility 5, 111, 111–113, 114–116
utilitarian values, children 19

validating difference 142
value changes 14–15
value conflict 238
Value-of-Children and Intergenerational Relations Study (VOC-IR) 13, 17–20, *18*
value orientations 29–30, 31–34
value plurality 238
values 2, 4; home-school partnerships 217; and integration 160–161, 162; intergenerational relations 12, 14, 15–20, 21–22; legitimacy 56–57; promotive narratives 114, 121–122, 124–126; social science context 27, 29–31; transmission of 4, 15–16, 21–22, 27–29; working class 234, 236–242, 244–245
Vatz Laaroussi, M. 6, 215, 219, 225, 253
vertical transmission 4, 15–16, 27, 29
Vincent, Carol 144
'virtual school bags' 243
vocational education (BSO), Flanders 172–174, 179, 183, 185
VOC-IR (Value-of-Children and Intergenerational Relations Study) 13, 17–20, *18*
voluntary migrants 104

Wallonia 67
Warren, M. R. 146, 147
waterfall system, Flanders 173, 183, 186
WEIRD (Western, Educated, Industrialized, Rich, and Democratic) 13
Weisz, J. 17
Western countries: ethnic minority groups 46–47; intergenerational relations 19–20; language 51; *see also individually named countries*
Wets, J. 4, 67, 251
whites 6; and diversity 141–142; working class 233–245
Wilson, W. J. 240–241

working class 6, 233–245, 254; educational mobility 115–116; and school practices 242–244; Steeltown 234–235; and success 197, 199; values 234, 236–242
workshops, 'Youth, Education & Value Change' 4
*World City* (Massey) 240
World Value Survey 19, 30

'Youth, Education & Value Change' (workshop) 4

Zeitgeist 21, 28–29, 31, 37
zerolingualism 198

# Taylor & Francis eBooks

## Helping you to choose the right eBooks for your Library

Add Routledge titles to your library's digital collection today. Taylor and Francis ebooks contains over 50,000 titles in the Humanities, Social Sciences, Behavioural Sciences, Built Environment and Law.

**Choose from a range of subject packages or create your own!**

**Benefits for you**
- Free MARC records
- COUNTER-compliant usage statistics
- Flexible purchase and pricing options
- All titles DRM-free.

**REQUEST YOUR FREE INSTITUTIONAL TRIAL TODAY**

**Free Trials Available**
We offer free trials to qualifying academic, corporate and government customers.

**Benefits for your user**
- Off-site, anytime access via Athens or referring URL
- Print or copy pages or chapters
- Full content search
- Bookmark, highlight and annotate text
- Access to thousands of pages of quality research at the click of a button.

## eCollections – Choose from over 30 subject eCollections, including:

| | |
|---|---|
| Archaeology | Language Learning |
| Architecture | Law |
| Asian Studies | Literature |
| Business & Management | Media & Communication |
| Classical Studies | Middle East Studies |
| Construction | Music |
| Creative & Media Arts | Philosophy |
| Criminology & Criminal Justice | Planning |
| Economics | Politics |
| Education | Psychology & Mental Health |
| Energy | Religion |
| Engineering | Security |
| English Language & Linguistics | Social Work |
| Environment & Sustainability | Sociology |
| Geography | Sport |
| Health Studies | Theatre & Performance |
| History | Tourism, Hospitality & Events |

For more information, pricing enquiries or to order a free trial, please contact your local sales team:
**www.tandfebooks.com/page/sales**

 The home of Routledge books

**www.tandfebooks.com**